Fruits Basket™

Volume 20

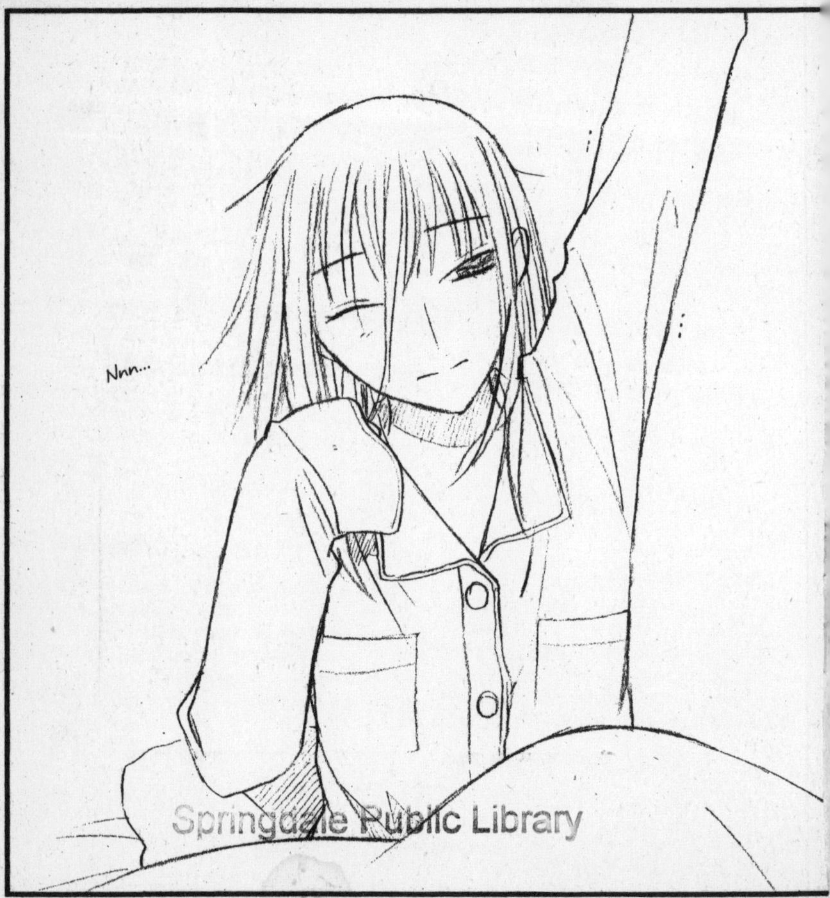
Nnn...

Natsuki Takaya

Fruits Basket Volume 20
Created by Natsuki Takaya

Translation - Alethea & Athena Nibley
English Adaptation - Lianne Sentar
Copy Editor - Shannon Watters
Retouch and Lettering - Star Print Brokers
Production Artist - Keila N. Ramos
Graphic Designer - Tina Corrales

Editor - Paul Morrisey
Digital Imaging Manager - Chris Buford
Pre-Production Supervisor - Lucas Rivera
Production Manager - Elisabeth Brizzi
Managing Editor - Vy Nguyen
Creative Director - Anne Marie Horne
Editor-in-Chief - Rob Tokar
Publisher - Mike Kiley
President and C.O.O. - John Parker
C.E.O. and Chief Creative Officer - Stu Levy

A  Manga

TOKYOPOP and 🐱 are trademarks or registered trademarks of TOKYOPOP Inc.

TOKYOPOP Inc.
5900 Wilshire Blvd. Suite 2000
Los Angeles, CA 90036

E-mail: info@TOKYOPOP.com
Come visit us online at www.TOKYOPOP.com

FRUITS BASKET by Natsuki Takaya
© 2006 Natsuki Takaya
All rights reserved.
First published in Japan in 2006 by HAKUSENSHA, INC., Tokyo
English language translation rights in the United States of
America, Canada and United Kingdom arranged with
HAKUSENSHA, INC., Tokyo through Tuttle-Mori Agency Inc.,
Tokyo
English text copyright © 2008 TOKYOPOP Inc.

All rights reserved. No portion of this book may be
reproduced or transmitted in any form or by any means
without written permission from the copyright holders.
This manga is a work of fiction. Any resemblance to
actual events or locales or persons, living or dead, is
entirely coincidental.

ISBN: 978-1-4278-0009-1

First TOKYOPOP printing: July 2008
10 9 8 7 6 5 4 3 2 1
Printed in the USA

Fruits Basket™

Volume 20

By
Natsuki Takaya

SPRINGDALE PUBLIC LIBRARY
405 South Pleasant
Springdale, Arkansas 72764

HAMBURG // LONDON // LOS ANGELES // TOKYO

Fruits Basket

Table of Contents

STORY SO FAR...

Hello, I'm Tohru Honda, and I have come to know a terrible secret. After the death of my mother, I was living by myself in a tent, when the Sohma family took me in. I soon learned that the Sohma family lives with a curse! Each family member is possessed by the vengeful spirit of an animal from the Chinese Zodiac. Whenever one of them becomes weak or is hugged by a member of the opposite sex, that person changes into his or her Zodiac animal!

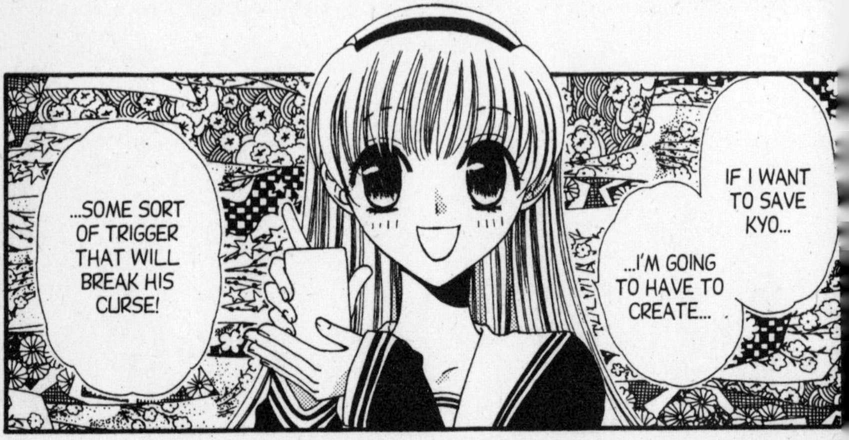
IF I WANT TO SAVE KYO...
...I'M GOING TO HAVE TO CREATE...
...SOME SORT OF TRIGGER THAT WILL BREAK HIS CURSE!

Tohru Honda

The ever-optimistic heroine of our story. An orphan, she now lives in Shigure's house, along with Yuki and Kyo, and is the only person outside of the family who knows the Sohma family's curse.

Yuki Sohma, the Rat

Soft-spoken. Self-esteem issues. At school, he's called "Prince Yuki."

Kyo Sohma, the Cat

The Cat who was left out of the Zodiac. Hates Yuki, leeks and miso. But mostly Yuki.

Kagura Sohma, the Boar

Bashful, yet headstrong. Determined to marry Kyo, even if it kills him.

Fruits Basket Characters

Mabudachi Trio

Shigure Sohma, the Dog

Enigmatic, mischievous and a little perverted. A popular novelist.

Hatori Sohma, the Dragon

Family doctor to the Sohmas. Only thing he can't cure is his broken heart.

Ayame Sohma, the Snake

Yuki's older brother. A proud and playful drama queen...er, king. Runs a costume shop.

Saki Hanajima

"Hana-chan." Can sense people's "waves." Goth demeanor scares her classmates.

Arisa Uotani

"Uo-chan." A tough-talking "Yankee" who looks out for her friends.

Tohru's Best Friends

Hiro Sohma, the Ram (or sheep)

This caustic tyke is skilled at throwing verbal barbs, but he has a soft spot for Kisa.

Momiji Sohma, the Rabbit

Half German. He's older than he looks. His mother rejected him because of the Sohma curse. His little sister, Momo, has been kept from him most of her life.

Hatsuharu Sohma, the Ox

The nicest of guys, except when he goes "Black." Then you'd better watch out. He was once in a relationship with Rin.

Kisa Sohma, the Tiger

Kisa became shy and self-conscious due to constant teasing by her classmates. Yuki, who has similar insecurities, feels particularly close to Kisa.

Fruits Basket Characters

Isuzu "Rin" Sohma, the Horse

She was once in a relationship with Hatsuharu (Haru)...and Tohru leaves her rather cold. Rin is full of pride, and she can't stand the amount of deference the other Sohma family members give Akito.

Ritsu Sohma, the Monkey

This shy, kimono-wearing member of the Sohma family is gorgeous. But this "she" is really a he!! Cross-dressing calms his nerves.

Kureno Sohma, the Rooster (or bird)

He is Akito's very favorite, and spends almost all of his time on the Sohma estate, tending to Akito's every desire. Kureno was born possessed by the spirit of the Bird, but his curse broke long ago...which means we've never seen him transformed. He pities Akito's loneliness, and can't bring himself to leave her.

"God"

Akito Sohma

The head of the Sohma clan. A dark figure of many secrets. Treated with fear and reverence. It has recently been revealed that Akito is actually a woman!

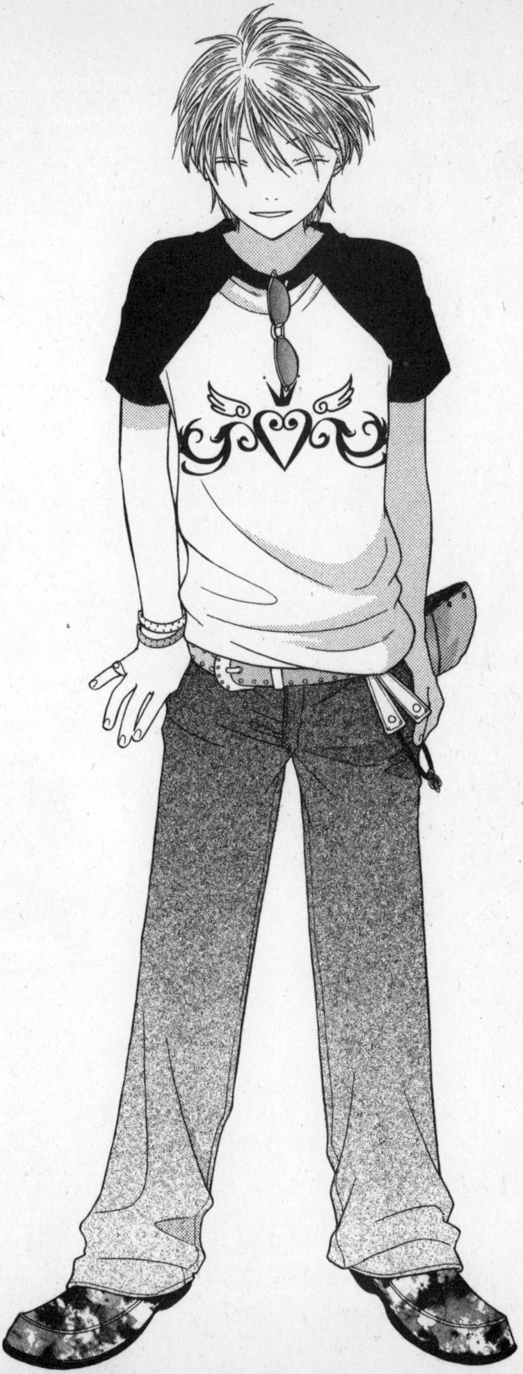

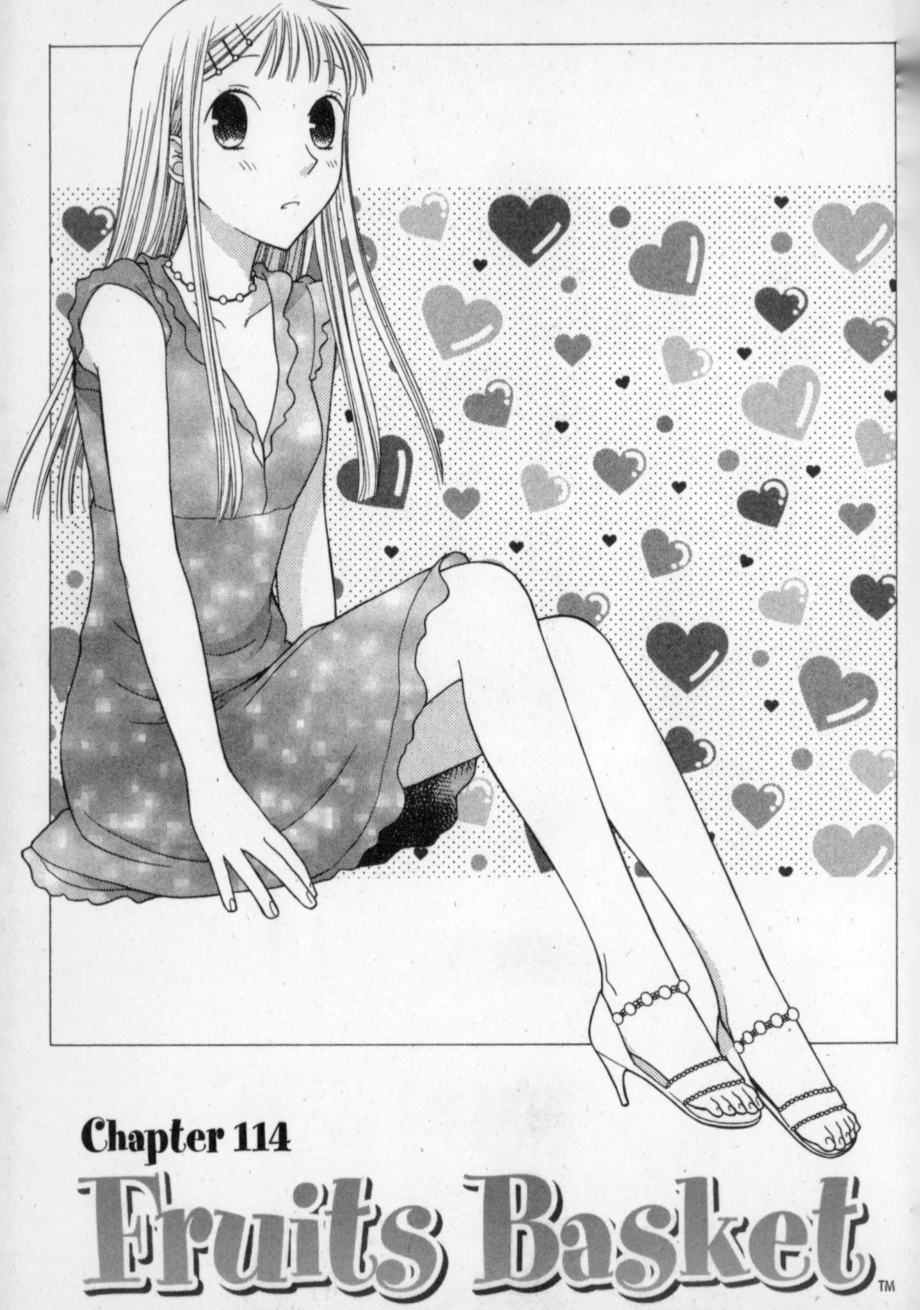

Chapter 114

Fruits Basket™

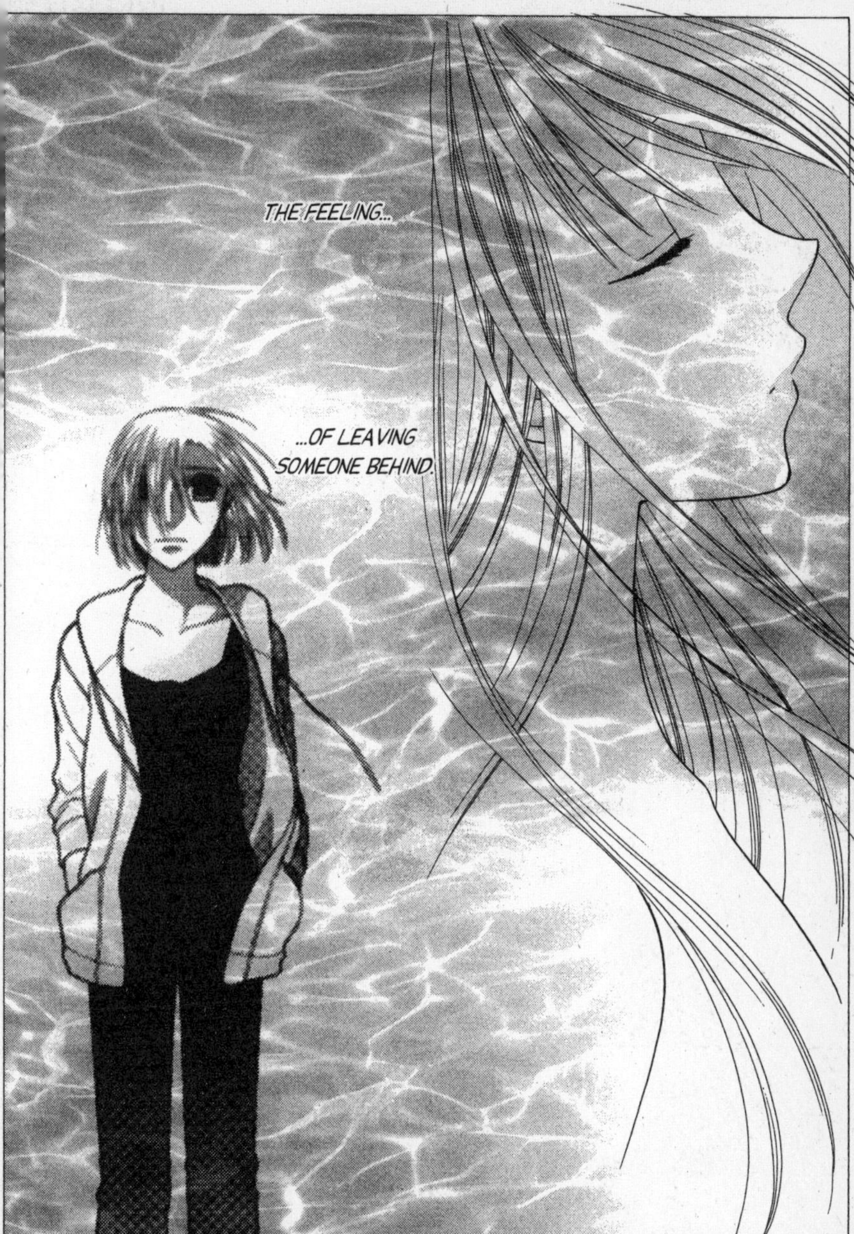
THE FEELING...
...OF LEAVING SOMEONE BEHIND.

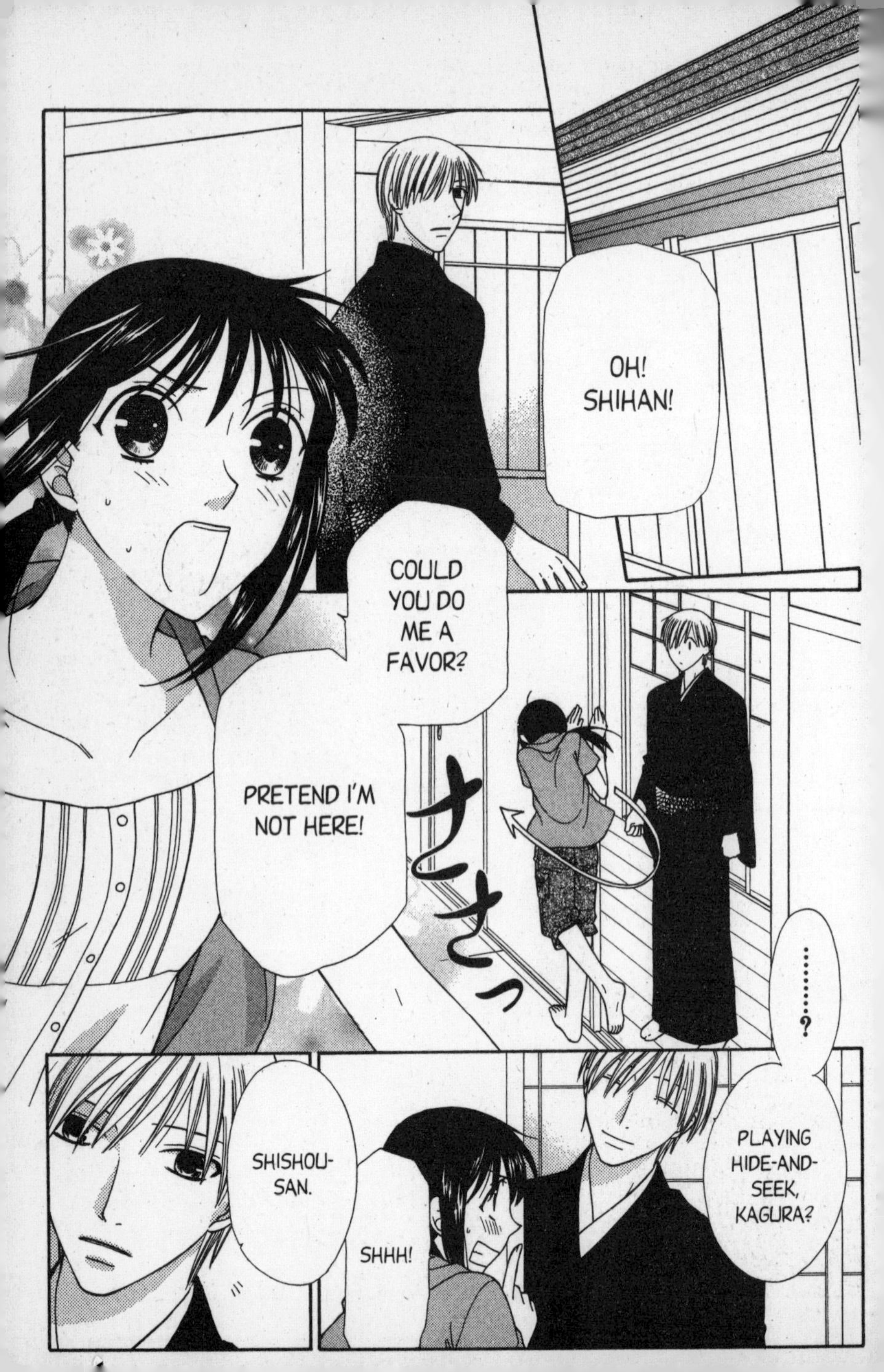
OH! SHIHAN!
COULD YOU DO ME A FAVOR?
PRETEND I'M NOT HERE!
ささっ
......?
PLAYING HIDE-AND-SEEK, KAGURA?
SHHH!
SHISHOU-SAN.

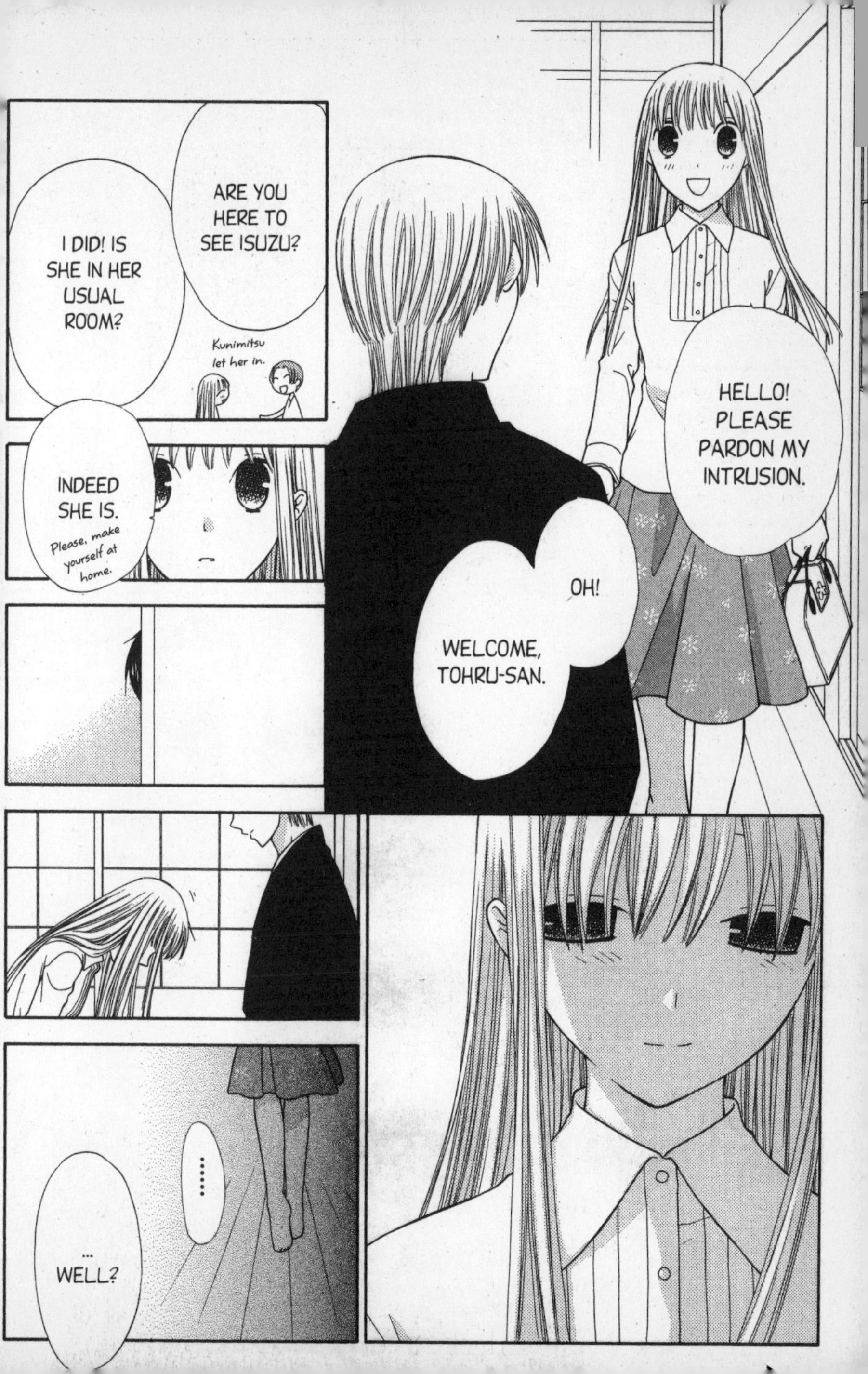
HELLO! PLEASE PARDON MY INTRUSION.
OH!
WELCOME, TOHRU-SAN.
ARE YOU HERE TO SEE ISUZU?
I DID! IS SHE IN HER USUAL ROOM?
Kunimitsu let her in.
INDEED SHE IS.
Please, make yourself at home.
......
...WELL?

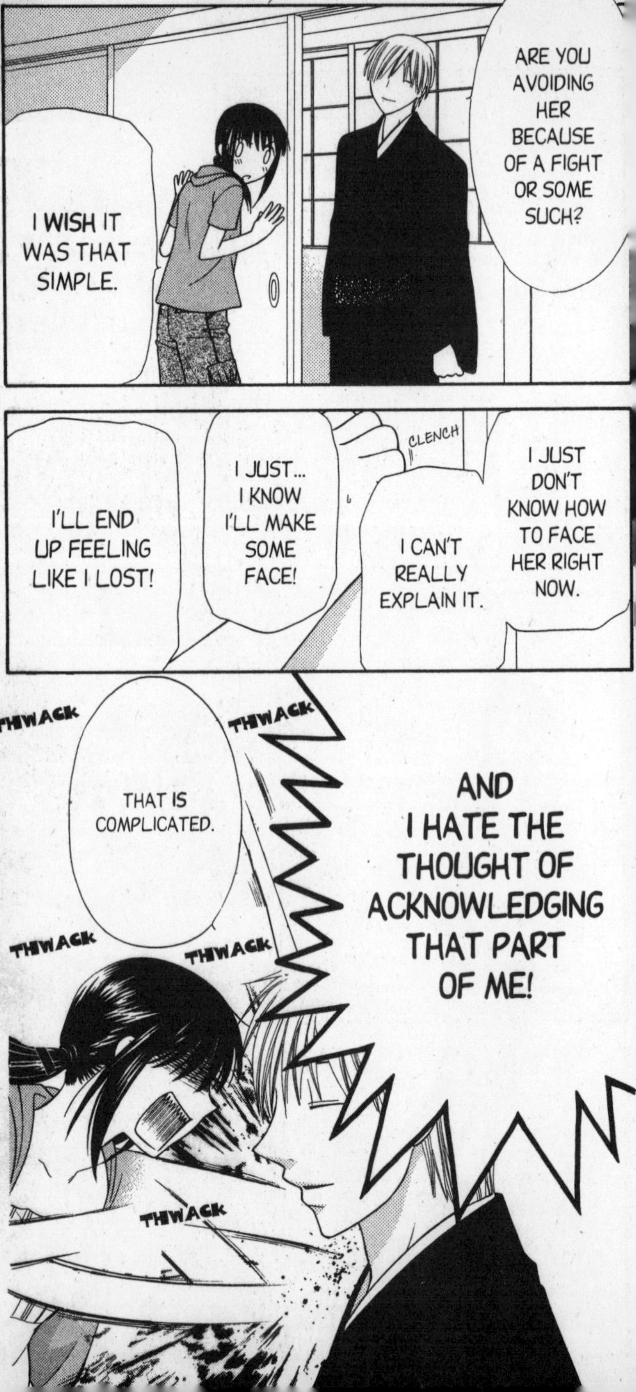
ARE YOU AVOIDING HER BECAUSE OF A FIGHT OR SOME SUCH?
I WISH IT WAS THAT SIMPLE.
I JUST DON'T KNOW HOW TO FACE HER RIGHT NOW.
I CAN'T REALLY EXPLAIN IT.
CLENCH
I JUST... I KNOW I'LL MAKE SOME FACE!
I'LL END UP FEELING LIKE I LOST!
AND I HATE THE THOUGHT OF ACKNOWLEDGING THAT PART OF ME!
THWACK
THWACK
THAT IS COMPLICATED.
THWACK
THWACK
THWACK

Fruits Basket

Nice to meet you and hello. This is Takaya, presenting Furuba Volume 20.

Volume 20...this has actually reached Volume 20.

Machi's on the cover this time around. At first I thought about having the Mogeta paperweight that Yuki gave her on the back cover, but I ended up going with the footprints. (It might be hard to tell from the picture, but those are the footprints Yuki and Machi put in the snow (laugh).)

Speaking of Mogeta, I first planned that Machi liked rabbits, and she sat behind Momiji, and since her heart thundered over rabbit merchandise, she liked Mogeta because Mogeta looks like a rabbit (only not really (laugh).) That was the story I thought of, anyway. But in the end, I couldn't fit that in, so Machi just became a simple Mogeta fangirl (laugh).

Now then, please enjoy Furuba 20.

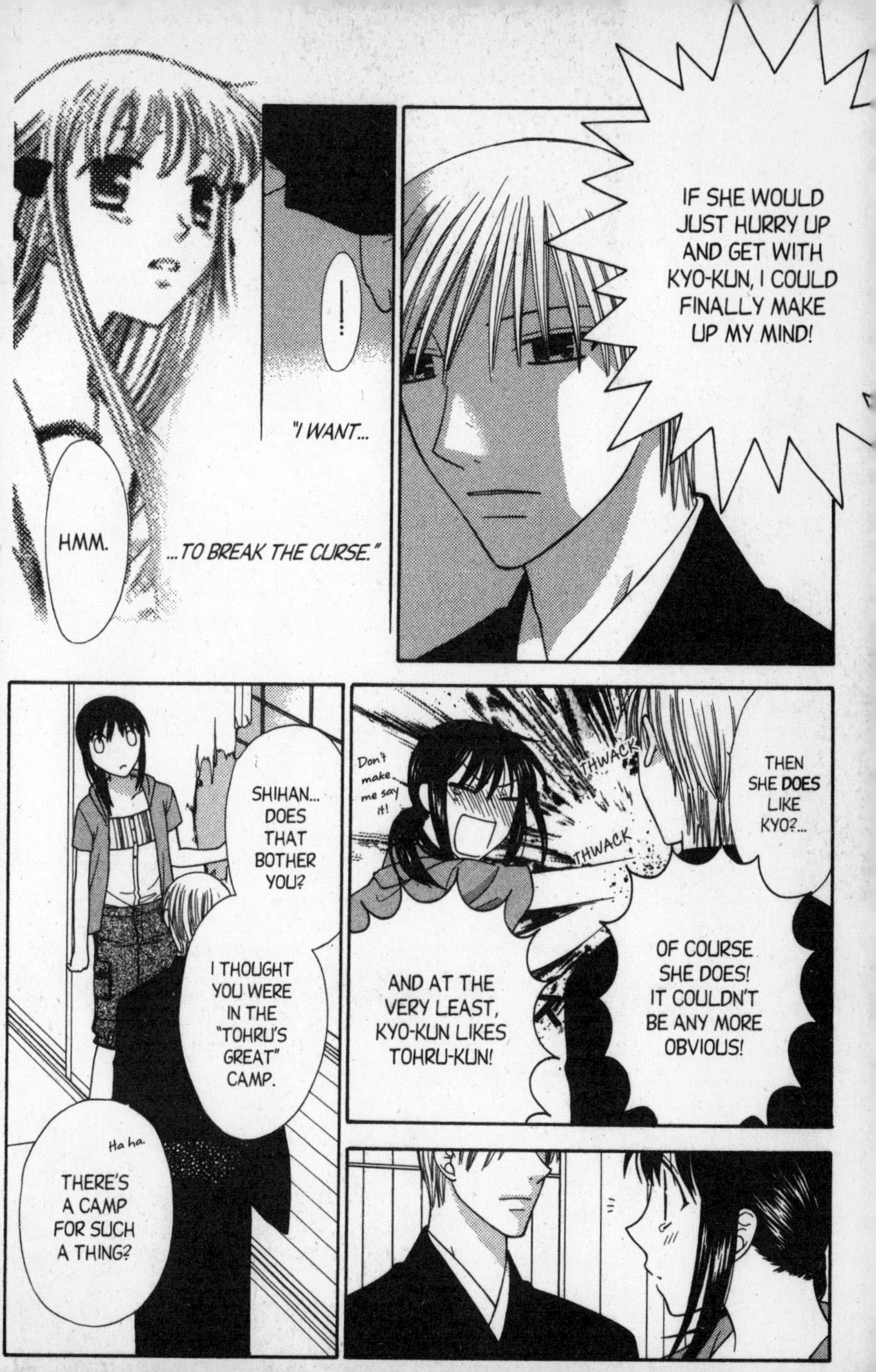
IF SHE WOULD JUST HURRY UP AND GET WITH KYO-KUN, I COULD FINALLY MAKE UP MY MIND!
!...
"I WANT...
...TO BREAK THE CURSE."
HMM.
THEN SHE **DOES** LIKE KYO?...
Don't make me say it!
THWACK
THWACK
OF COURSE SHE DOES! IT COULDN'T BE ANY MORE OBVIOUS!
AND AT THE VERY LEAST, KYO-KUN LIKES TOHRU-KUN!
SHIHAN... DOES THAT BOTHER YOU?
I THOUGHT YOU WERE IN THE "TOHRU'S GREAT" CAMP.
Ha ha.
THERE'S A CAMP FOR SUCH A THING?

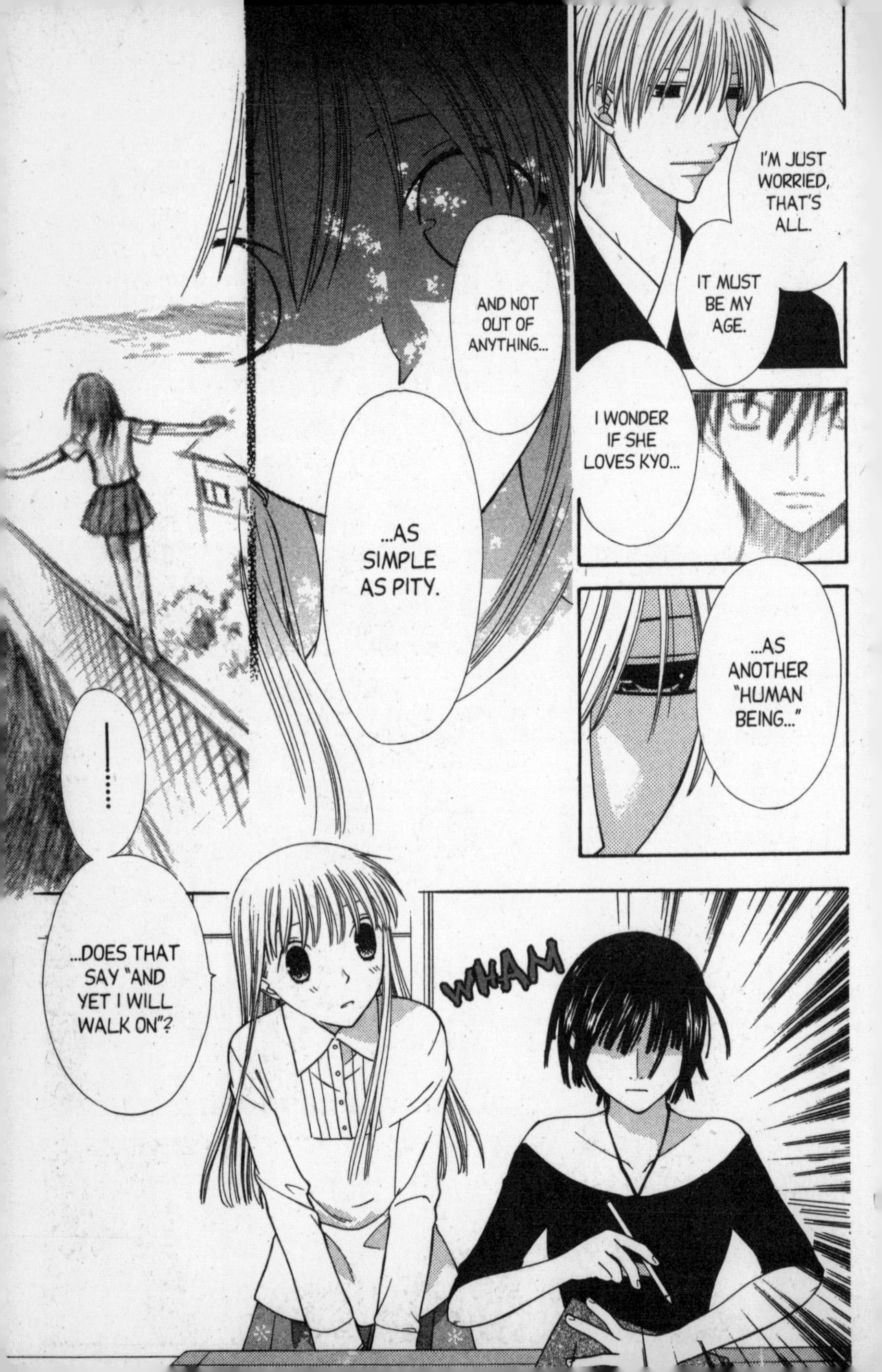
I'M JUST WORRIED, THAT'S ALL.
IT MUST BE MY AGE.
I WONDER IF SHE LOVES KYO...
...AS ANOTHER "HUMAN BEING..."
AND NOT OUT OF ANYTHING...
...AS SIMPLE AS PITY.
!......
...DOES THAT SAY "AND YET I WILL WALK ON"?
WHAM

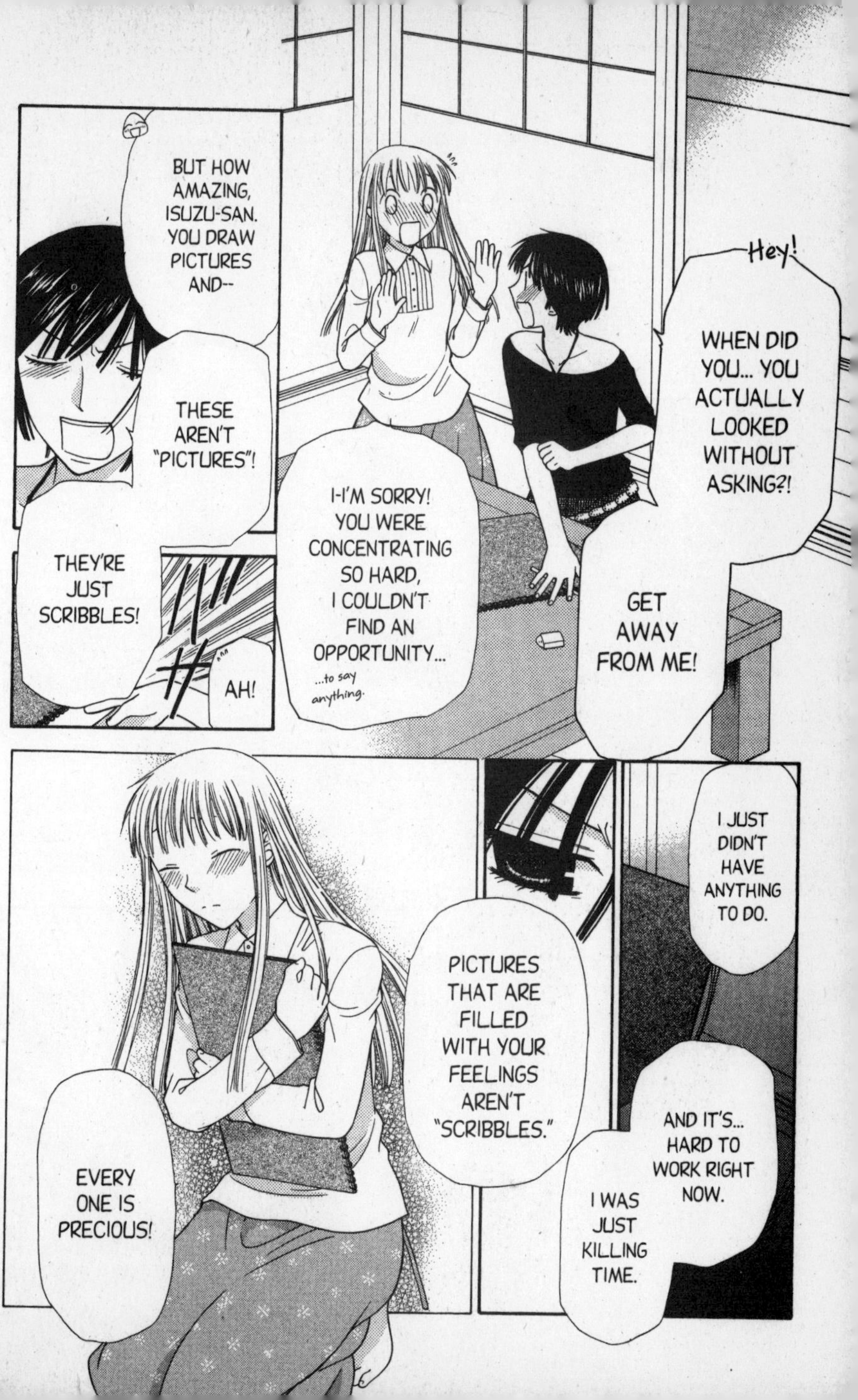
Hey!
WHEN DID YOU... YOU ACTUALLY LOOKED WITHOUT ASKING?!
GET AWAY FROM ME!
I-I'M SORRY! YOU WERE CONCENTRATING SO HARD, I COULDN'T FIND AN OPPORTUNITY...
...to say anything.
BUT HOW AMAZING, ISUZU-SAN. YOU DRAW PICTURES AND--
THESE AREN'T "PICTURES"!
THEY'RE JUST SCRIBBLES!
AH!
I JUST DIDN'T HAVE ANYTHING TO DO.
AND IT'S... HARD TO WORK RIGHT NOW.
I WAS JUST KILLING TIME.
PICTURES THAT ARE FILLED WITH YOUR FEELINGS AREN'T "SCRIBBLES."
EVERY ONE IS PRECIOUS!

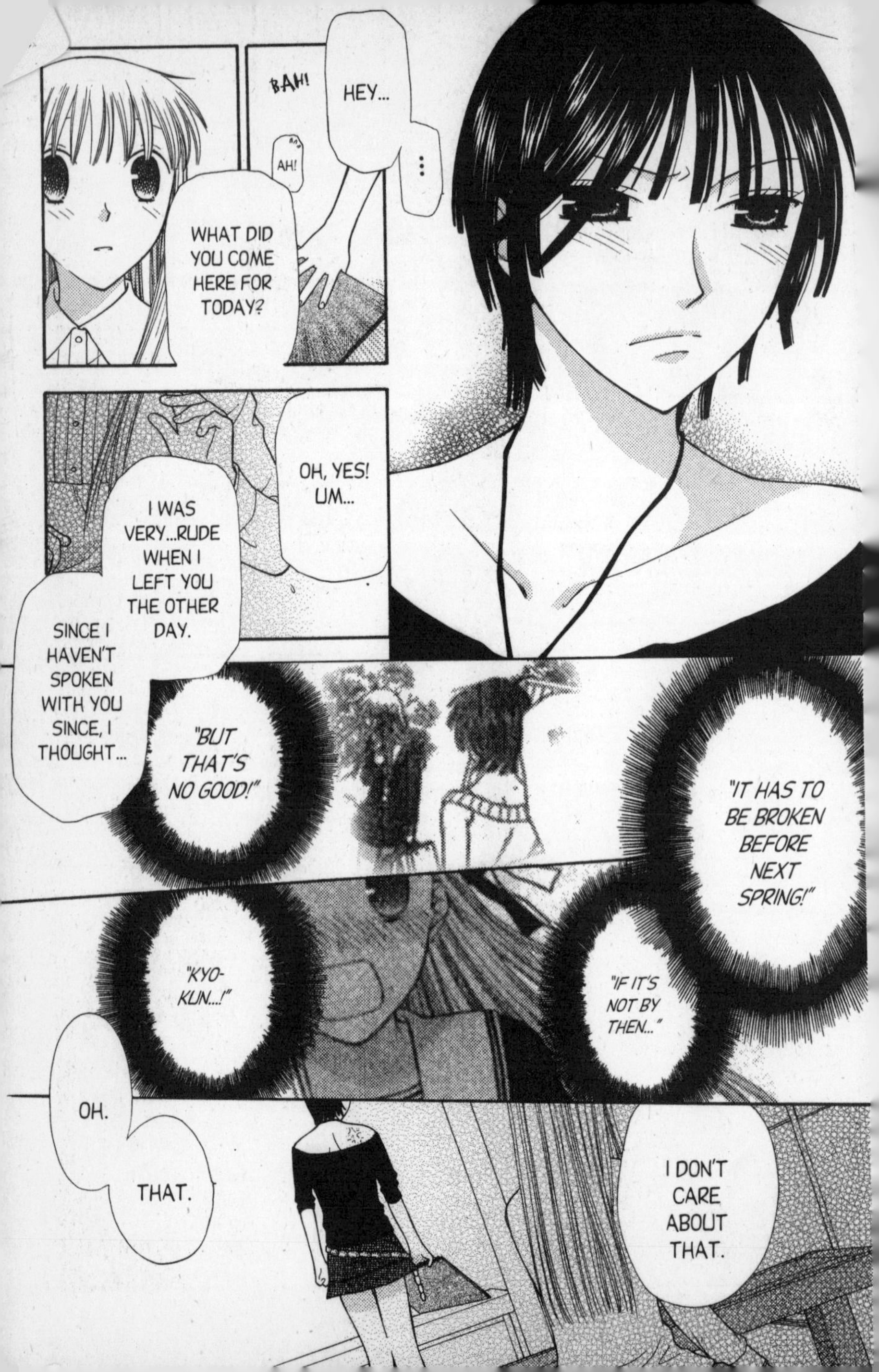
HEY...
BAH!
...
AH!
WHAT DID YOU COME HERE FOR TODAY?
OH, YES! UM...
I WAS VERY...RUDE WHEN I LEFT YOU THE OTHER DAY.
SINCE I HAVEN'T SPOKEN WITH YOU SINCE, I THOUGHT...
"IT HAS TO BE BROKEN BEFORE NEXT SPRING!"
"BUT THAT'S NO GOOD!"
"IF IT'S NOT BY THEN..."
"KYO-KUN...!"
I DON'T CARE ABOUT THAT.
OH.
THAT.

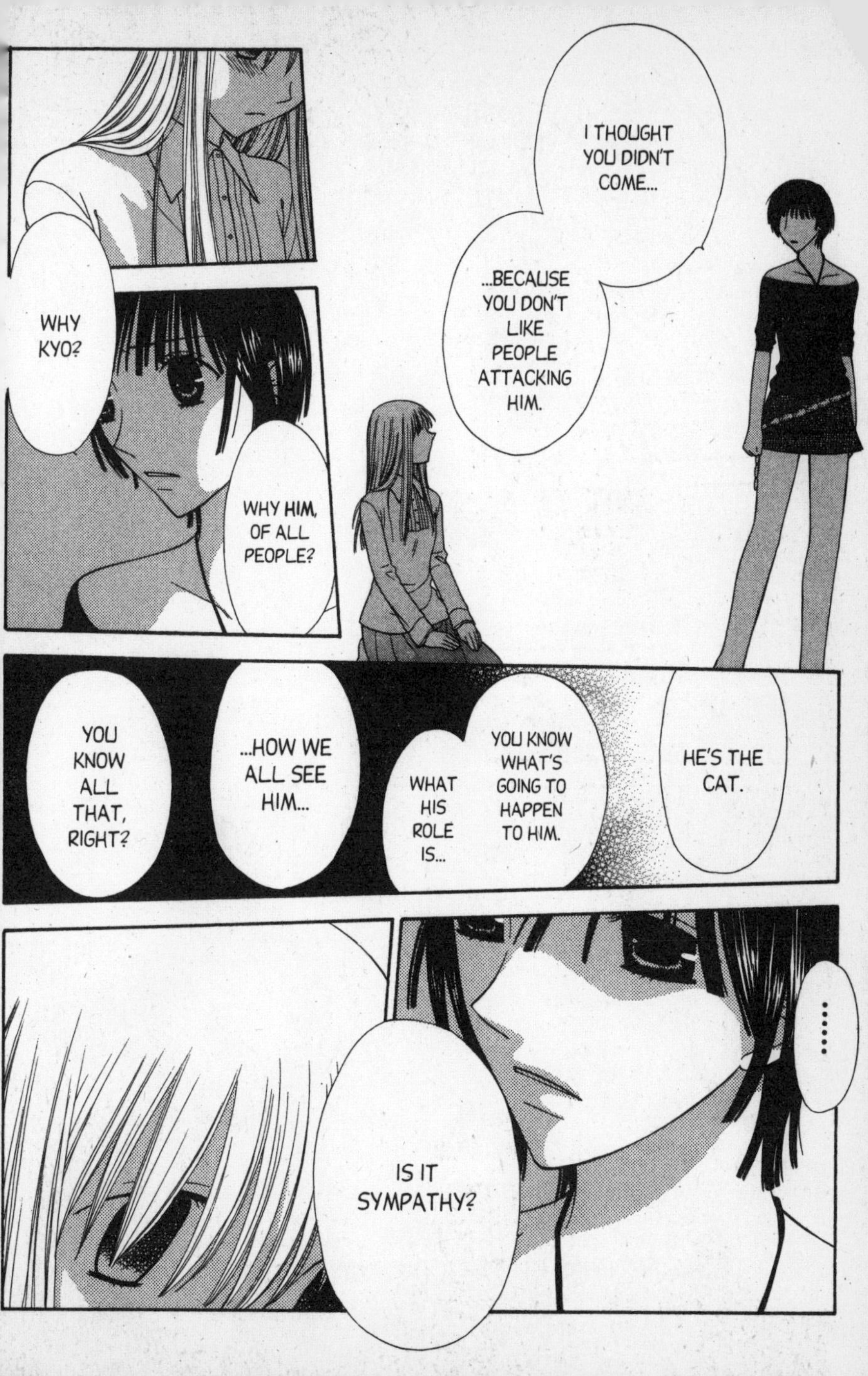
I THOUGHT YOU DIDN'T COME...
...BECAUSE YOU DON'T LIKE PEOPLE ATTACKING HIM.
WHY KYO?
WHY HIM, OF ALL PEOPLE?
HE'S THE CAT.
YOU KNOW WHAT'S GOING TO HAPPEN TO HIM.
WHAT HIS ROLE IS...
...HOW WE ALL SEE HIM...
YOU KNOW ALL THAT, RIGHT?
......
IS IT SYMPATHY?

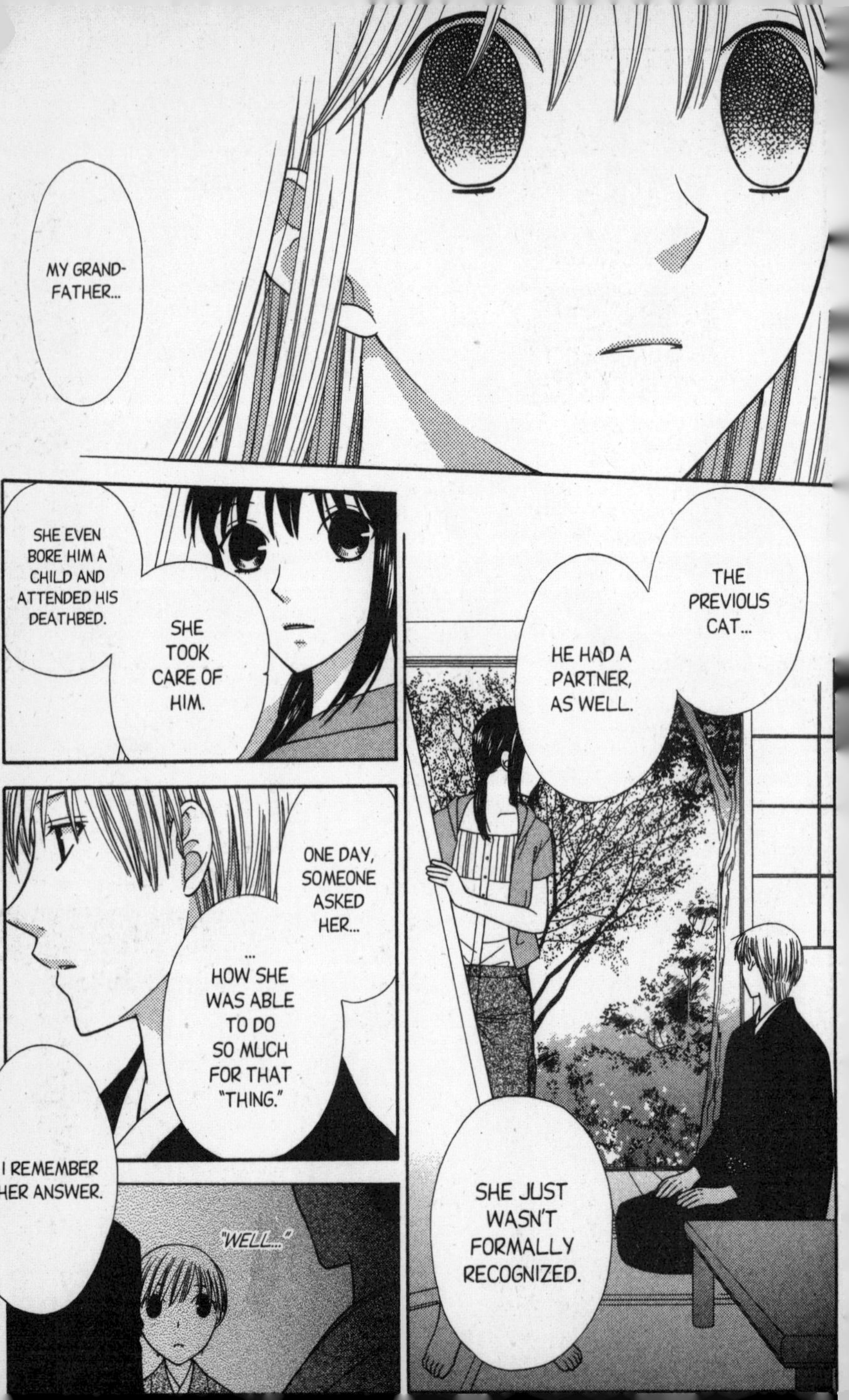
MY GRAND-FATHER...
THE PREVIOUS CAT...
HE HAD A PARTNER, AS WELL.
SHE JUST WASN'T FORMALLY RECOGNIZED.
SHE TOOK CARE OF HIM.
SHE EVEN BORE HIM A CHILD AND ATTENDED HIS DEATHBED.
ONE DAY, SOMEONE ASKED HER...
...HOW SHE WAS ABLE TO DO SO MUCH FOR THAT "THING."
I REMEMBER HER ANSWER.
"WELL..."

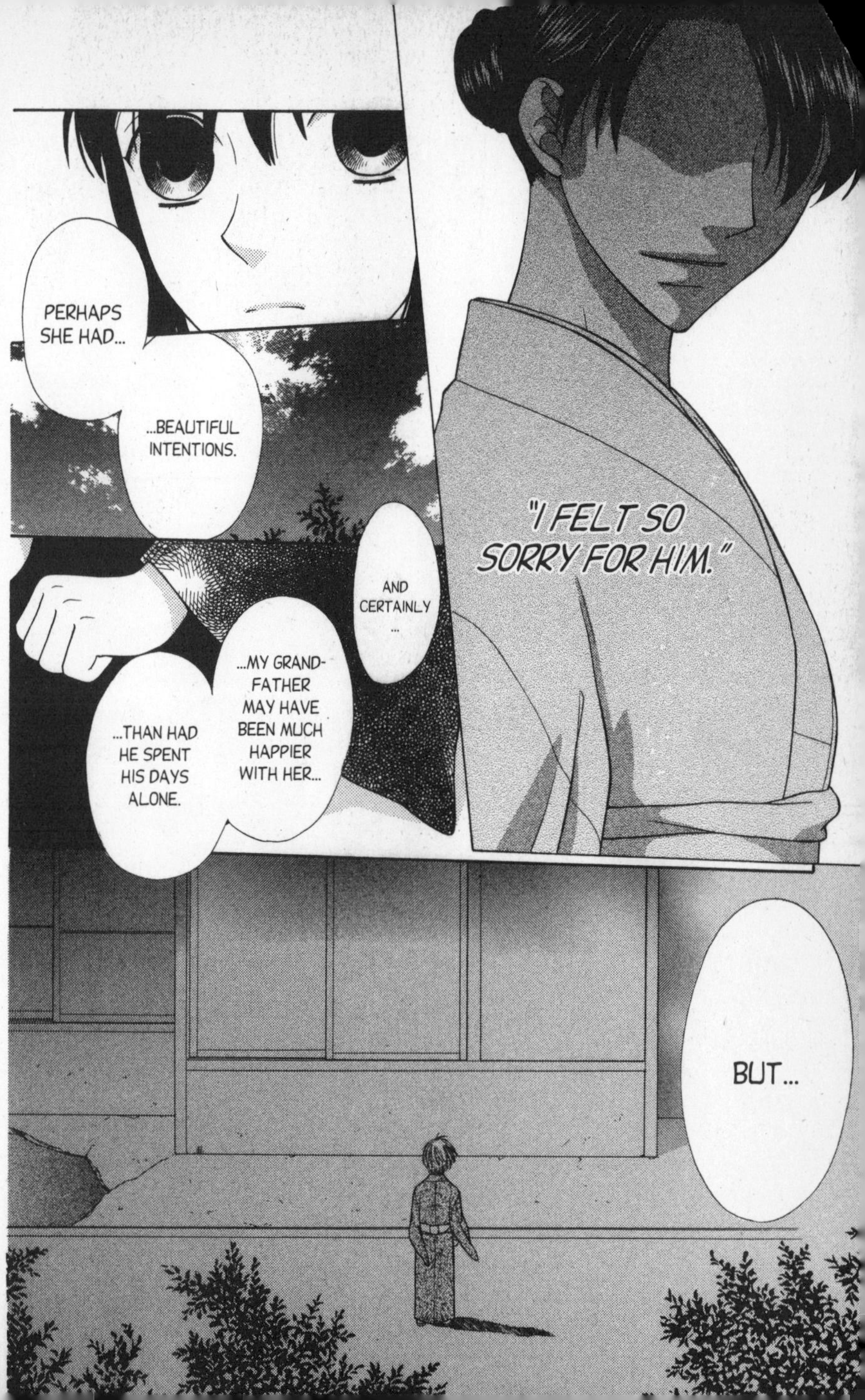
"I FELT SO SORRY FOR HIM."
PERHAPS SHE HAD...
...BEAUTIFUL INTENTIONS.
AND CERTAINLY ...
...MY GRAND-FATHER MAY HAVE BEEN MUCH HAPPIER WITH HER...
...THAN HAD HE SPENT HIS DAYS ALONE.
BUT...

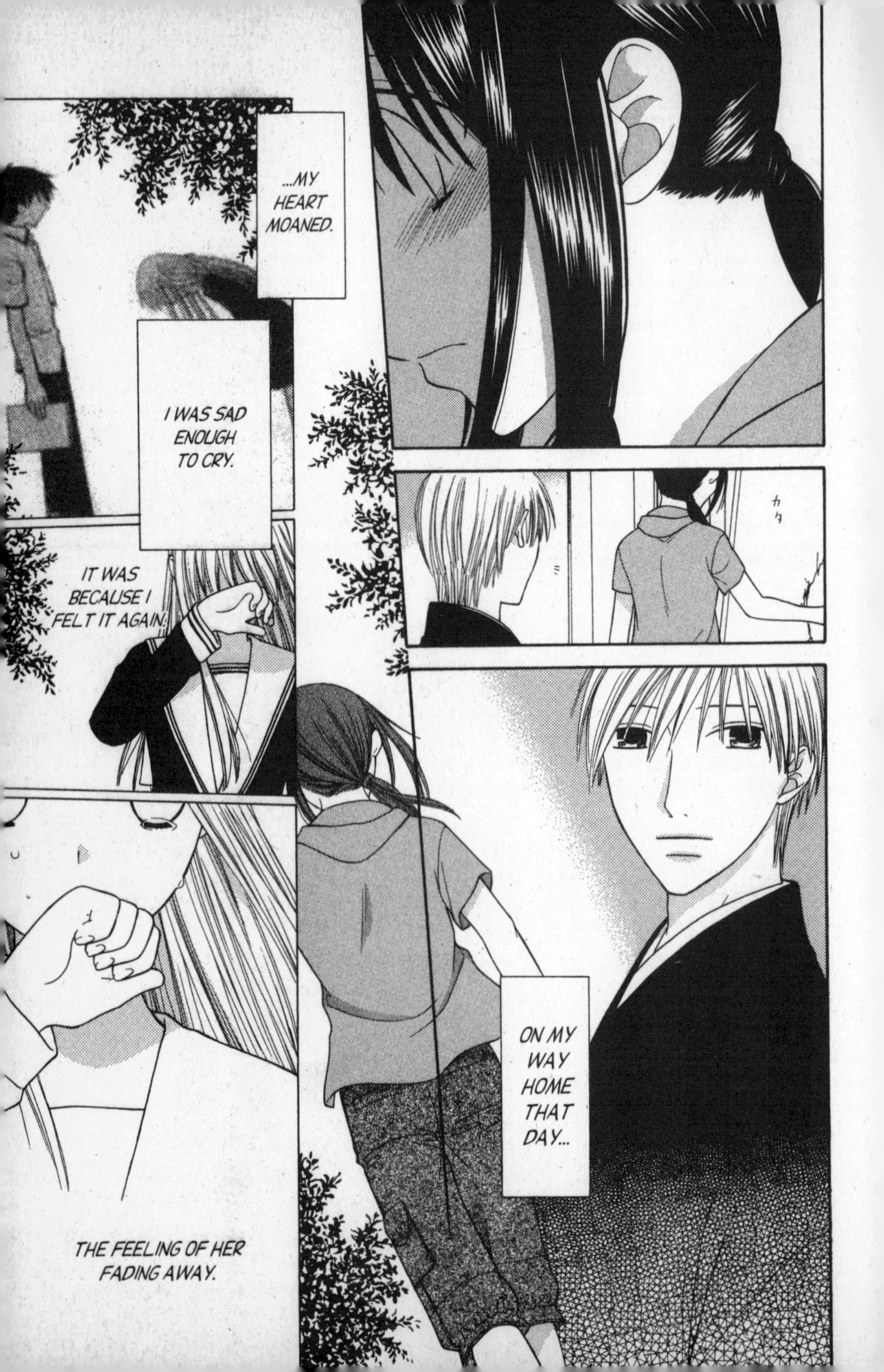
カチ
ON MY WAY HOME THAT DAY...
...MY HEART MOANED.
I WAS SAD ENOUGH TO CRY.
IT WAS BECAUSE I FELT IT AGAIN.
THE FEELING OF HER FADING AWAY.

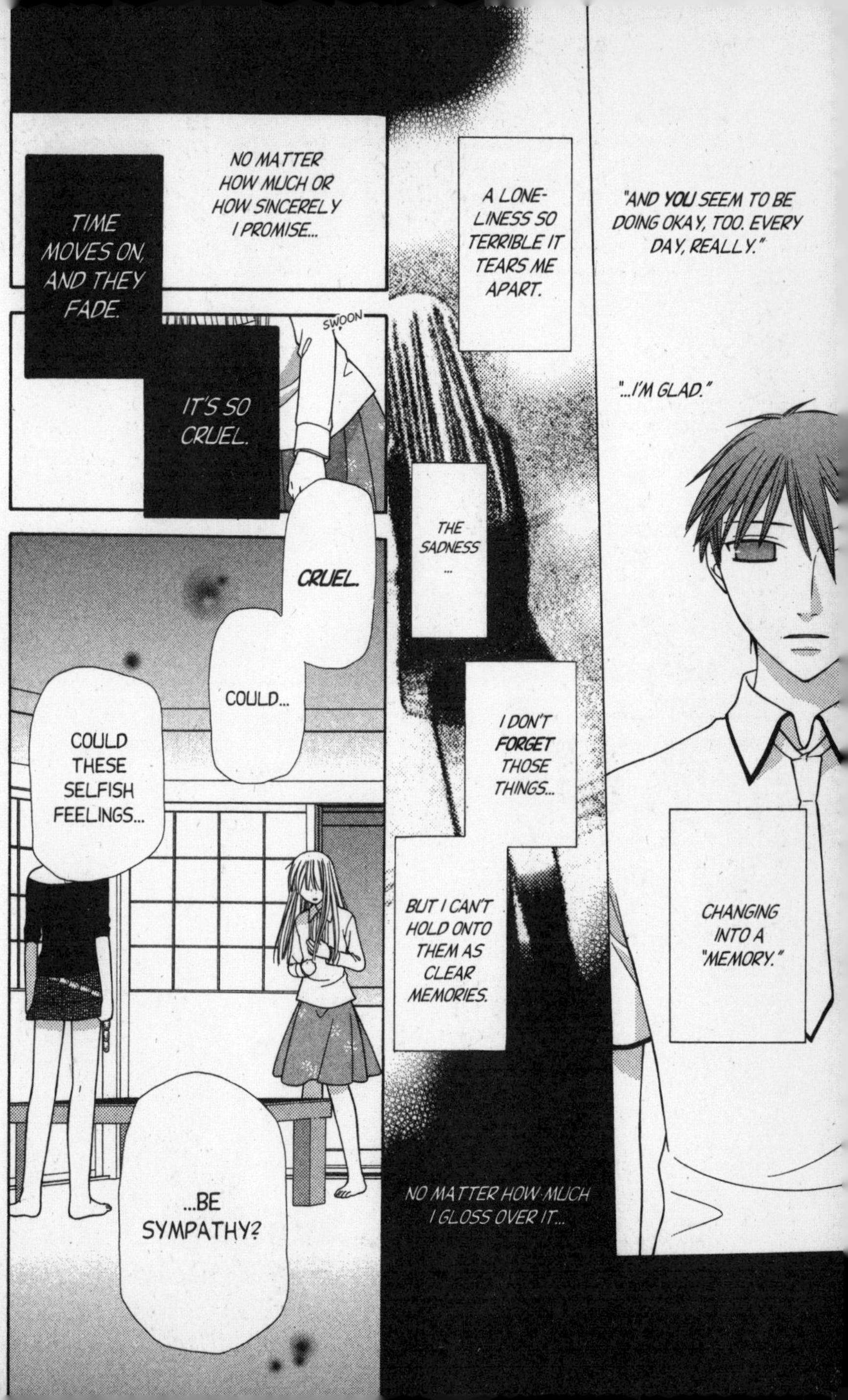
"AND YOU SEEM TO BE DOING OKAY, TOO. EVERY DAY, REALLY."
"...I'M GLAD."
CHANGING INTO A "MEMORY."
A LONELINESS SO TERRIBLE IT TEARS ME APART.
THE SADNESS...
I DON'T FORGET THOSE THINGS...
BUT I CAN'T HOLD ONTO THEM AS CLEAR MEMORIES.
NO MATTER HOW MUCH I GLOSS OVER IT...
NO MATTER HOW MUCH OR HOW SINCERELY I PROMISE...
TIME MOVES ON, AND THEY FADE.
SWOON
IT'S SO CRUEL.
CRUEL.
COULD...
COULD THESE SELFISH FEELINGS...
...BE SYMPATHY?

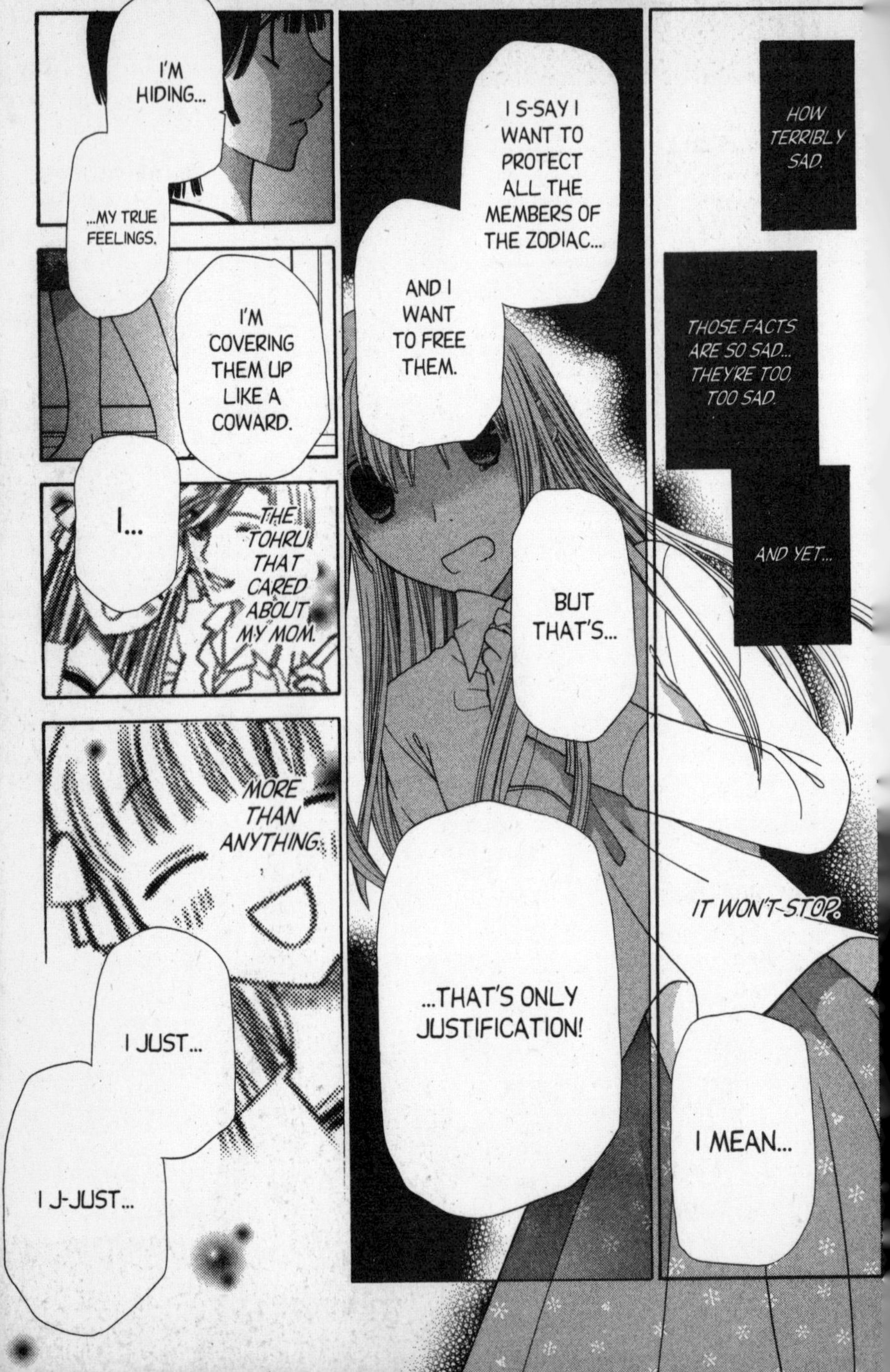
HOW TERRIBLY SAD.
THOSE FACTS ARE SO SAD... THEY'RE TOO, TOO SAD.
AND YET...
IT WON'T STOP.
I MEAN...
I S-SAY I WANT TO PROTECT ALL THE MEMBERS OF THE ZODIAC...
AND I WANT TO FREE THEM.
BUT THAT'S...
...THAT'S ONLY JUSTIFICATION!
I'M HIDING...
...MY TRUE FEELINGS.
I'M COVERING THEM UP LIKE A COWARD.
I...
THE TOHRU THAT CARED ABOUT MY MOM.
MORE THAN ANYTHING.
I JUST...
I J-JUST...

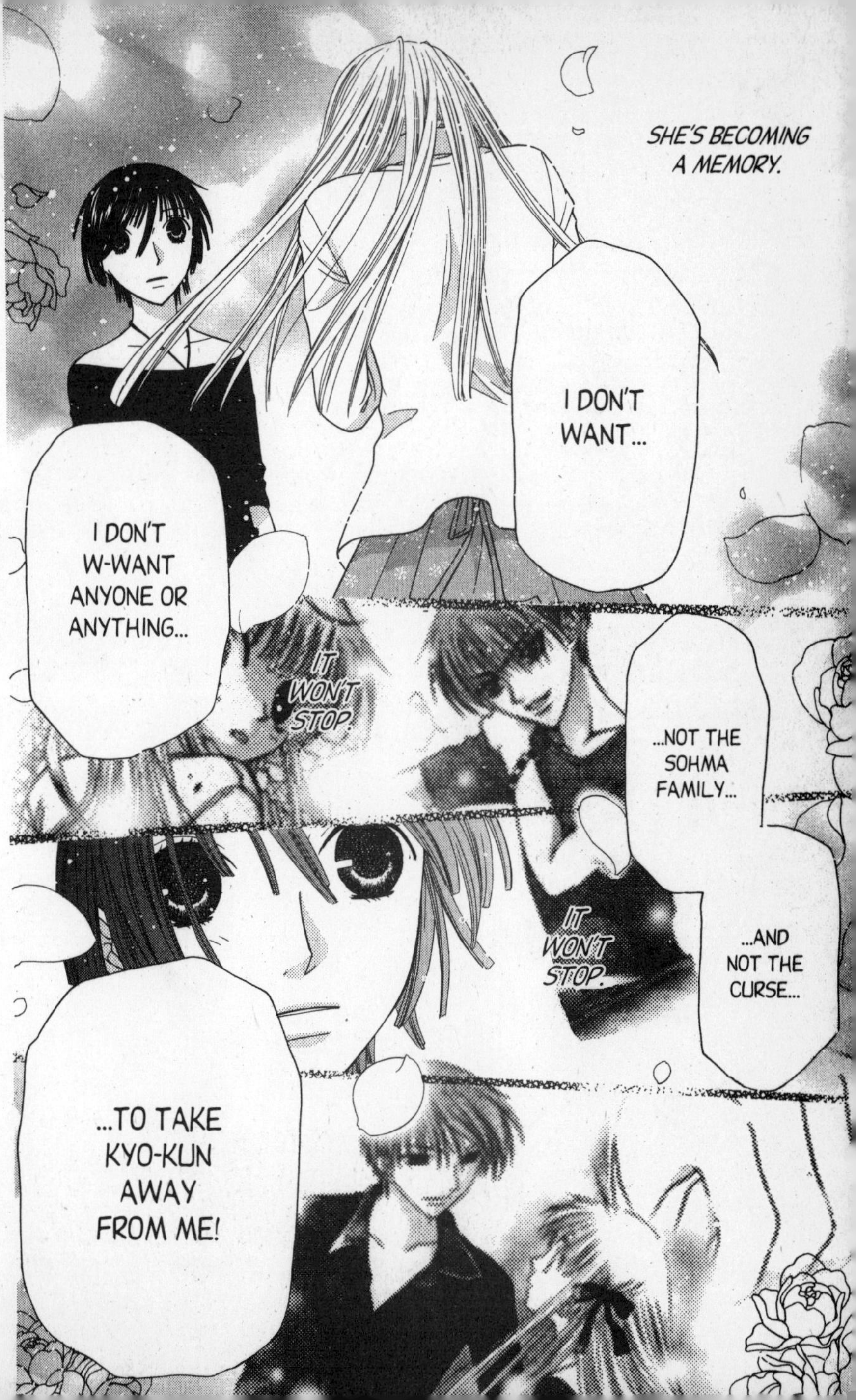
SHE'S BECOMING A MEMORY.
I DON'T WANT...
I DON'T W-WANT ANYONE OR ANYTHING...
...NOT THE SOHMA FAMILY...
IT WON'T STOP.
...AND NOT THE CURSE...
IT WON'T STOP.
...TO TAKE KYO-KUN AWAY FROM ME!

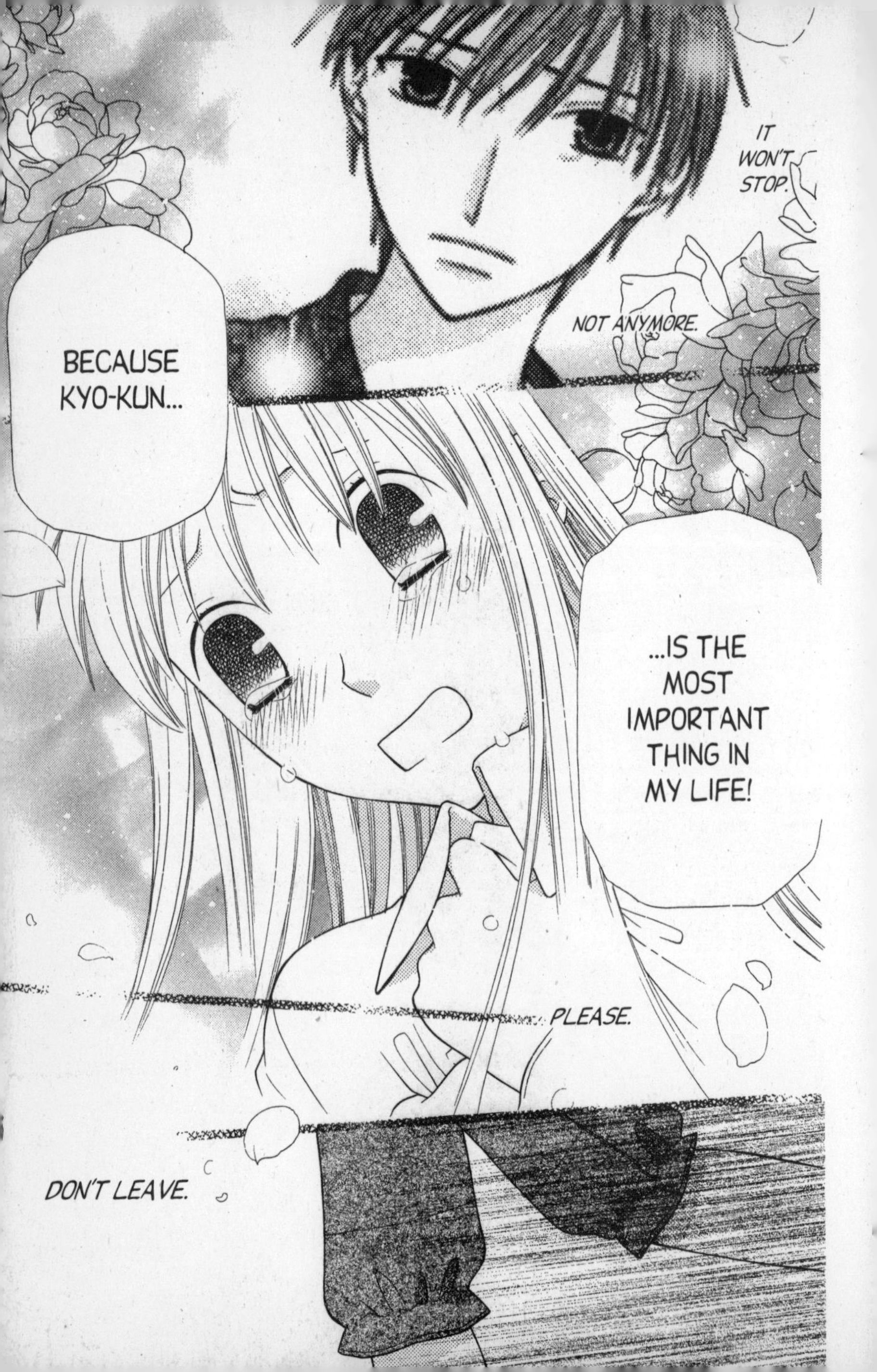
IT WON'T STOP.
NOT ANYMORE.
BECAUSE KYO-KUN...
...IS THE MOST IMPORTANT THING IN MY LIFE!
PLEASE.
DON'T LEAVE.

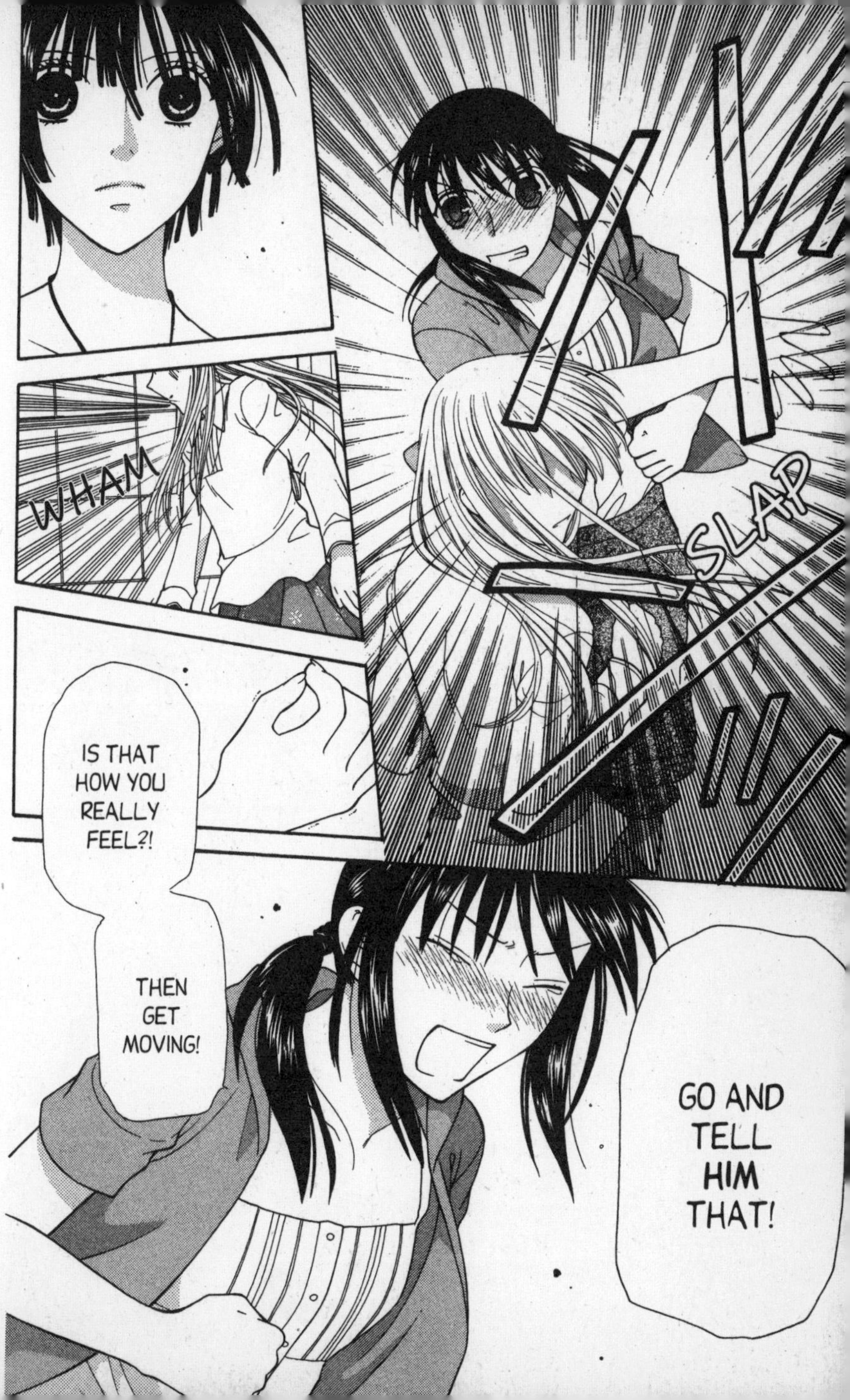
SLAP
WHAM
IS THAT HOW YOU REALLY FEEL?!
THEN GET MOVING!
GO AND TELL HIM THAT!

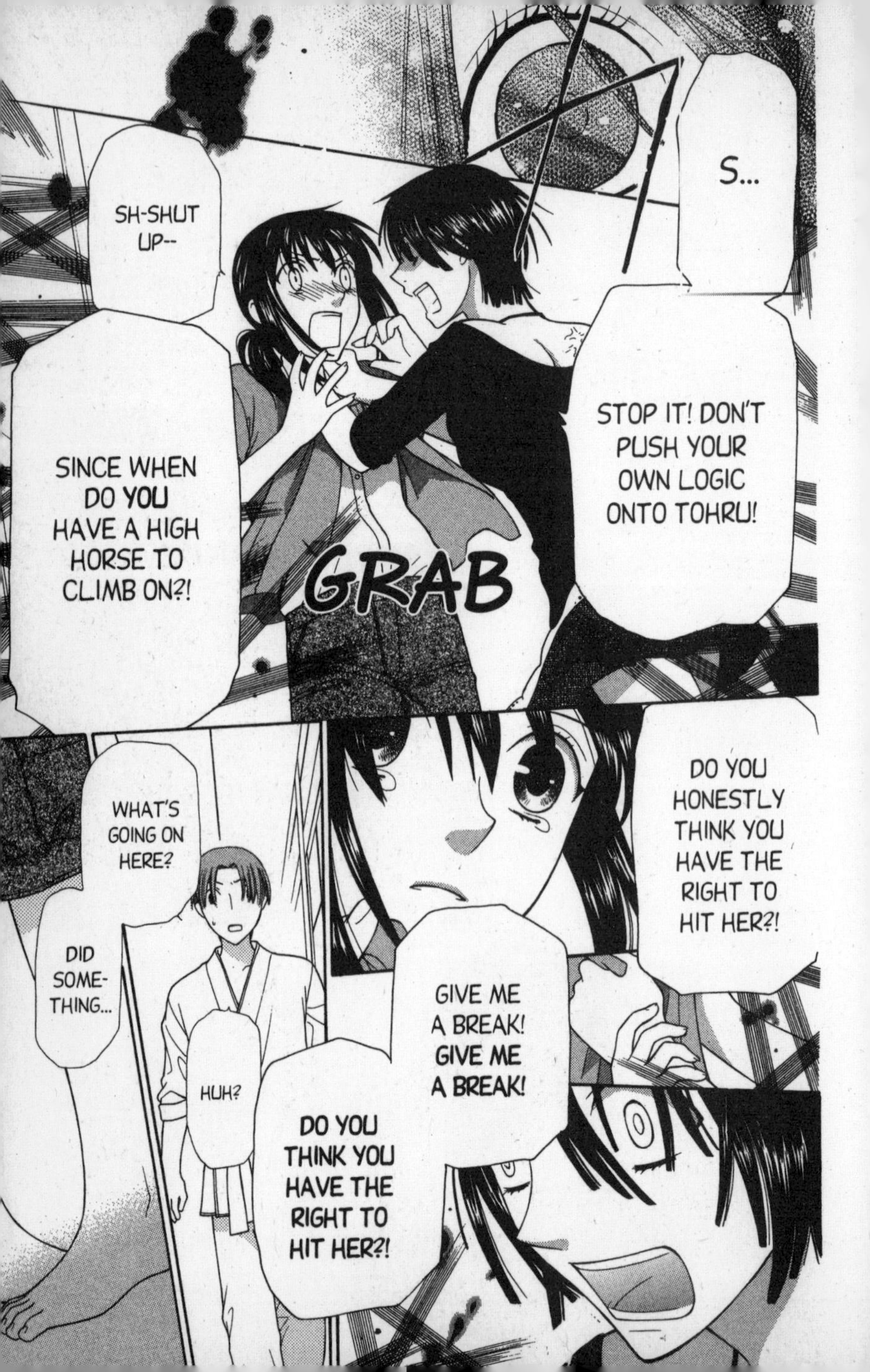
S...
STOP IT! DON'T PUSH YOUR OWN LOGIC ONTO TOHRU!
SH-SHUT UP--
SINCE WHEN DO YOU HAVE A HIGH HORSE TO CLIMB ON?!
GRAB
DO YOU HONESTLY THINK YOU HAVE THE RIGHT TO HIT HER?!
GIVE ME A BREAK! GIVE ME A BREAK!
DO YOU THINK YOU HAVE THE RIGHT TO HIT HER?!
WHAT'S GOING ON HERE?
DID SOMETHING...
HUH?

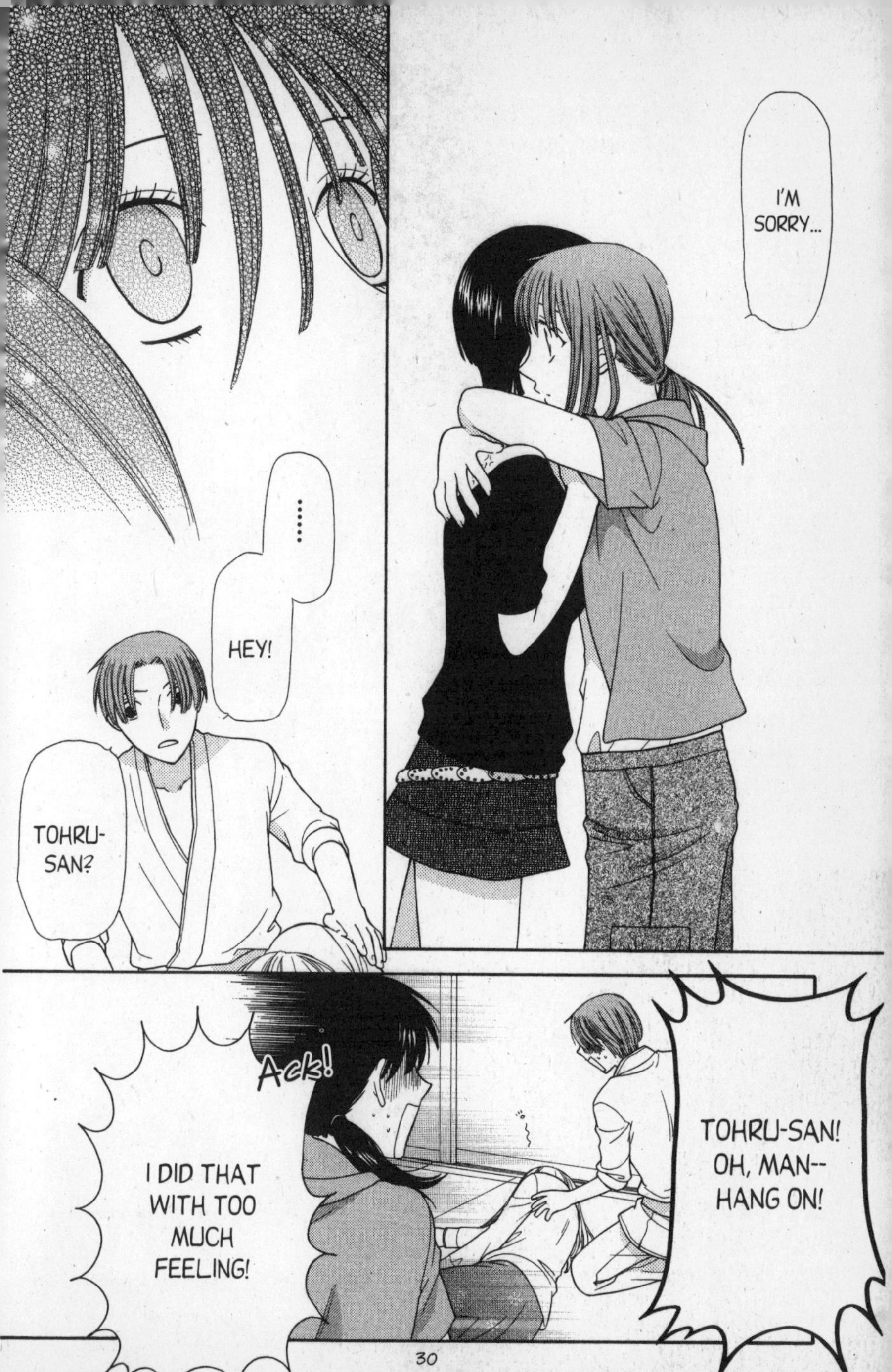
I'M SORRY...
......
HEY!
TOHRU-SAN?
TOHRU-SAN! OH, MAN-- HANG ON!
Ack!
I DID THAT WITH TOO MUCH FEELING!

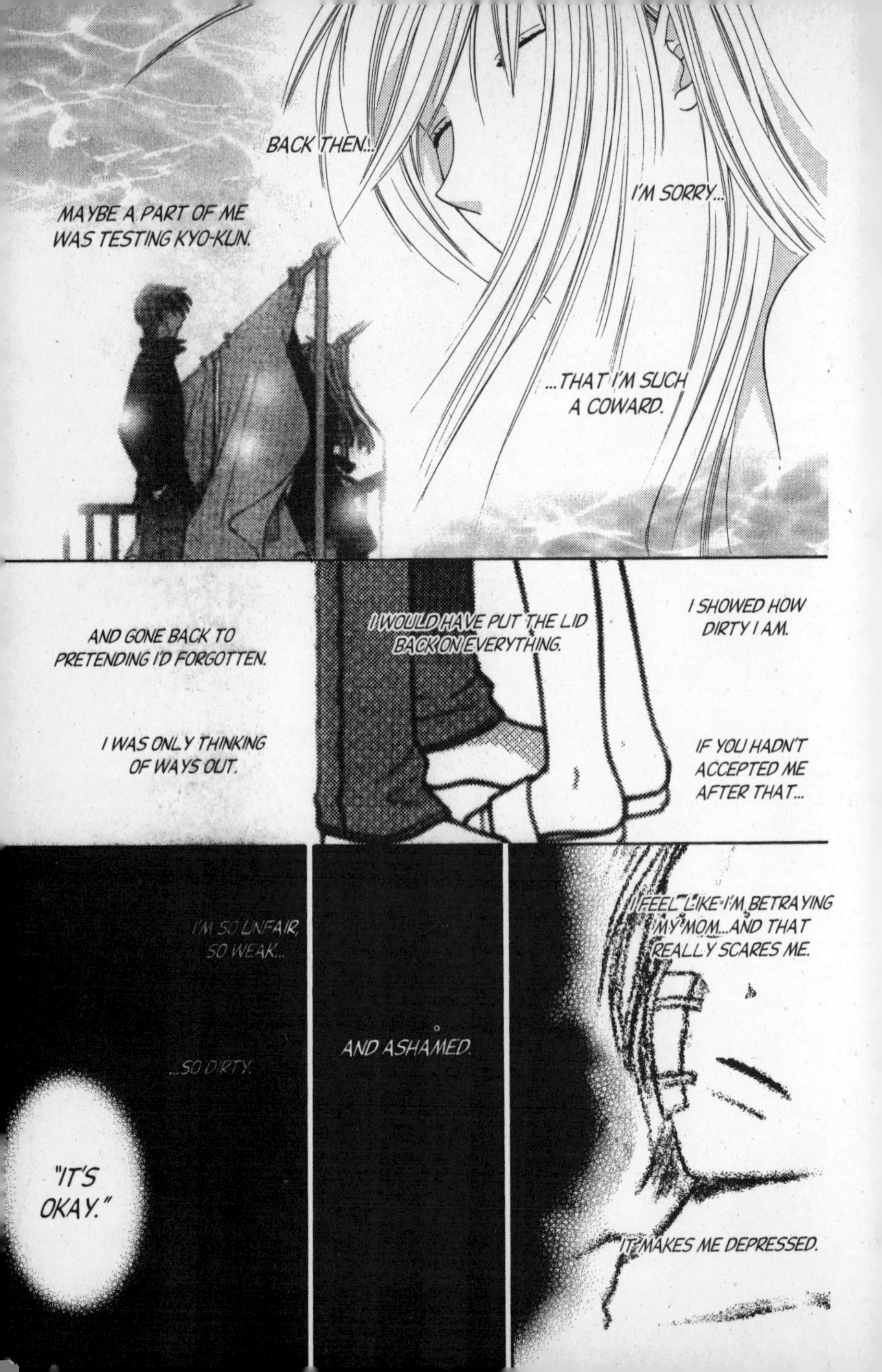
I'M SORRY...
...THAT I'M SUCH A COWARD.
BACK THEN...
MAYBE A PART OF ME WAS TESTING KYO-KUN.
I SHOWED HOW DIRTY I AM.
IF YOU HADN'T ACCEPTED ME AFTER THAT...
I WOULD HAVE PUT THE LID BACK ON EVERYTHING.
AND GONE BACK TO PRETENDING I'D FORGOTTEN.
I WAS ONLY THINKING OF WAYS OUT.
I FEEL LIKE I'M BETRAYING MY MOM...AND THAT REALLY SCARES ME.
IT MAKES ME DEPRESSED.
AND ASHAMED.
I'M SO UNFAIR, SO WEAK...
...SO DIRTY.
"IT'S OKAY."

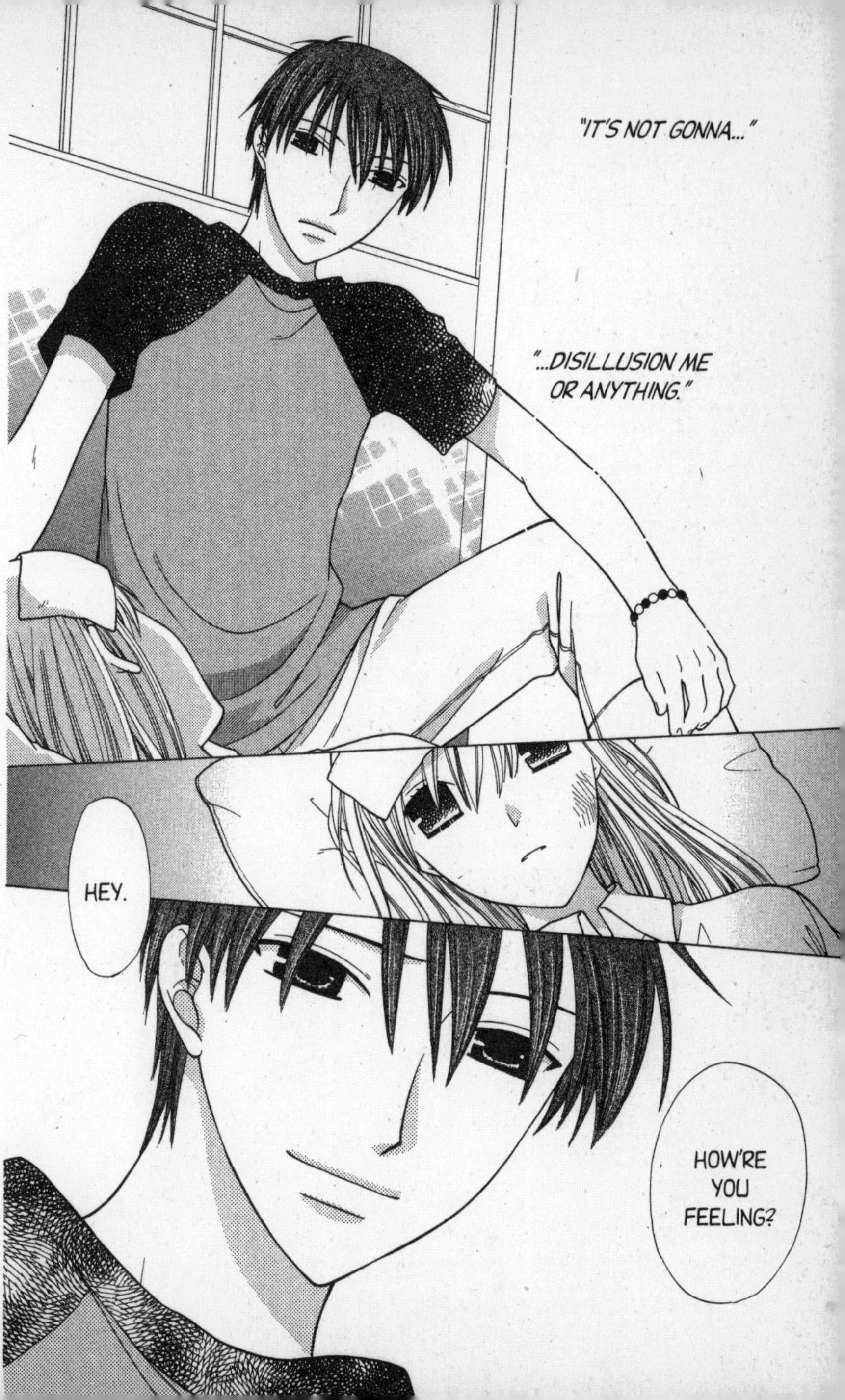
"IT'S NOT GONNA..."
"...DISILLUSION ME OR ANYTHING."
HEY.
HOW'RE YOU FEELING?

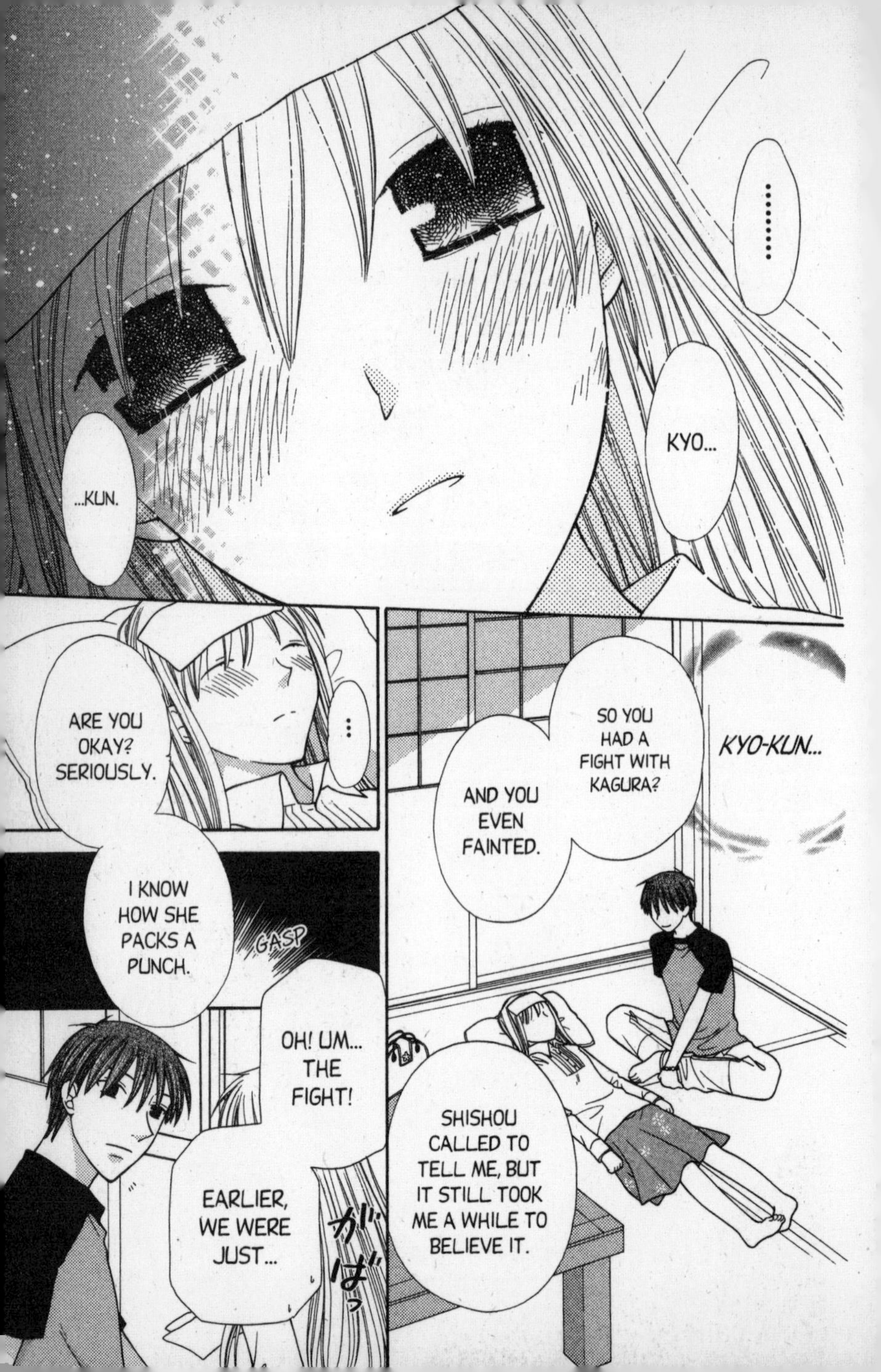

......
KYO...
...KUN.
KYO-KUN...
SO YOU HAD A FIGHT WITH KAGURA?
AND YOU EVEN FAINTED.
SHISHOU CALLED TO TELL ME, BUT IT STILL TOOK ME A WHILE TO BELIEVE IT.
...
ARE YOU OKAY? SERIOUSLY.
I KNOW HOW SHE PACKS A PUNCH.
GASP
OH! UM... THE FIGHT!
EARLIER, WE WERE JUST...
がばっ

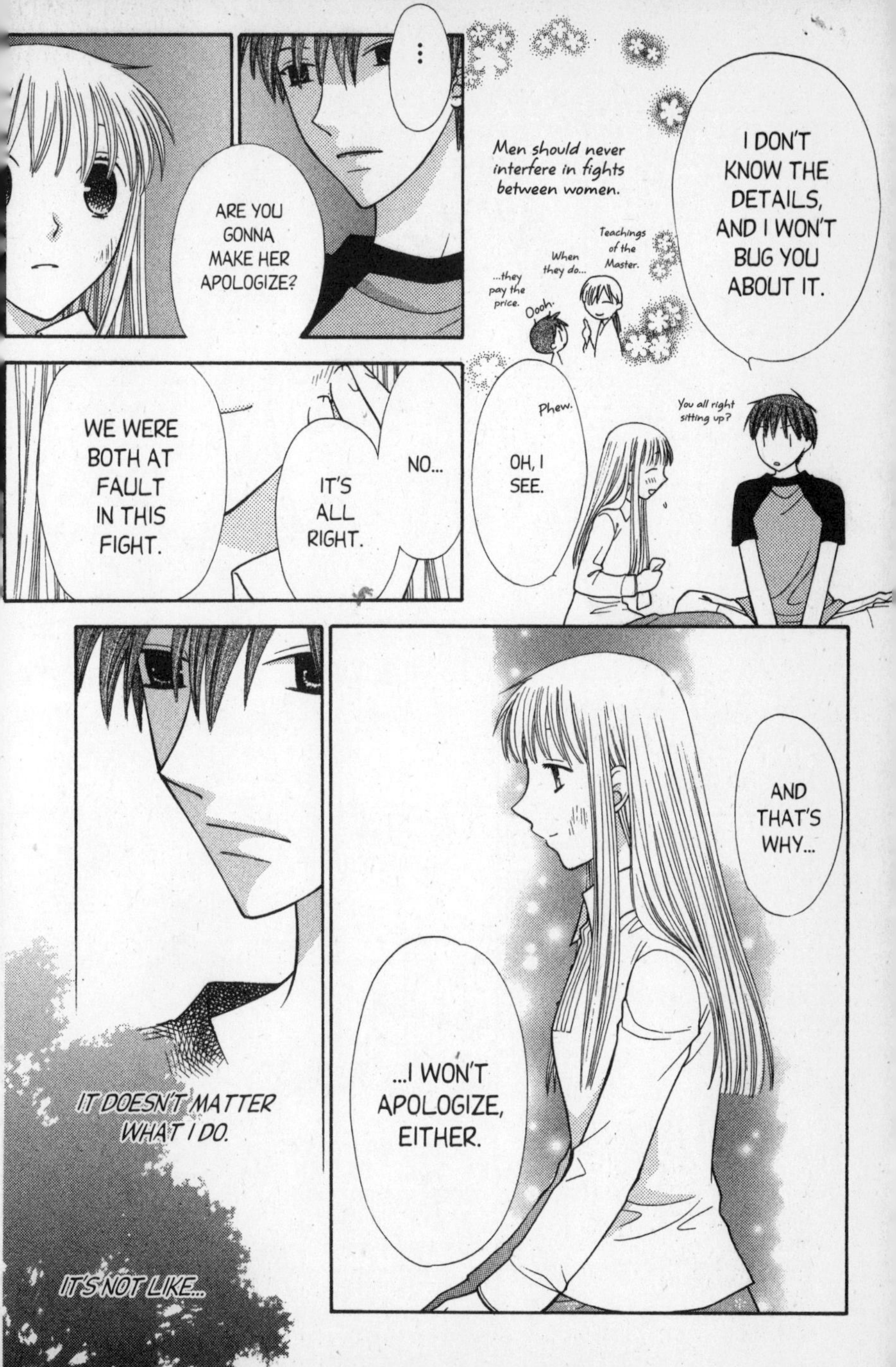
I DON'T KNOW THE DETAILS, AND I WON'T BUG YOU ABOUT IT.
Men should never interfere in fights between women.
Teachings of the Master.
When they do...
...they pay the price.
Oooh.
You all right sitting up?
Phew.
OH, I SEE.
...
ARE YOU GONNA MAKE HER APOLOGIZE?
NO...
IT'S ALL RIGHT.
WE WERE BOTH AT FAULT IN THIS FIGHT.
AND THAT'S WHY...
...I WON'T APOLOGIZE, EITHER.
IT DOESN'T MATTER WHAT I DO.
IT'S NOT LIKE...

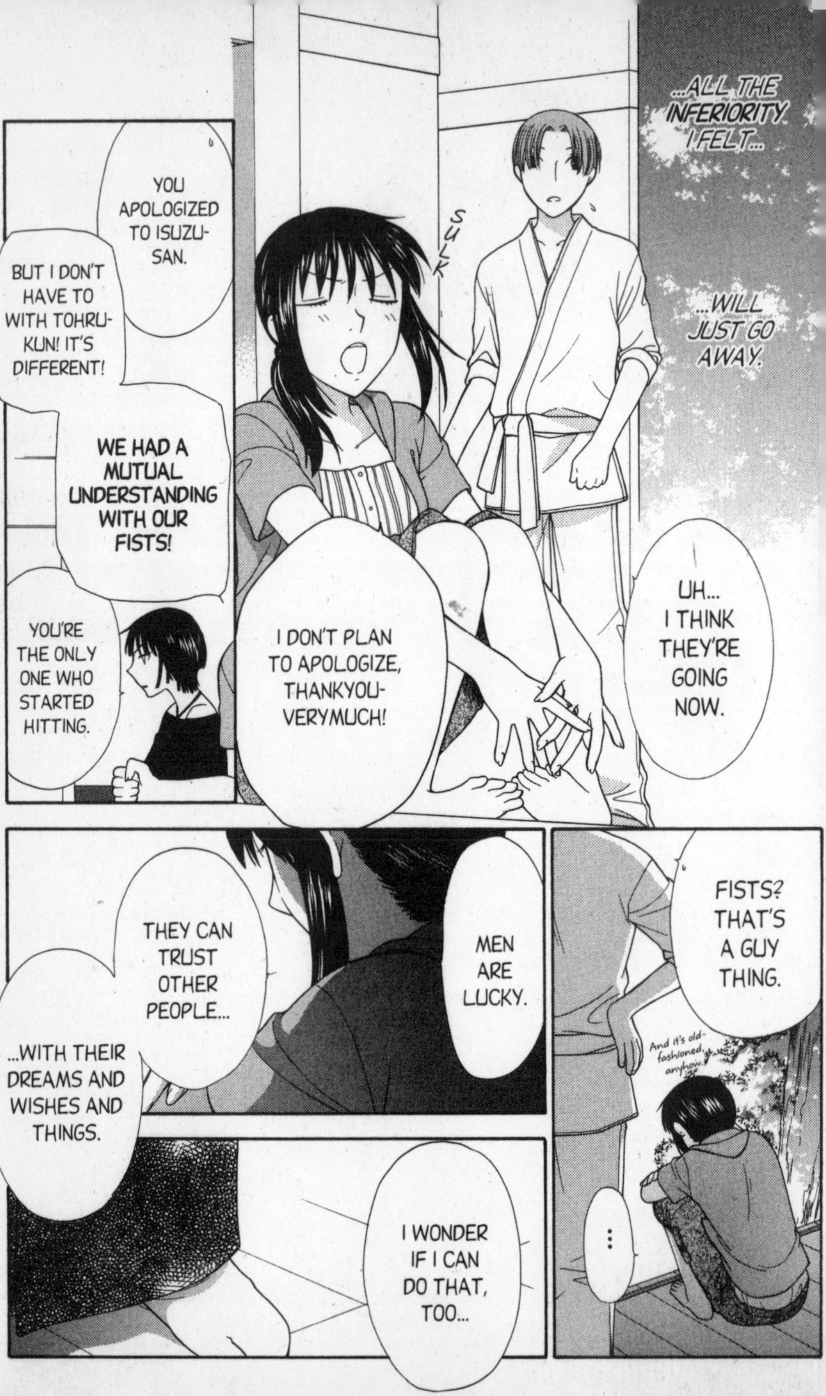
...ALL THE INFERIORITY I FELT...
...WILL JUST GO AWAY.
UH... I THINK THEY'RE GOING NOW.
SULK
YOU APOLOGIZED TO ISUZU-SAN.
BUT I DON'T HAVE TO WITH TOHRU-KUN! IT'S DIFFERENT!
WE HAD A MUTUAL UNDERSTANDING WITH OUR FISTS!
YOU'RE THE ONLY ONE WHO STARTED HITTING.
I DON'T PLAN TO APOLOGIZE, THANKYOU-VERYMUCH!
FISTS? THAT'S A GUY THING.
And it's old-fashioned, anyhow.
...
MEN ARE LUCKY.
THEY CAN TRUST OTHER PEOPLE...
...WITH THEIR DREAMS AND WISHES AND THINGS.
I WONDER IF I CAN DO THAT, TOO...

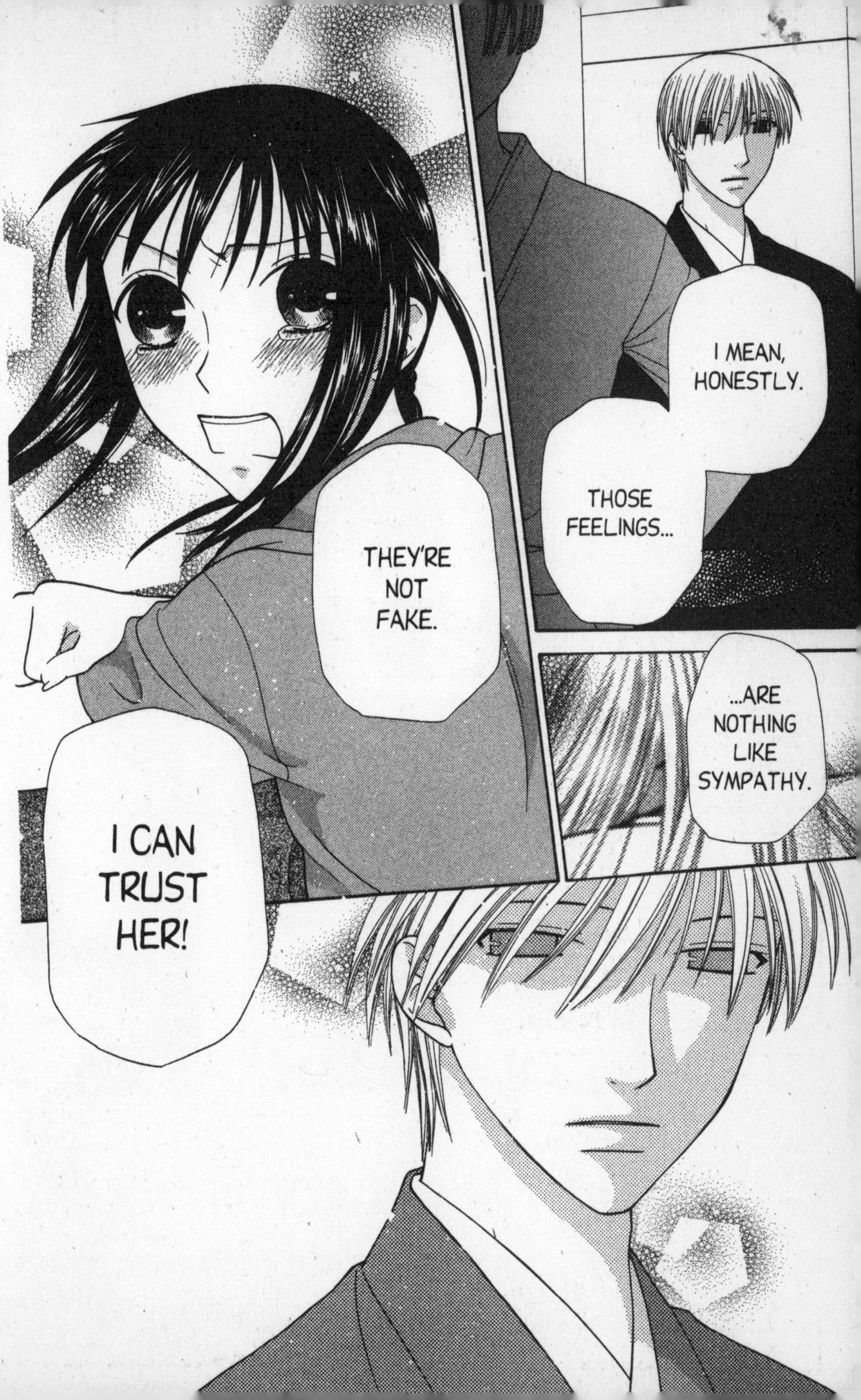
I MEAN, HONESTLY.
THOSE FEELINGS...
...ARE NOTHING LIKE SYMPATHY.
THEY'RE NOT FAKE.
I CAN TRUST HER!

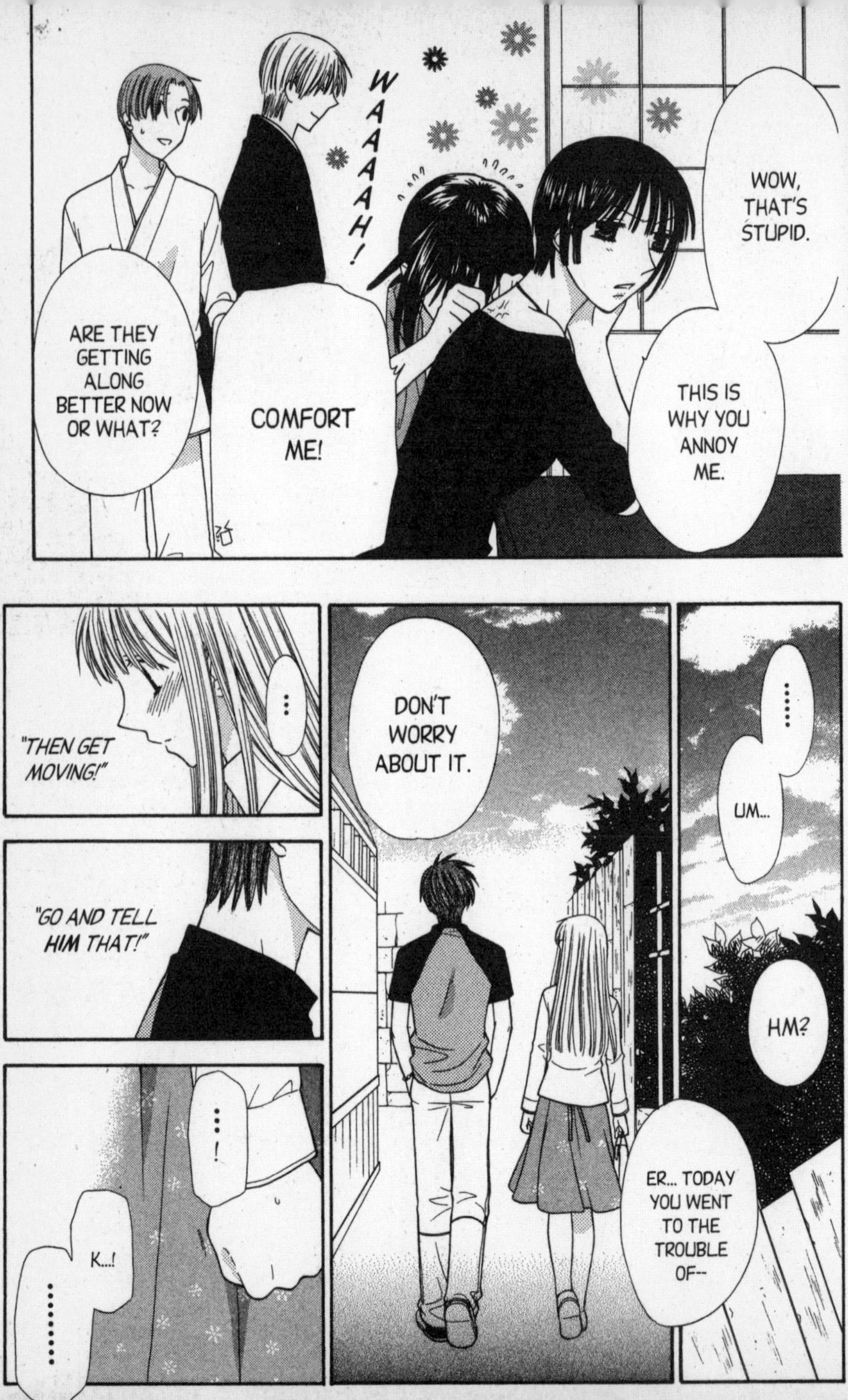
WOW, THAT'S STUPID.
THIS IS WHY YOU ANNOY ME.
WAAAAAH!
COMFORT ME!
ARE THEY GETTING ALONG BETTER NOW OR WHAT?
......
UM...
HM?
ER... TODAY YOU WENT TO THE TROUBLE OF--
DON'T WORRY ABOUT IT.
...
"THEN GET MOVING!"
"GO AND TELL HIM THAT!"
...!
K...!
....

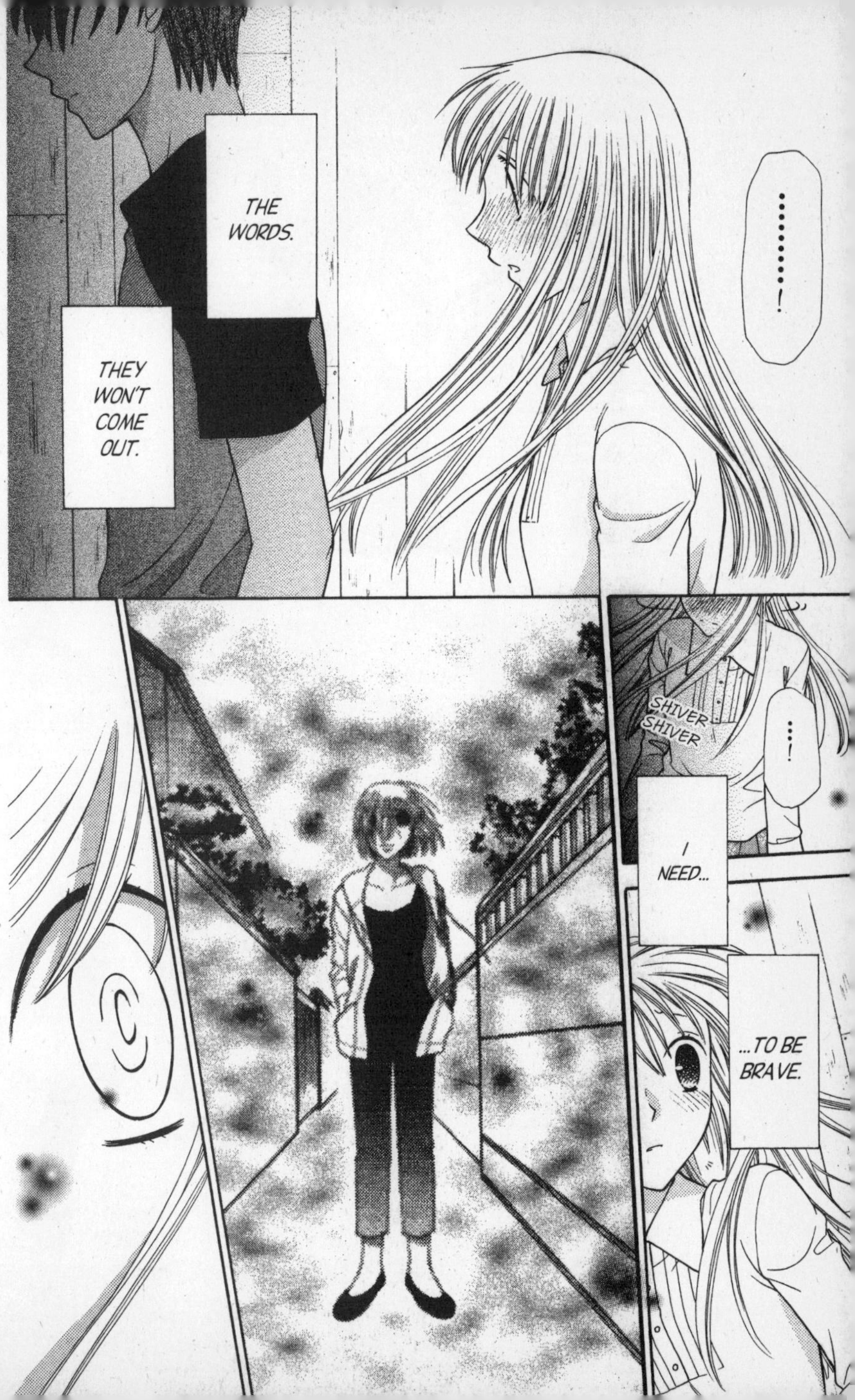
........!
THE WORDS.
THEY WON'T COME OUT.
...!
SHIVER SHIVER
I NEED...
...TO BE BRAVE.

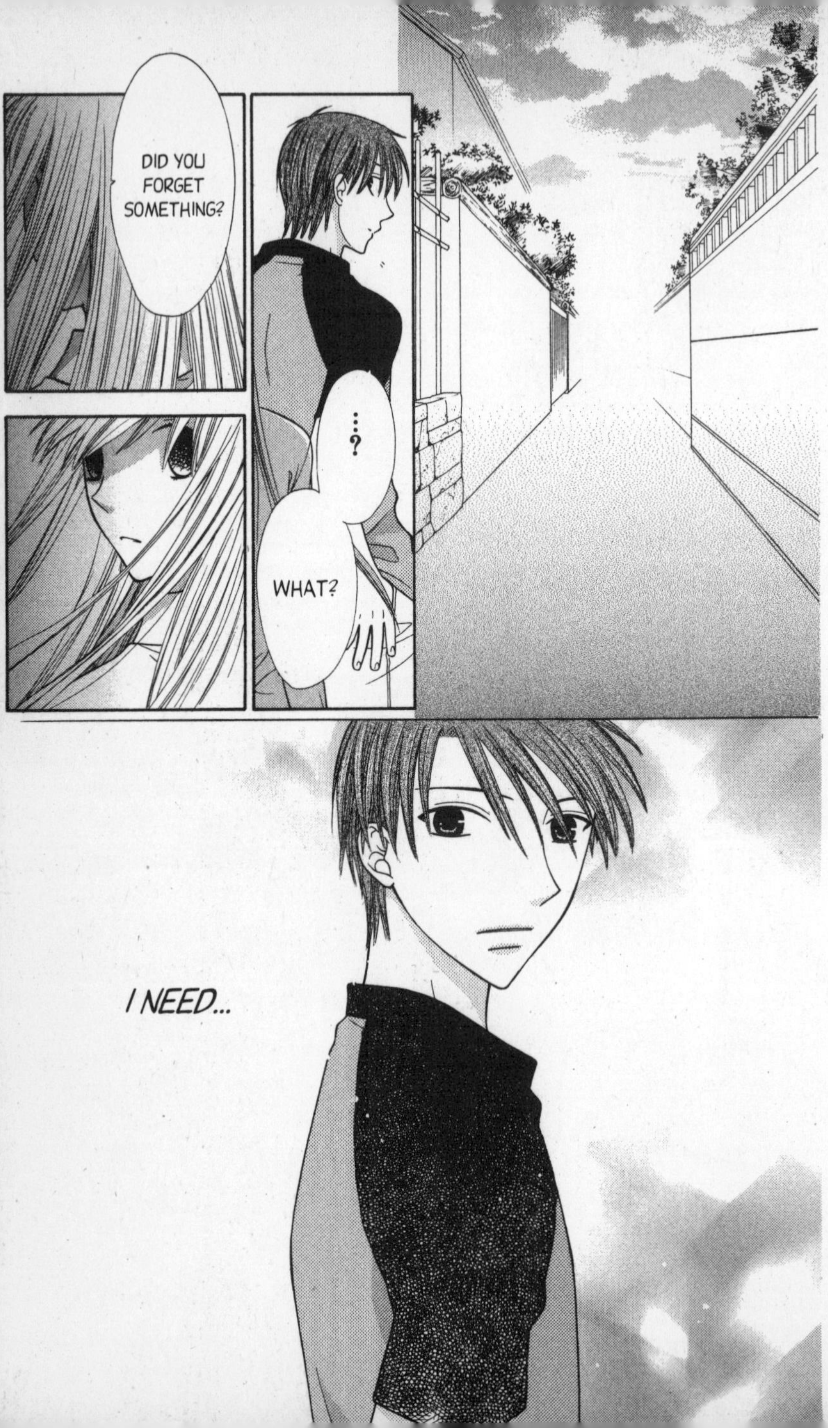
DID YOU FORGET SOMETHING?
...?
WHAT?
I NEED...

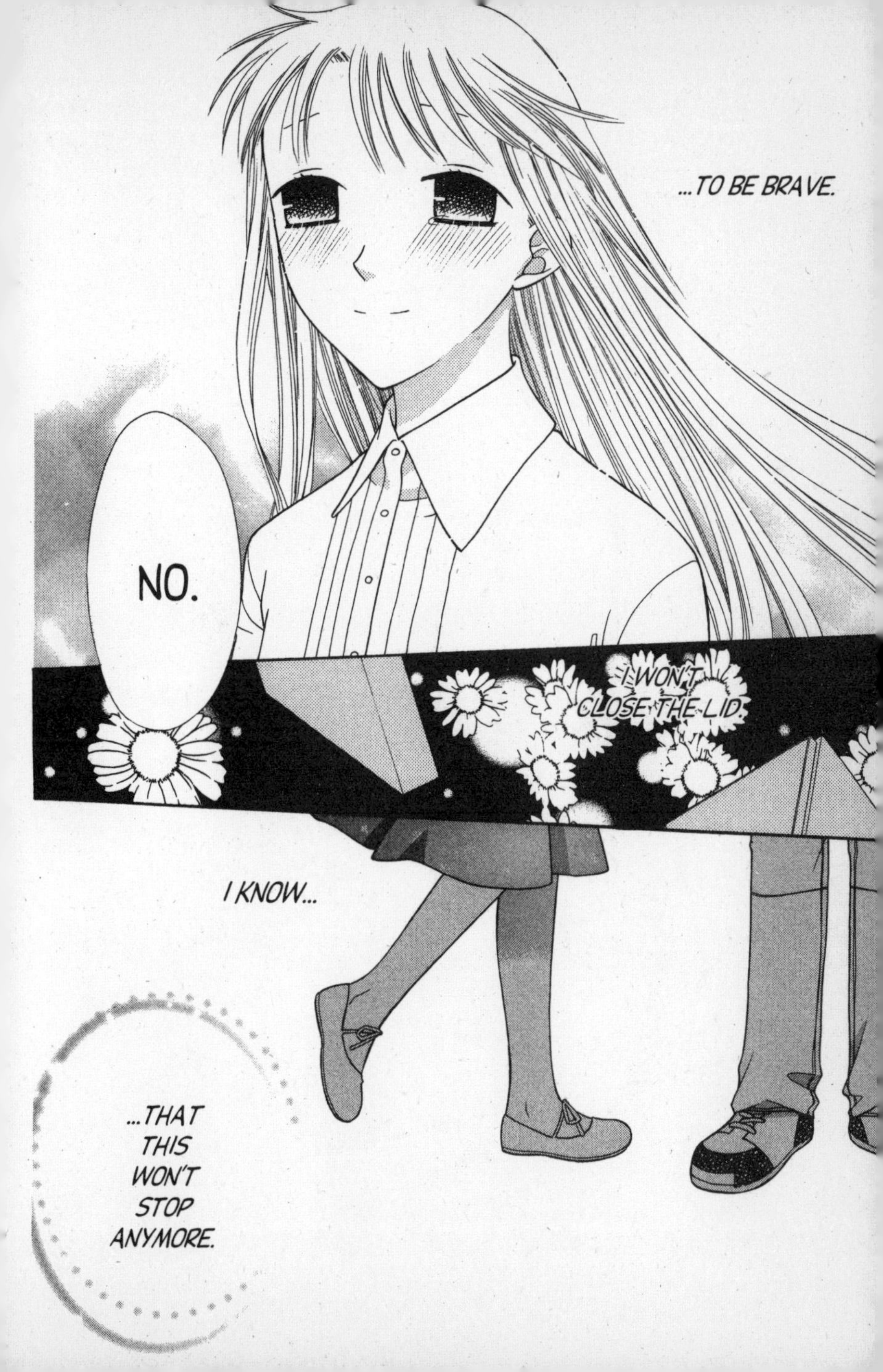
...TO BE BRAVE.
NO.
I WON'T CLOSE THE LID.
I KNOW...
...THAT THIS WON'T STOP ANYMORE.

Filler Sketch

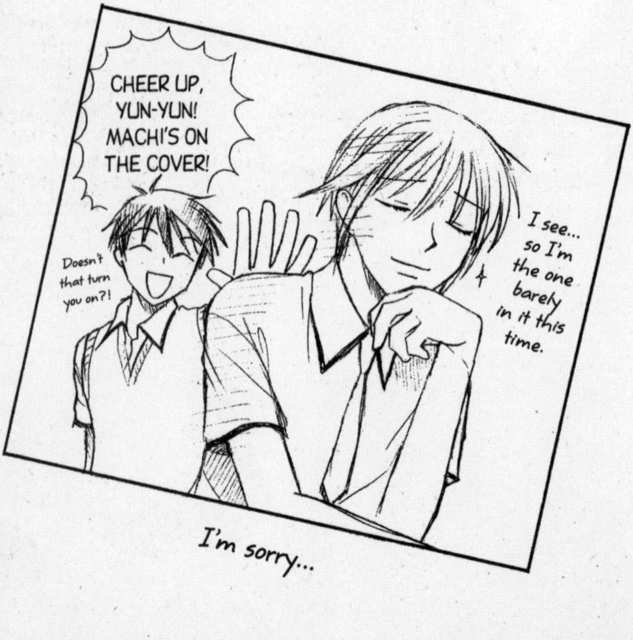
I see... so I'm the one barely in it this time.
CHEER UP, YUN-YUN! MACHI'S ON THE COVER!
Doesn't that turn you on?!
I'm sorry...

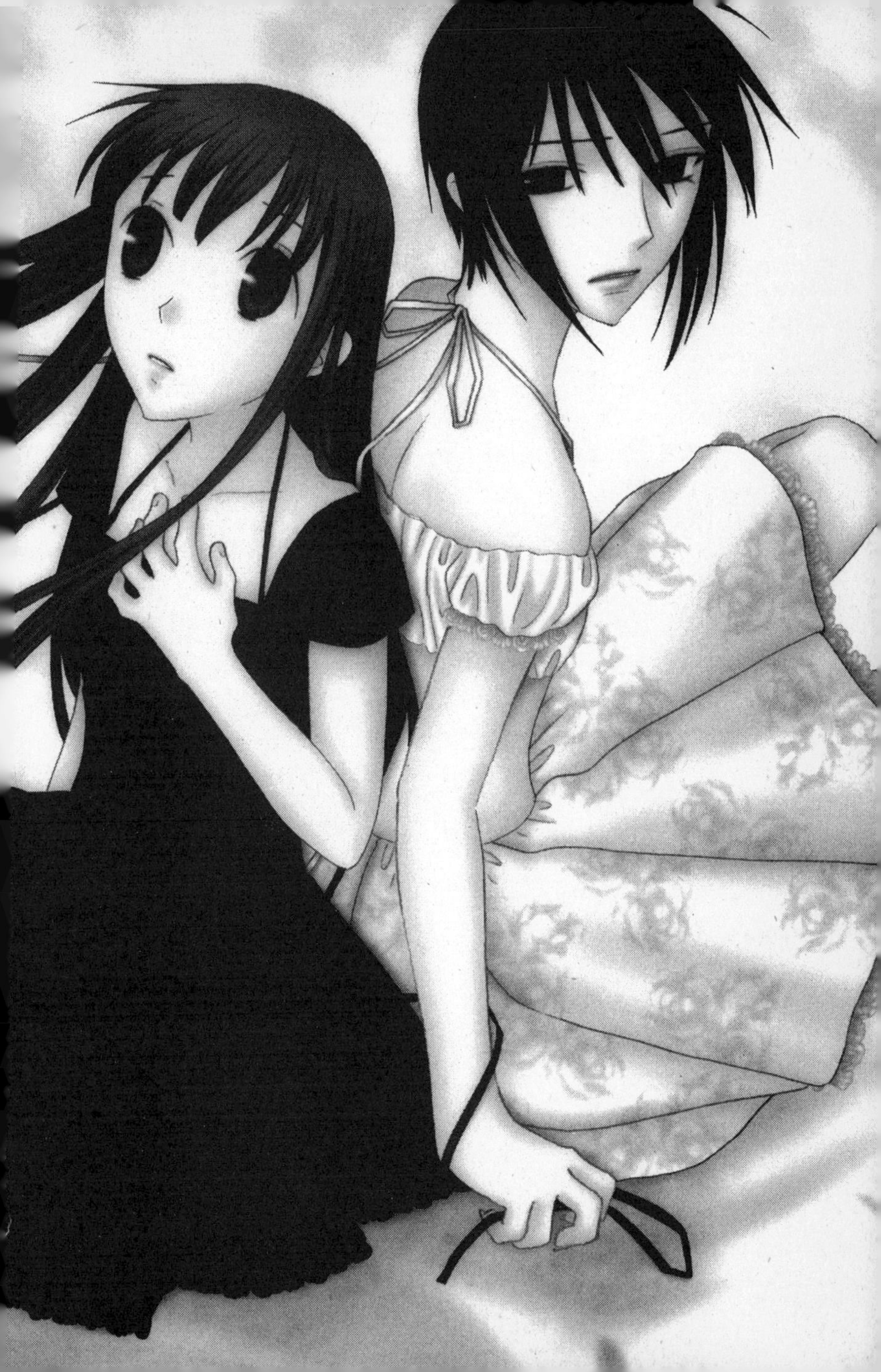

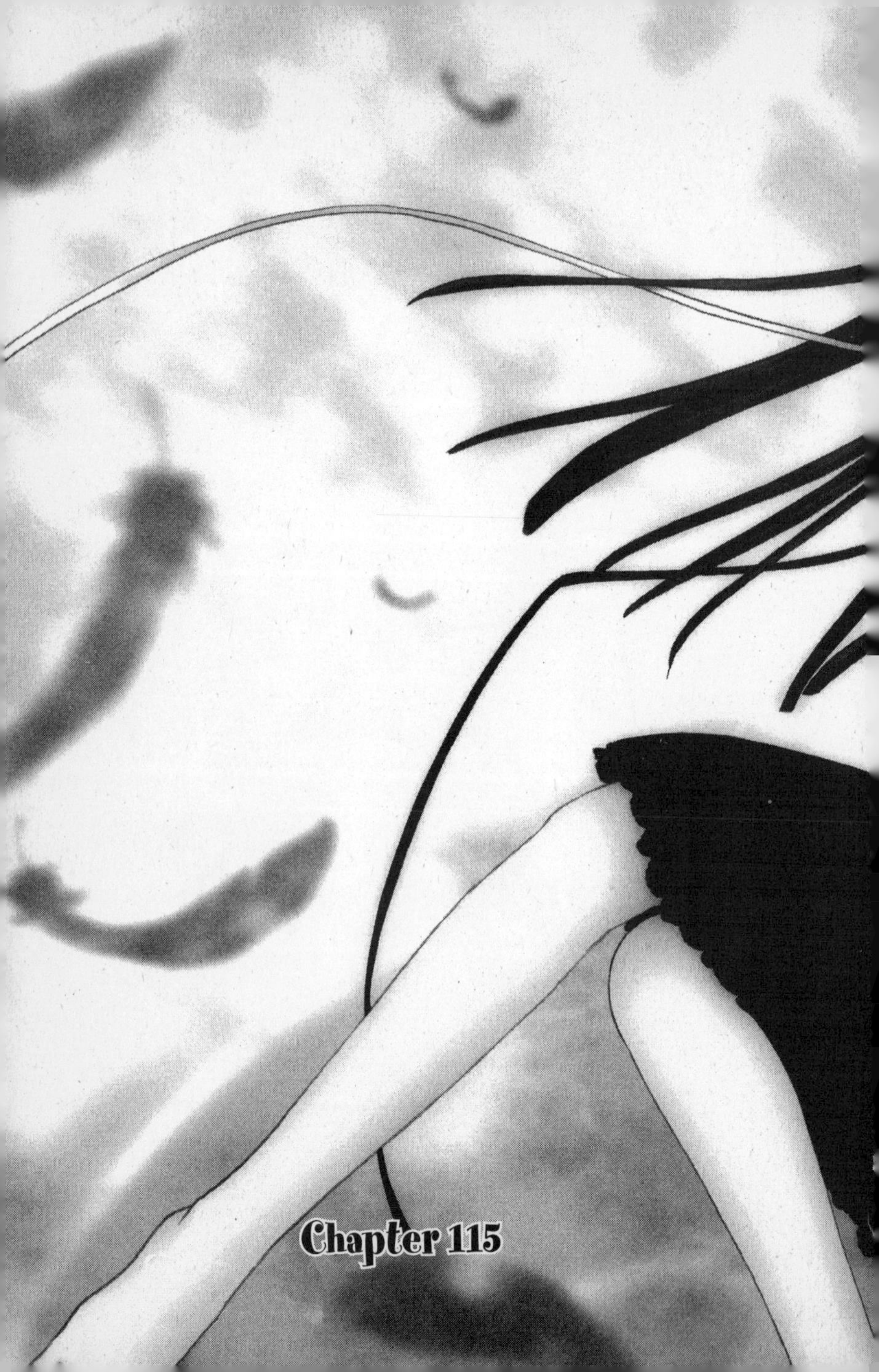
Chapter 115

Filler Sketch

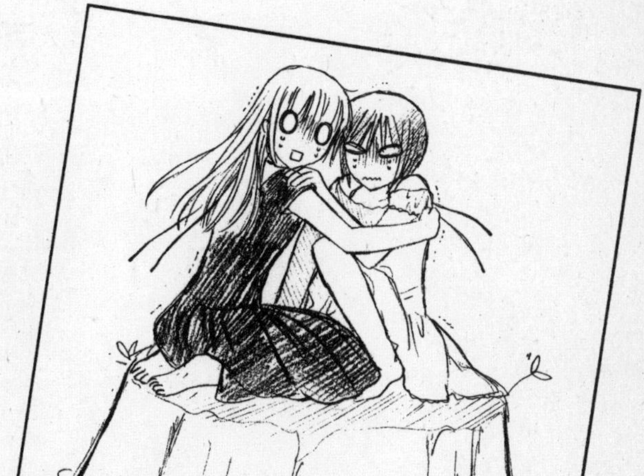
And the two approach the height of tribulation.

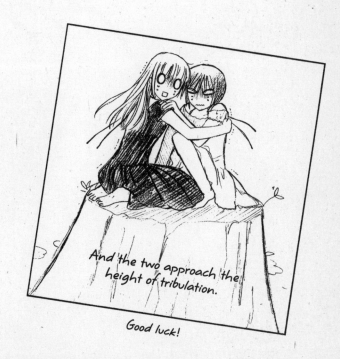

Good luck!

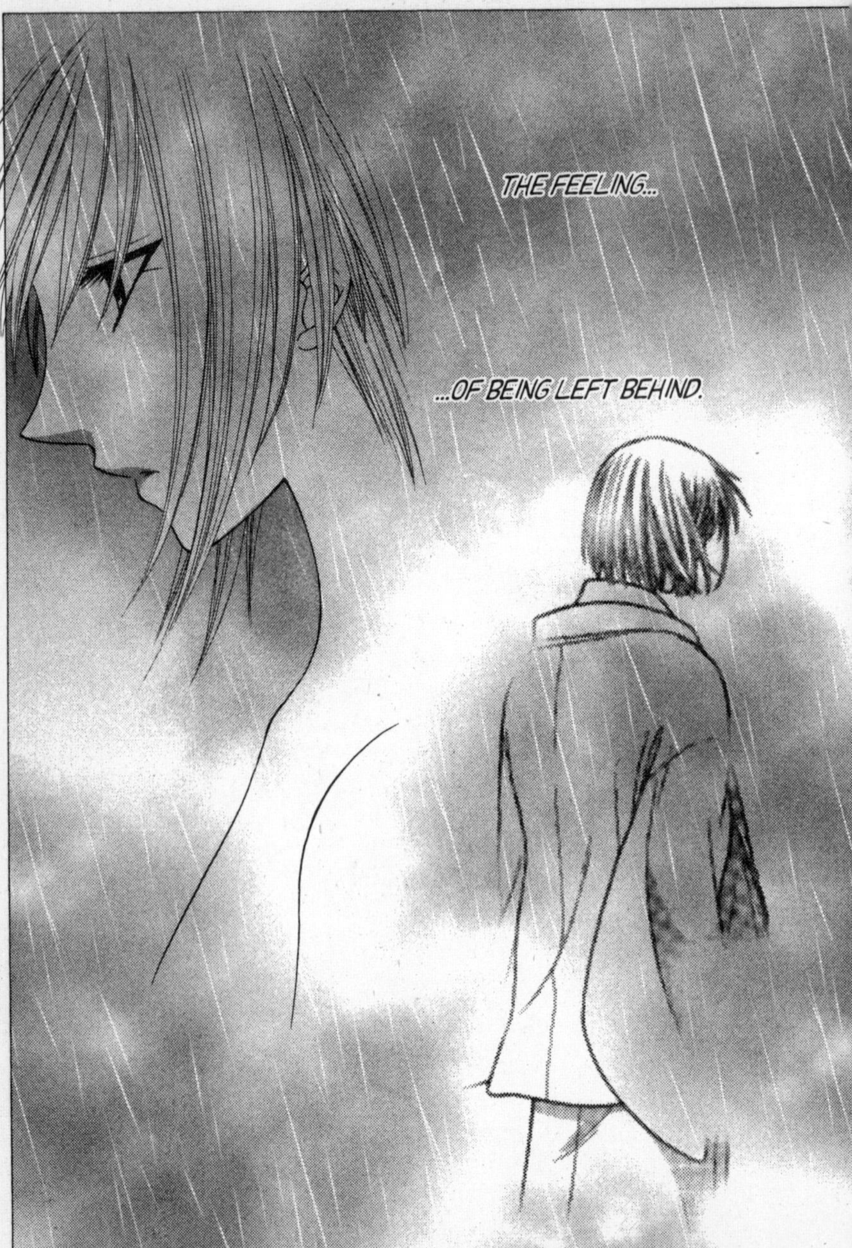
THE FEELING...
...OF BEING LEFT BEHIND.

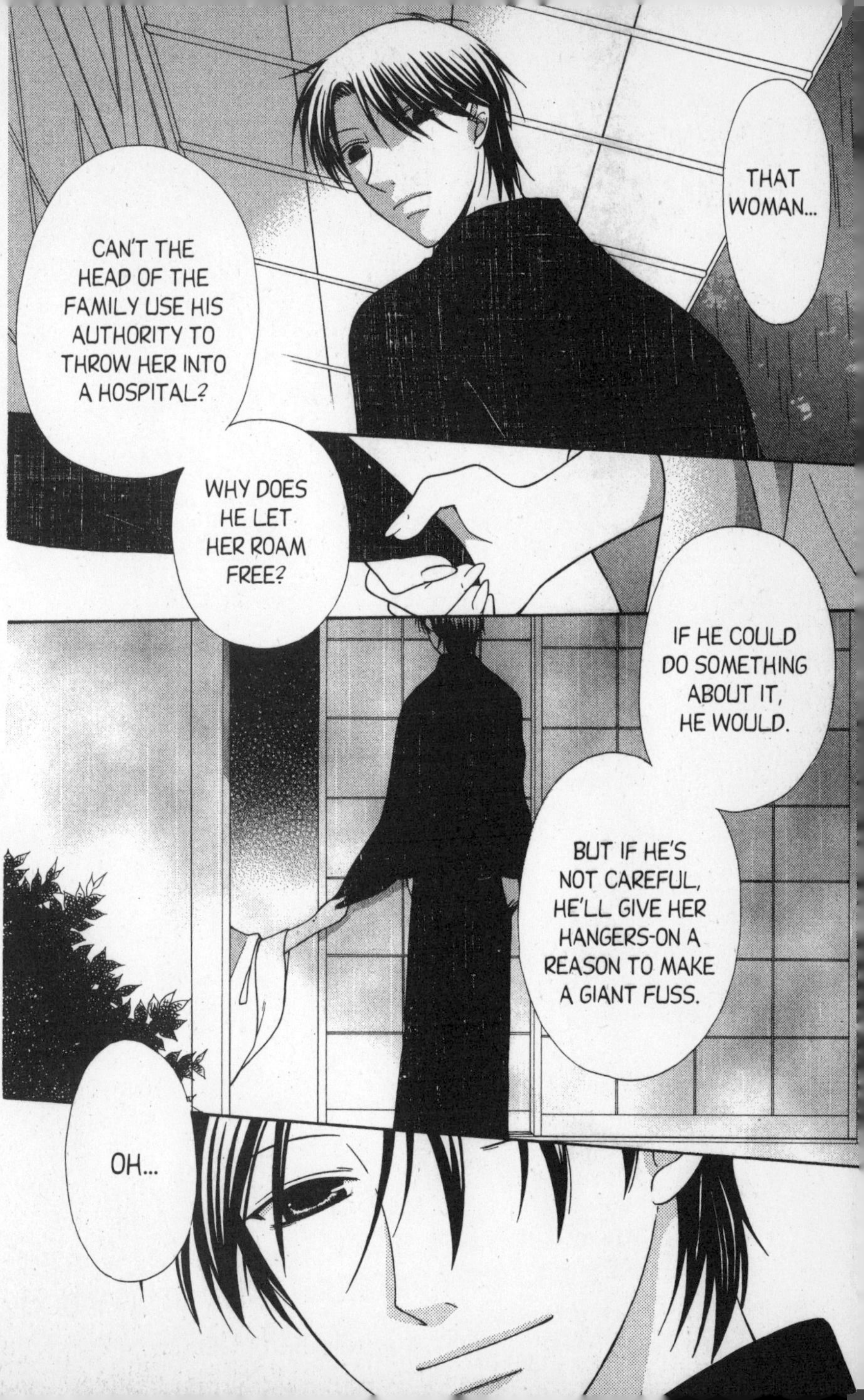
THAT WOMAN...
CAN'T THE HEAD OF THE FAMILY USE HIS AUTHORITY TO THROW HER INTO A HOSPITAL?
WHY DOES HE LET HER ROAM FREE?
IF HE COULD DO SOMETHING ABOUT IT, HE WOULD.
BUT IF HE'S NOT CAREFUL, HE'LL GIVE HER HANGERS-ON A REASON TO MAKE A GIANT FUSS.
OH...

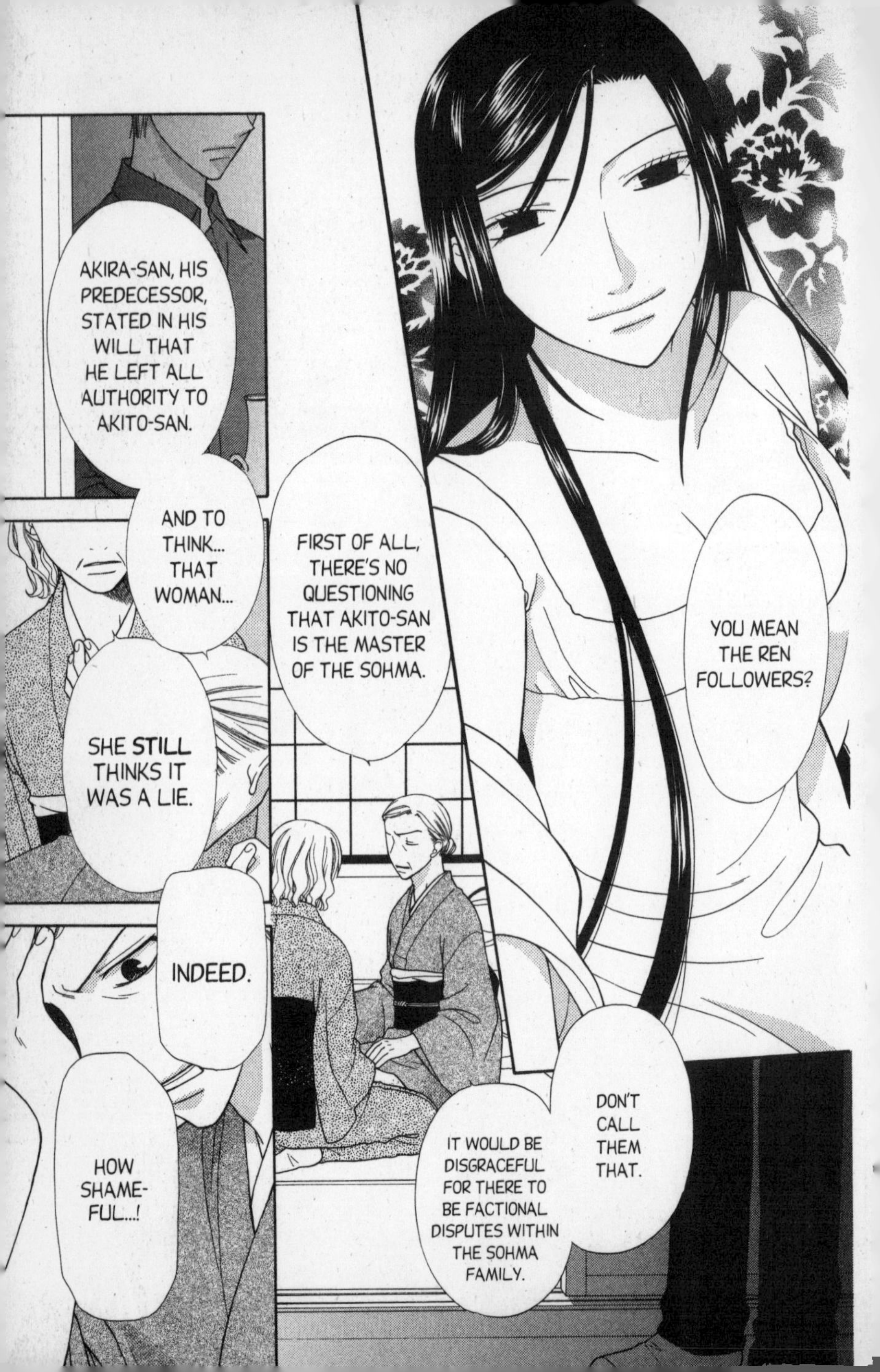
YOU MEAN THE REN FOLLOWERS?
DON'T CALL THEM THAT.
IT WOULD BE DISGRACEFUL FOR THERE TO BE FACTIONAL DISPUTES WITHIN THE SOHMA FAMILY.
FIRST OF ALL, THERE'S NO QUESTIONING THAT AKITO-SAN IS THE MASTER OF THE SOHMA.
AKIRA-SAN, HIS PREDECESSOR, STATED IN HIS WILL THAT HE LEFT ALL AUTHORITY TO AKITO-SAN.
AND TO THINK... THAT WOMAN...
SHE STILL THINKS IT WAS A LIE.
INDEED.
HOW SHAME-FUL...!

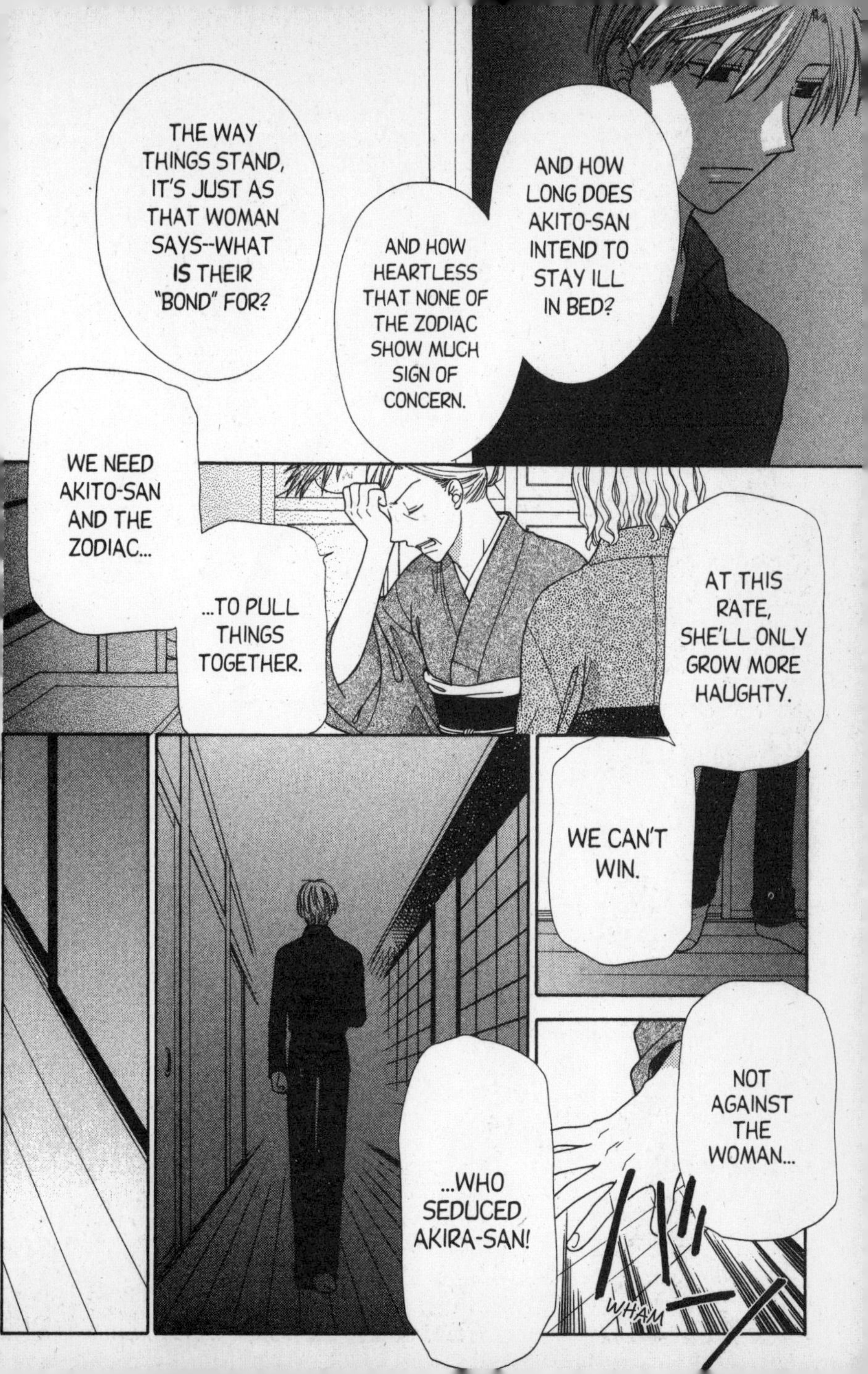
AND HOW LONG DOES AKITO-SAN INTEND TO STAY ILL IN BED?
AND HOW HEARTLESS THAT NONE OF THE ZODIAC SHOW MUCH SIGN OF CONCERN.
THE WAY THINGS STAND, IT'S JUST AS THAT WOMAN SAYS--WHAT **IS** THEIR "BOND" FOR?
AT THIS RATE, SHE'LL ONLY GROW MORE HAUGHTY.
WE NEED AKITO-SAN AND THE ZODIAC...
...TO PULL THINGS TOGETHER.
WE CAN'T WIN.
NOT AGAINST THE WOMAN...
...WHO SEDUCED AKIRA-SAN!
WHAM

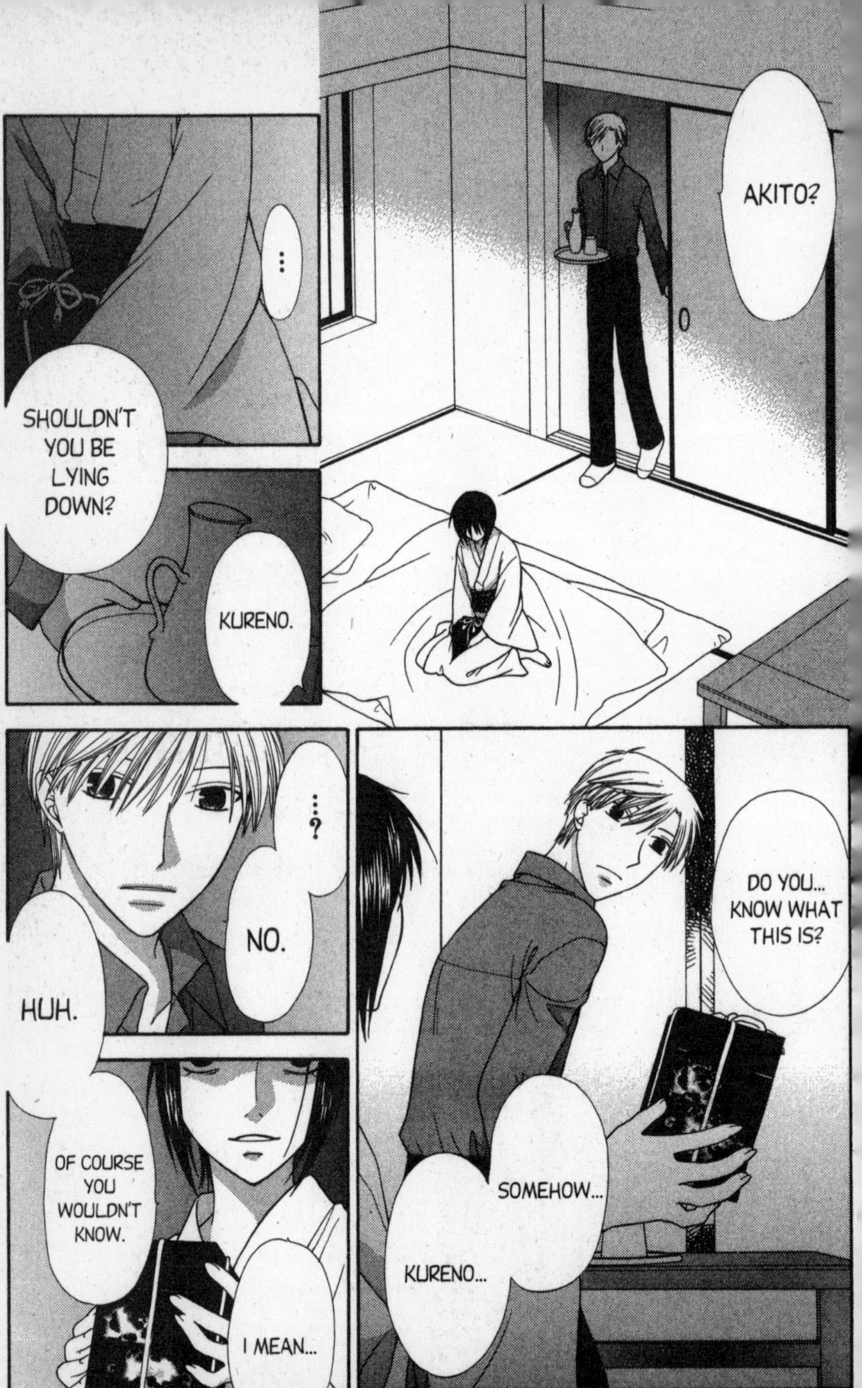
AKITO?
...
SHOULDN'T YOU BE LYING DOWN?
KURENO.
DO YOU... KNOW WHAT THIS IS?
...?
NO.
HUH.
OF COURSE YOU WOULDN'T KNOW.
I MEAN...
SOMEHOW...
KURENO...

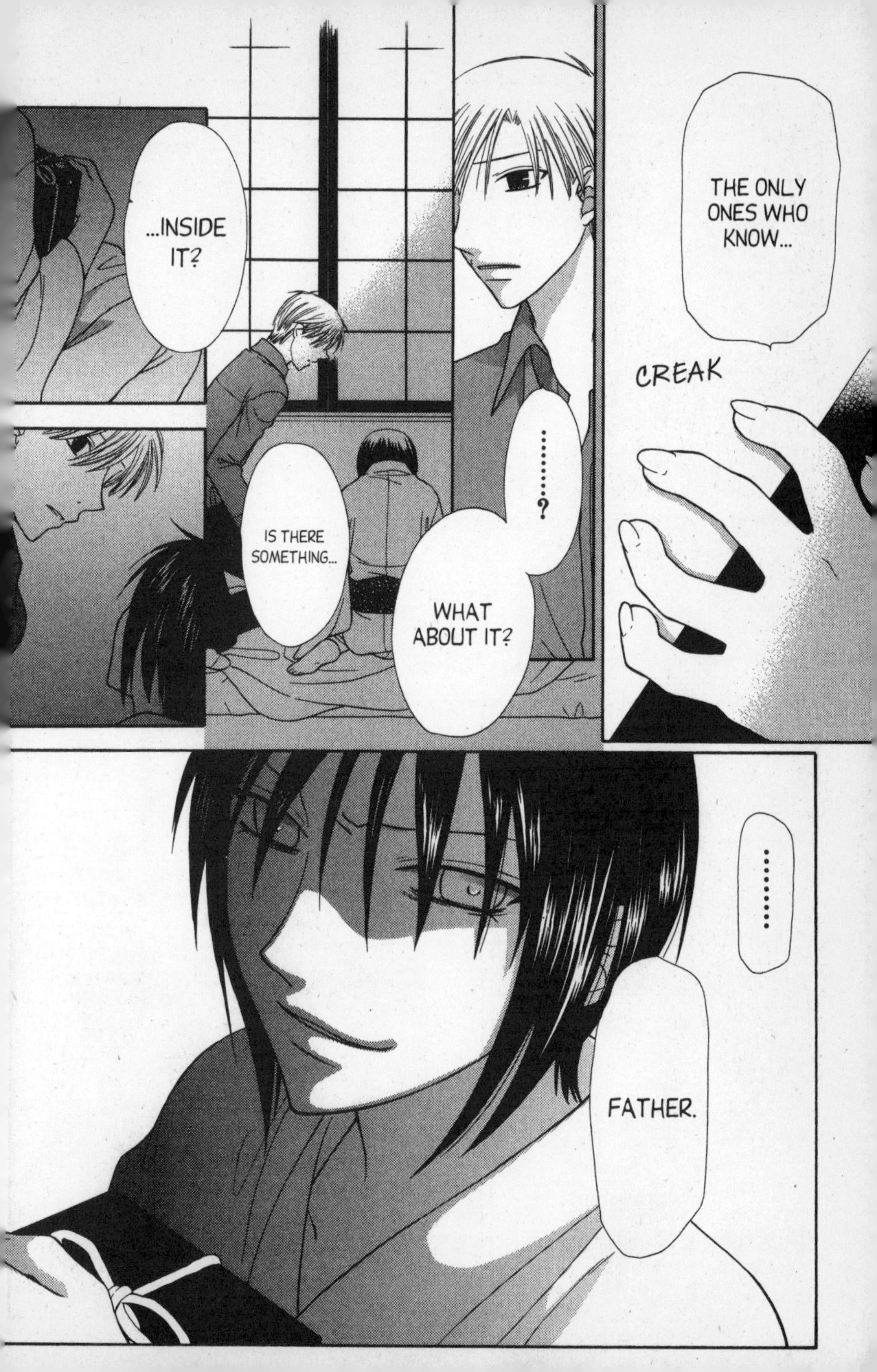
THE ONLY ONES WHO KNOW...
CREAK
......?
WHAT ABOUT IT?
IS THERE SOMETHING...
...INSIDE IT?
....
FATHER.

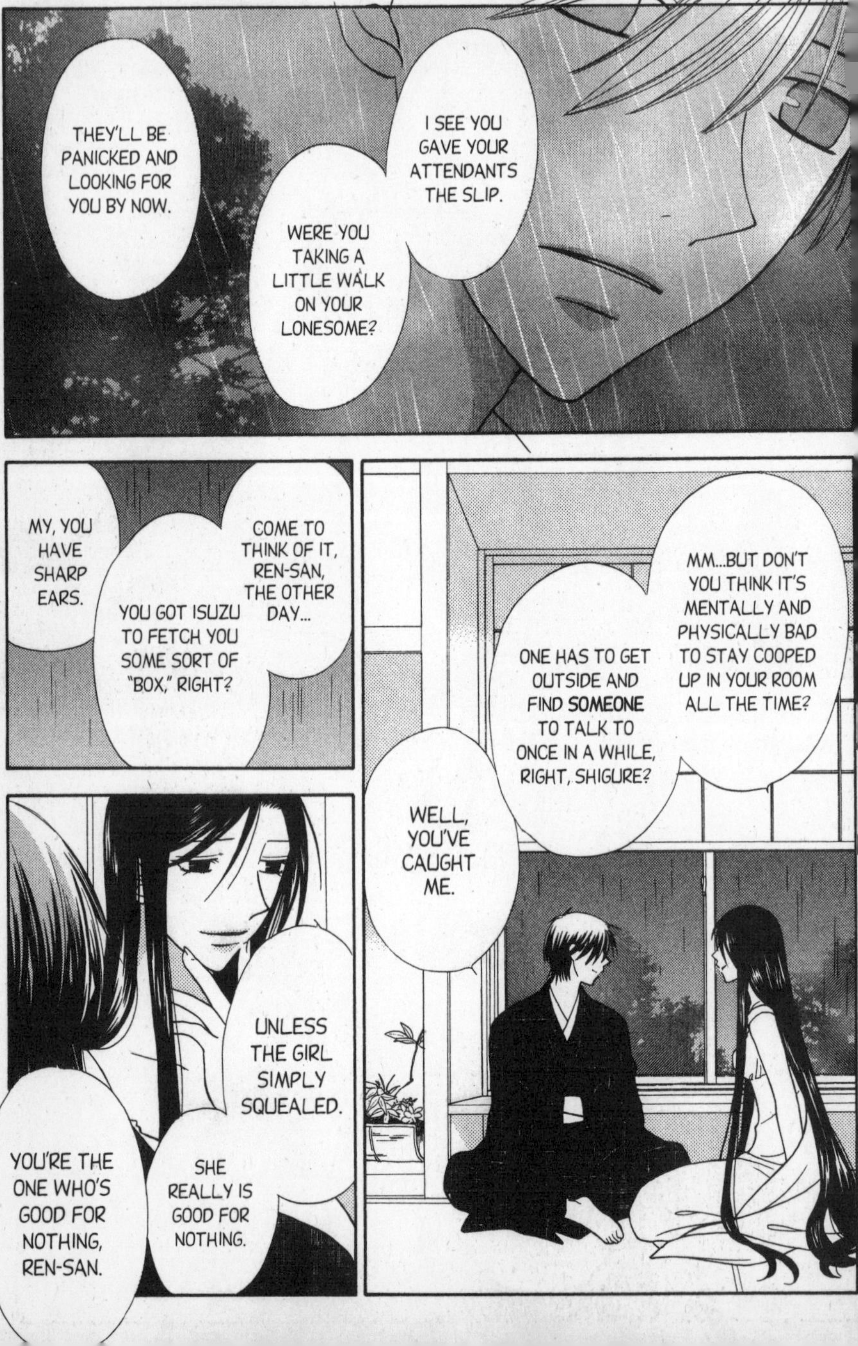
I SEE YOU GAVE YOUR ATTENDANTS THE SLIP.
WERE YOU TAKING A LITTLE WALK ON YOUR LONESOME?
THEY'LL BE PANICKED AND LOOKING FOR YOU BY NOW.
MM...BUT DON'T YOU THINK IT'S MENTALLY AND PHYSICALLY BAD TO STAY COOPED UP IN YOUR ROOM ALL THE TIME?
ONE HAS TO GET OUTSIDE AND FIND **SOMEONE** TO TALK TO ONCE IN A WHILE, RIGHT, SHIGURE?
WELL, YOU'VE CAUGHT ME.
COME TO THINK OF IT, REN-SAN, THE OTHER DAY...
YOU GOT ISUZU TO FETCH YOU SOME SORT OF "BOX," RIGHT?
MY, YOU HAVE SHARP EARS.
UNLESS THE GIRL SIMPLY SQUEALED.
SHE REALLY IS GOOD FOR NOTHING.
YOU'RE THE ONE WHO'S GOOD FOR NOTHING, REN-SAN.

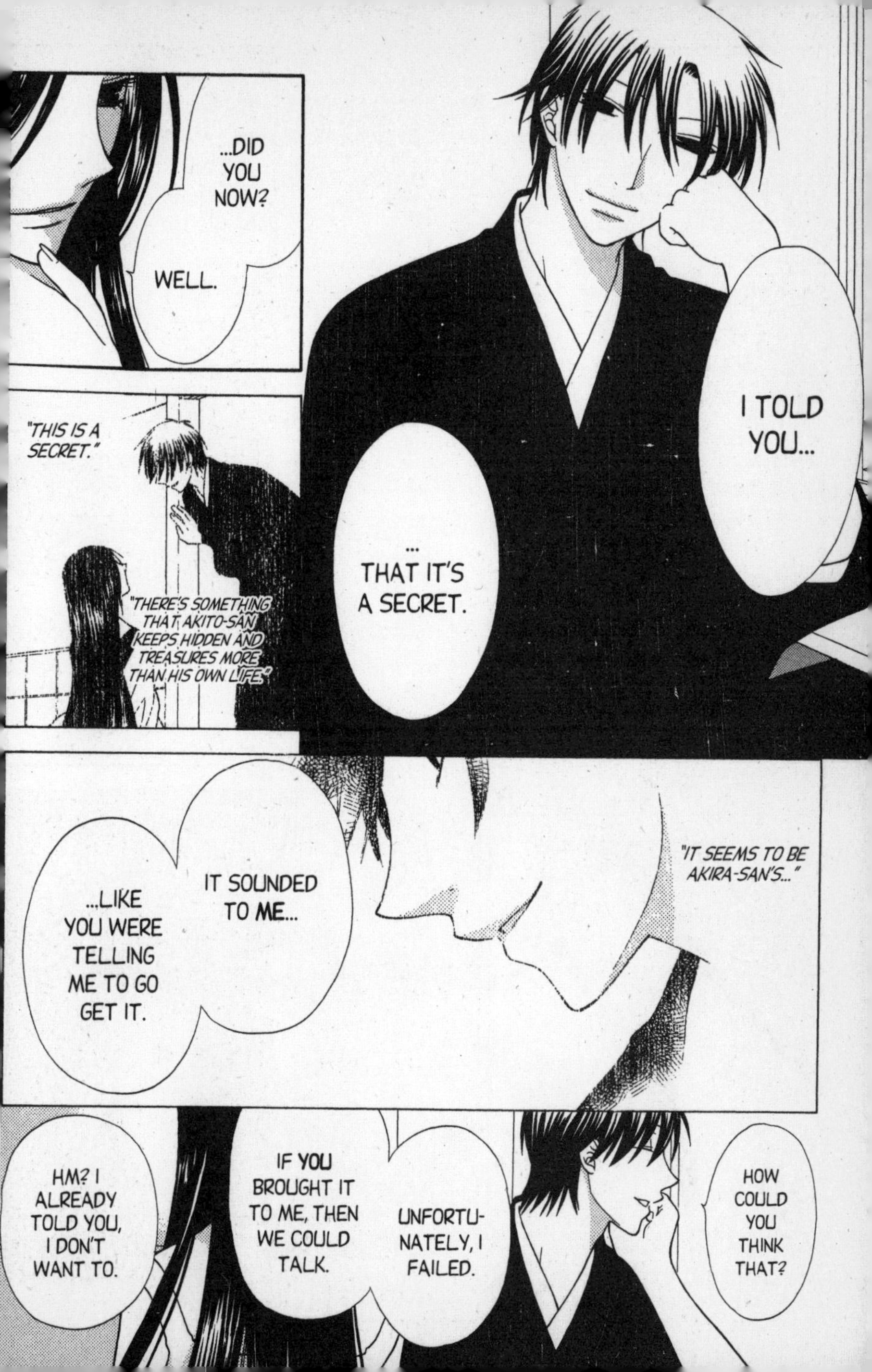
I TOLD YOU...
...THAT IT'S A SECRET.
...DID YOU NOW?
WELL.
"THIS IS A SECRET."
"THERE'S SOMETHING THAT AKITO-SAN KEEPS HIDDEN AND TREASURES MORE THAN HIS OWN LIFE."
"IT SEEMS TO BE AKIRA-SAN'S..."
IT SOUNDED TO ME...
...LIKE YOU WERE TELLING ME TO GO GET IT.
HOW COULD YOU THINK THAT?
UNFORTU-NATELY, I FAILED.
IF YOU BROUGHT IT TO ME, THEN WE COULD TALK.
HM? I ALREADY TOLD YOU, I DON'T WANT TO.

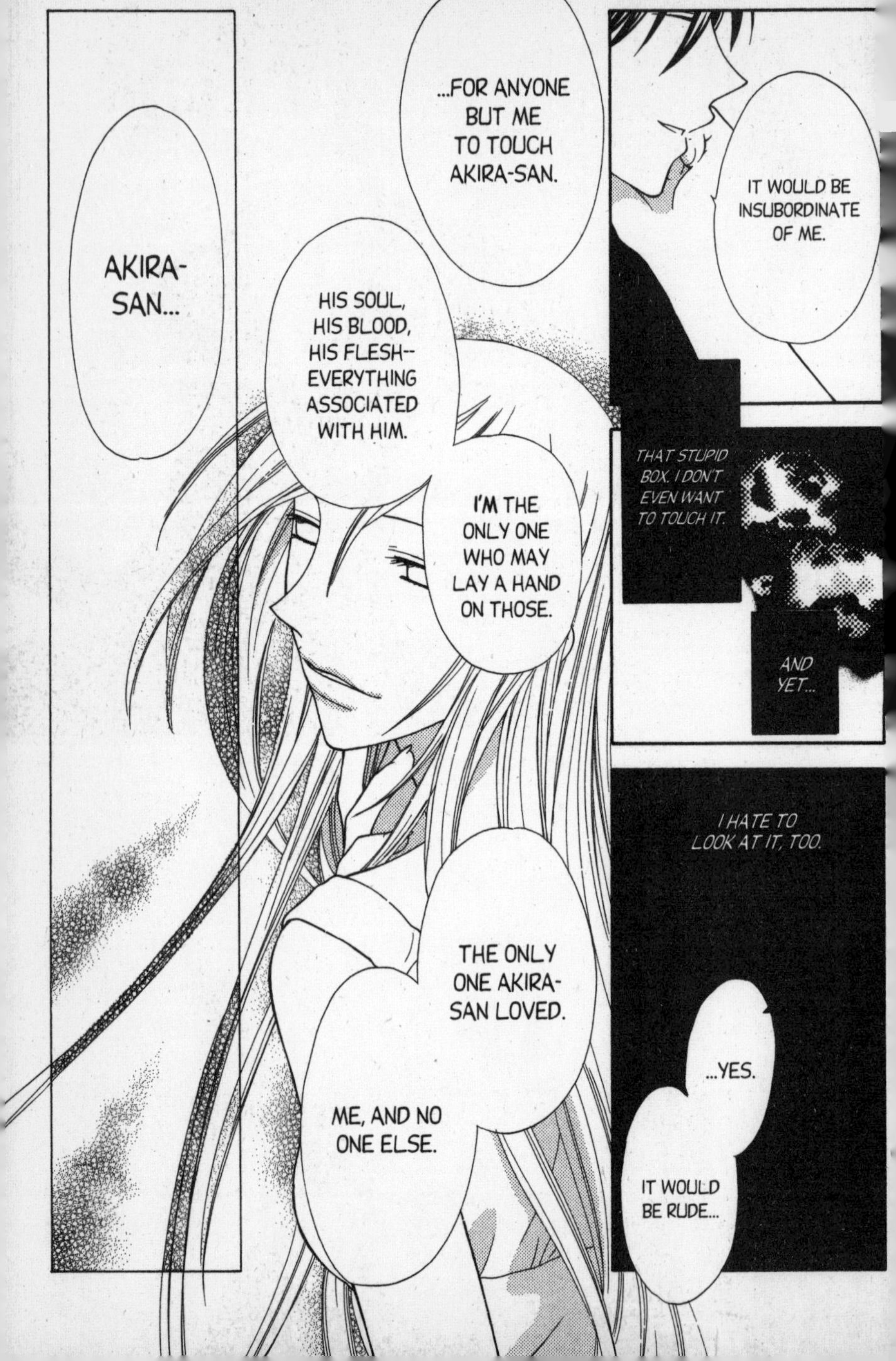
IT WOULD BE INSUBORDINATE OF ME.
THAT STUPID BOX. I DON'T EVEN WANT TO TOUCH IT.
AND YET...
I HATE TO LOOK AT IT, TOO.
...YES.
IT WOULD BE RUDE...
...FOR ANYONE BUT ME TO TOUCH AKIRA-SAN.
HIS SOUL, HIS BLOOD, HIS FLESH-- EVERYTHING ASSOCIATED WITH HIM.
I'M THE ONLY ONE WHO MAY LAY A HAND ON THOSE.
THE ONLY ONE AKIRA-SAN LOVED.
ME, AND NO ONE ELSE.
AKIRA-SAN...

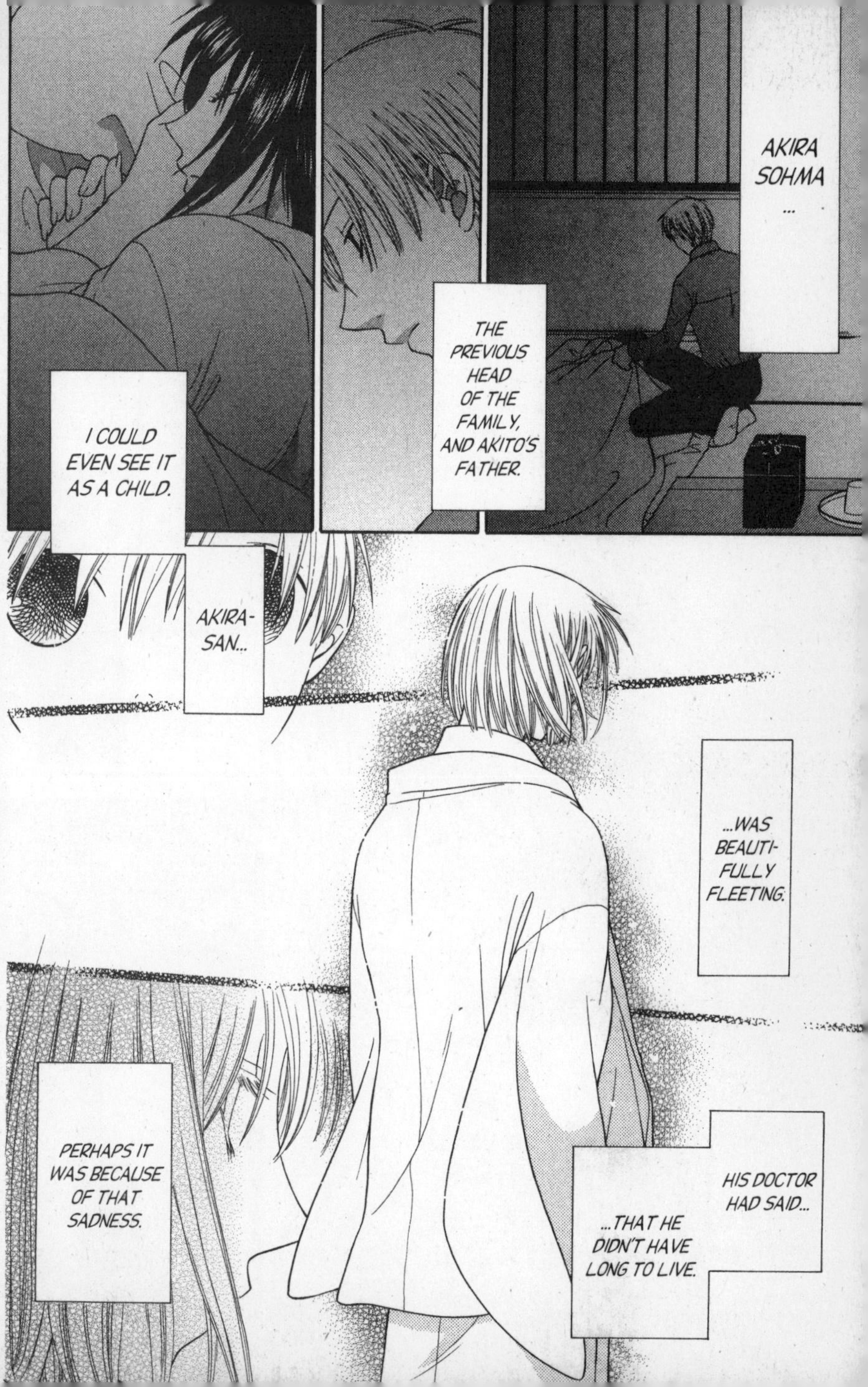
AKIRA SOHMA ...
THE PREVIOUS HEAD OF THE FAMILY, AND AKITO'S FATHER.
I COULD EVEN SEE IT AS A CHILD.
AKIRA-SAN...
...WAS BEAUTIFULLY FLEETING.
HIS DOCTOR HAD SAID...
...THAT HE DIDN'T HAVE LONG TO LIVE.
PERHAPS IT WAS BECAUSE OF THAT SADNESS.

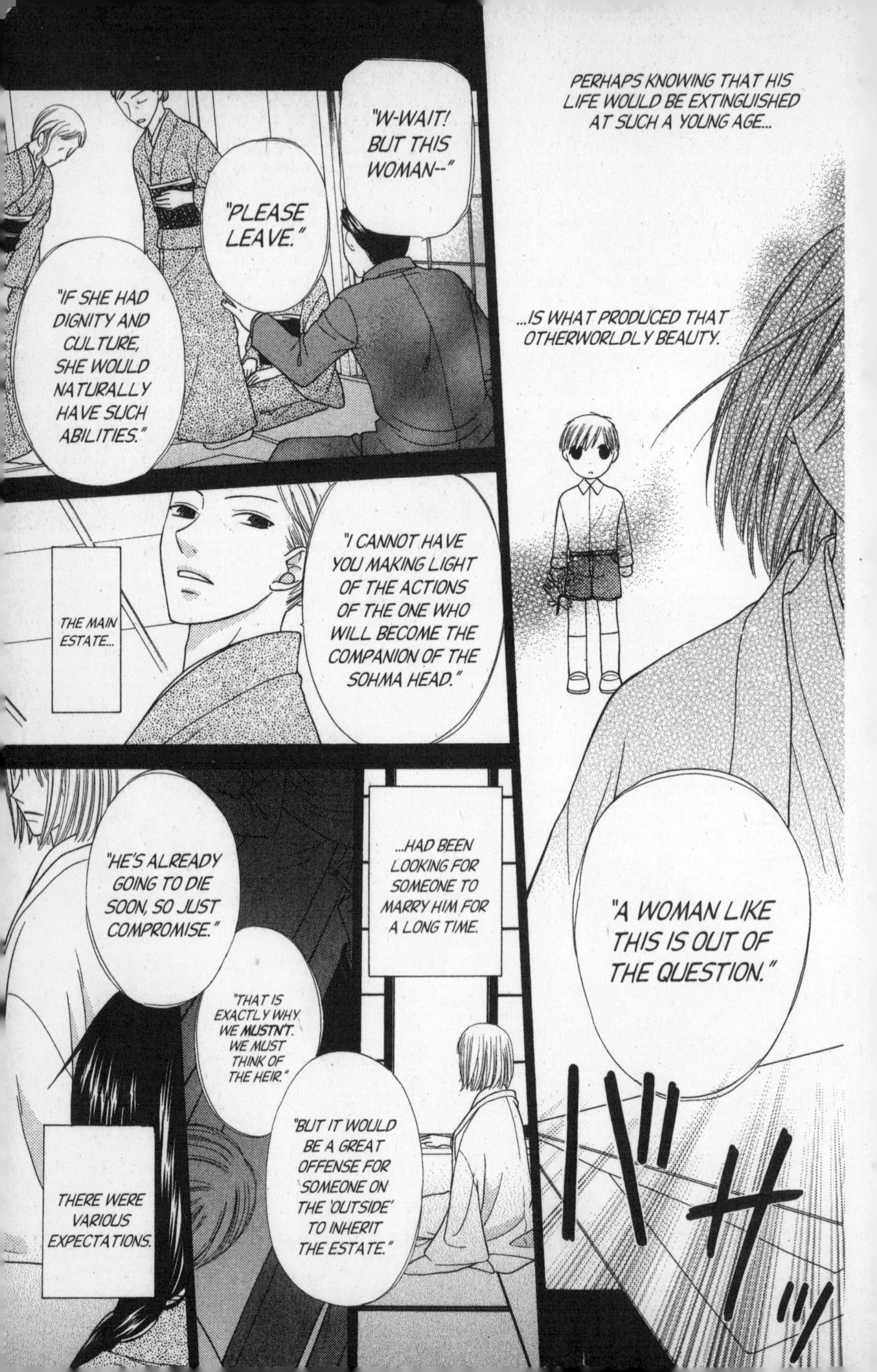
PERHAPS KNOWING THAT HIS LIFE WOULD BE EXTINGUISHED AT SUCH A YOUNG AGE...
...IS WHAT PRODUCED THAT OTHERWORLDLY BEAUTY.
"A WOMAN LIKE THIS IS OUT OF THE QUESTION."
バッ
"W-WAIT! BUT THIS WOMAN--"
"PLEASE LEAVE."
"IF SHE HAD DIGNITY AND CULTURE, SHE WOULD NATURALLY HAVE SUCH ABILITIES."
"I CANNOT HAVE YOU MAKING LIGHT OF THE ACTIONS OF THE ONE WHO WILL BECOME THE COMPANION OF THE SOHMA HEAD."
THE MAIN ESTATE...
...HAD BEEN LOOKING FOR SOMEONE TO MARRY HIM FOR A LONG TIME.
"HE'S ALREADY GOING TO DIE SOON, SO JUST COMPROMISE."
"THAT IS EXACTLY WHY WE MUSTN'T. WE MUST THINK OF THE HEIR."
"BUT IT WOULD BE A GREAT OFFENSE FOR SOMEONE ON THE 'OUTSIDE' TO INHERIT THE ESTATE."
THERE WERE VARIOUS EXPECTATIONS.

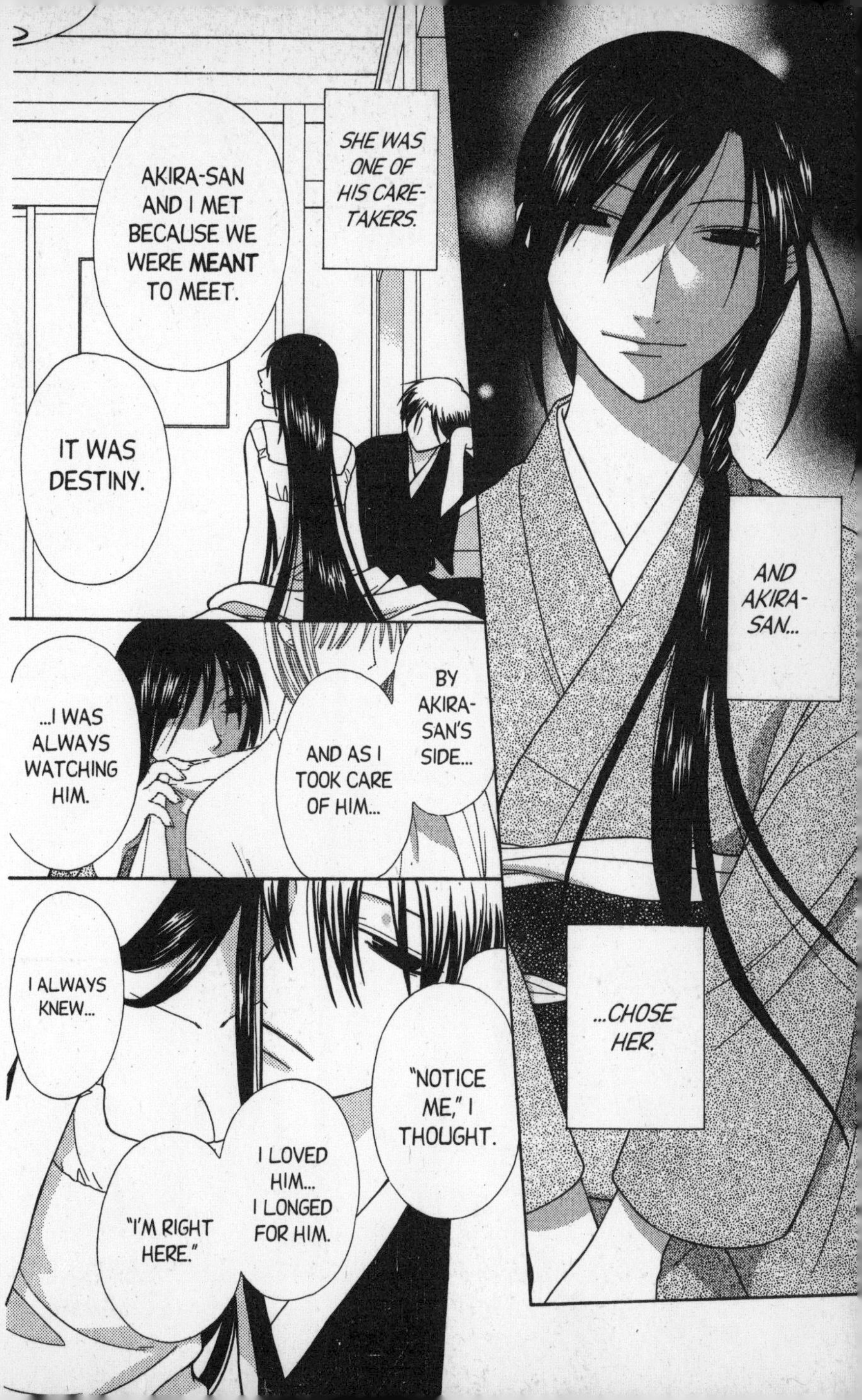
AND AKIRA-SAN...
...CHOSE HER.
SHE WAS ONE OF HIS CARE-TAKERS.
AKIRA-SAN AND I MET BECAUSE WE WERE MEANT TO MEET.
IT WAS DESTINY.
BY AKIRA-SAN'S SIDE...
AND AS I TOOK CARE OF HIM...
...I WAS ALWAYS WATCHING HIM.
I ALWAYS KNEW...
"NOTICE ME," I THOUGHT.
I LOVED HIM... I LONGED FOR HIM.
"I'M RIGHT HERE."

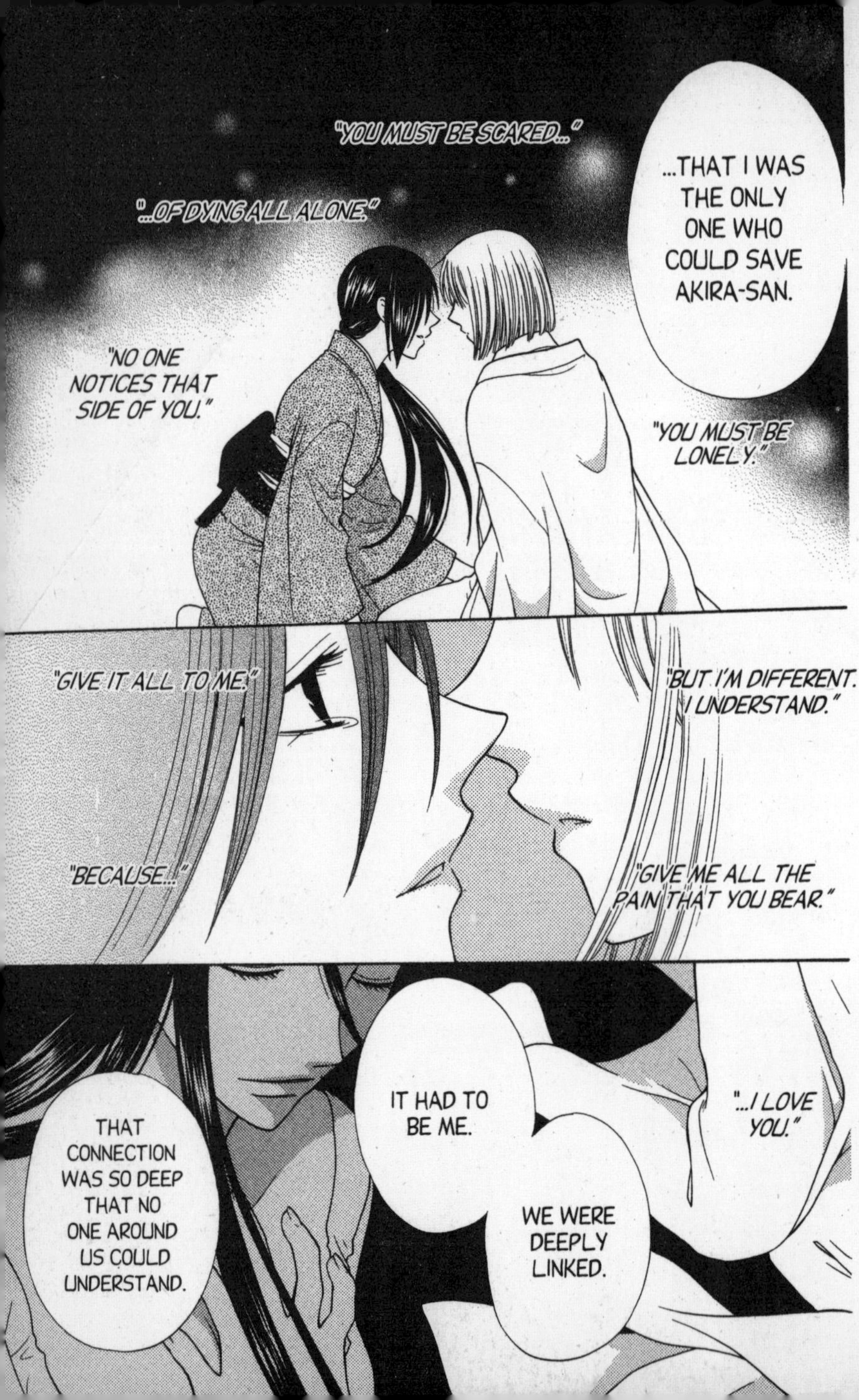
...THAT I WAS THE ONLY ONE WHO COULD SAVE AKIRA-SAN.
"YOU MUST BE SCARED..."
"...OF DYING ALL ALONE."
"NO ONE NOTICES THAT SIDE OF YOU."
"YOU MUST BE LONELY."
"BUT I'M DIFFERENT. I UNDERSTAND."
"GIVE ME ALL THE PAIN THAT YOU BEAR."
"GIVE IT ALL TO ME."
"BECAUSE..."
"...I LOVE YOU."
IT HAD TO BE ME.
WE WERE DEEPLY LINKED.
THAT CONNECTION WAS SO DEEP THAT NO ONE AROUND US COULD UNDERSTAND.

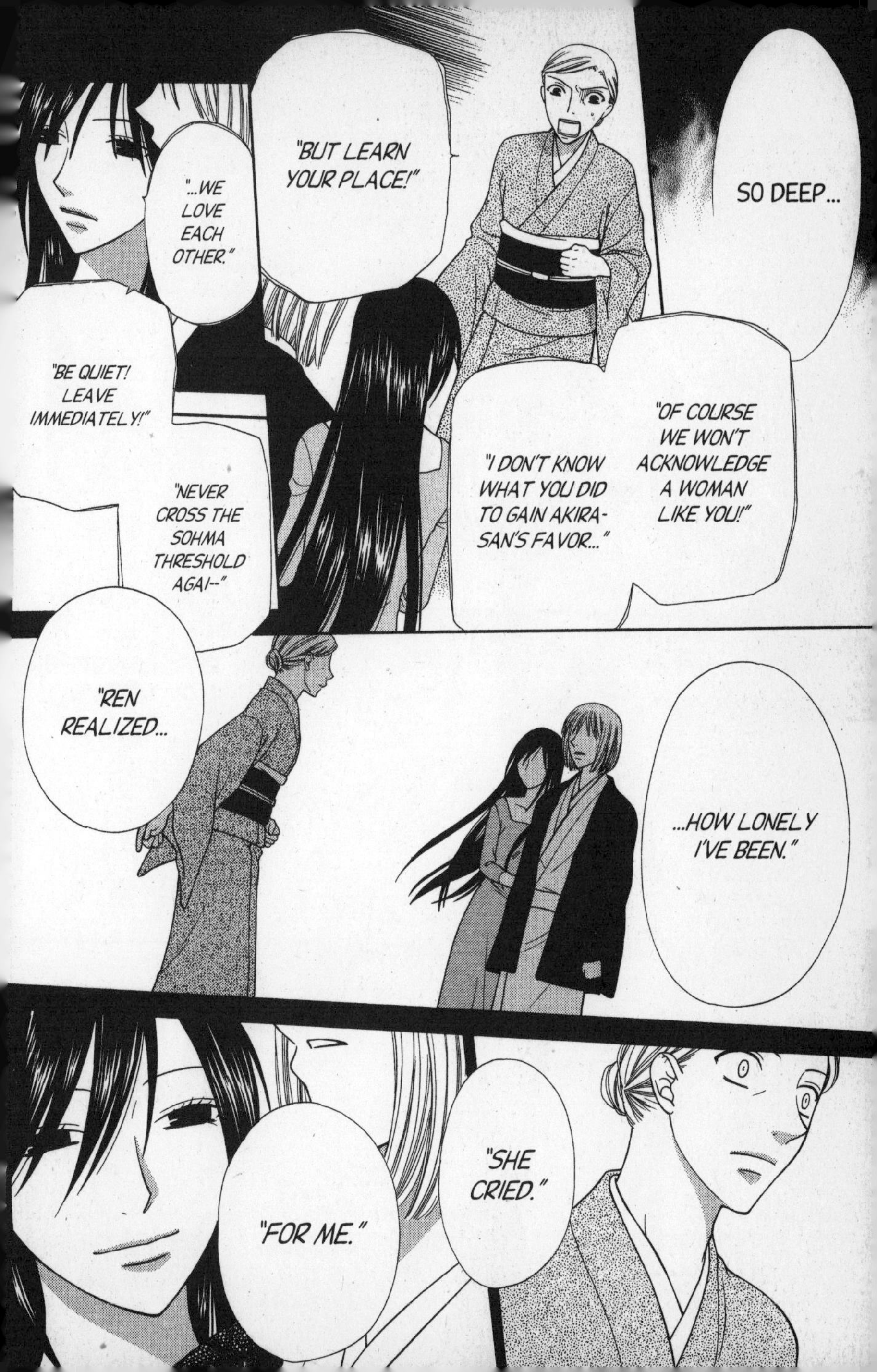
SO DEEP...
"OF COURSE WE WON'T ACKNOWLEDGE A WOMAN LIKE YOU!"
"I DON'T KNOW WHAT YOU DID TO GAIN AKIRA-SAN'S FAVOR..."
"BUT LEARN YOUR PLACE!"
"...WE LOVE EACH OTHER."
"BE QUIET! LEAVE IMMEDIATELY!"
"NEVER CROSS THE SOHMA THRESHOLD AGAI--"
"REN REALIZED...
...HOW LONELY I'VE BEEN."
"SHE CRIED."
"FOR ME."

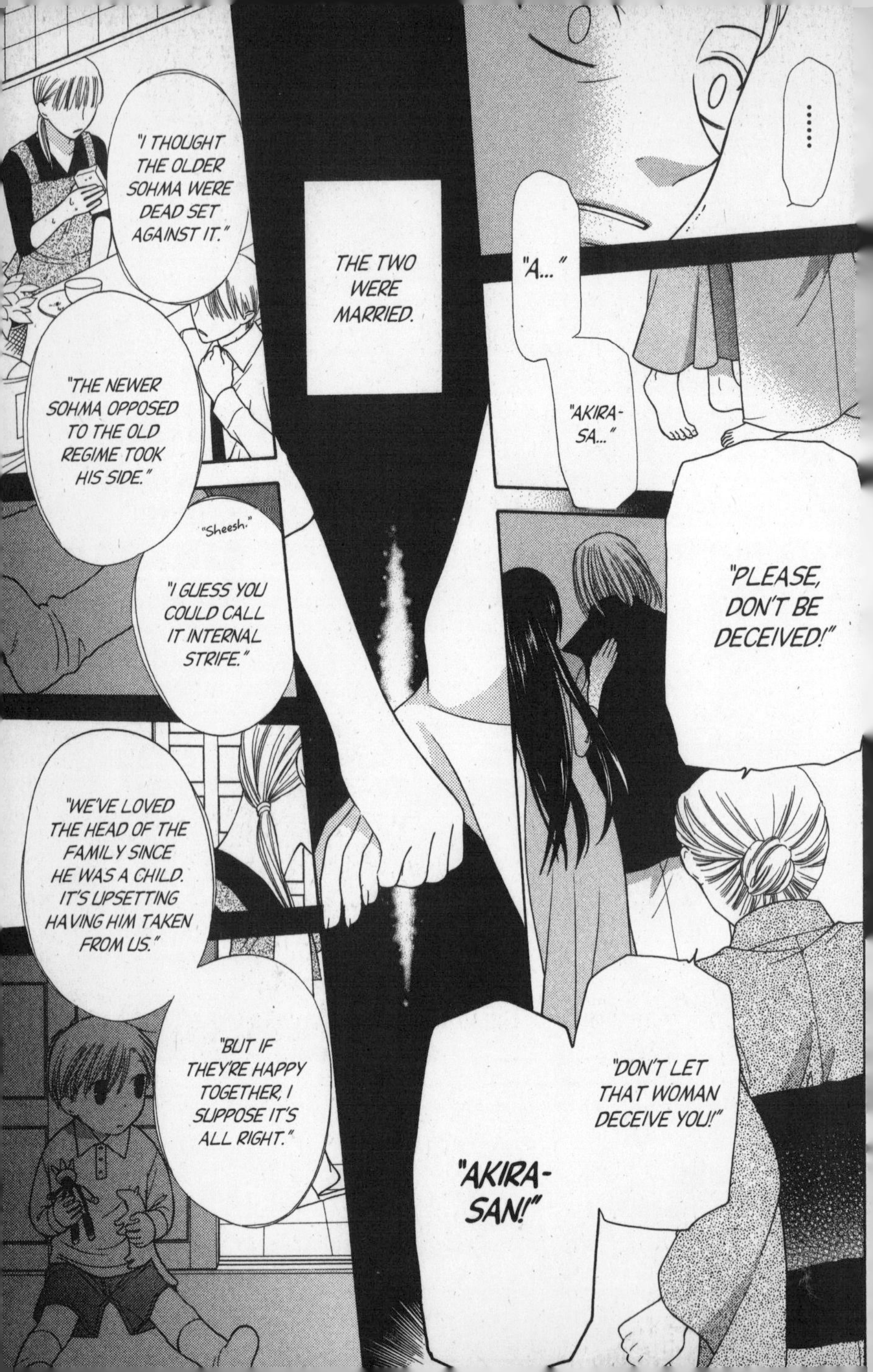
......
"A..."
"AKIRA-SA..."
"PLEASE, DON'T BE DECEIVED!"
"DON'T LET THAT WOMAN DECEIVE YOU!"
"AKIRA-SAN!"
THE TWO WERE MARRIED.
"I THOUGHT THE OLDER SOHMA WERE DEAD SET AGAINST IT."
"THE NEWER SOHMA OPPOSED TO THE OLD REGIME TOOK HIS SIDE."
"Sheesh."
"I GUESS YOU COULD CALL IT INTERNAL STRIFE."
"WE'VE LOVED THE HEAD OF THE FAMILY SINCE HE WAS A CHILD. IT'S UPSETTING HAVING HIM TAKEN FROM US."
"BUT IF THEY'RE HAPPY TOGETHER, I SUPPOSE IT'S ALL RIGHT."

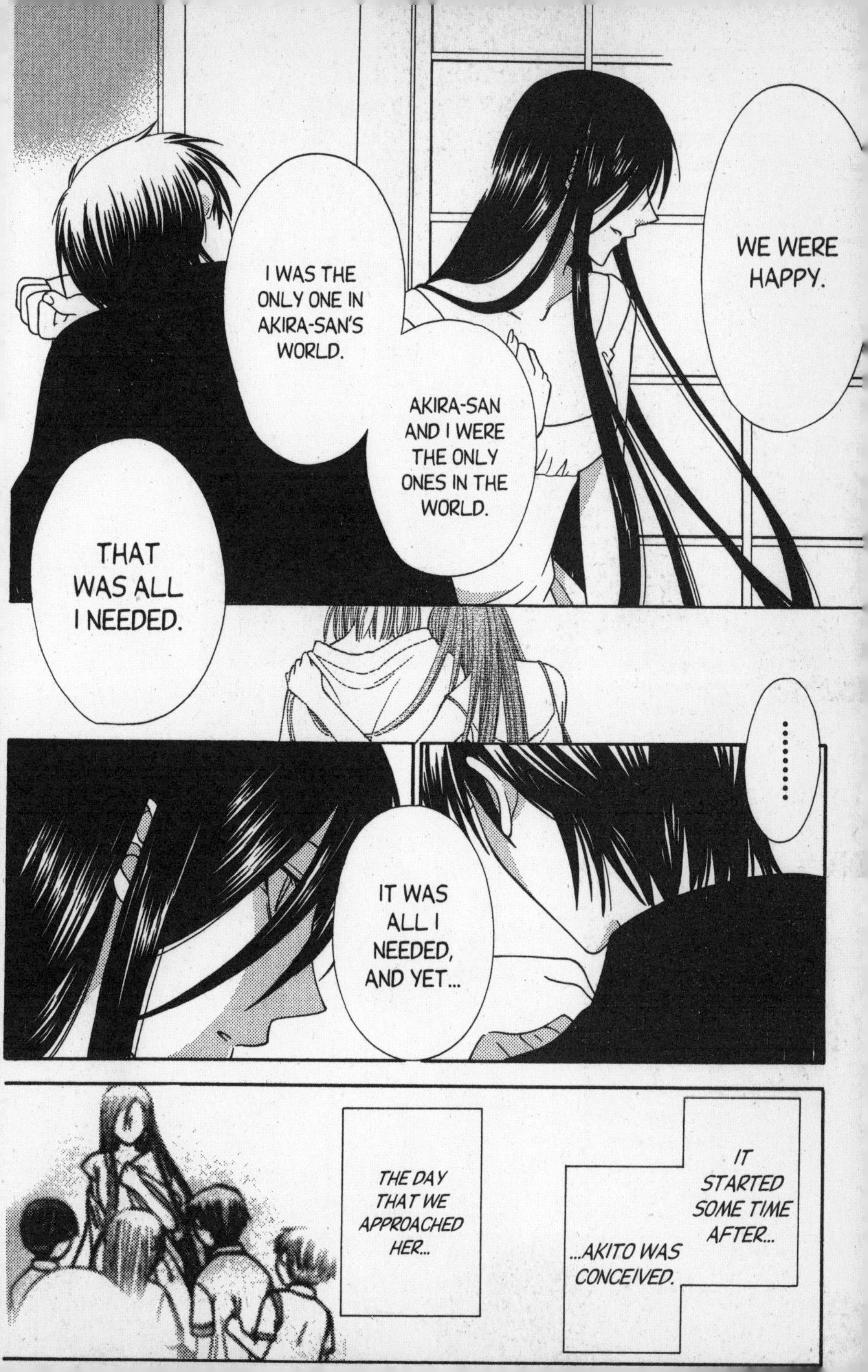
WE WERE HAPPY.
I WAS THE ONLY ONE IN AKIRA-SAN'S WORLD.
AKIRA-SAN AND I WERE THE ONLY ONES IN THE WORLD.
THAT WAS ALL I NEEDED.
......
IT WAS ALL I NEEDED, AND YET...
IT STARTED SOME TIME AFTER...
...AKITO WAS CONCEIVED.
THE DAY THAT WE APPROACHED HER...

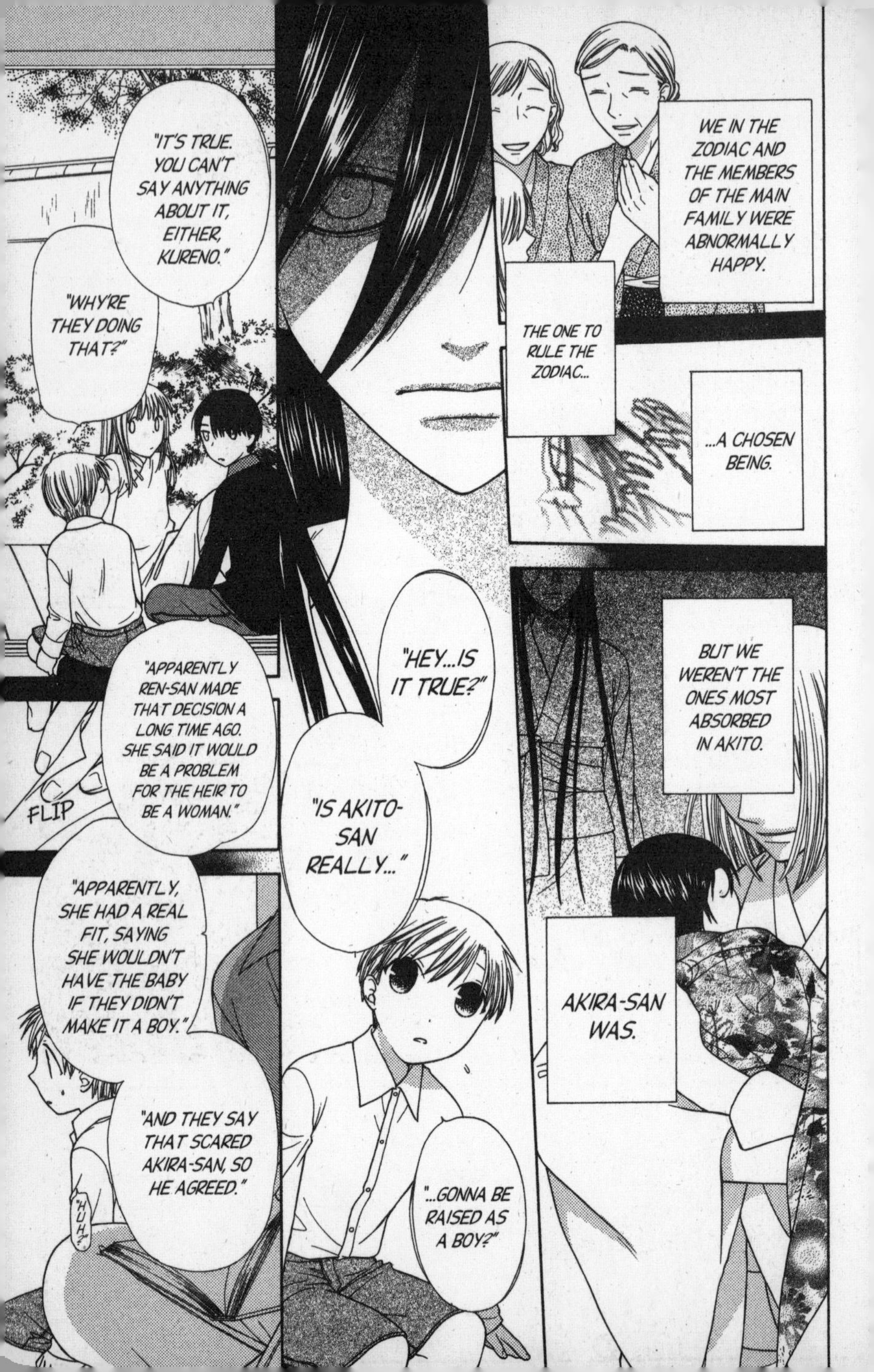
WE IN THE ZODIAC AND THE MEMBERS OF THE MAIN FAMILY WERE ABNORMALLY HAPPY.
THE ONE TO RULE THE ZODIAC...
...A CHOSEN BEING.
BUT WE WEREN'T THE ONES MOST ABSORBED IN AKITO.
AKIRA-SAN WAS.
"HEY...IS IT TRUE?"
"IS AKITO-SAN REALLY..."
"...GONNA BE RAISED AS A BOY?"
"IT'S TRUE. YOU CAN'T SAY ANYTHING ABOUT IT, EITHER, KURENO."
"WHY'RE THEY DOING THAT?"
"APPARENTLY REN-SAN MADE THAT DECISION A LONG TIME AGO. SHE SAID IT WOULD BE A PROBLEM FOR THE HEIR TO BE A WOMAN."
FLIP
"APPARENTLY, SHE HAD A REAL FIT, SAYING SHE WOULDN'T HAVE THE BABY IF THEY DIDN'T MAKE IT A BOY."
"AND THEY SAY THAT SCARED AKIRA-SAN, SO HE AGREED."
"HUH?"

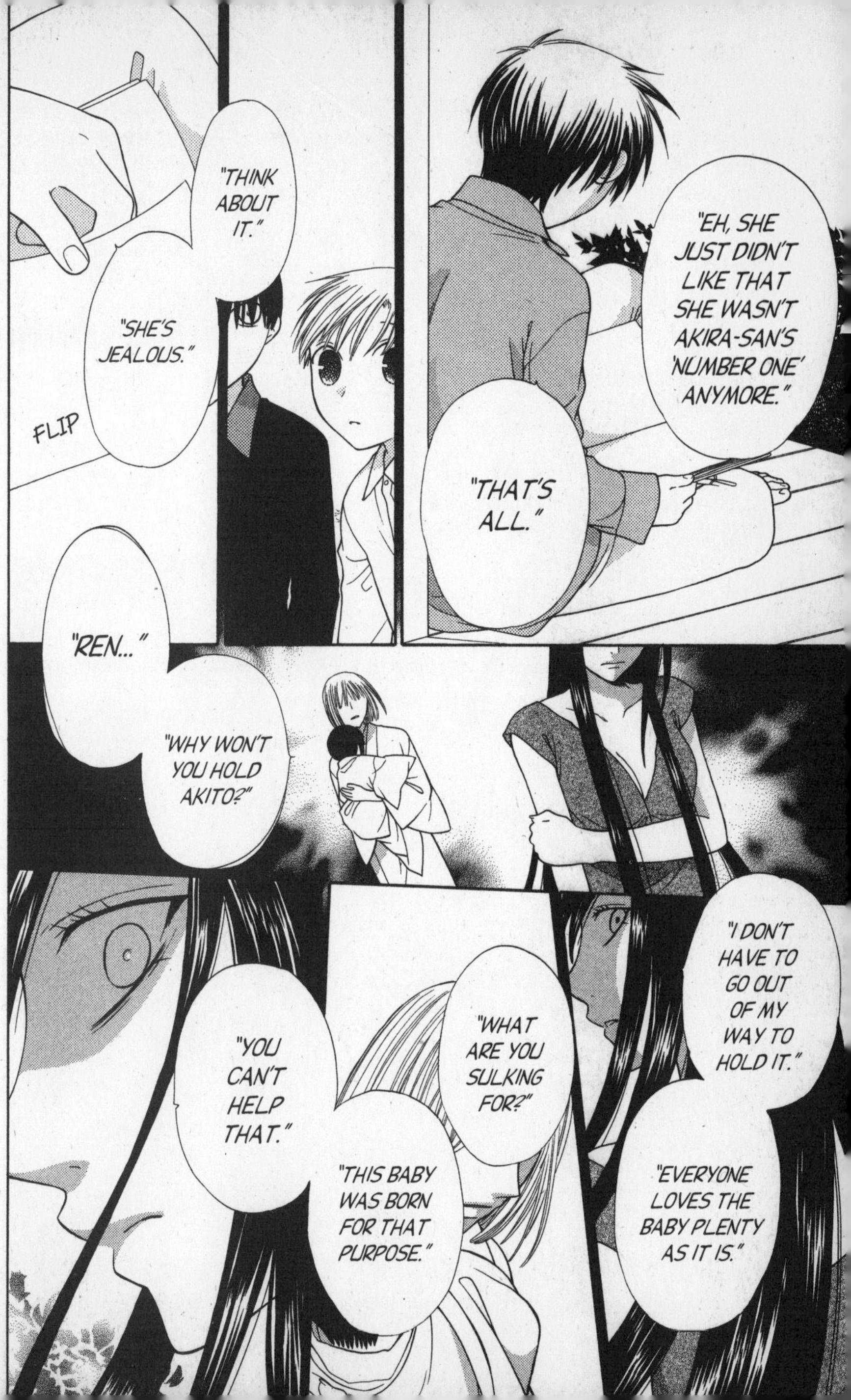
"EH, SHE JUST DIDN'T LIKE THAT SHE WASN'T AKIRA-SAN'S 'NUMBER ONE' ANYMORE."
"THAT'S ALL."
"THINK ABOUT IT."
"SHE'S JEALOUS."
FLIP
"REN..."
"WHY WON'T YOU HOLD AKITO?"
"I DON'T HAVE TO GO OUT OF MY WAY TO HOLD IT."
"EVERYONE LOVES THE BABY PLENTY AS IT IS."
"WHAT ARE YOU SULKING FOR?"
"THIS BABY WAS BORN FOR THAT PURPOSE."
"YOU CAN'T HELP THAT."

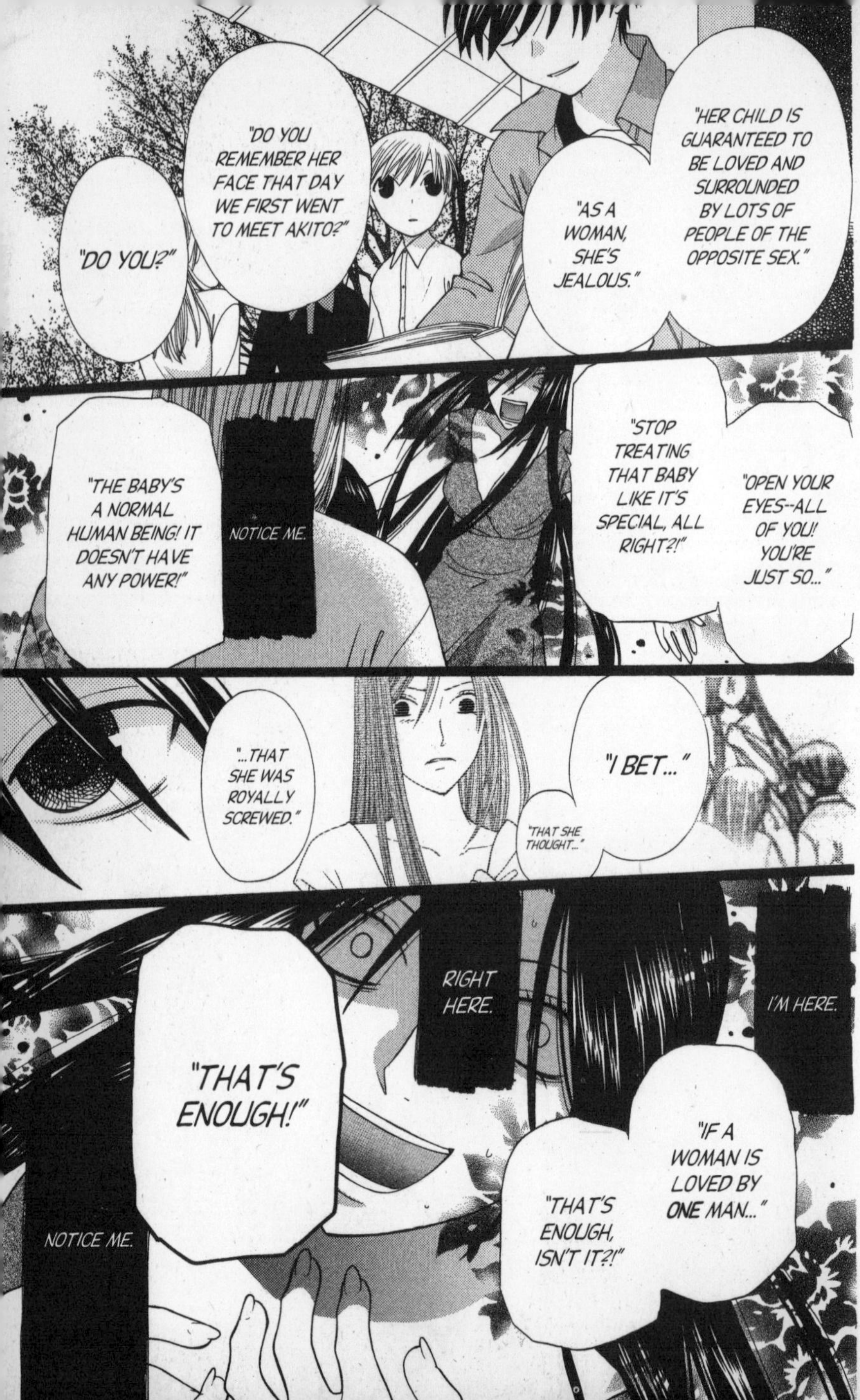
"HER CHILD IS GUARANTEED TO BE LOVED AND SURROUNDED BY LOTS OF PEOPLE OF THE OPPOSITE SEX."
"AS A WOMAN, SHE'S JEALOUS."
"DO YOU REMEMBER HER FACE THAT DAY WE FIRST WENT TO MEET AKITO?"
"DO YOU?"
"OPEN YOUR EYES--ALL OF YOU! YOU'RE JUST SO..."
"STOP TREATING THAT BABY LIKE IT'S SPECIAL, ALL RIGHT?!"
NOTICE ME.
"THE BABY'S A NORMAL HUMAN BEING! IT DOESN'T HAVE ANY POWER!"
"I BET..."
"THAT SHE THOUGHT..."
"...THAT SHE WAS ROYALLY SCREWED."
I'M HERE.
"IF A WOMAN IS LOVED BY ONE MAN..."
"THAT'S ENOUGH, ISN'T IT?!"
RIGHT HERE.
"THAT'S ENOUGH!"
NOTICE ME.

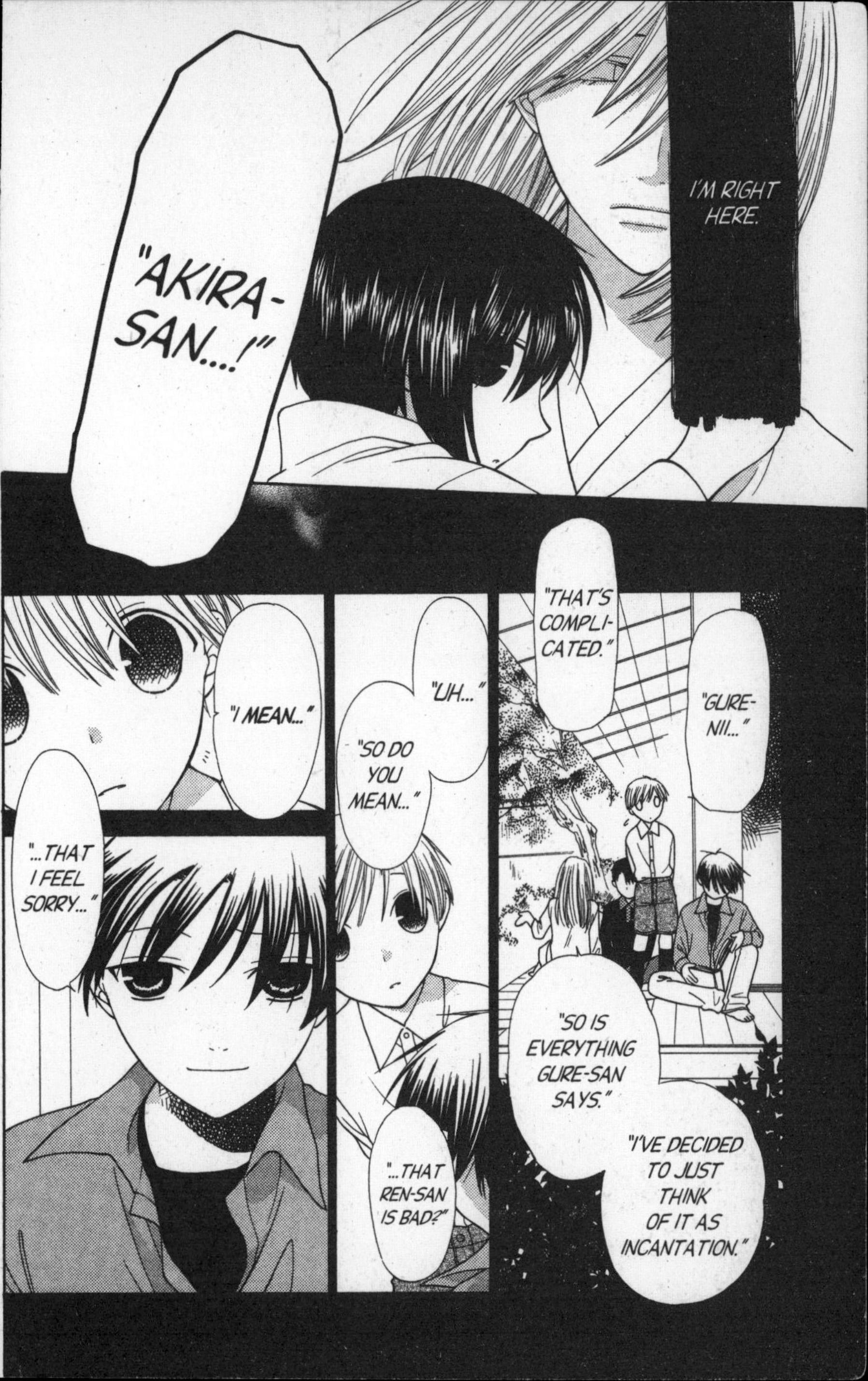
I'M RIGHT HERE.
"AKIRA-SAN...!"
"GURE-NII..."
"THAT'S COMPLI-CATED."
"SO IS EVERYTHING GURE-SAN SAYS."
"I'VE DECIDED TO JUST THINK OF IT AS INCANTATION."
"UH..."
"SO DO YOU MEAN..."
"...THAT REN-SAN IS BAD?"
"I MEAN..."
"...THAT I FEEL SORRY..."

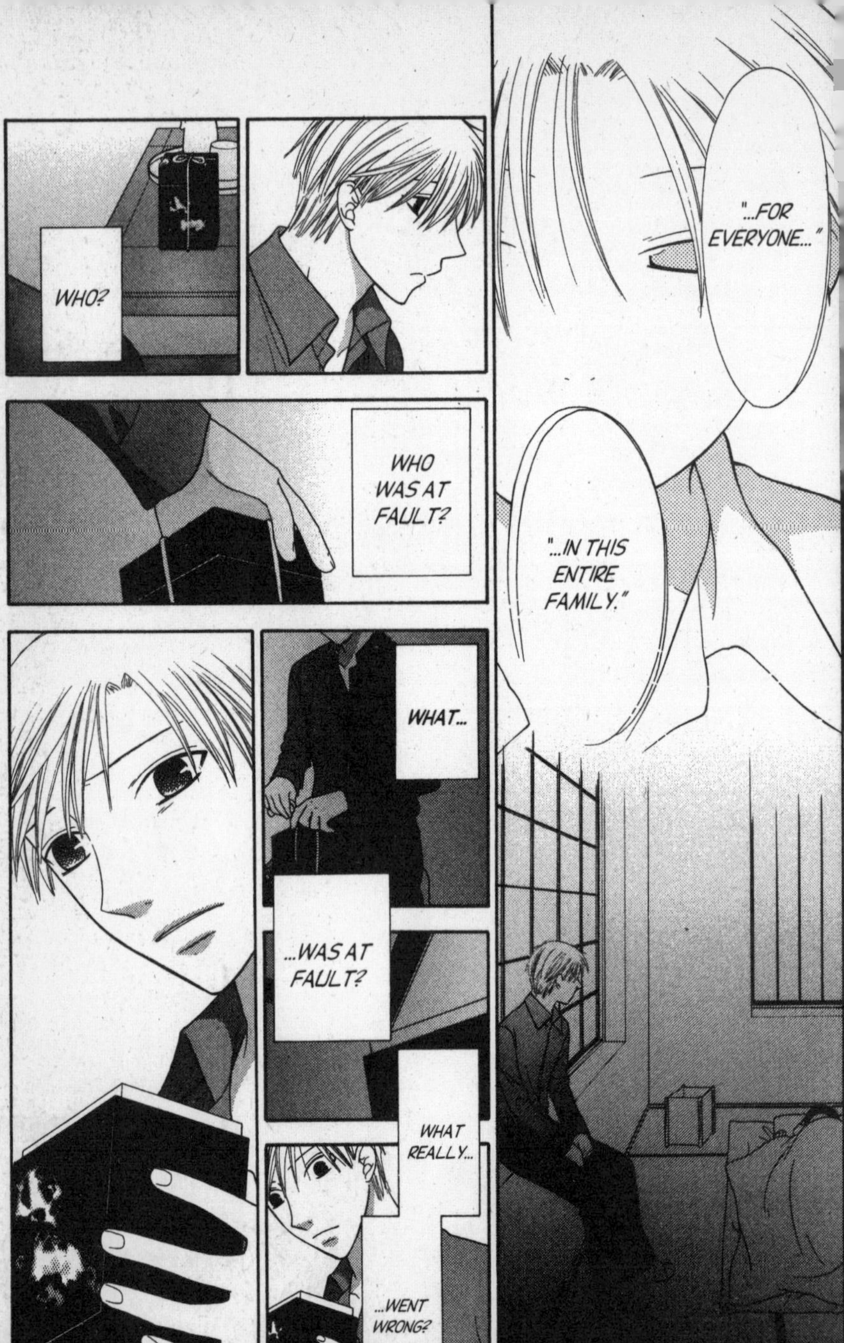
"...FOR EVERYONE..."
"...IN THIS ENTIRE FAMILY."
WHO?
WHO WAS AT FAULT?
WHAT...
...WAS AT FAULT?
WHAT REALLY...
...WENT WRONG?

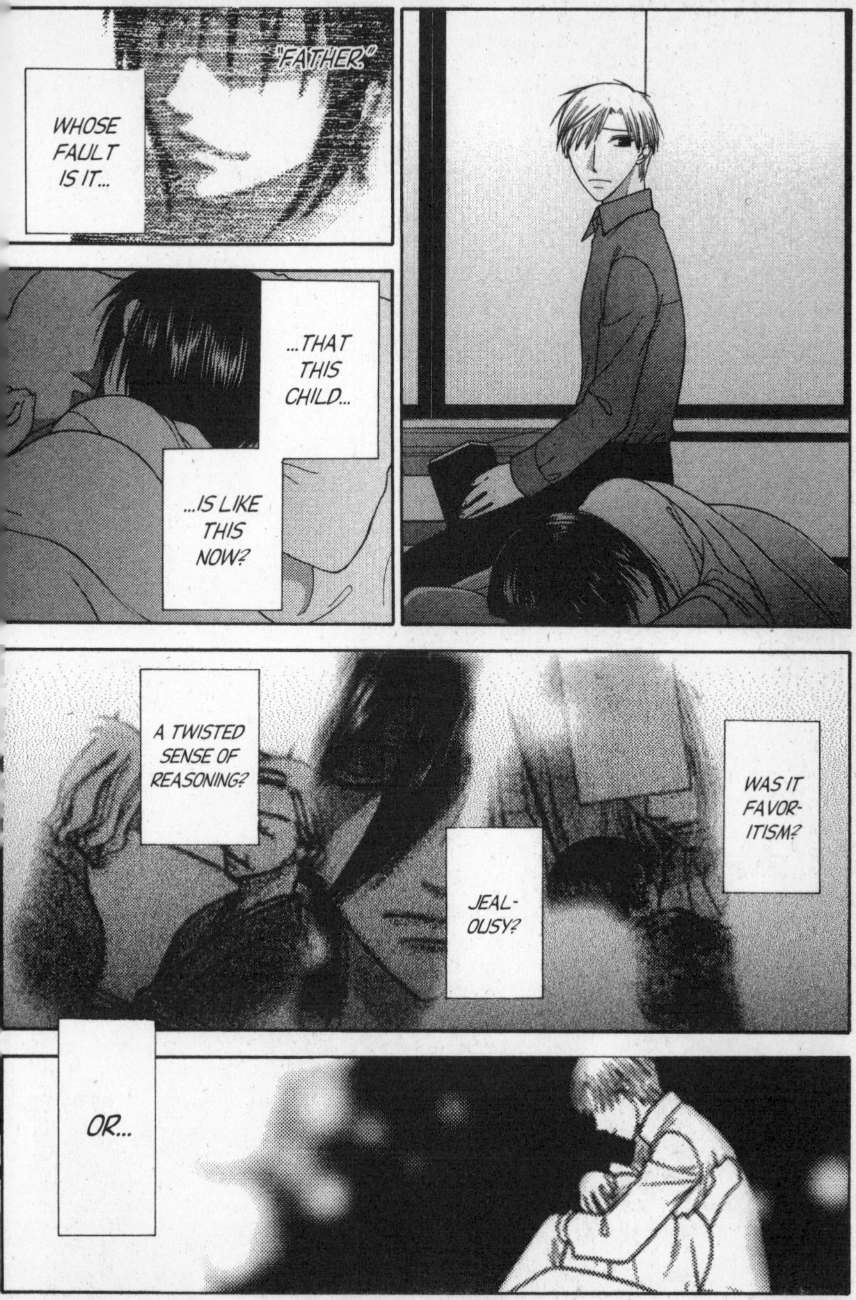
"FATHER."
WHOSE FAULT IS IT...
...THAT THIS CHILD...
...IS LIKE THIS NOW?
WAS IT FAVOR-ITISM?
JEAL-OUSY?
A TWISTED SENSE OF REASONING?
OR...

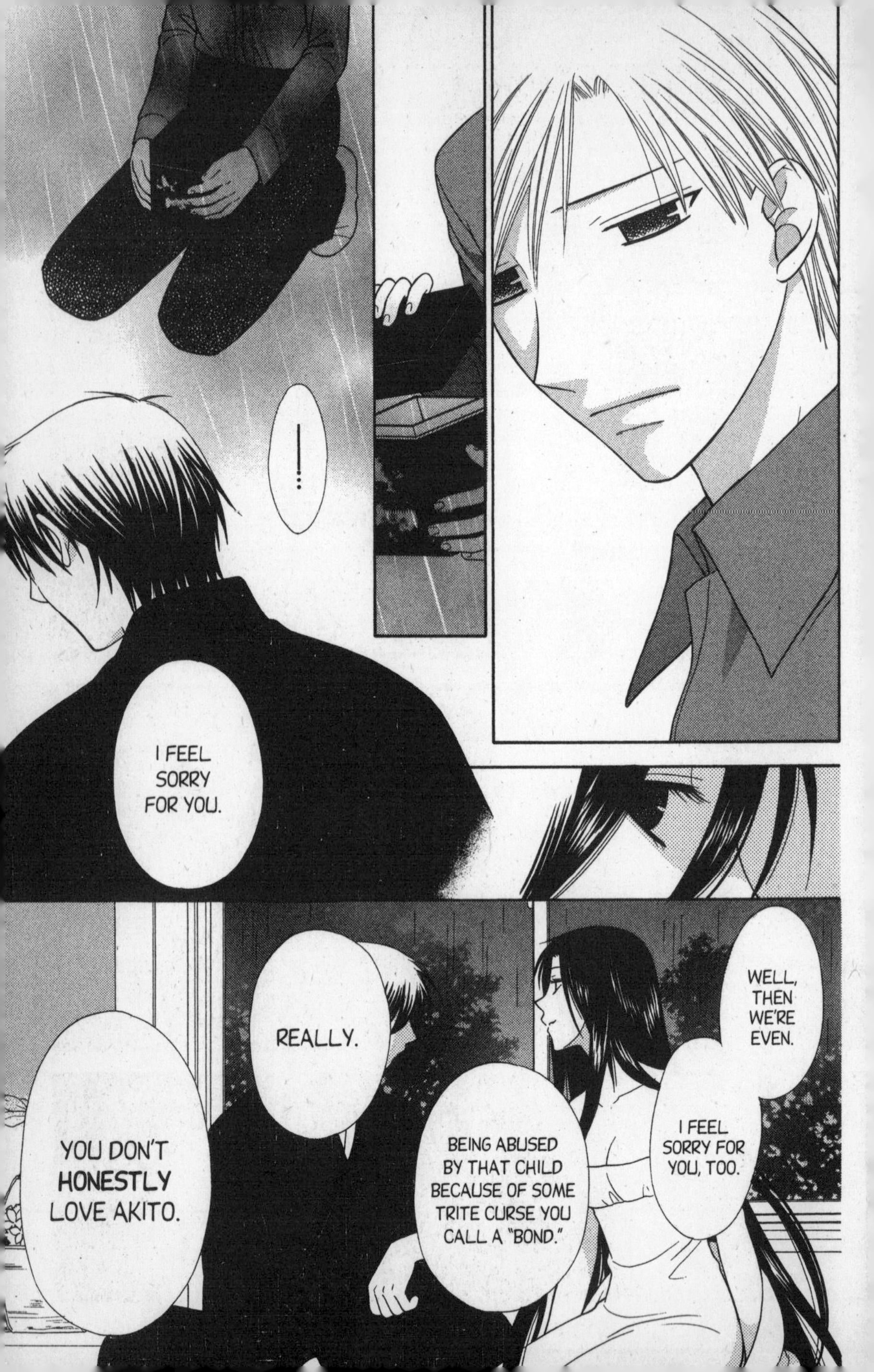
!...
I FEEL SORRY FOR YOU.
WELL, THEN WE'RE EVEN.
I FEEL SORRY FOR YOU, TOO.
BEING ABUSED BY THAT CHILD BECAUSE OF SOME TRITE CURSE YOU CALL A "BOND."
REALLY.
YOU DON'T **HONESTLY** LOVE AKITO.

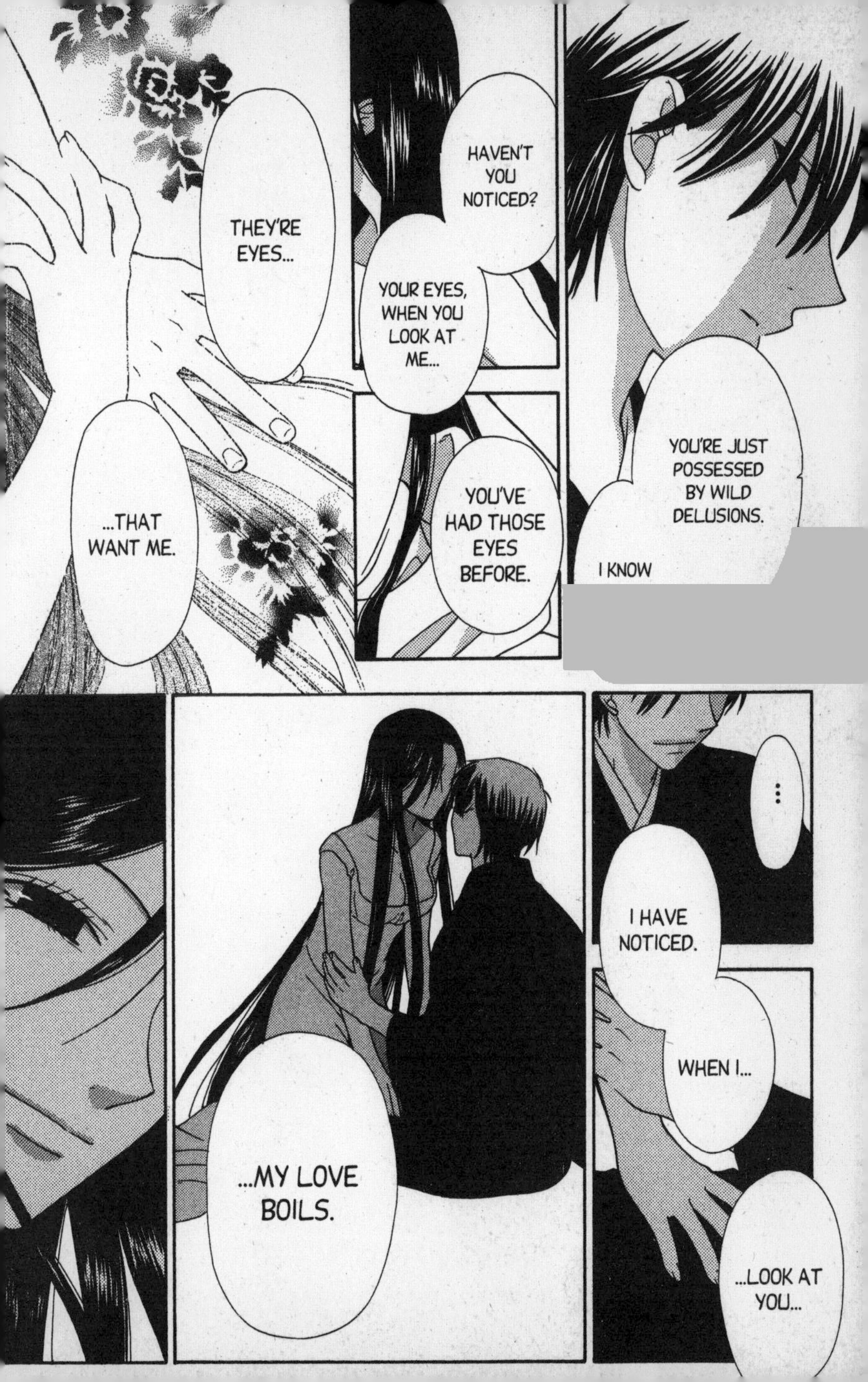
YOU'RE JUST POSSESSED BY WILD DELUSIONS.
I KNOW
HAVEN'T YOU NOTICED?
YOUR EYES, WHEN YOU LOOK AT ME...
YOU'VE HAD THOSE EYES BEFORE.
THEY'RE EYES...
...THAT WANT ME.
...
I HAVE NOTICED.
WHEN I...
...LOOK AT YOU...
...MY LOVE BOILS.

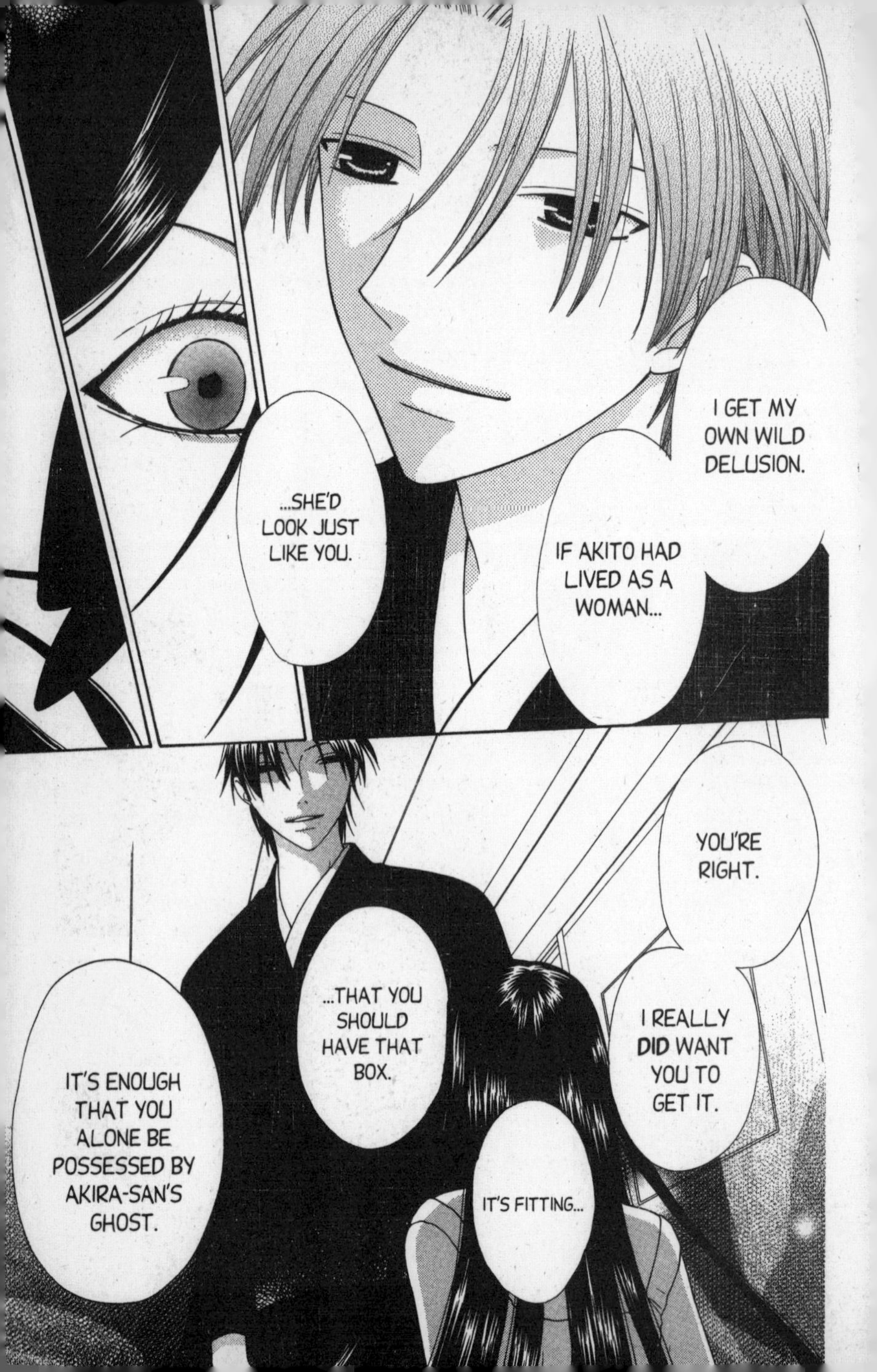
I GET MY OWN WILD DELUSION.
IF AKITO HAD LIVED AS A WOMAN...
...SHE'D LOOK JUST LIKE YOU.
YOU'RE RIGHT.
I REALLY **DID** WANT YOU TO GET IT.
IT'S FITTING...
...THAT YOU SHOULD HAVE THAT BOX.
IT'S ENOUGH THAT YOU ALONE BE POSSESSED BY AKIRA-SAN'S GHOST.

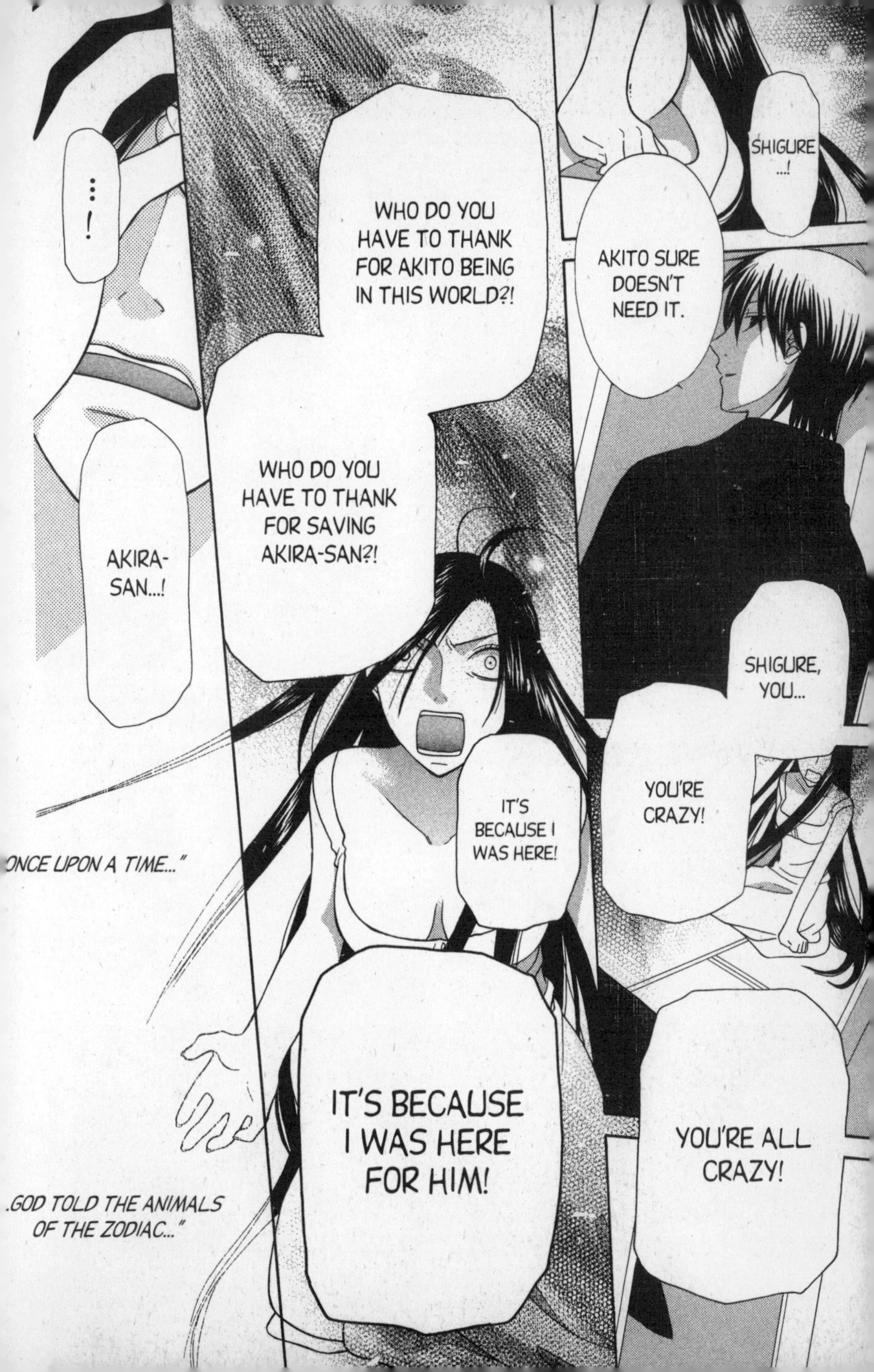
SHIGURE ...!
AKITO SURE DOESN'T NEED IT.
SHIGURE, YOU...
YOU'RE CRAZY!
YOU'RE ALL CRAZY!
WHO DO YOU HAVE TO THANK FOR AKITO BEING IN THIS WORLD?!
WHO DO YOU HAVE TO THANK FOR SAVING AKIRA-SAN?!
IT'S BECAUSE I WAS HERE!
IT'S BECAUSE I WAS HERE FOR HIM!
...!
AKIRA-SAN...!
ONCE UPON A TIME..."
.GOD TOLD THE ANIMALS OF THE ZODIAC..."

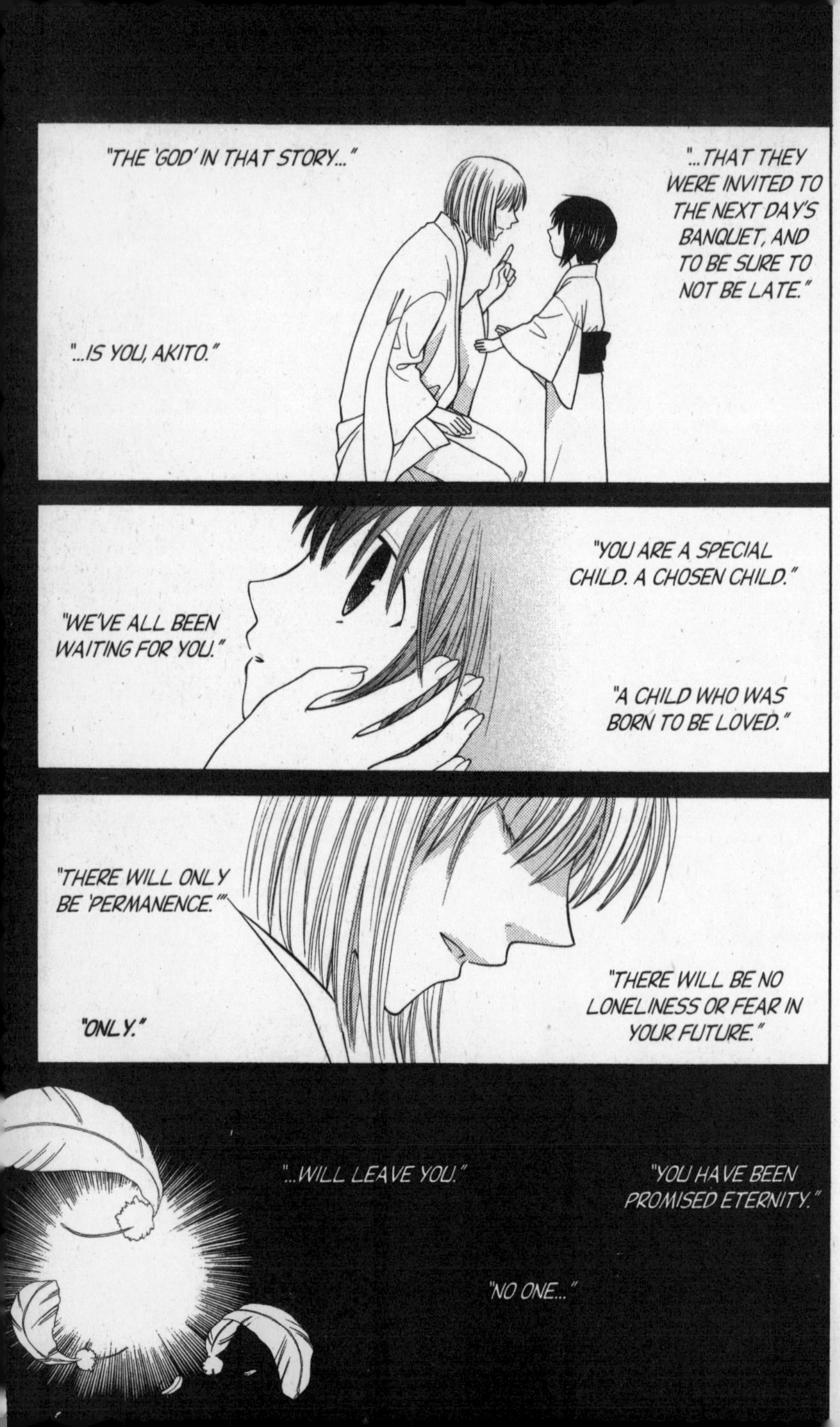
"...THAT THEY WERE INVITED TO THE NEXT DAY'S BANQUET, AND TO BE SURE TO NOT BE LATE."
"THE 'GOD' IN THAT STORY..."
"...IS YOU, AKITO."
"YOU ARE A SPECIAL CHILD. A CHOSEN CHILD."
"WE'VE ALL BEEN WAITING FOR YOU."
"A CHILD WHO WAS BORN TO BE LOVED."
"THERE WILL BE NO LONELINESS OR FEAR IN YOUR FUTURE."
"THERE WILL ONLY BE 'PERMANENCE.'"
"ONLY."
"YOU HAVE BEEN PROMISED ETERNITY."
"...WILL LEAVE YOU."
"NO ONE..."

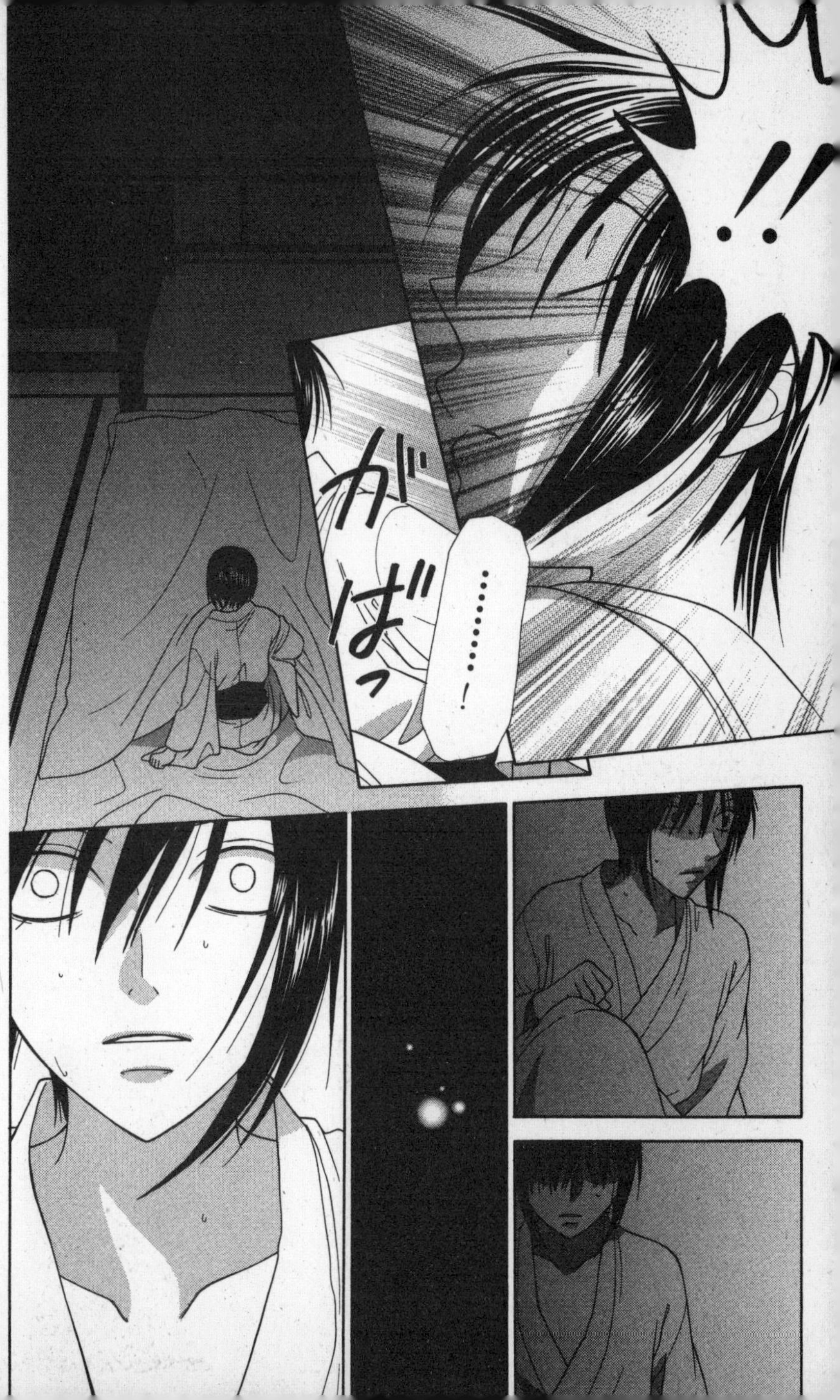
がばっ
……!

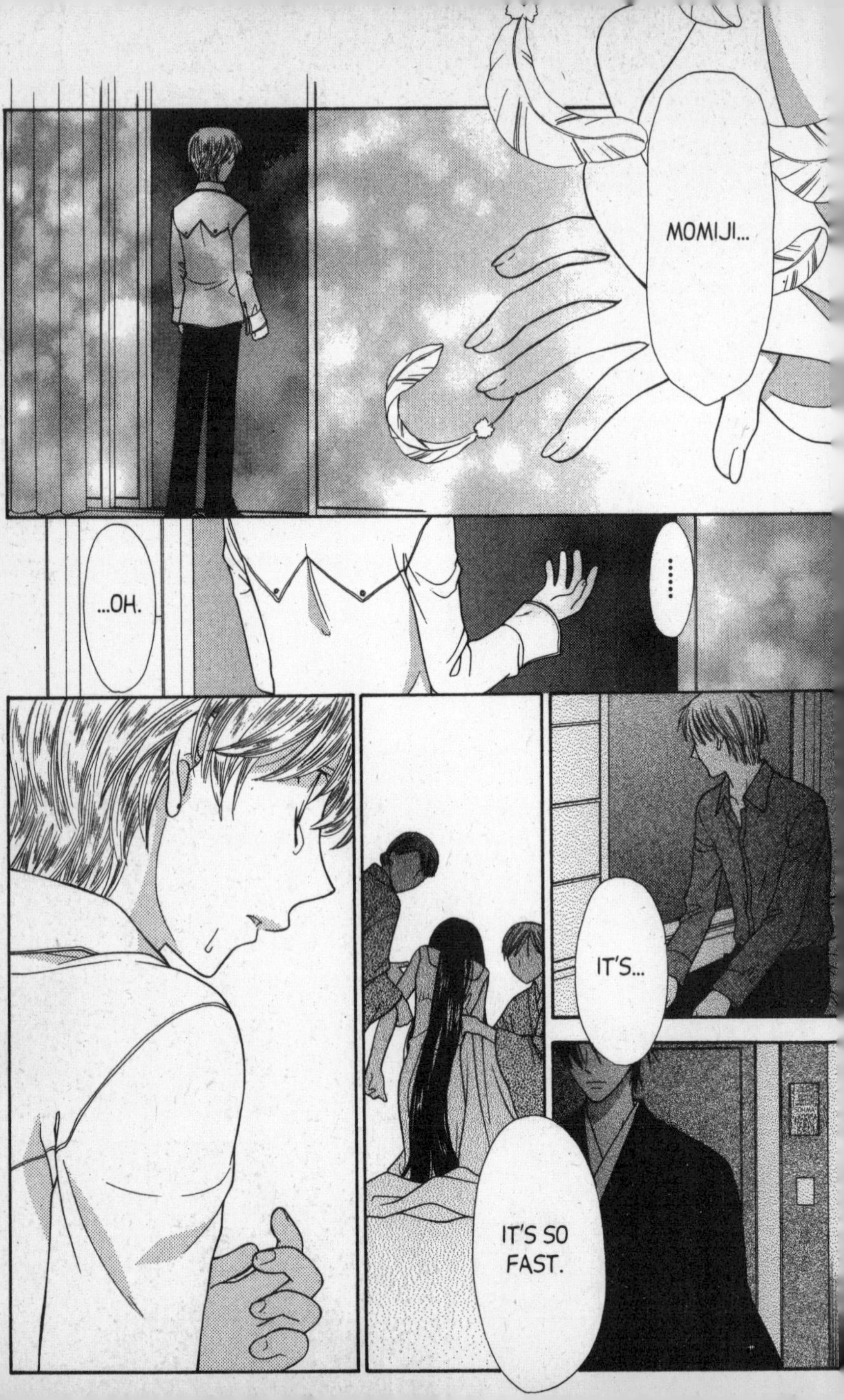
MOMIJI...
......
...OH.
IT'S...
IT'S SO FAST.

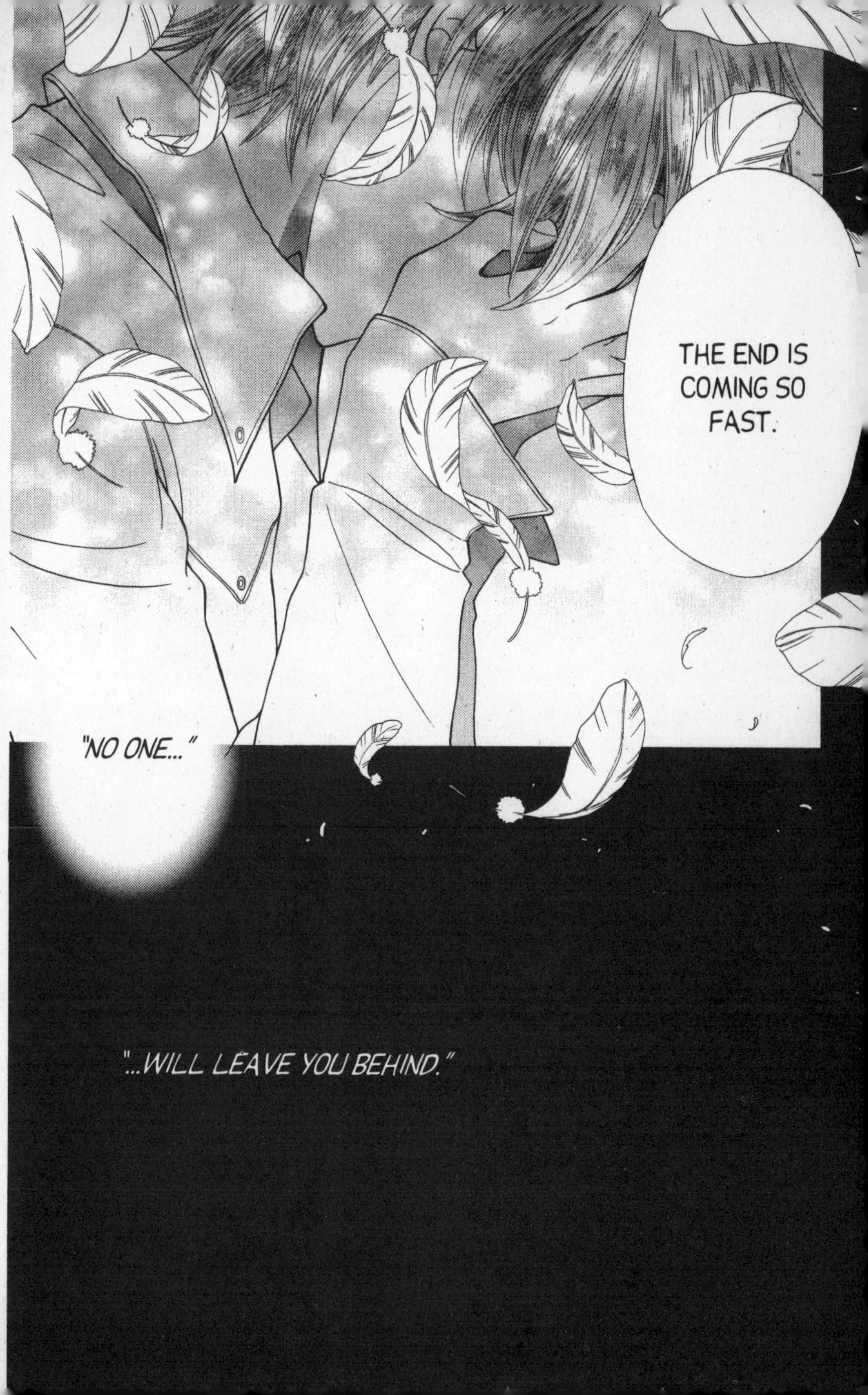
THE END IS COMING SO FAST.
"NO ONE..."
"...WILL LEAVE YOU BEHIND."

Chapter 116

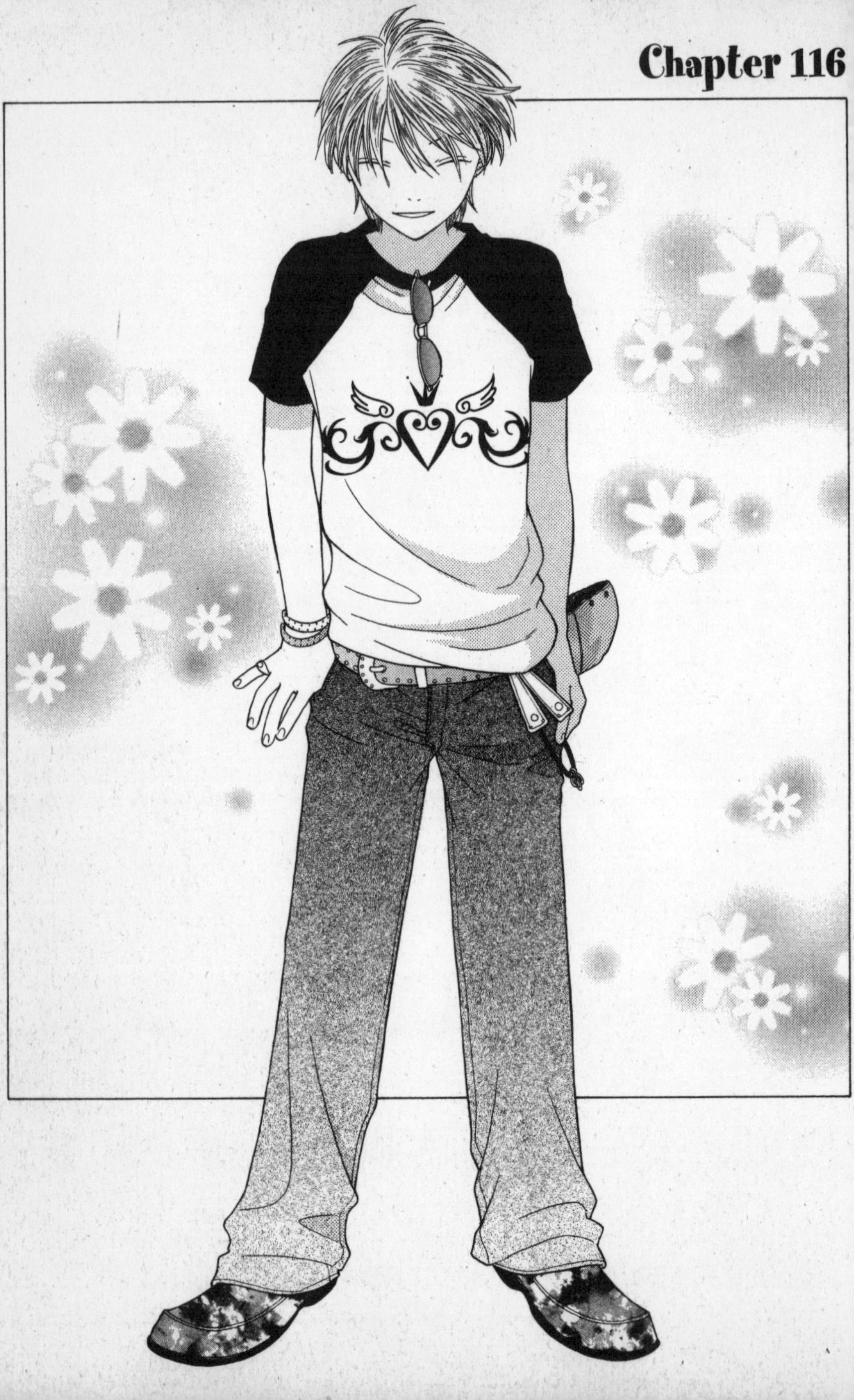

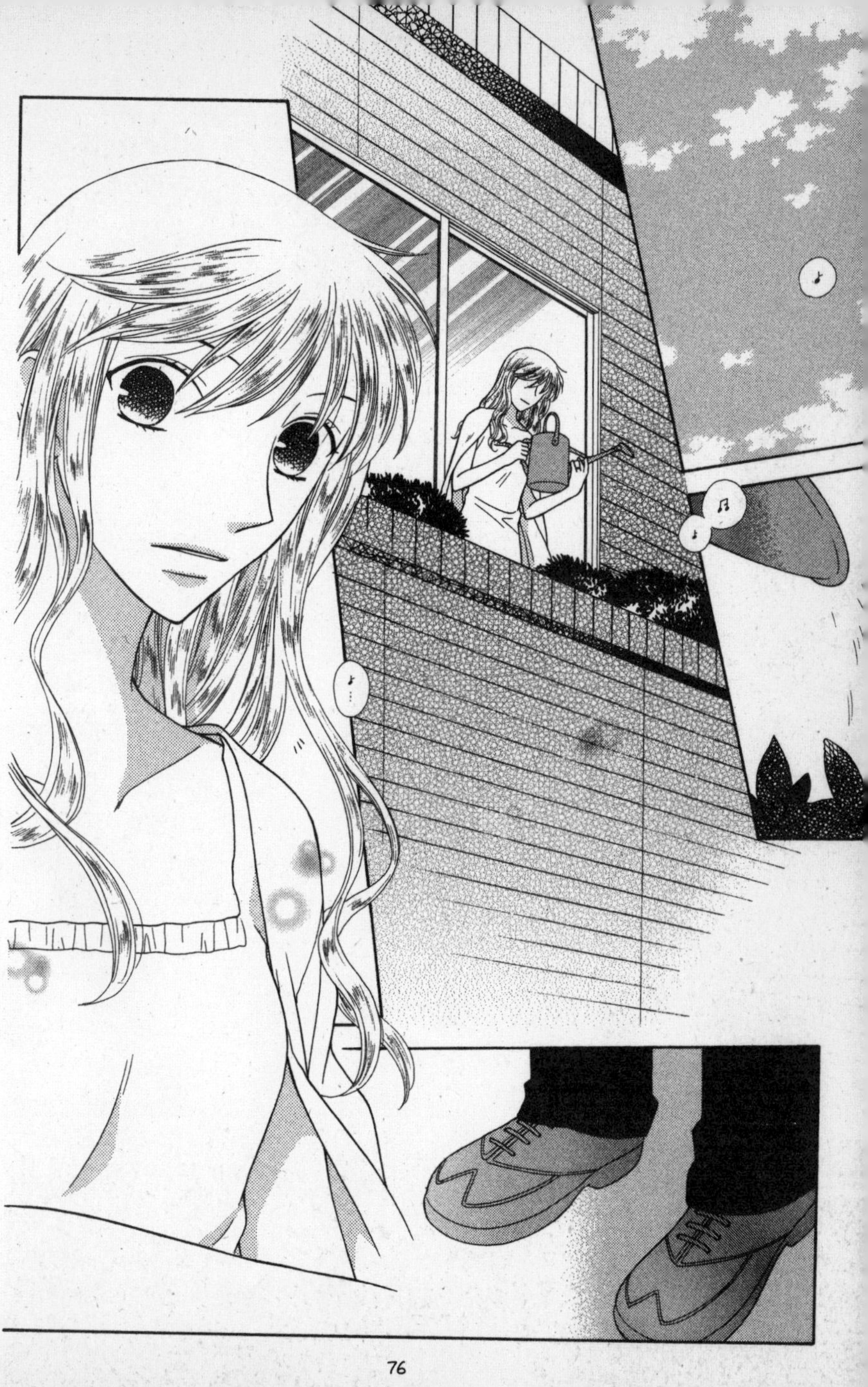

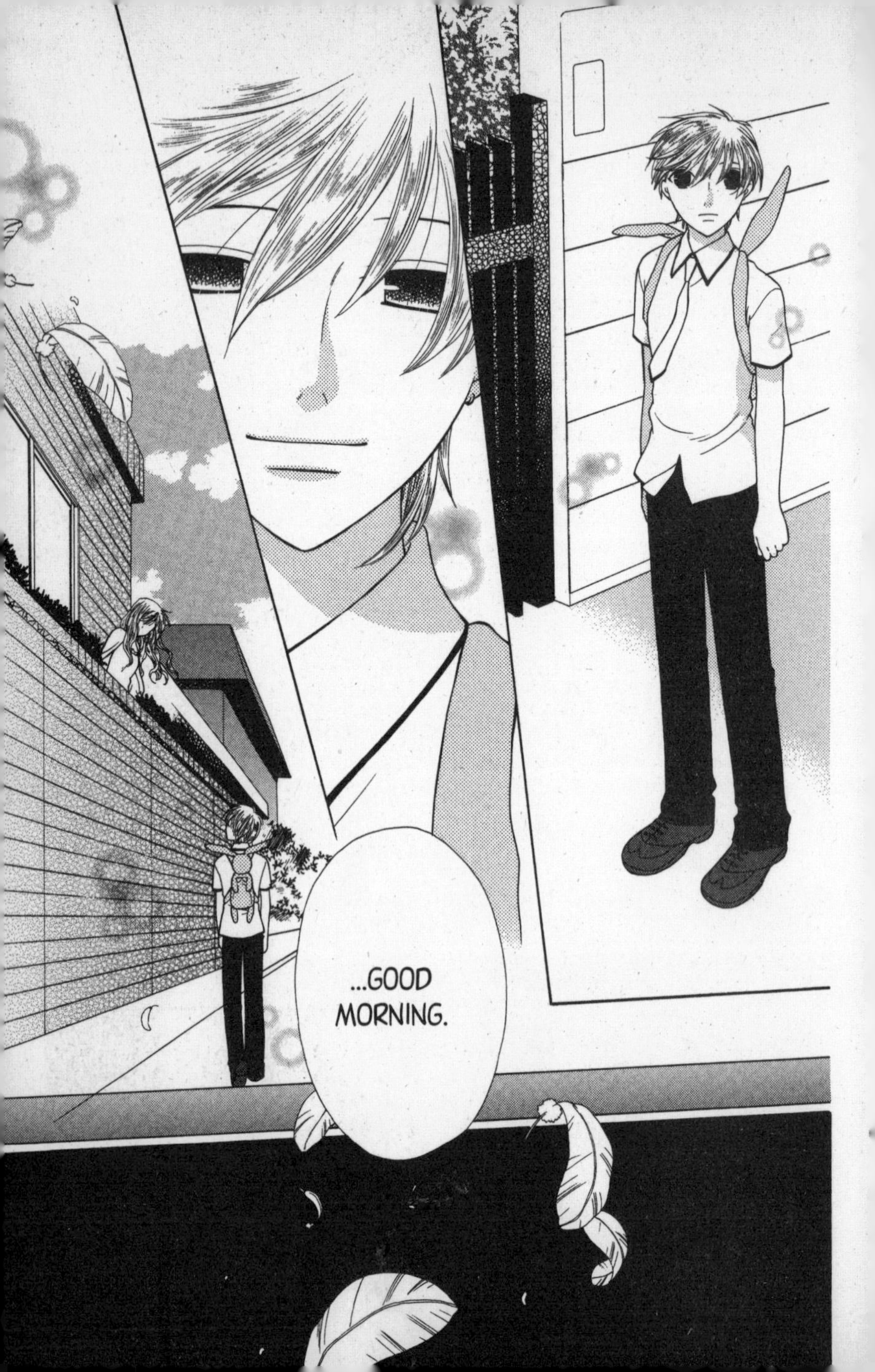
...GOOD MORNING.

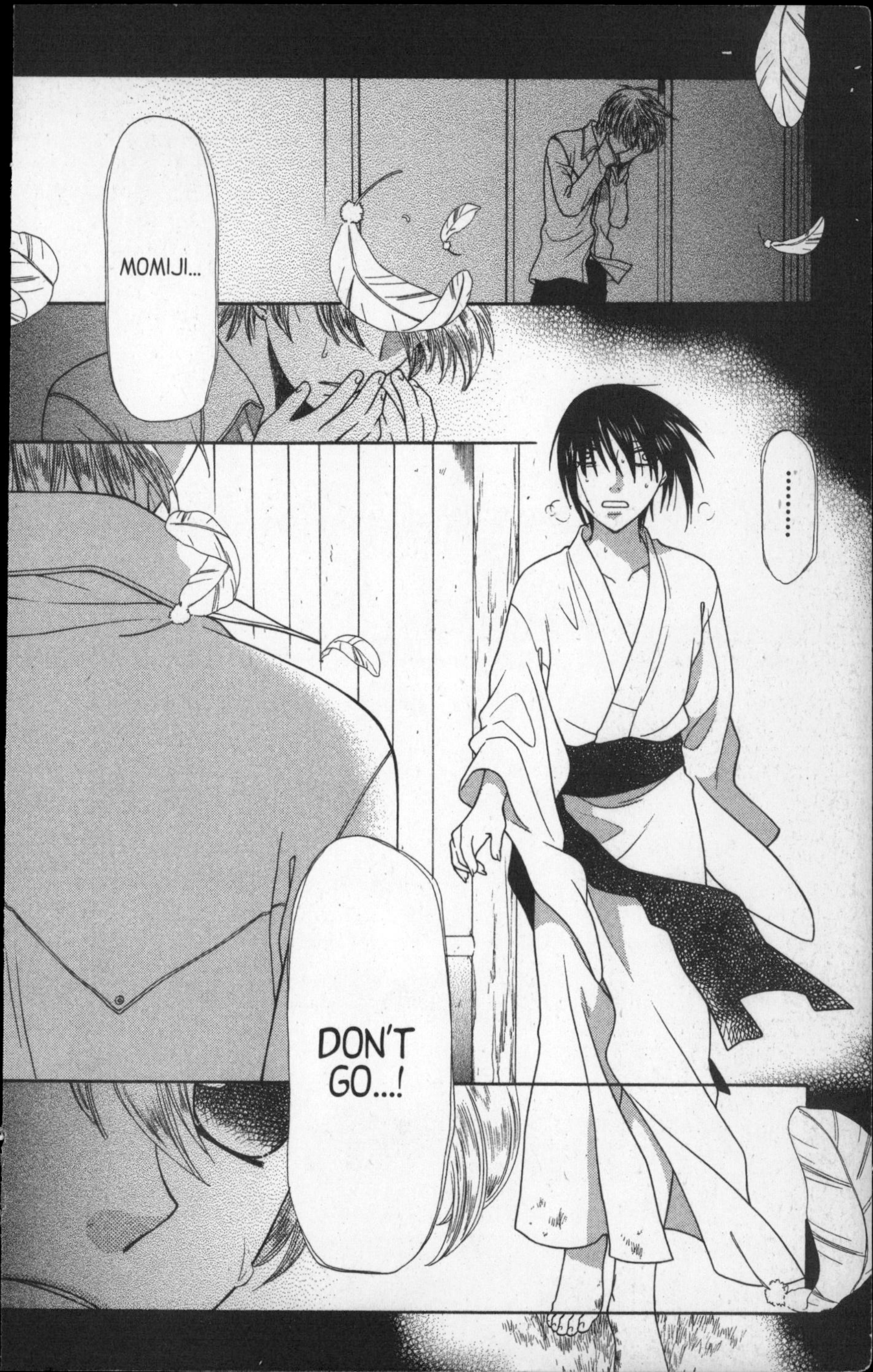
MOMIJI...
......
DON'T GO...!

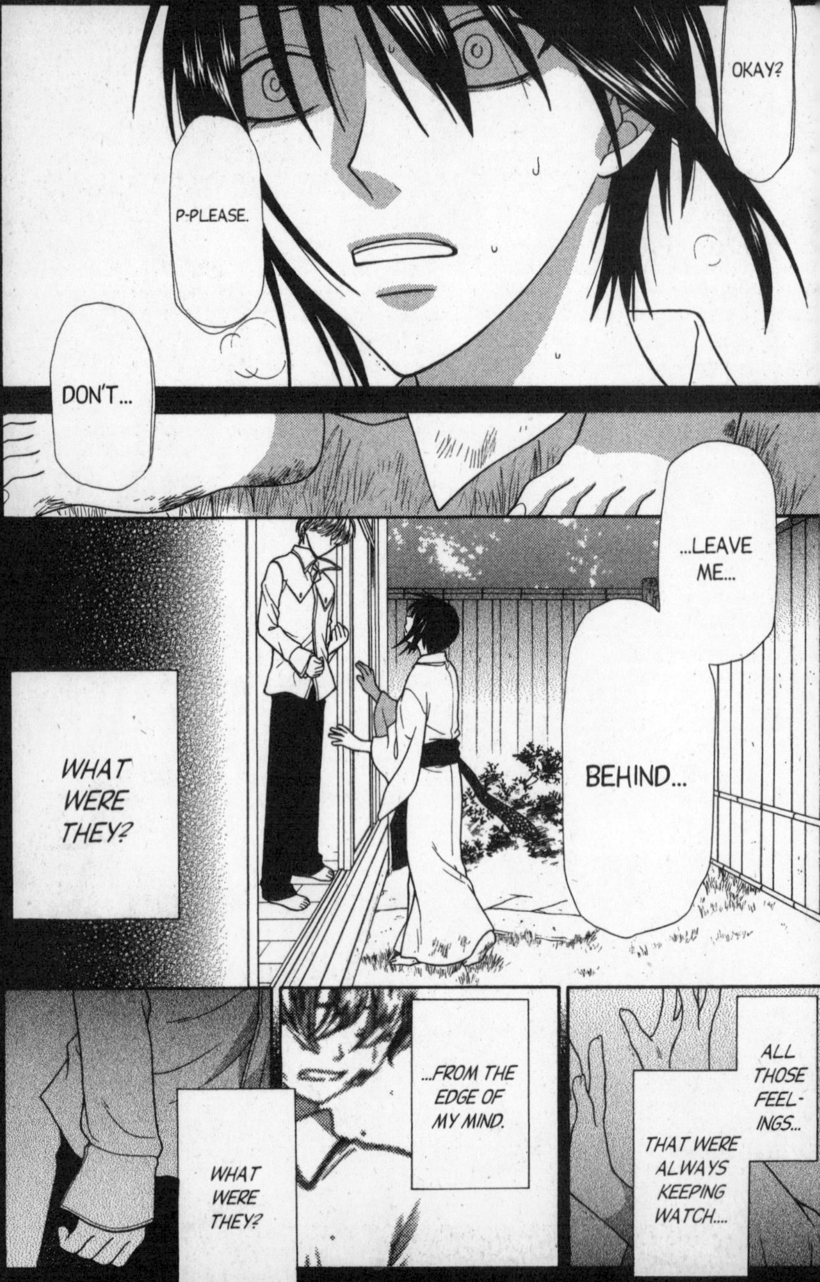
OKAY?
P-PLEASE.
DON'T...
...LEAVE ME...
BEHIND...
WHAT WERE THEY?
ALL THOSE FEEL-INGS...
THAT WERE ALWAYS KEEPING WATCH....
...FROM THE EDGE OF MY MIND.
WHAT WERE THEY?

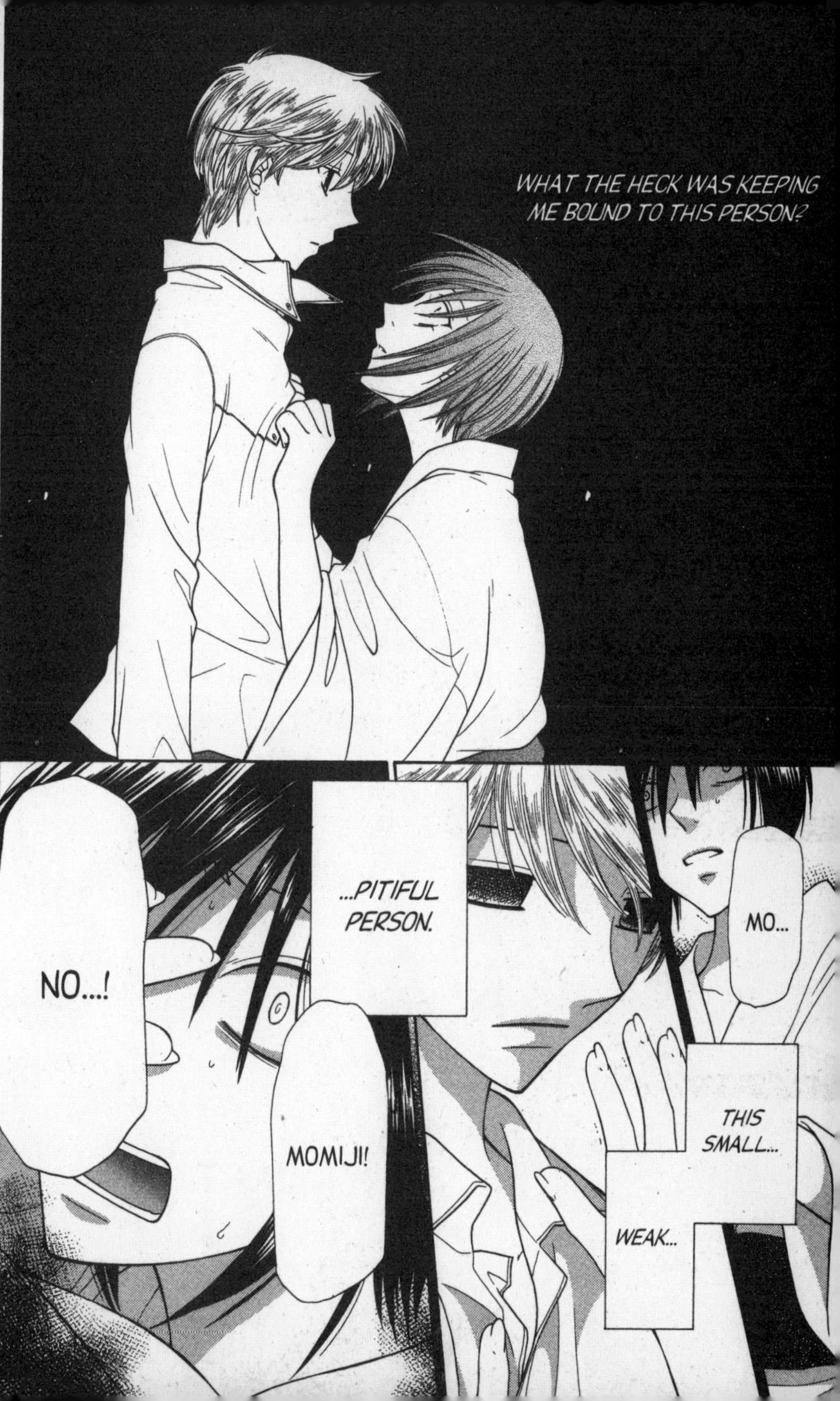
WHAT THE HECK WAS KEEPING ME BOUND TO THIS PERSON?
MO...
THIS SMALL...
WEAK...
...PITIFUL PERSON.
NO...!
MOMIJI!

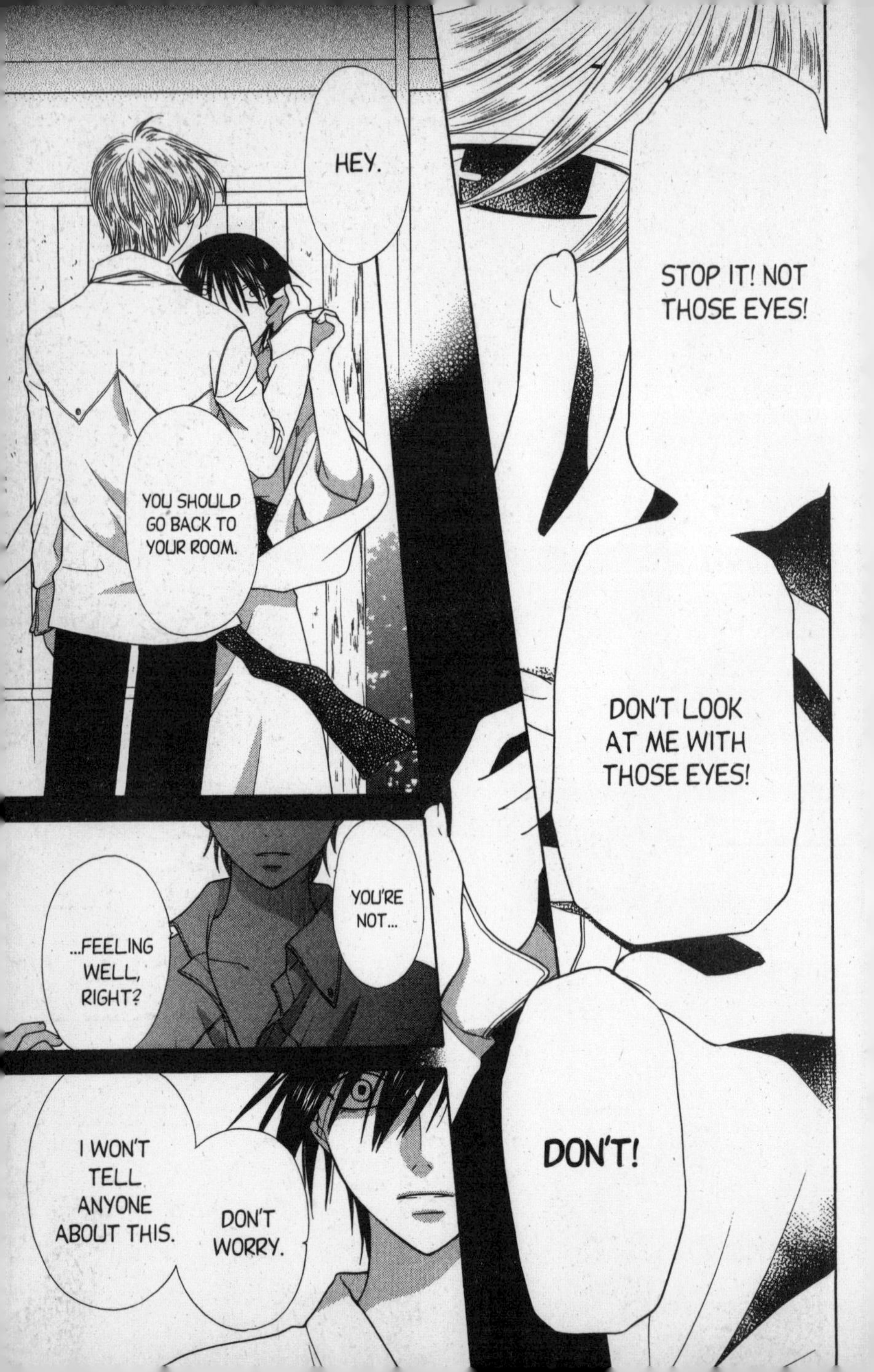
STOP IT! NOT THOSE EYES!
DON'T LOOK AT ME WITH THOSE EYES!
DON'T!
HEY.
YOU SHOULD GO BACK TO YOUR ROOM.
YOU'RE NOT...
...FEELING WELL, RIGHT?
DON'T WORRY.
I WON'T TELL ANYONE ABOUT THIS.

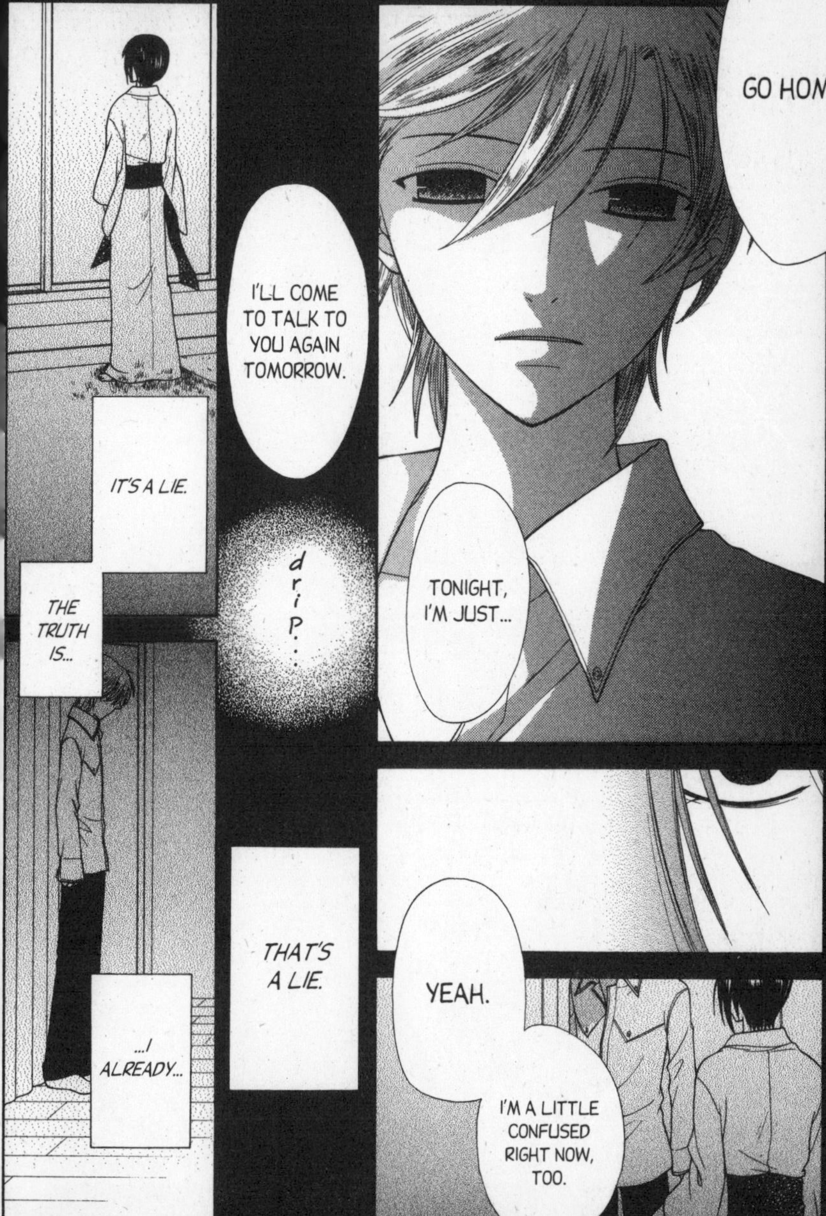
GO HOME.
I'LL COME TO TALK TO YOU AGAIN TOMORROW.
TONIGHT, I'M JUST...
IT'S A LIE.
THE TRUTH IS...
drip...
YEAH.
I'M A LITTLE CONFUSED RIGHT NOW, TOO.
THAT'S A LIE.
...I ALREADY...

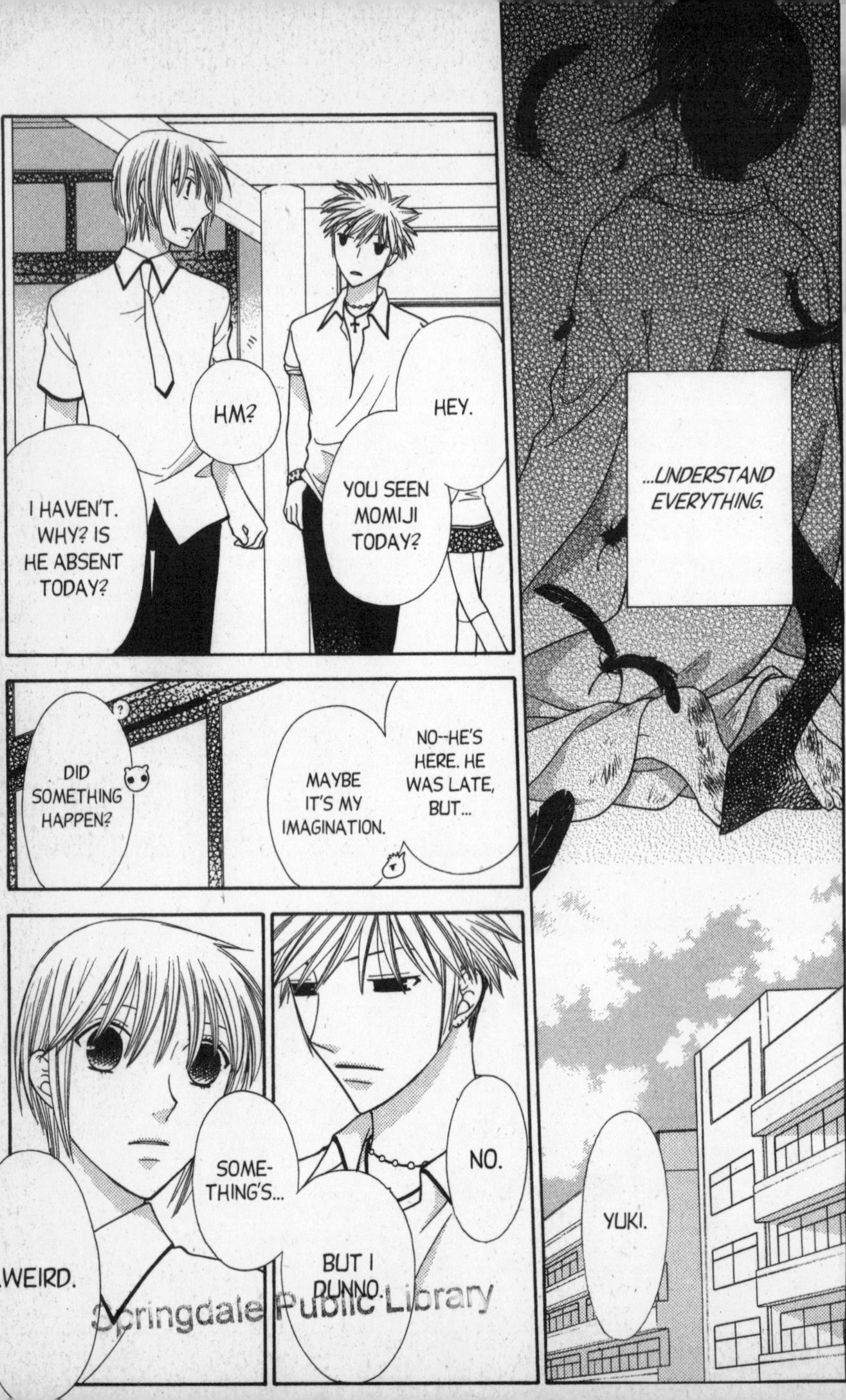
...UNDERSTAND EVERYTHING.
YUKI.
HEY.
YOU SEEN MOMIJI TODAY?
HM?
I HAVEN'T. WHY? IS HE ABSENT TODAY?
NO--HE'S HERE. HE WAS LATE, BUT...
MAYBE IT'S MY IMAGINATION.
DID SOMETHING HAPPEN?
NO.
BUT I DUNNO.
SOME-THING'S...
...WEIRD.

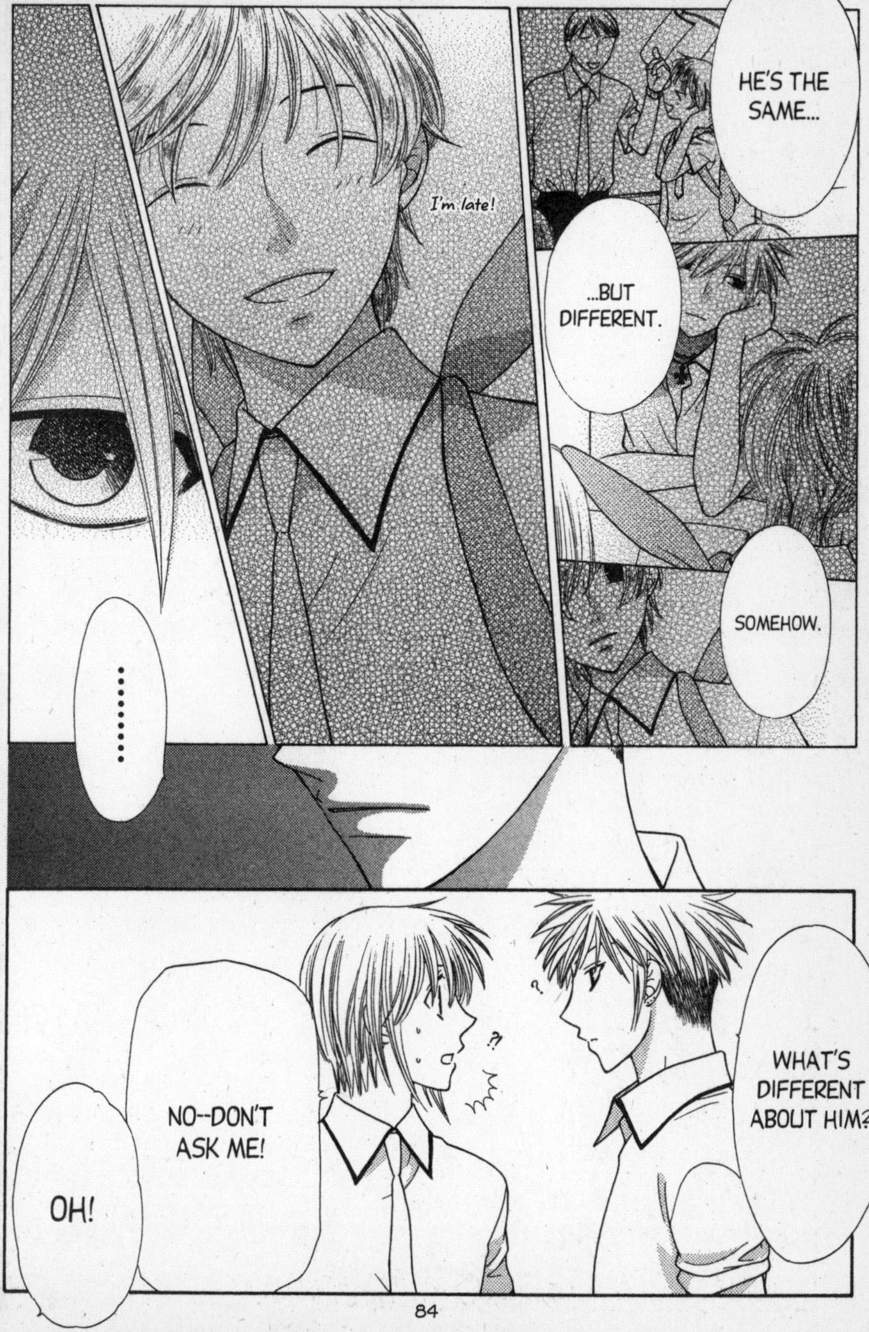
HE'S THE SAME...
...BUT DIFFERENT.
SOMEHOW.
I'm late!
....
WHAT'S DIFFERENT ABOUT HIM?
?
?!
NO--DON'T ASK ME!
OH!

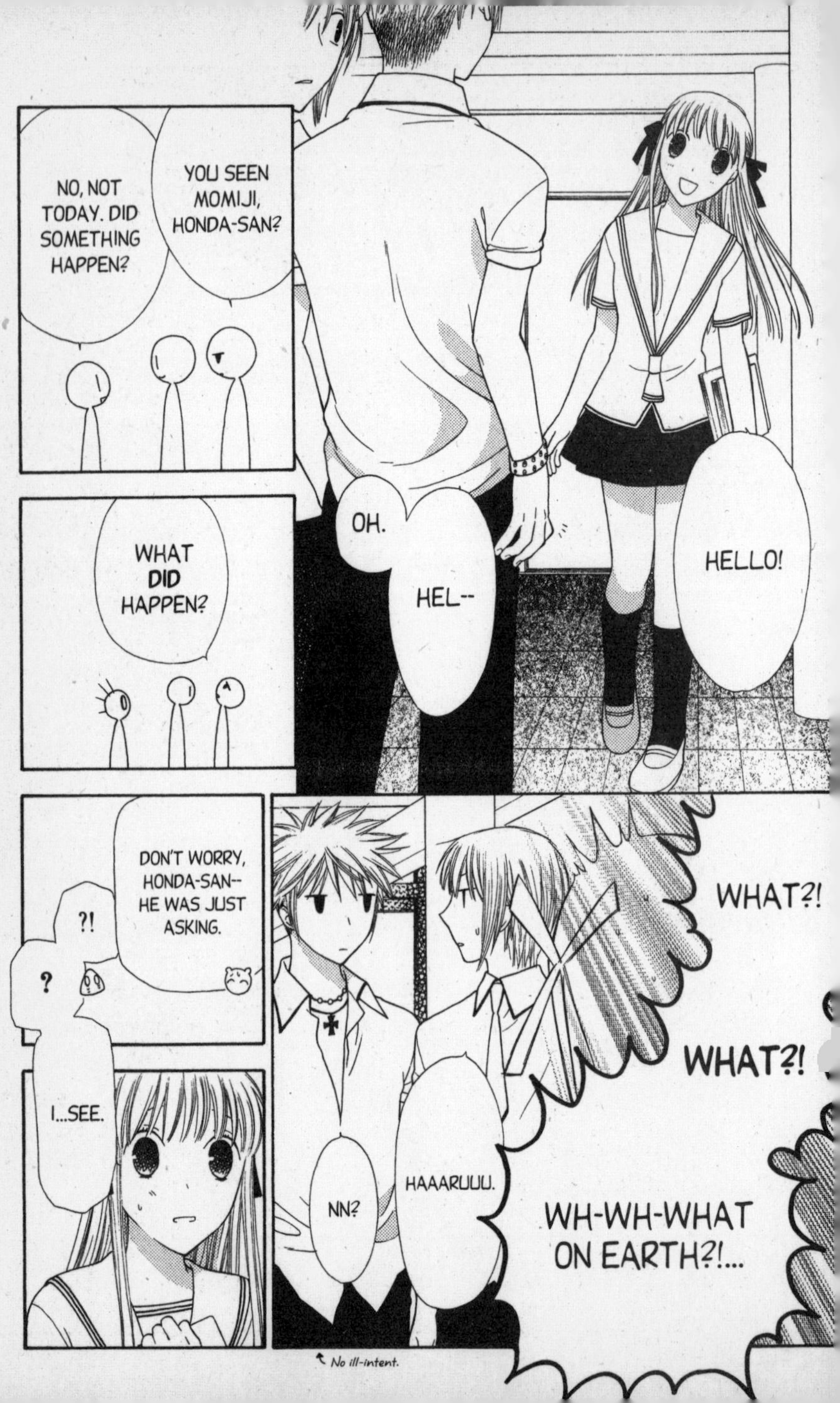
HELLO!
HEL--
OH.
YOU SEEN MOMIJI, HONDA-SAN?
NO, NOT TODAY. DID SOMETHING HAPPEN?
WHAT DID HAPPEN?
WHAT?!
WHAT?!
WH-WH-WHAT ON EARTH?!...
HAAARUUU.
NN?
DON'T WORRY, HONDA-SAN-- HE WAS JUST ASKING.
?!
?
I...SEE.
No ill-intent.

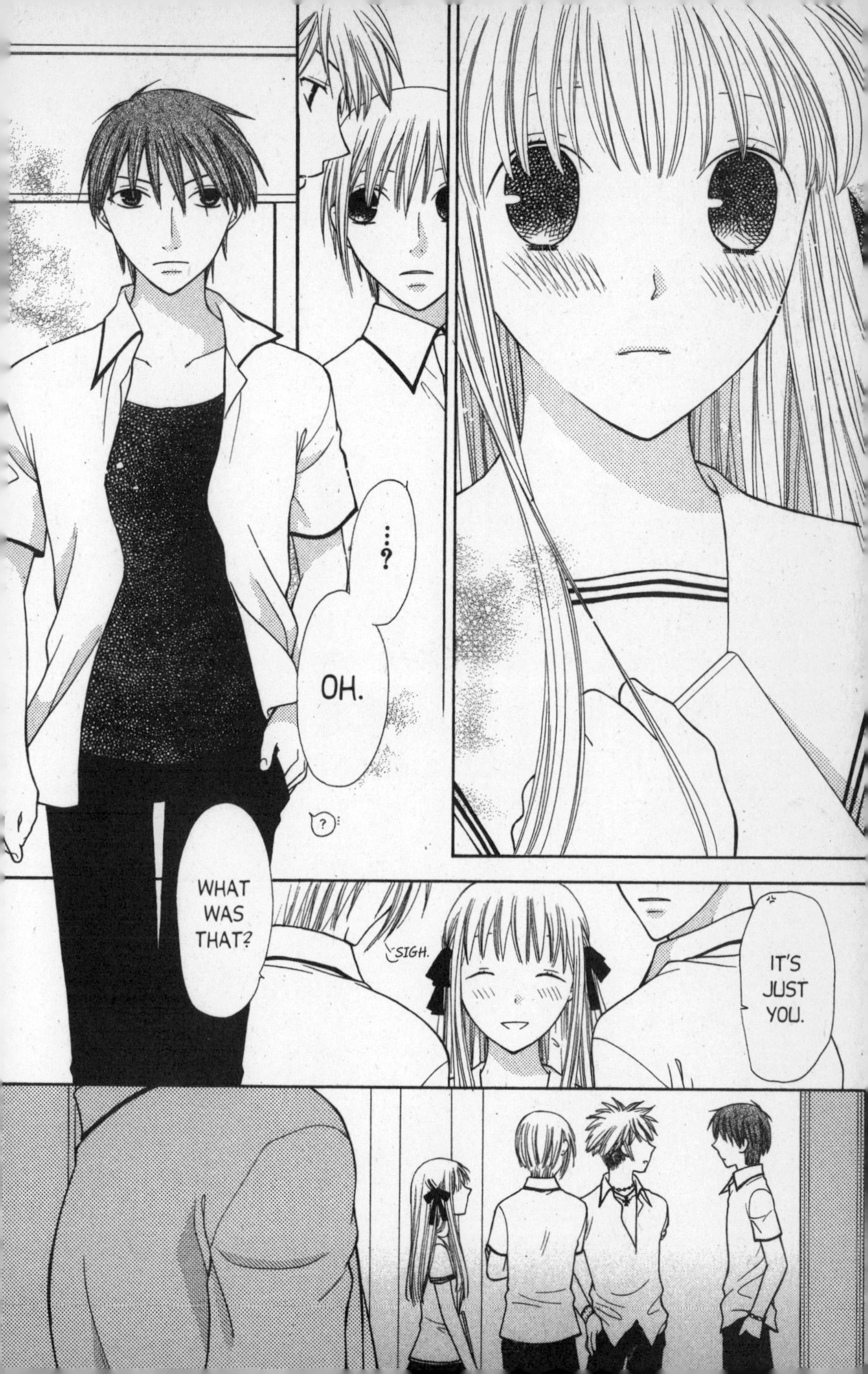
...?
OH.
?
IT'S JUST YOU.
SIGH.
WHAT WAS THAT?

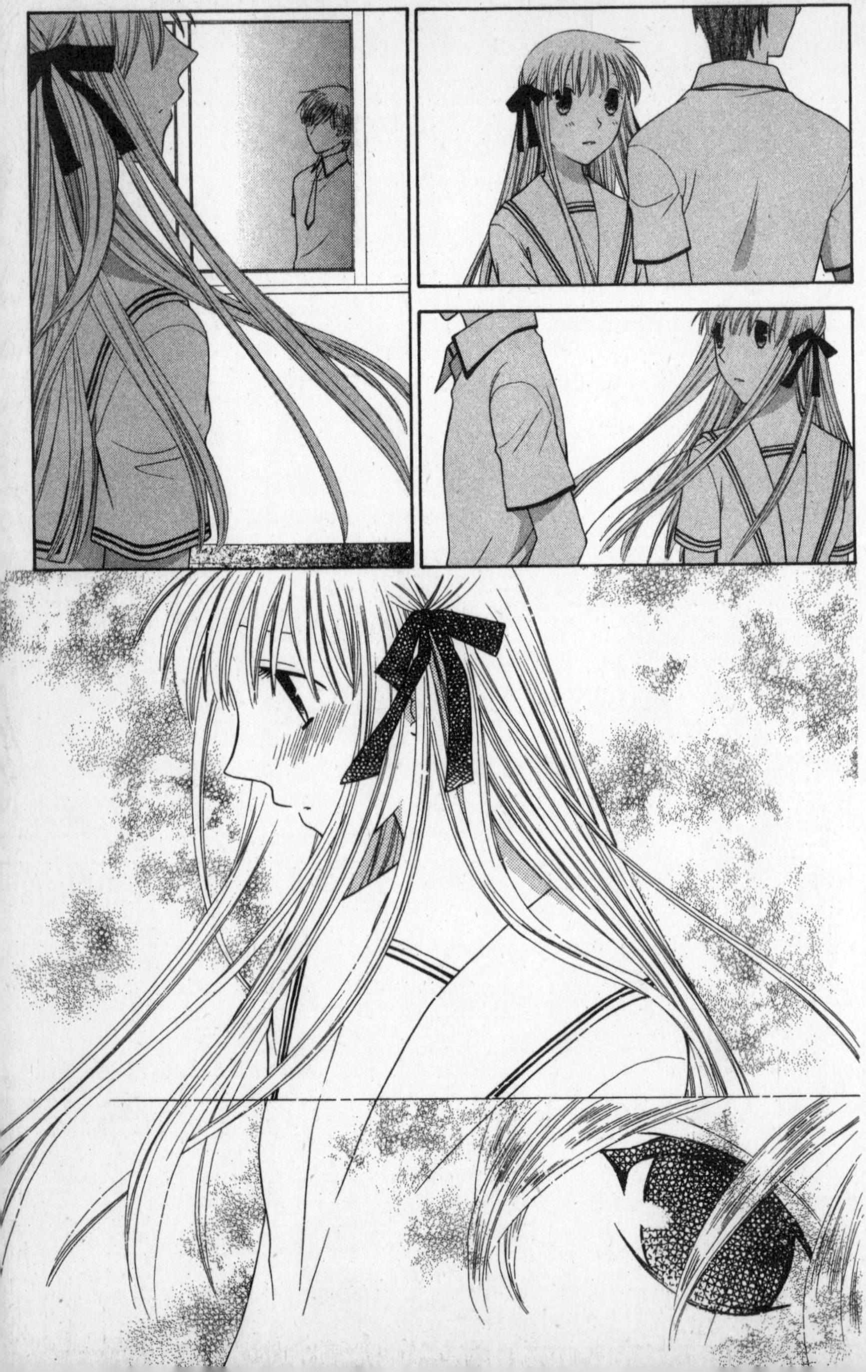

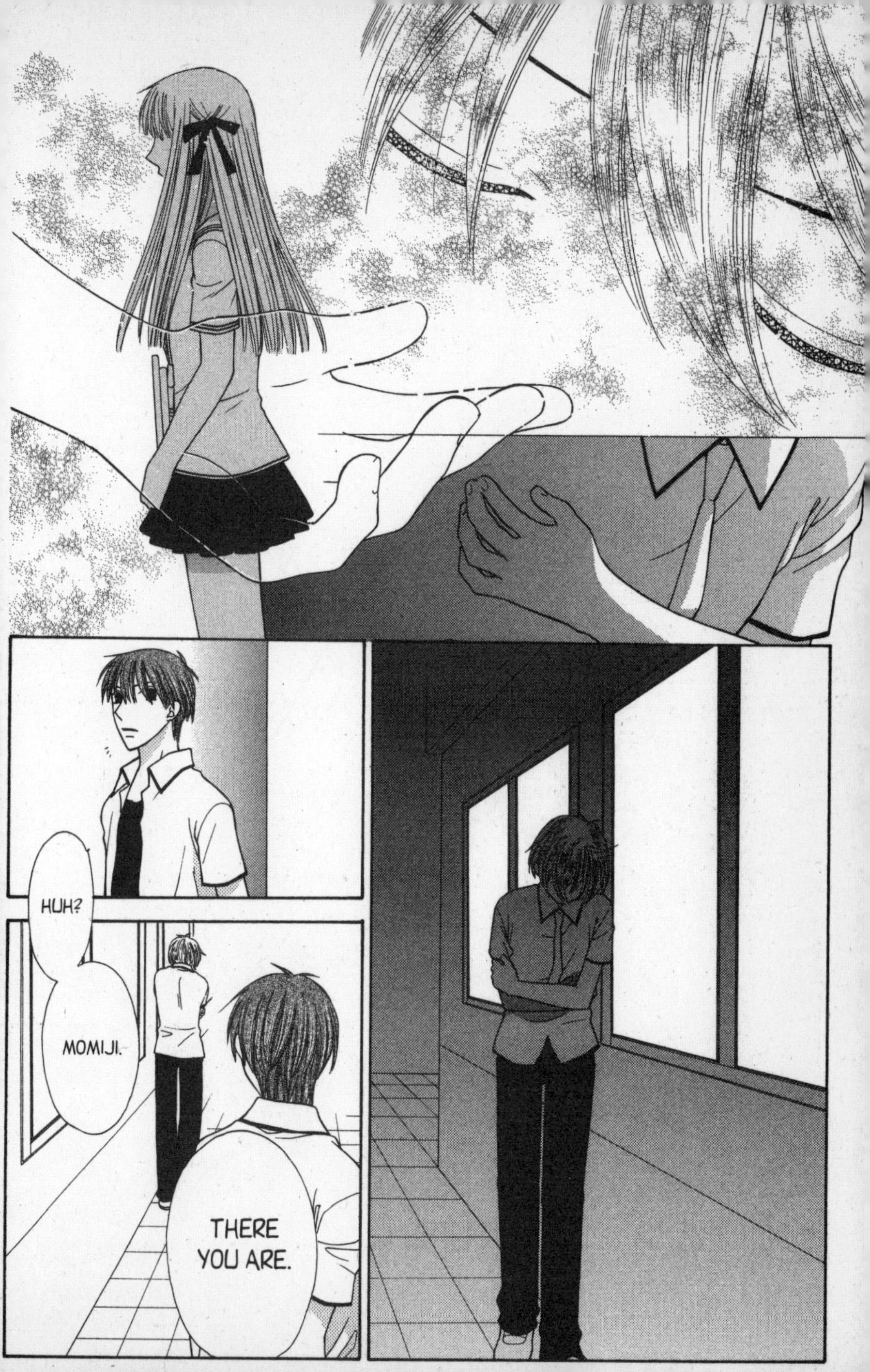
HUH?
MOMIJI.
THERE YOU ARE.

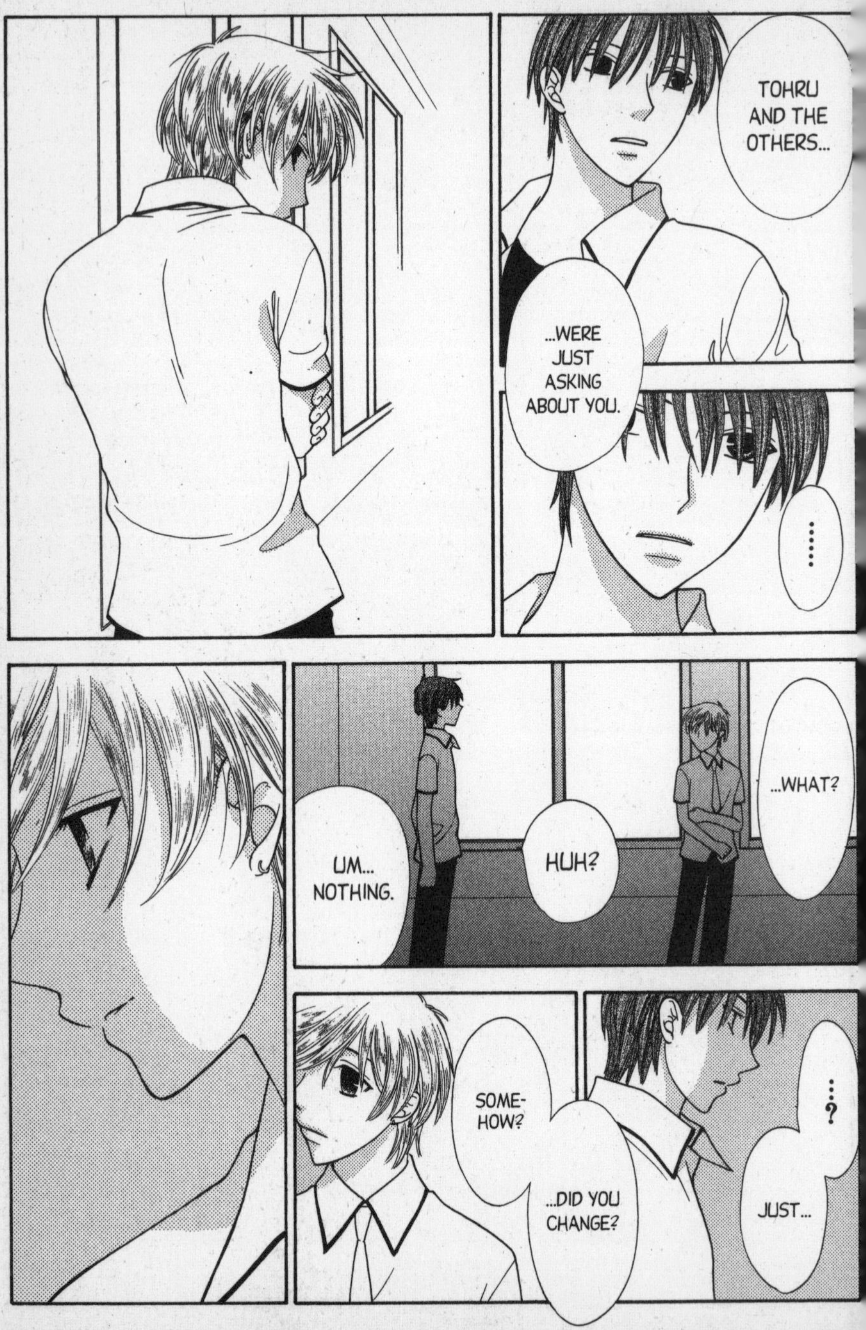
TOHRU AND THE OTHERS...
...WERE JUST ASKING ABOUT YOU.
......
...WHAT?
HUH?
UM... NOTHING.
...?
JUST...
SOME-HOW?
...DID YOU CHANGE?

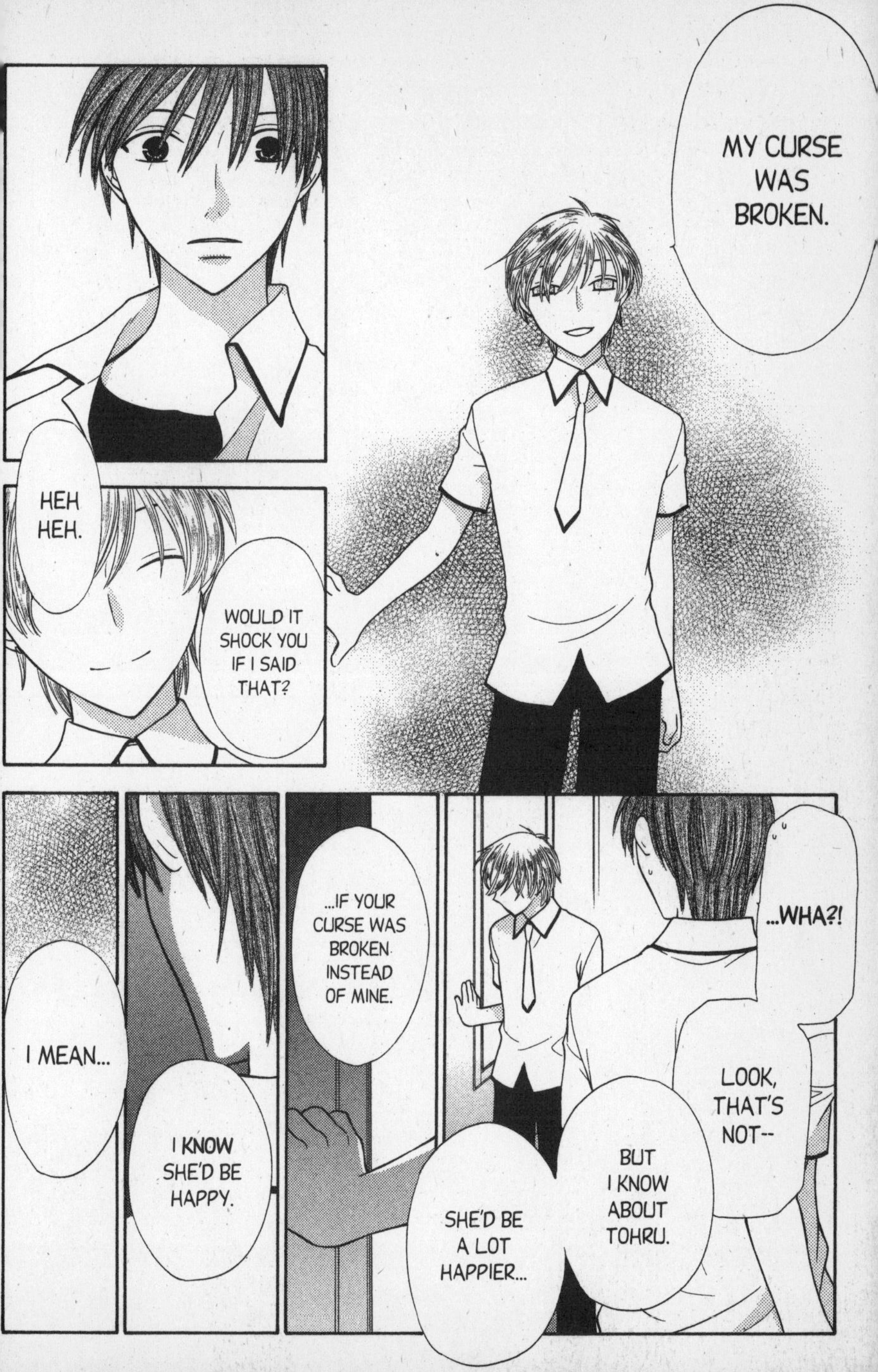
MY CURSE WAS BROKEN.
HEH HEH.
WOULD IT SHOCK YOU IF I SAID THAT?
...WHA?!
LOOK, THAT'S NOT--
BUT I KNOW ABOUT TOHRU.
SHE'D BE A LOT HAPPIER...
...IF YOUR CURSE WAS BROKEN INSTEAD OF MINE.
I KNOW SHE'D BE HAPPY.
I MEAN...

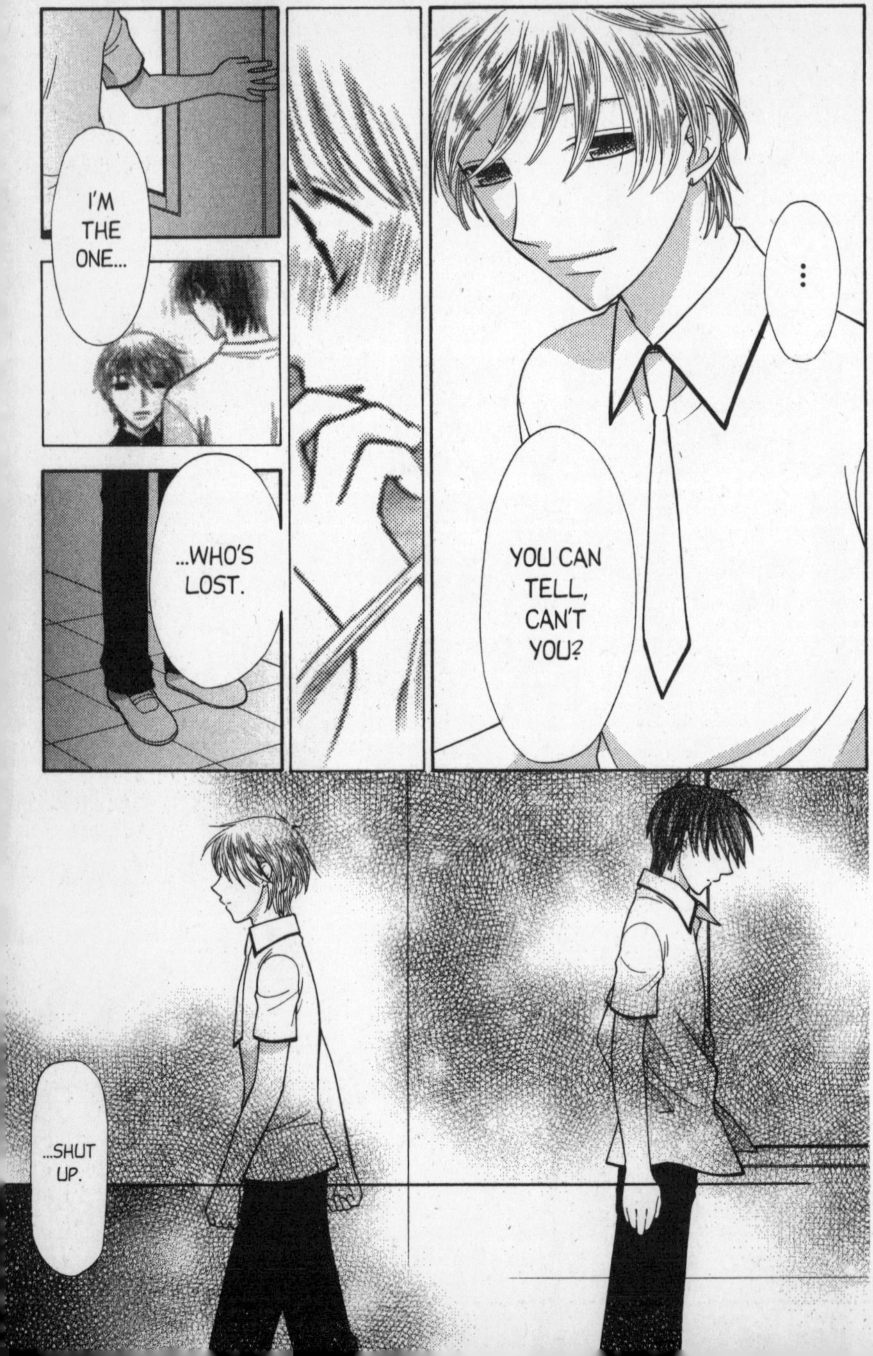
...
YOU CAN TELL, CAN'T YOU?
I'M THE ONE...
...WHO'S LOST.
...SHUT UP.

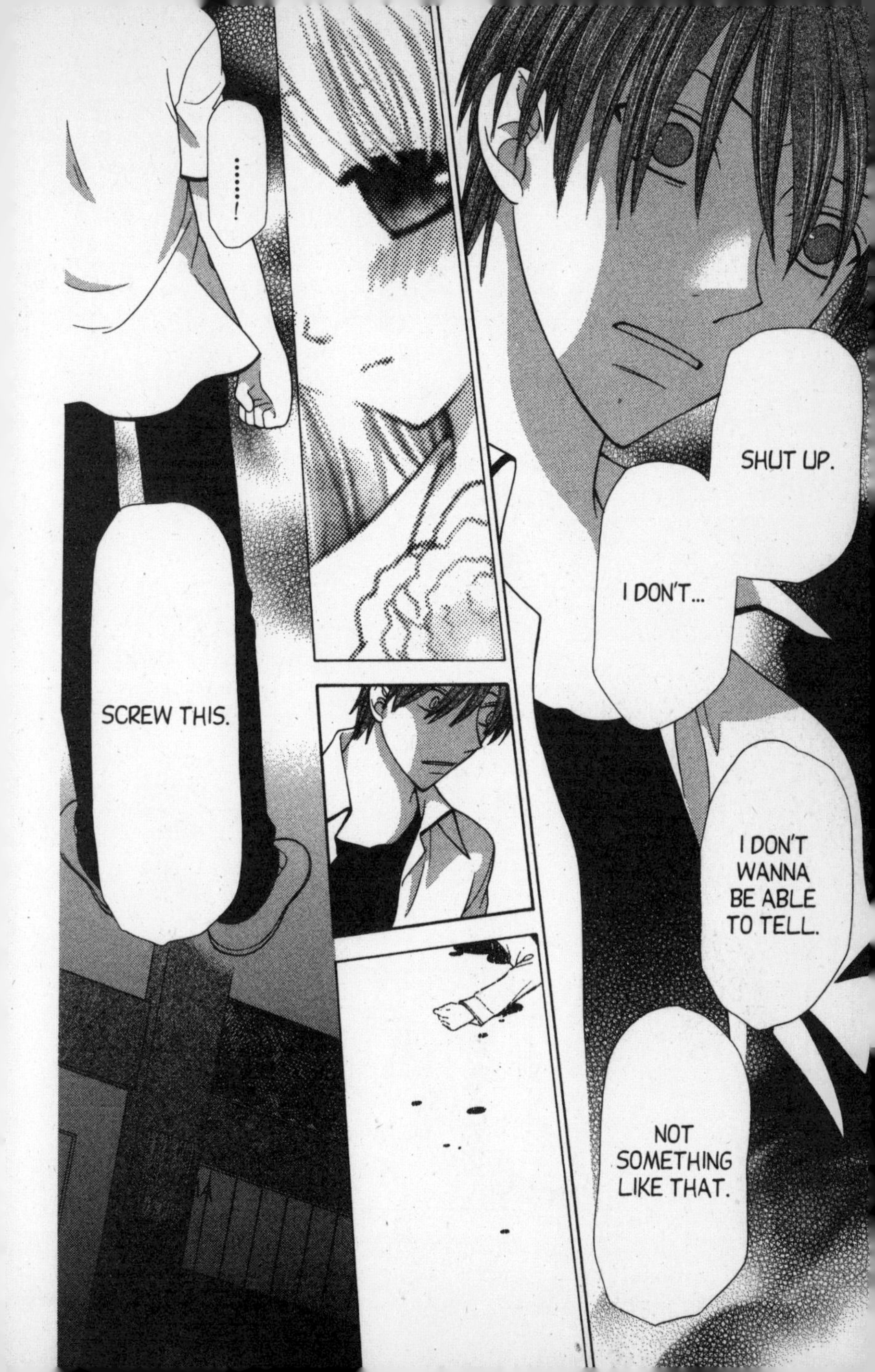
SHUT UP.
I DON'T...
I DON'T WANNA BE ABLE TO TELL.
NOT SOMETHING LIKE THAT.
......!
SCREW THIS.

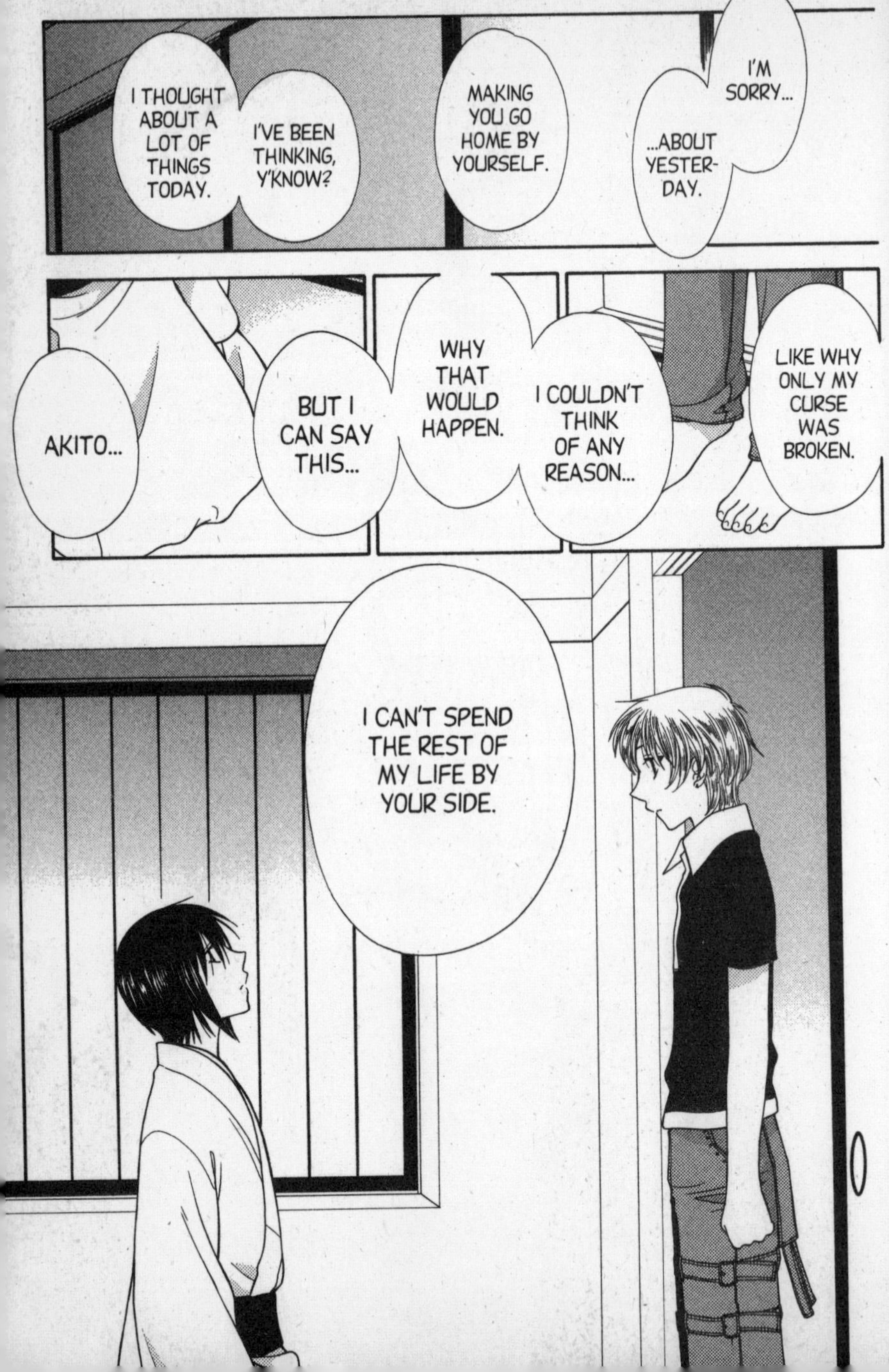
I'M SORRY...
...ABOUT YESTERDAY.
MAKING YOU GO HOME BY YOURSELF.
I'VE BEEN THINKING, Y'KNOW?
I THOUGHT ABOUT A LOT OF THINGS TODAY.
LIKE WHY ONLY MY CURSE WAS BROKEN.
I COULDN'T THINK OF ANY REASON...
WHY THAT WOULD HAPPEN.
BUT I CAN SAY THIS...
AKITO...
I CAN'T SPEND THE REST OF MY LIFE BY YOUR SIDE.

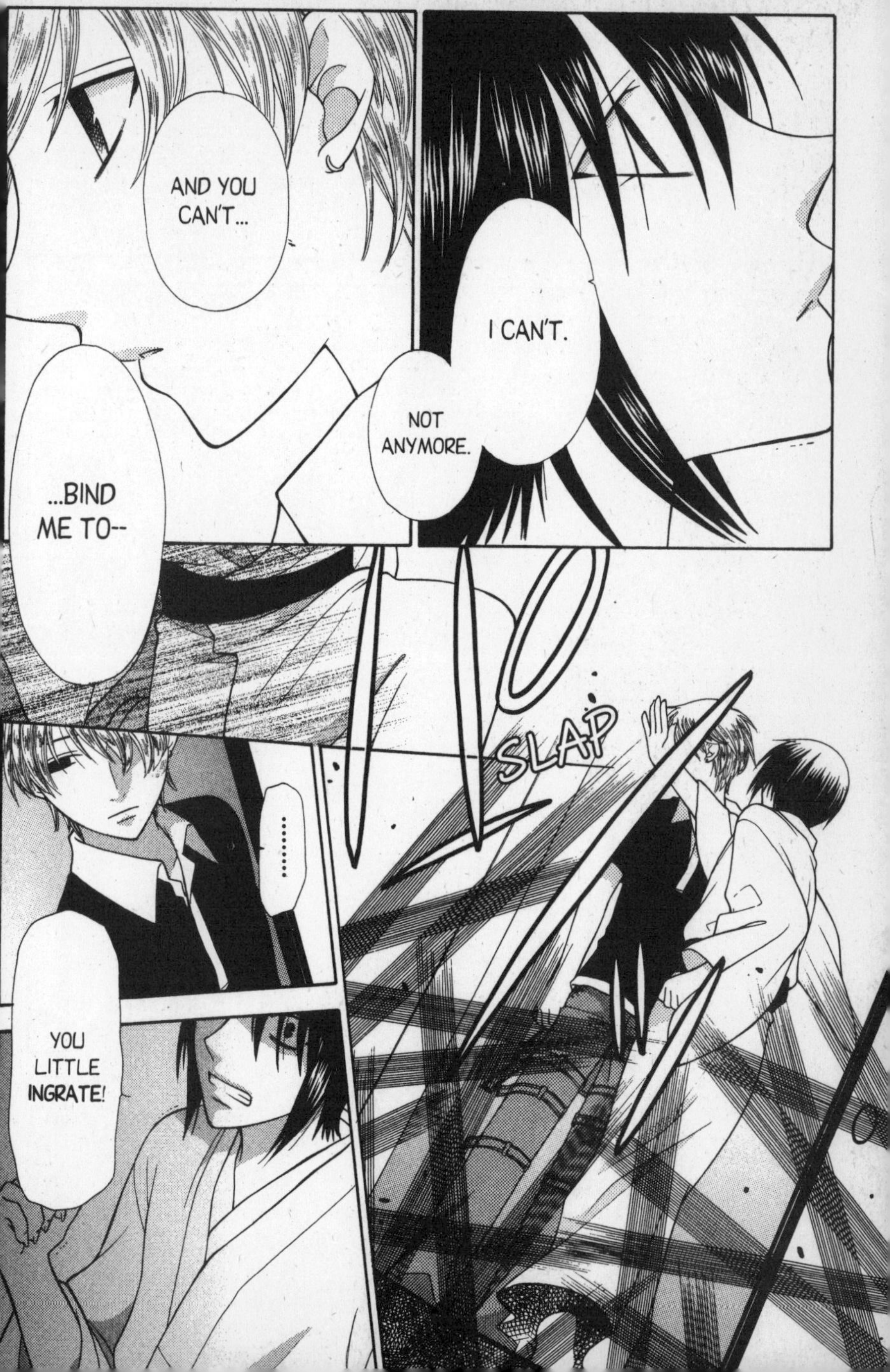
I CAN'T.
NOT ANYMORE.
AND YOU CAN'T...
...BIND ME TO--
SLAP
......
YOU LITTLE INGRATE!

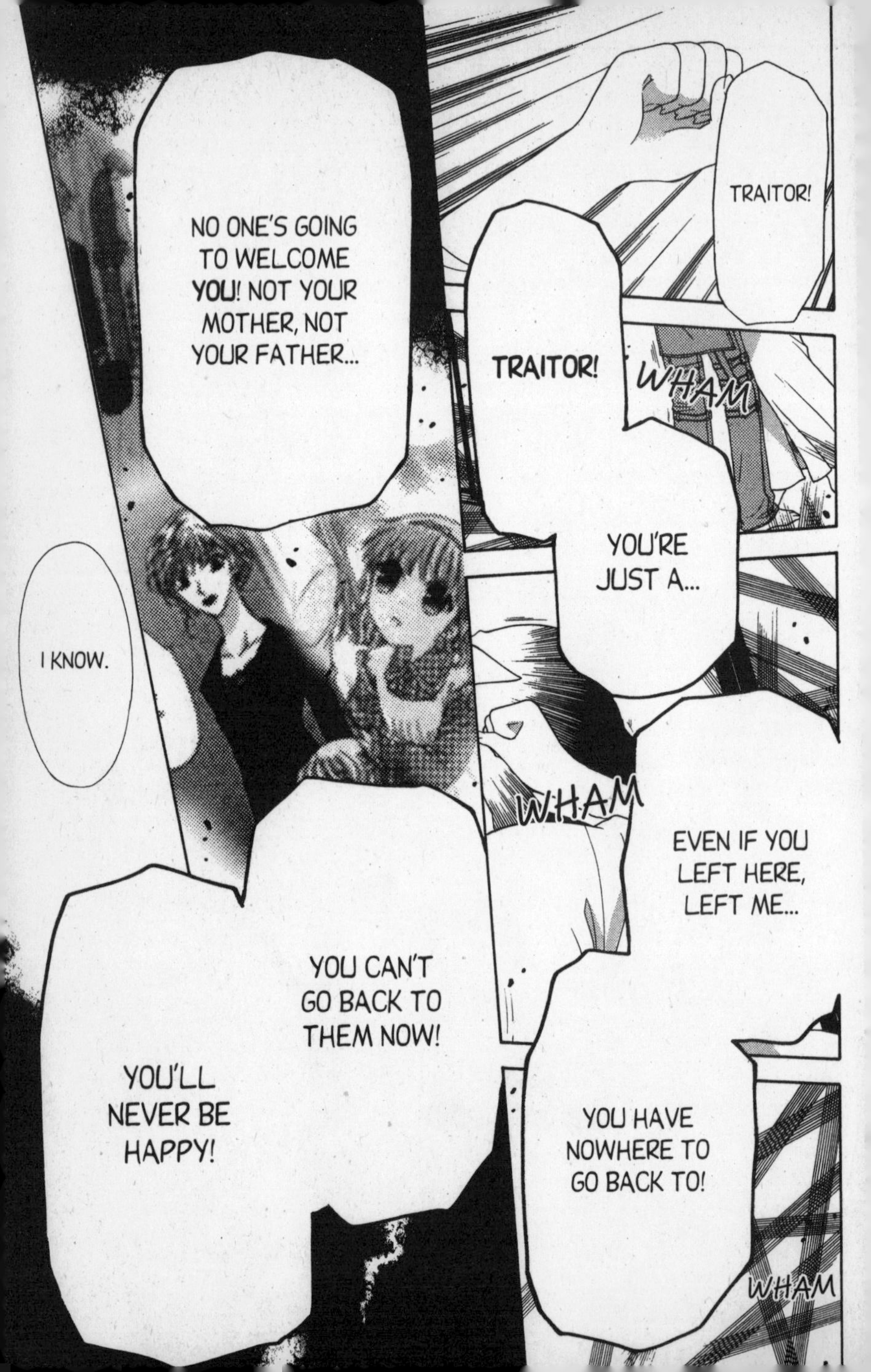
TRAITOR!
TRAITOR!
WHAM
YOU'RE JUST A...
WHAM
EVEN IF YOU LEFT HERE, LEFT ME...
YOU HAVE NOWHERE TO GO BACK TO!
WHAM
NO ONE'S GOING TO WELCOME YOU! NOT YOUR MOTHER, NOT YOUR FATHER...
I KNOW.
YOU CAN'T GO BACK TO THEM NOW!
YOU'LL NEVER BE HAPPY!

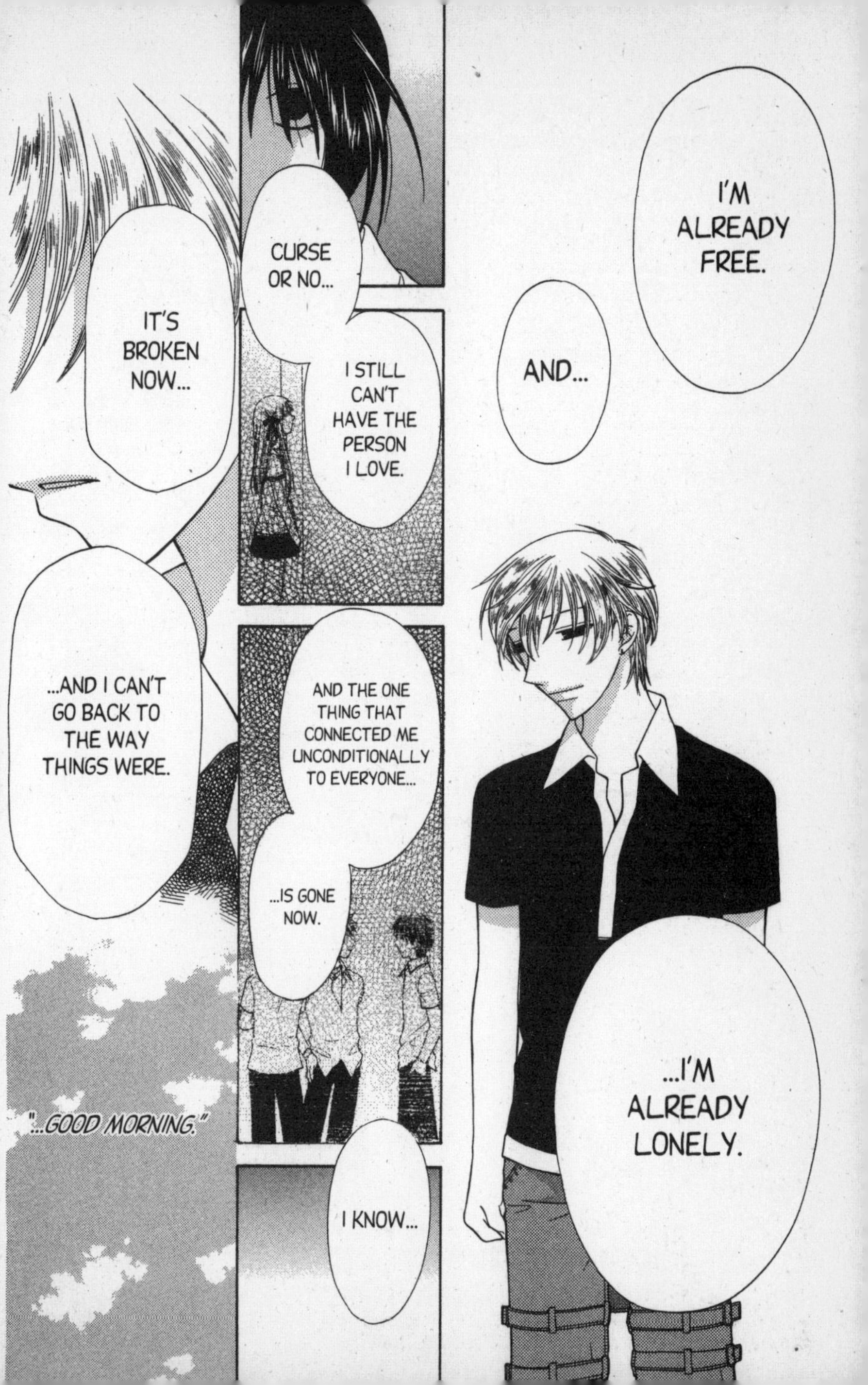
I'M ALREADY FREE.
AND...
...I'M ALREADY LONELY.
CURSE OR NO...
I STILL CAN'T HAVE THE PERSON I LOVE.
AND THE ONE THING THAT CONNECTED ME UNCONDITIONALLY TO EVERYONE...
...IS GONE NOW.
I KNOW...
IT'S BROKEN NOW...
...AND I CAN'T GO BACK TO THE WAY THINGS WERE.
"...GOOD MORNING."

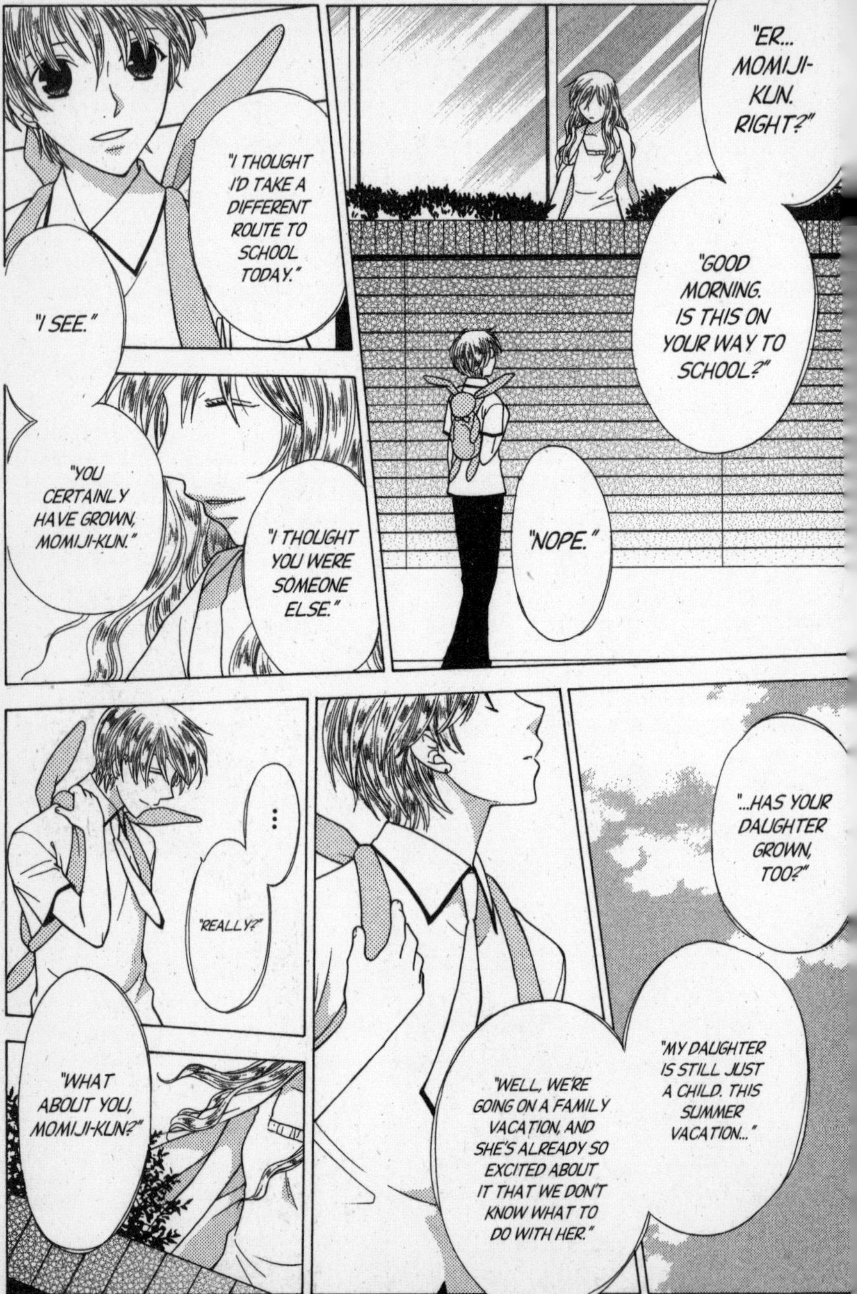
"ER... MOMIJI-KUN. RIGHT?"
"GOOD MORNING. IS THIS ON YOUR WAY TO SCHOOL?"
"NOPE."
"I THOUGHT I'D TAKE A DIFFERENT ROUTE TO SCHOOL TODAY."
"I SEE."
"I THOUGHT YOU WERE SOMEONE ELSE."
"YOU CERTAINLY HAVE GROWN, MOMIJI-KUN."
"...HAS YOUR DAUGHTER GROWN, TOO?"
"MY DAUGHTER IS STILL JUST A CHILD. THIS SUMMER VACATION..."
"WELL, WE'RE GOING ON A FAMILY VACATION, AND SHE'S ALREADY SO EXCITED ABOUT IT THAT WE DON'T KNOW WHAT TO DO WITH HER."
...
"REALLY?"
"WHAT ABOUT YOU, MOMIJI-KUN?"

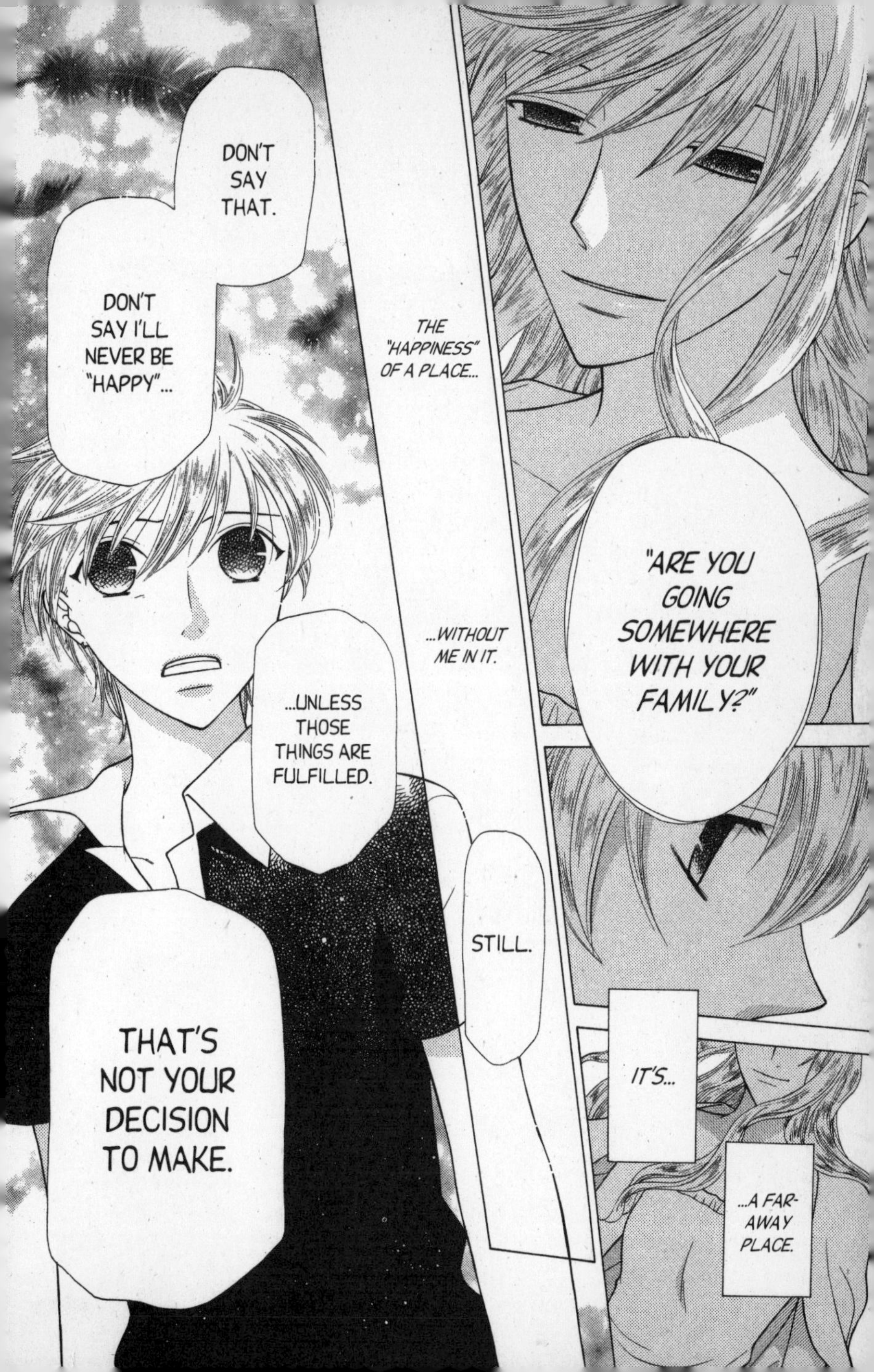
"ARE YOU GOING SOMEWHERE WITH YOUR FAMILY?"
IT'S...
...A FAR-AWAY PLACE.
THE "HAPPINESS" OF A PLACE...
...WITHOUT ME IN IT.
STILL.
DON'T SAY THAT.
DON'T SAY I'LL NEVER BE "HAPPY"...
...UNLESS THOSE THINGS ARE FULFILLED.
THAT'S NOT YOUR DECISION TO MAKE.

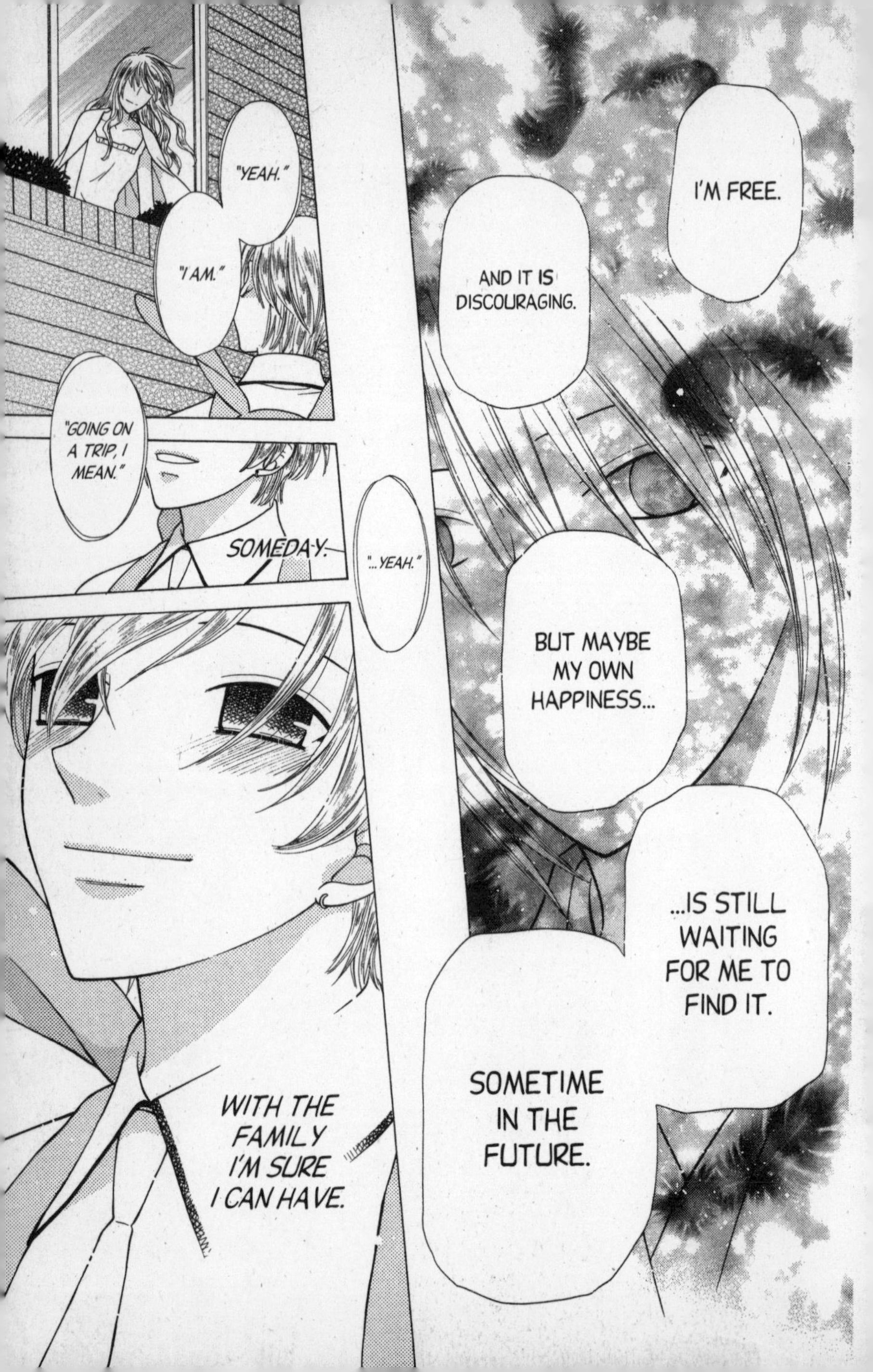

I'M FREE.
AND IT IS DISCOURAGING.
BUT MAYBE MY OWN HAPPINESS...
...IS STILL WAITING FOR ME TO FIND IT.
SOMETIME IN THE FUTURE.
"YEAH."
"I AM."
"GOING ON A TRIP, I MEAN."
SOMEDAY.
"...YEAH."
WITH THE FAMILY I'M SURE I CAN HAVE.

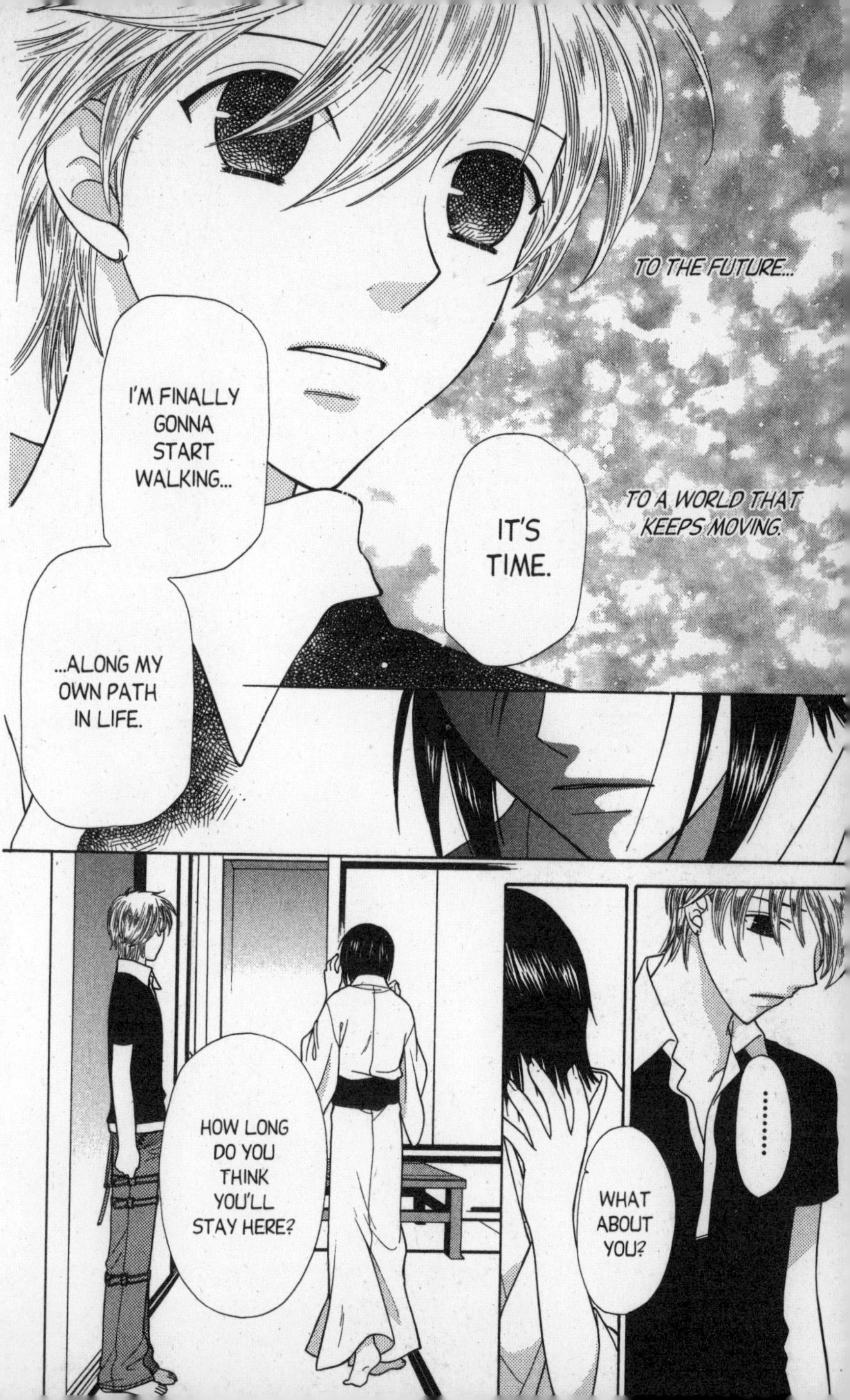
TO THE FUTURE...
TO A WORLD THAT KEEPS MOVING.
IT'S TIME.
I'M FINALLY GONNA START WALKING...
...ALONG MY OWN PATH IN LIFE.
......
WHAT ABOUT YOU?
HOW LONG DO YOU THINK YOU'LL STAY HERE?

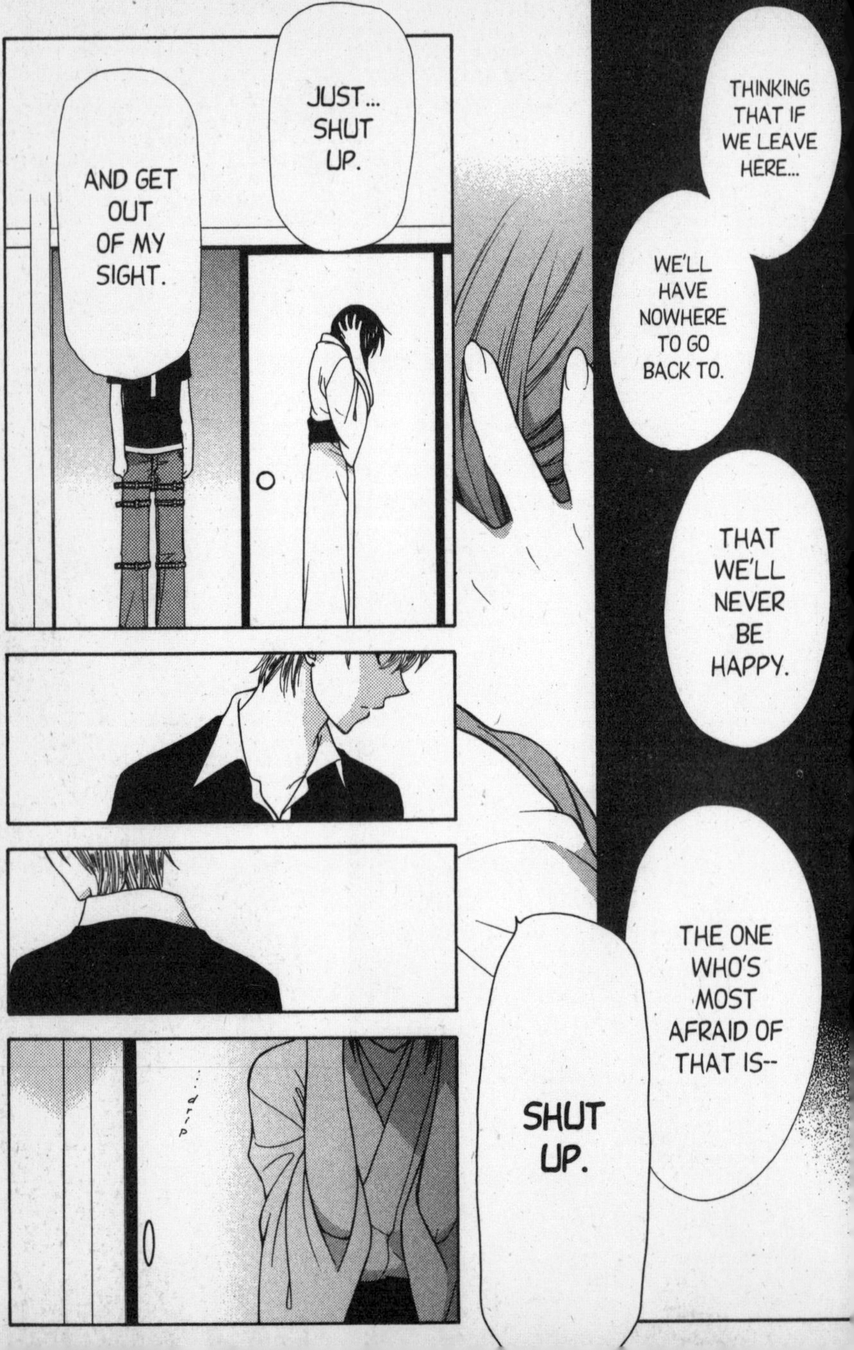
THINKING THAT IF WE LEAVE HERE...
WE'LL HAVE NOWHERE TO GO BACK TO.
THAT WE'LL NEVER BE HAPPY.
THE ONE WHO'S MOST AFRAID OF THAT IS--
SHUT UP.
JUST... SHUT UP.
AND GET OUT OF MY SIGHT.
...drip

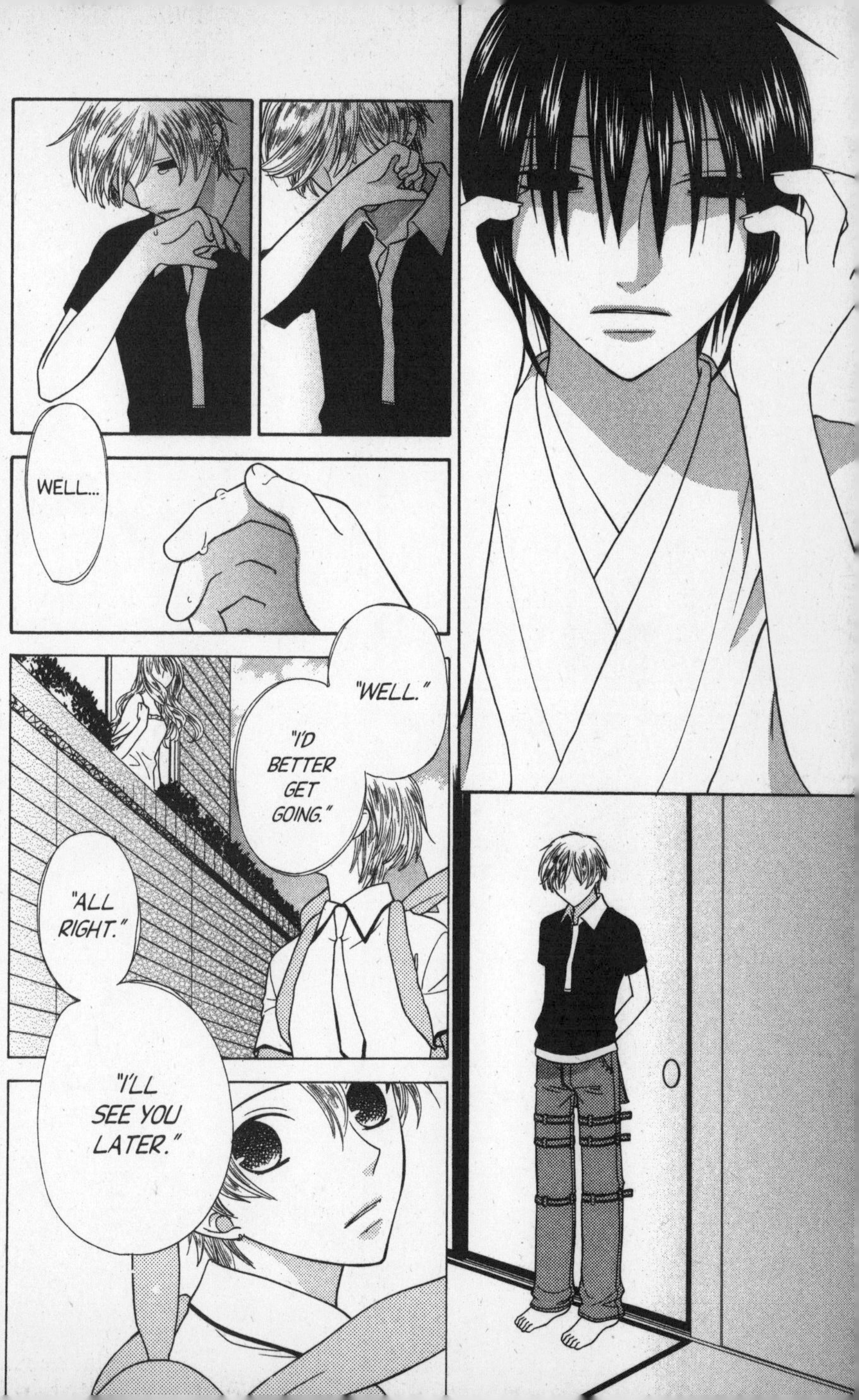
WELL...
"WELL."
"I'D BETTER GET GOING."
"ALL RIGHT."
"I'LL SEE YOU LATER."

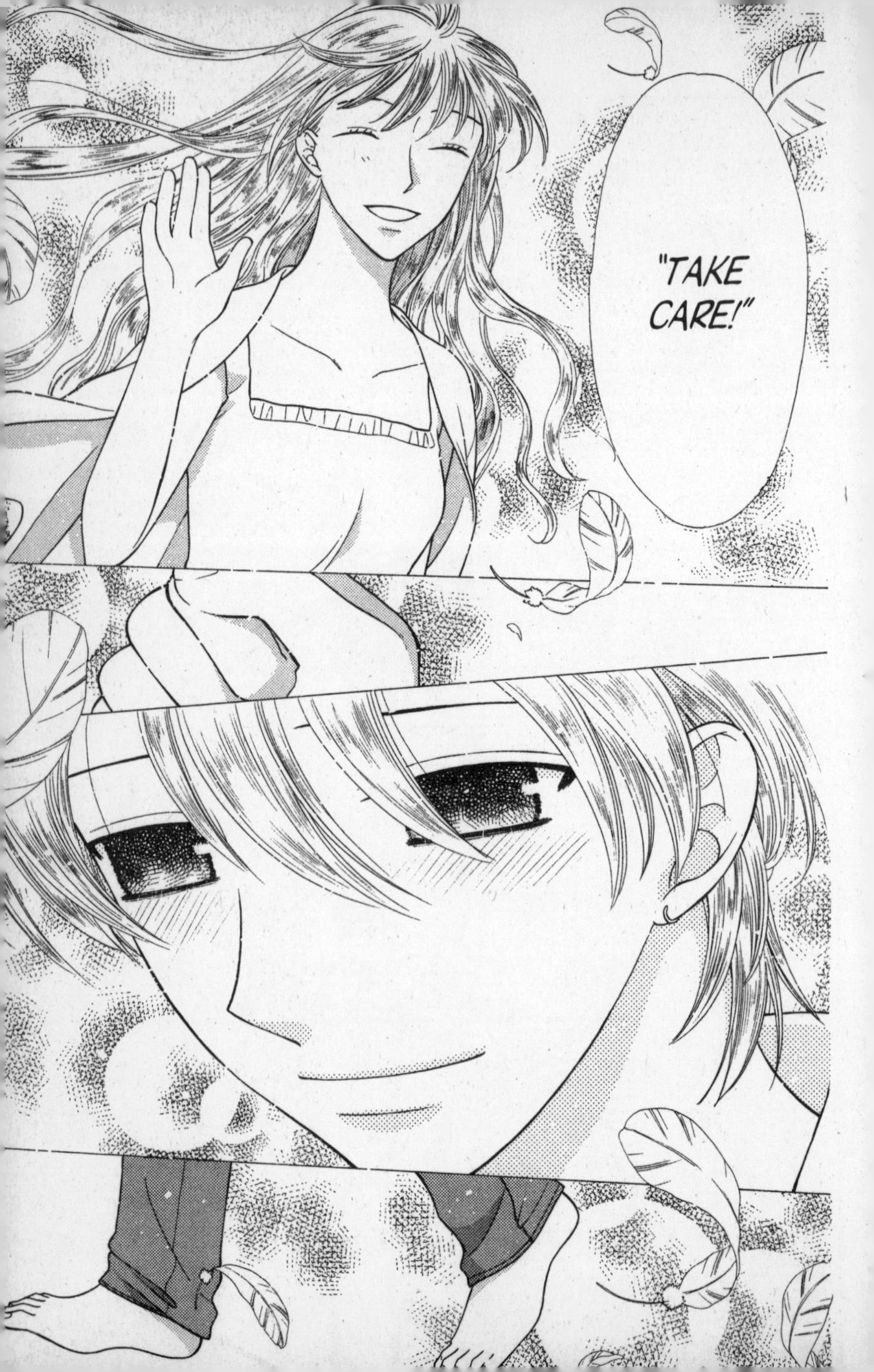
"TAKE CARE!"

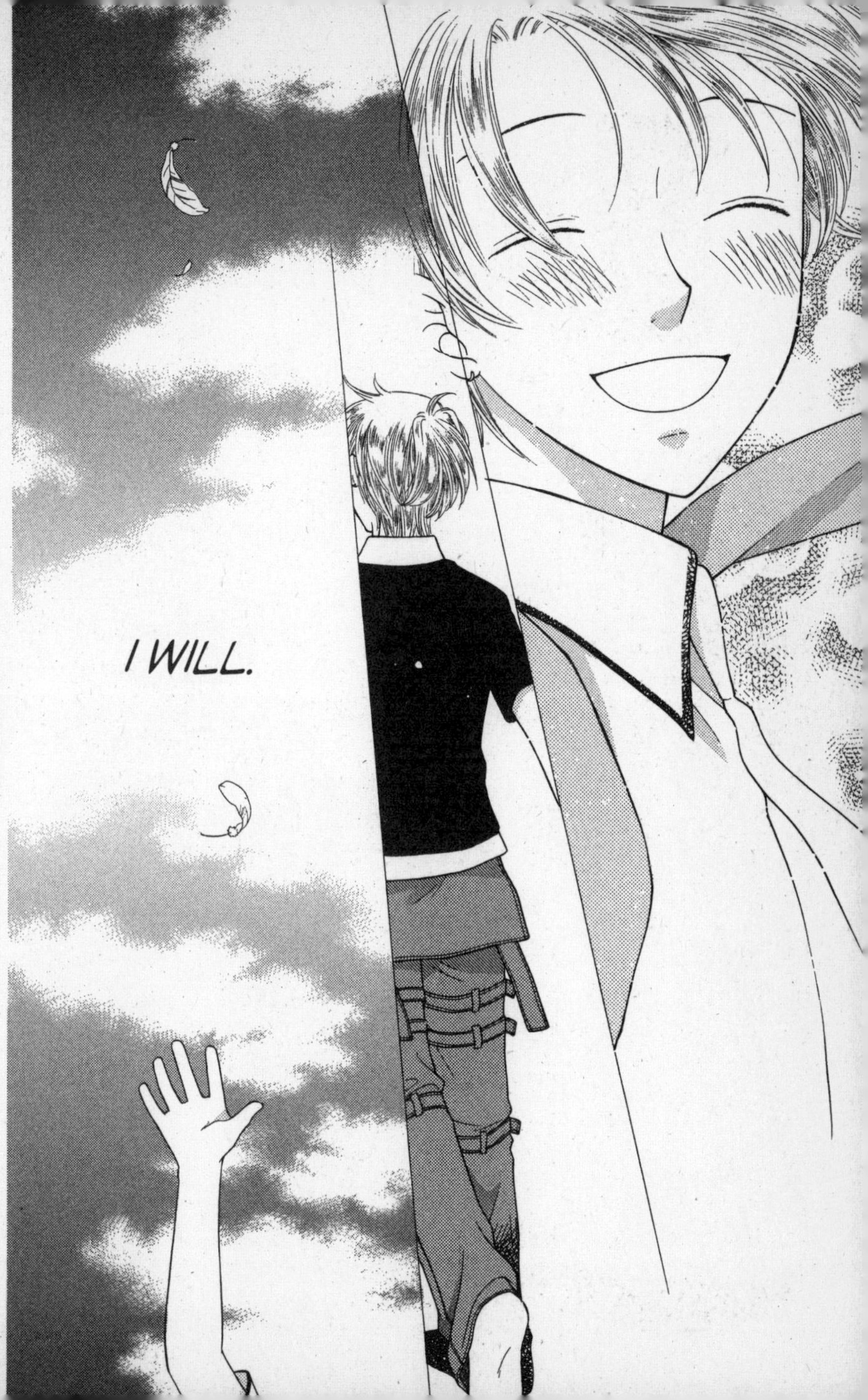
I WILL.

Chapter 117

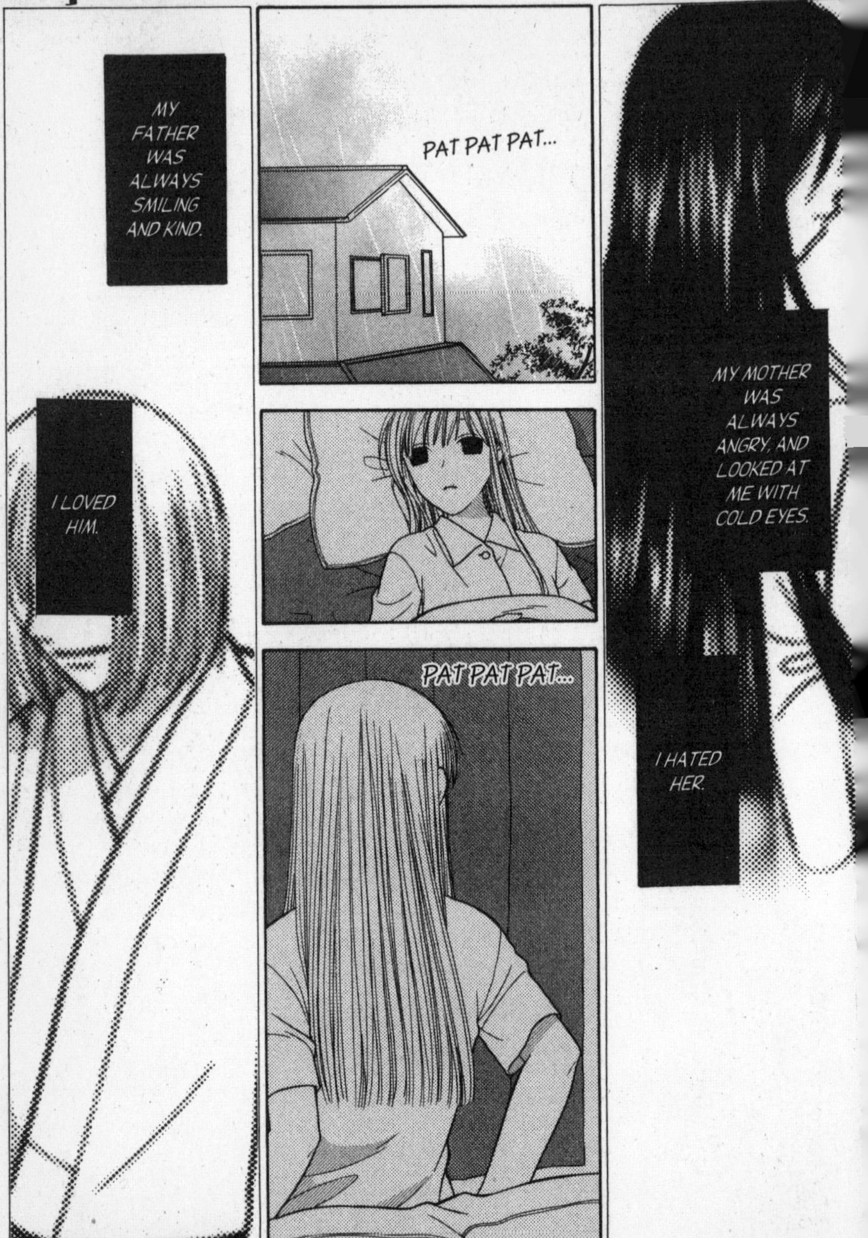
MY MOTHER WAS ALWAYS ANGRY, AND LOOKED AT ME WITH COLD EYES.
I HATED HER.
PAT PAT PAT...
PAT PAT PAT...
MY FATHER WAS ALWAYS SMILING AND KIND.
I LOVED HIM.

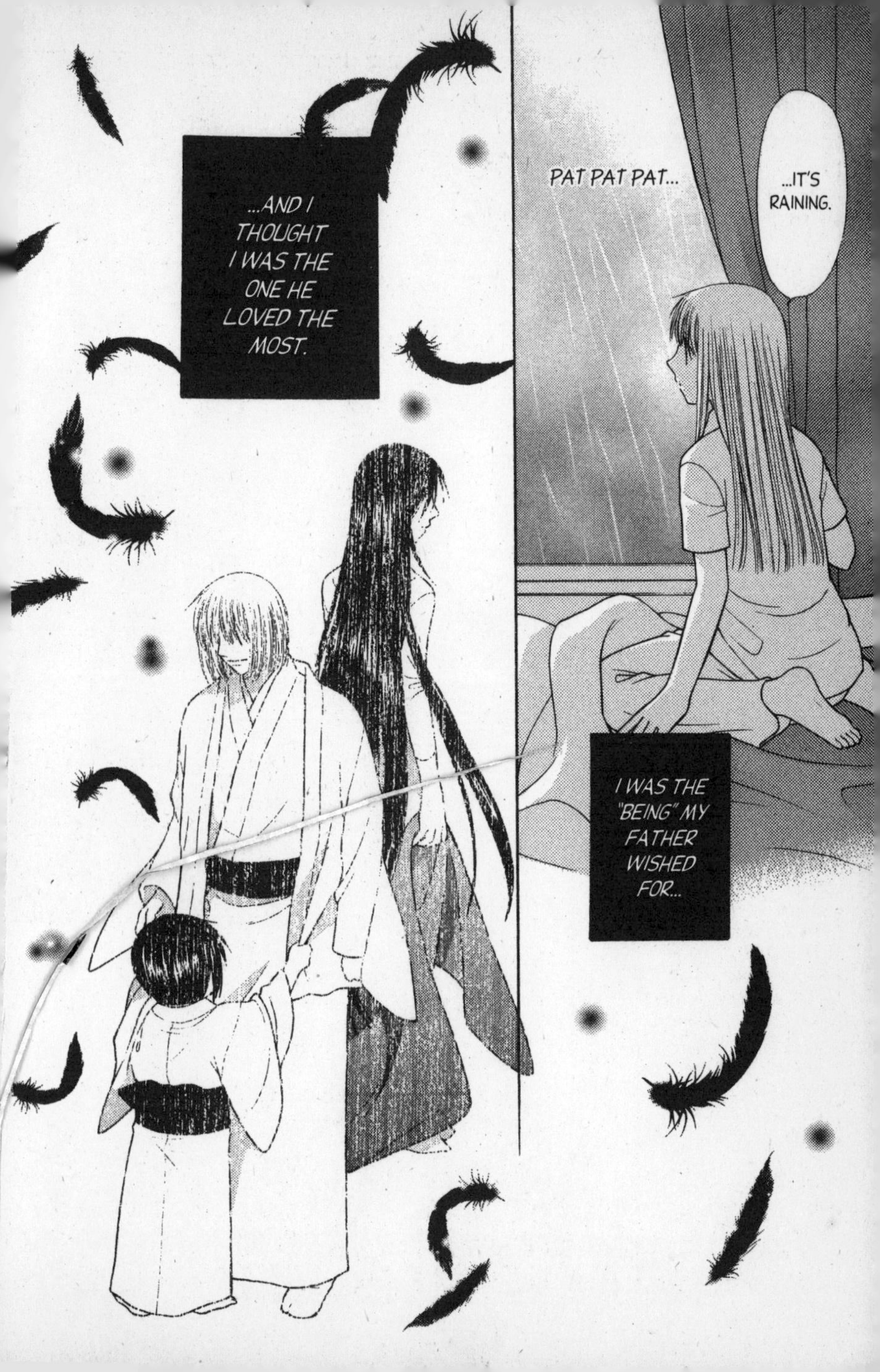
...IT'S RAINING.
PAT PAT PAT...
I WAS THE "BEING" MY FATHER WISHED FOR...
...AND I THOUGHT I WAS THE ONE HE LOVED THE MOST.

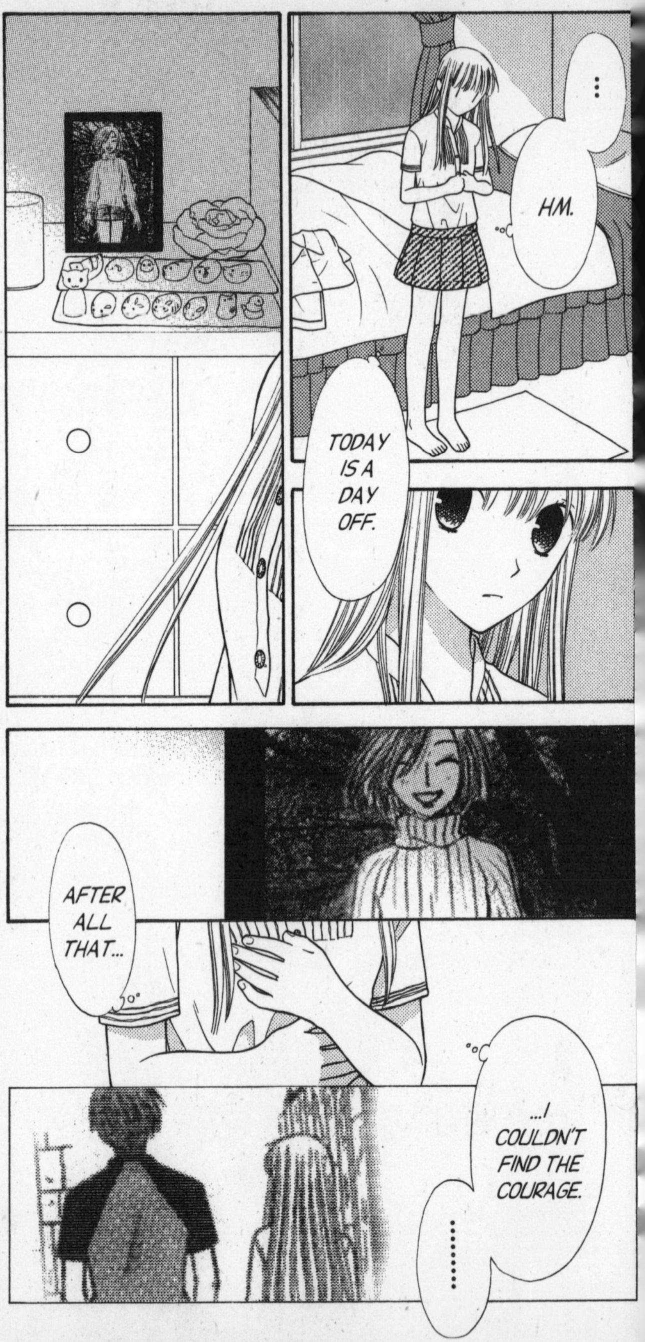
...
HM.
TODAY IS A DAY OFF.
AFTER ALL THAT...
...I COULDN'T FIND THE COURAGE.
....

Talking and such.

This time, I intentionally have fewer columns. I figured that with the story getting insanely serious, the columns might interrupt the mood. Thus there really aren't that many of them. (But that... might (?)...be a good thing. (laugh)) And the volume ends at a terrible place... It seems like Kyo's feelings were deeper than I was prepared for. When drawing, there aren't that many characters who give me trouble (like by not moving the way I planned, etc.), but he may have given me the next most trouble after Kureno-san.

Kureno-san was awful... He'd be like, "I don't want to do that. That won't work, either," and just wouldn't agree with the development that I, the author, would present to him (laugh). So I said, "Do what you want!" and let him walk freely, and the result is what you see now. It's fun to go along with my characters, but sometimes it wears me out (laugh).

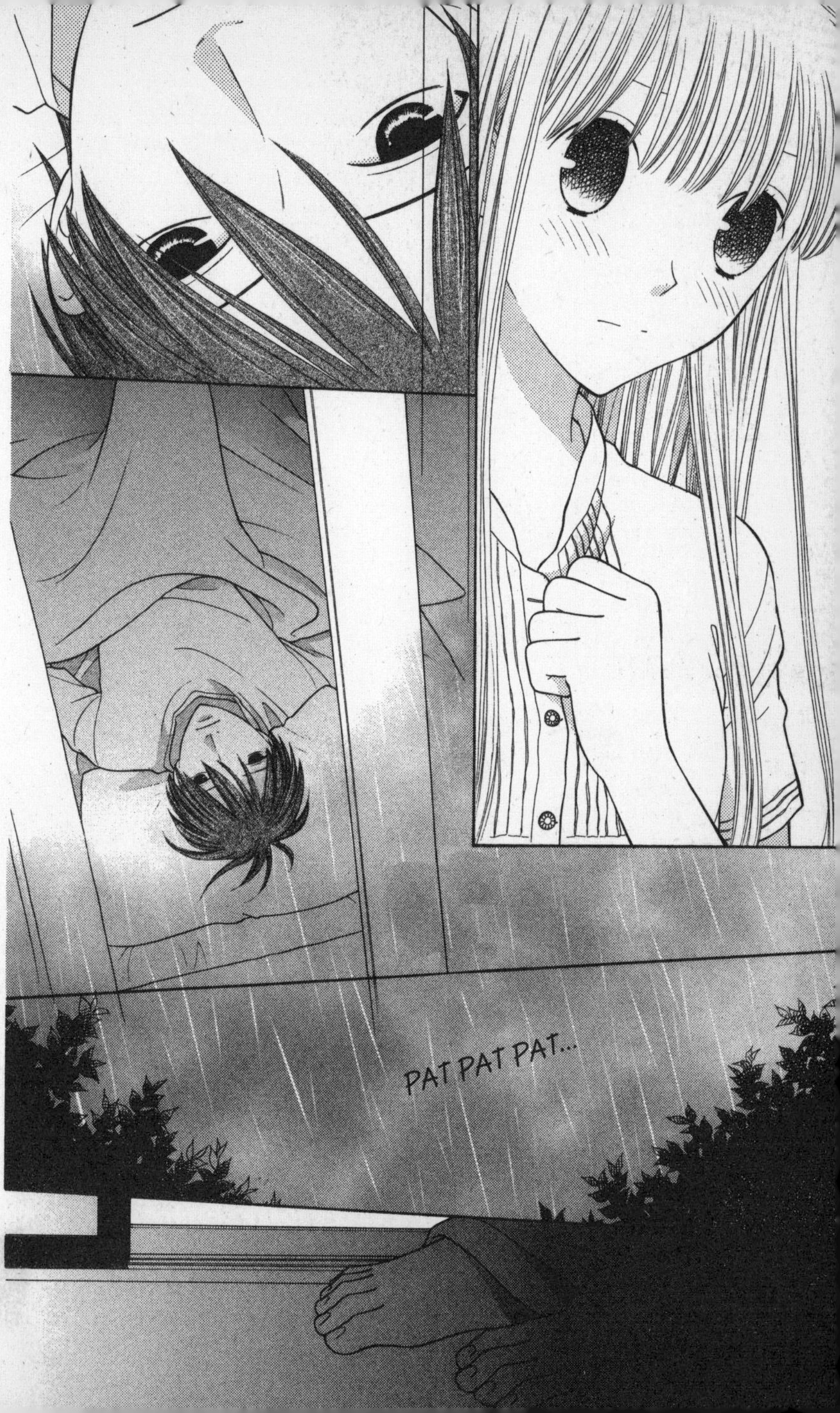
PAT PAT PAT...

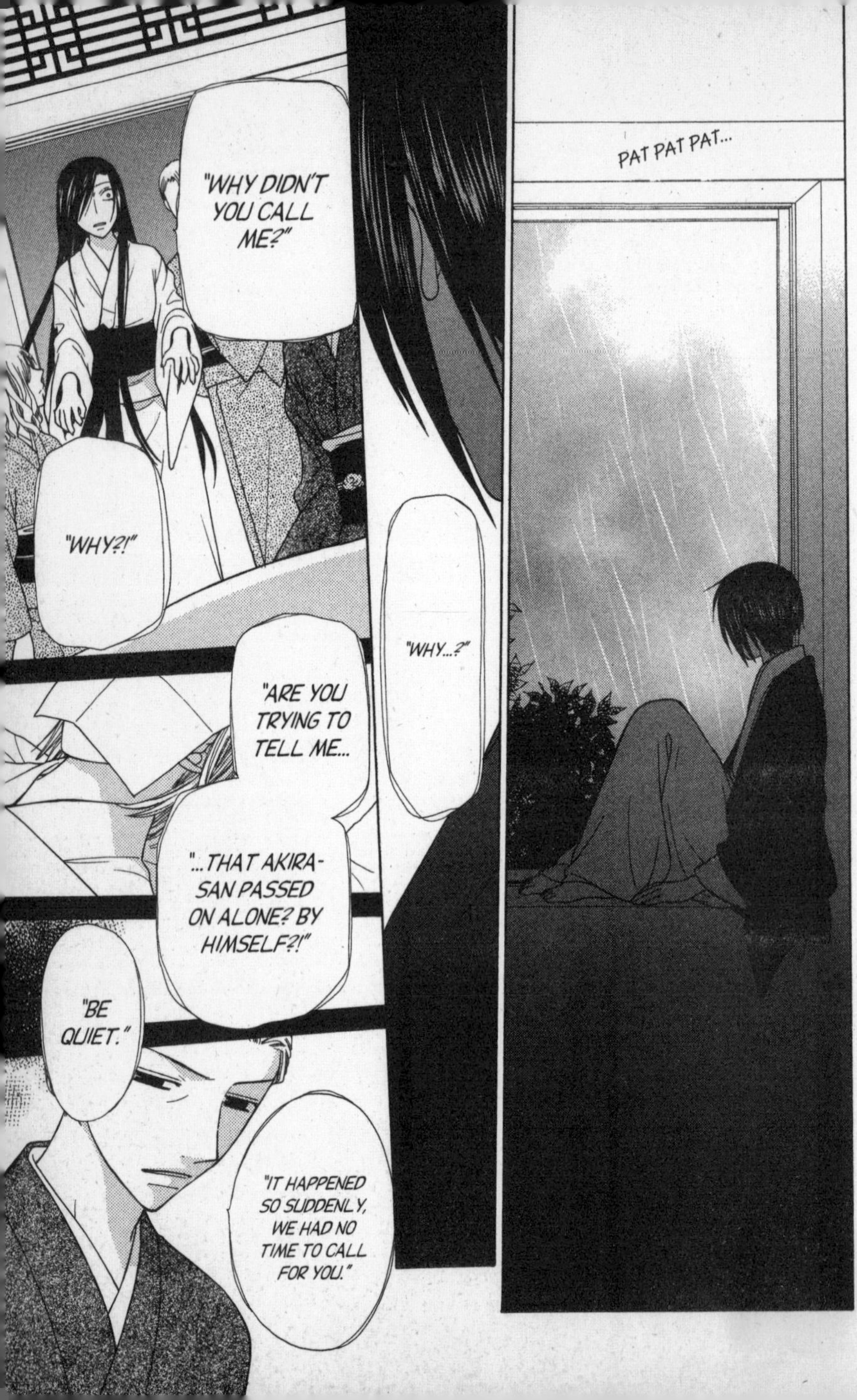
PAT PAT PAT...
"WHY...?"
"WHY DIDN'T YOU CALL ME?"
"WHY?!"
"ARE YOU TRYING TO TELL ME...
"...THAT AKIRA-SAN PASSED ON ALONE? BY HIMSELF?!"
"BE QUIET."
"IT HAPPENED SO SUDDENLY, WE HAD NO TIME TO CALL FOR YOU."

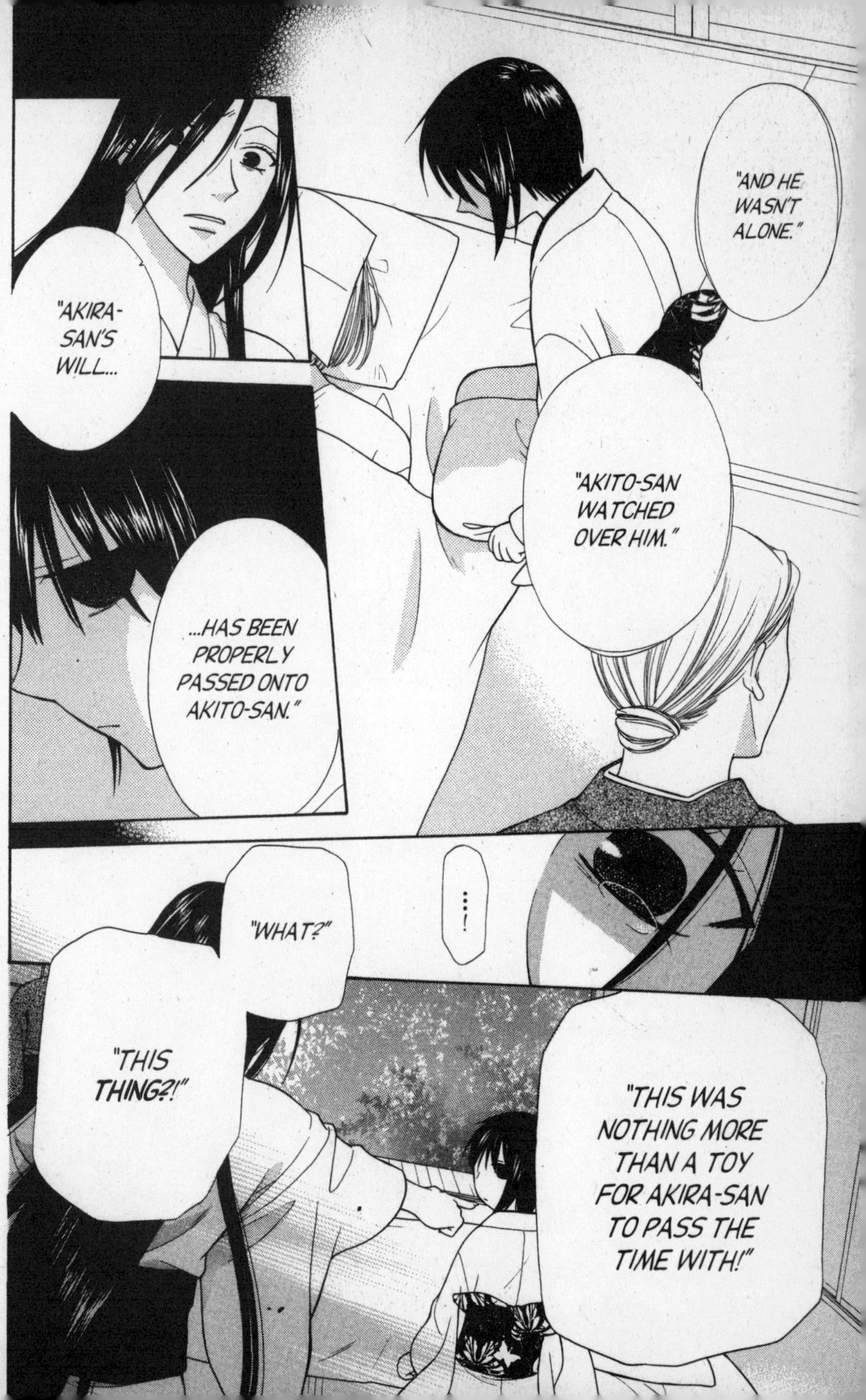
"AND HE WASN'T ALONE."
"AKITO-SAN WATCHED OVER HIM."
"AKIRA-SAN'S WILL...
...HAS BEEN PROPERLY PASSED ONTO AKITO-SAN."
...!
"WHAT?"
"THIS WAS NOTHING MORE THAN A TOY FOR AKIRA-SAN TO PASS THE TIME WITH!"
"THIS THING?!"

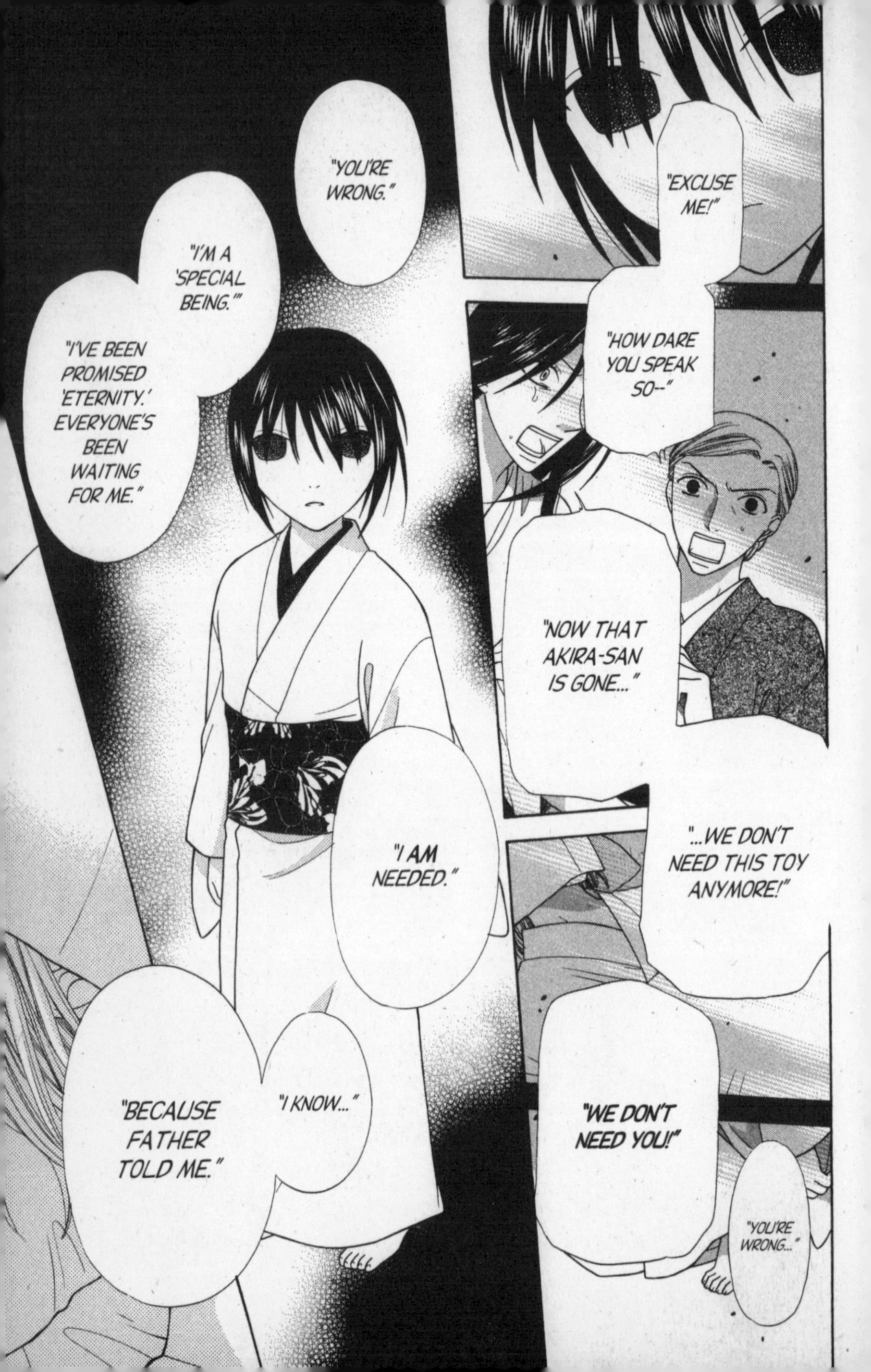
"EXCUSE ME!"
"HOW DARE YOU SPEAK SO--"
"NOW THAT AKIRA-SAN IS GONE..."
"...WE DON'T NEED THIS TOY ANYMORE!"
"WE DON'T NEED YOU!"
"YOU'RE WRONG..."
"YOU'RE WRONG."
"I'M A 'SPECIAL BEING.'"
"I'VE BEEN PROMISED 'ETERNITY.' EVERYONE'S BEEN WAITING FOR ME."
"I AM NEEDED."
"I KNOW..."
"BECAUSE FATHER TOLD ME."

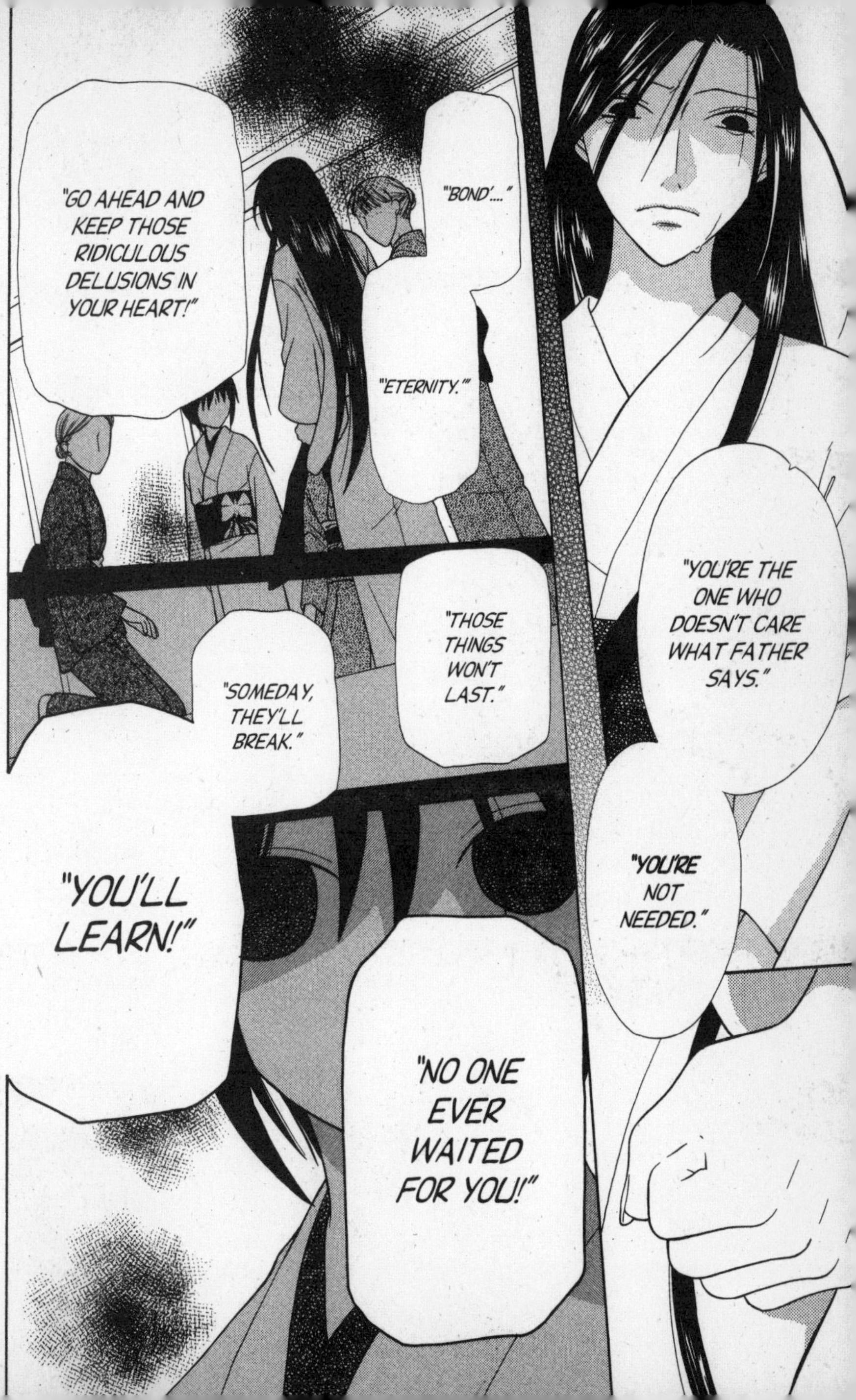
"'BOND'..."
"ETERNITY.'"
"GO AHEAD AND KEEP THOSE RIDICULOUS DELUSIONS IN YOUR HEART!"
"THOSE THINGS WON'T LAST."
"SOMEDAY, THEY'LL BREAK."
"YOU'LL LEARN!"
"YOU'RE THE ONE WHO DOESN'T CARE WHAT FATHER SAYS."
"YOU'RE NOT NEEDED."
"NO ONE EVER WAITED FOR YOU!"

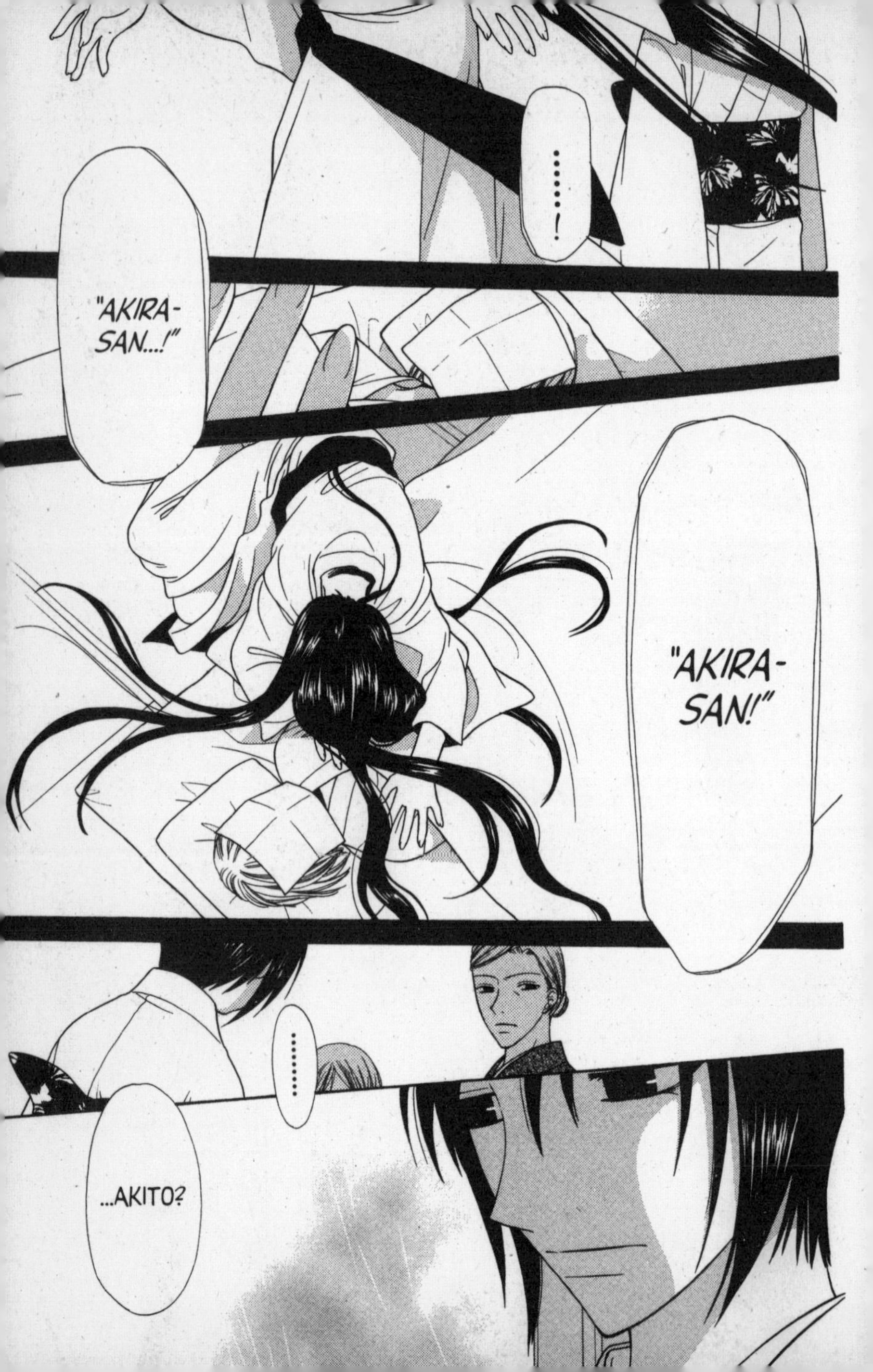
......!
"AKIRA-SAN...!"
"AKIRA-SAN!"
......
...AKITO?

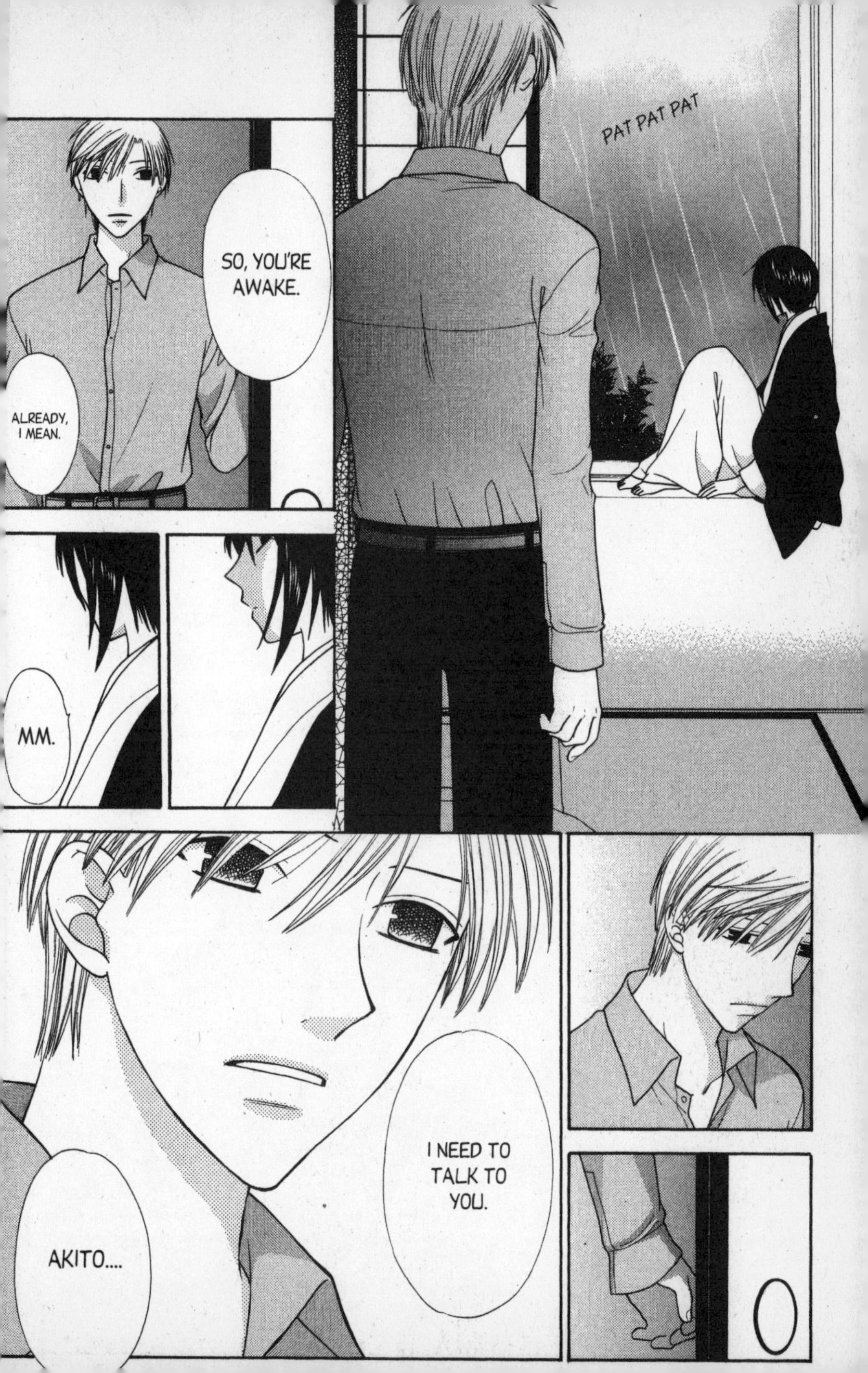
PAT PAT PAT
SO, YOU'RE AWAKE.
ALREADY, I MEAN.
MM.
I NEED TO TALK TO YOU.
AKITO....

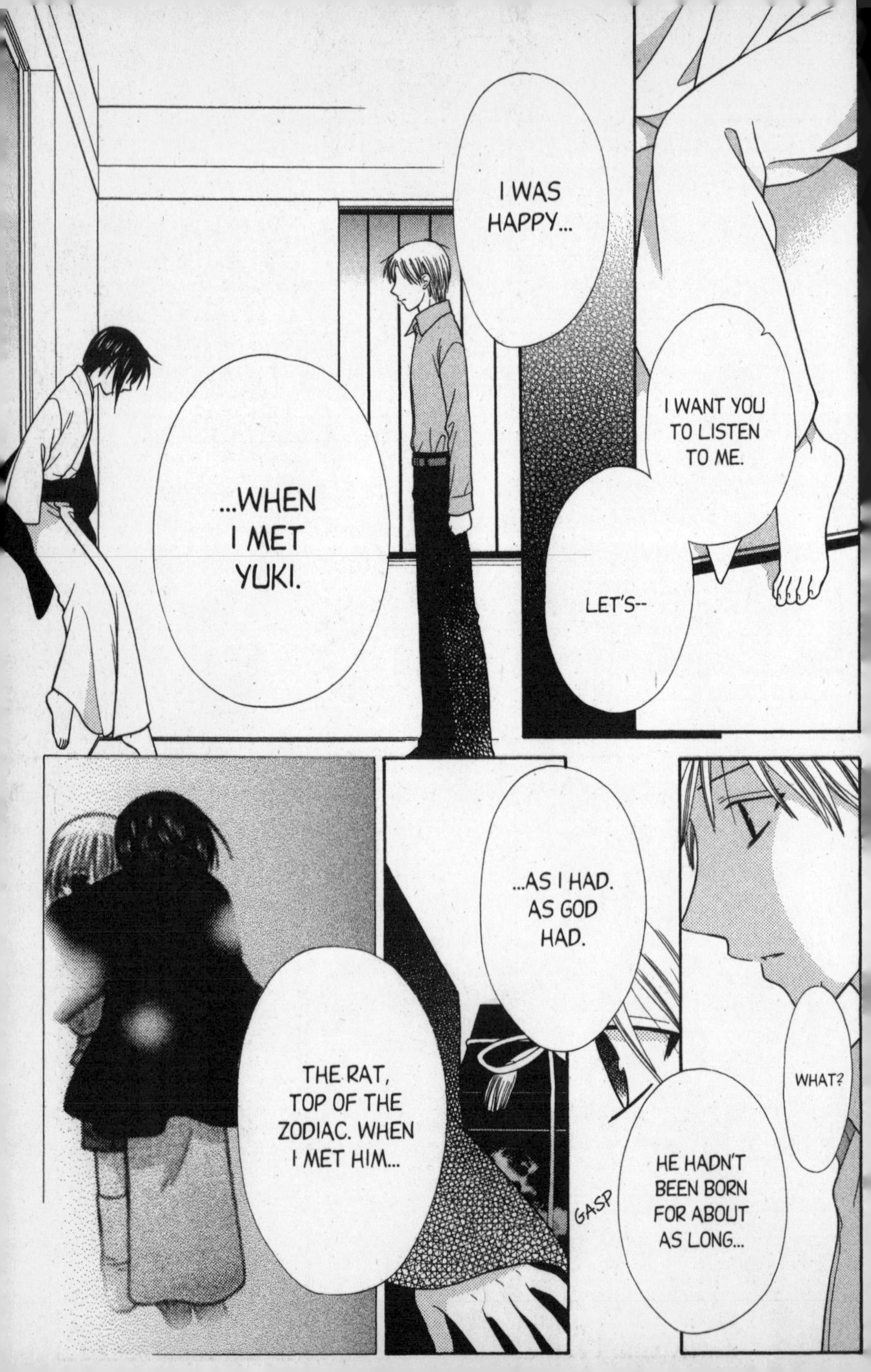
I WANT YOU TO LISTEN TO ME.
LET'S--
I WAS HAPPY...
...WHEN I MET YUKI.
WHAT?
HE HADN'T BEEN BORN FOR ABOUT AS LONG...
GASP
...AS I HAD. AS GOD HAD.
THE RAT, TOP OF THE ZODIAC. WHEN I MET HIM...

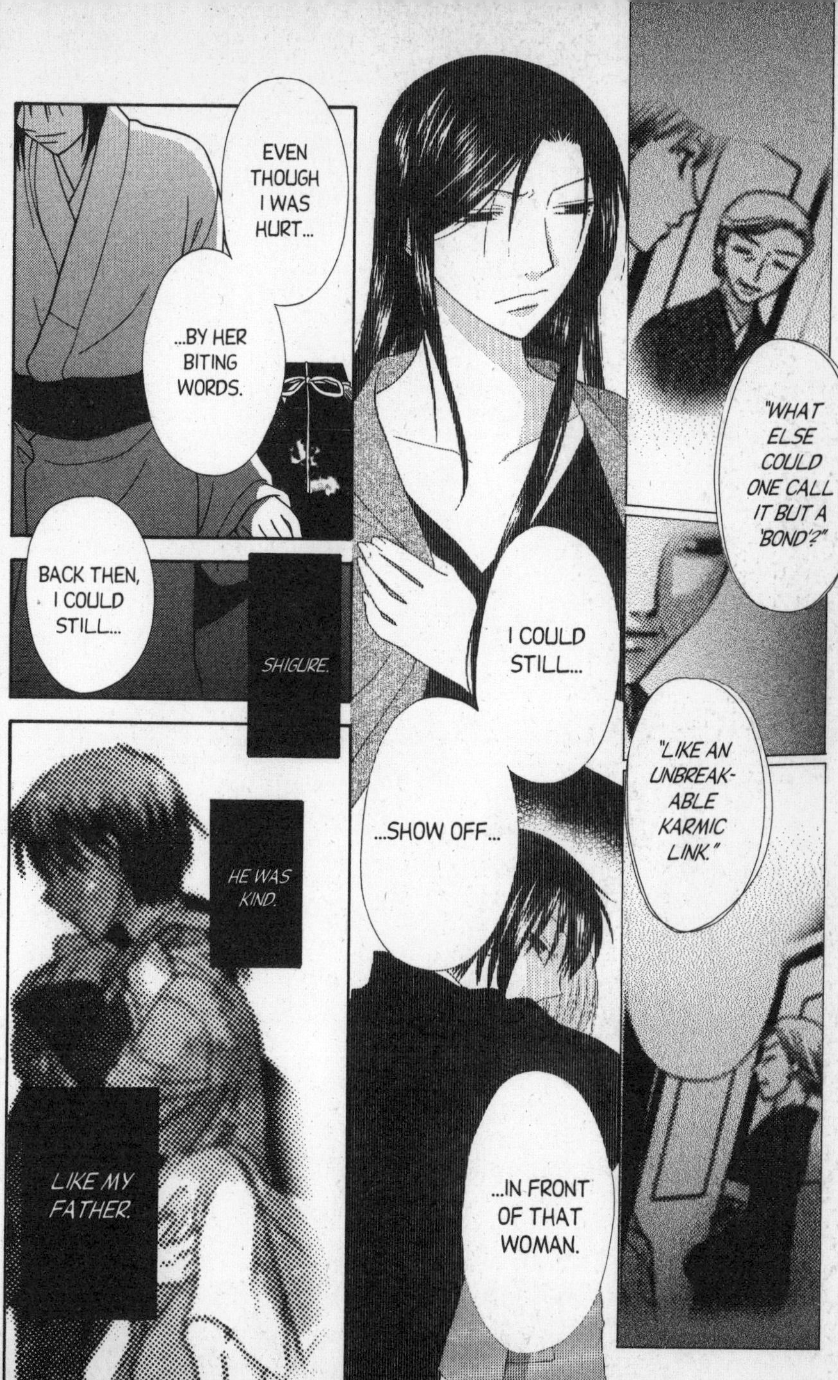
"WHAT ELSE COULD ONE CALL IT BUT A 'BOND'?"
"LIKE AN UNBREAK-ABLE KARMIC LINK."
I COULD STILL...
...SHOW OFF...
...IN FRONT OF THAT WOMAN.
EVEN THOUGH I WAS HURT...
...BY HER BITING WORDS.
BACK THEN, I COULD STILL...
SHIGURE.
HE WAS KIND.
LIKE MY FATHER.

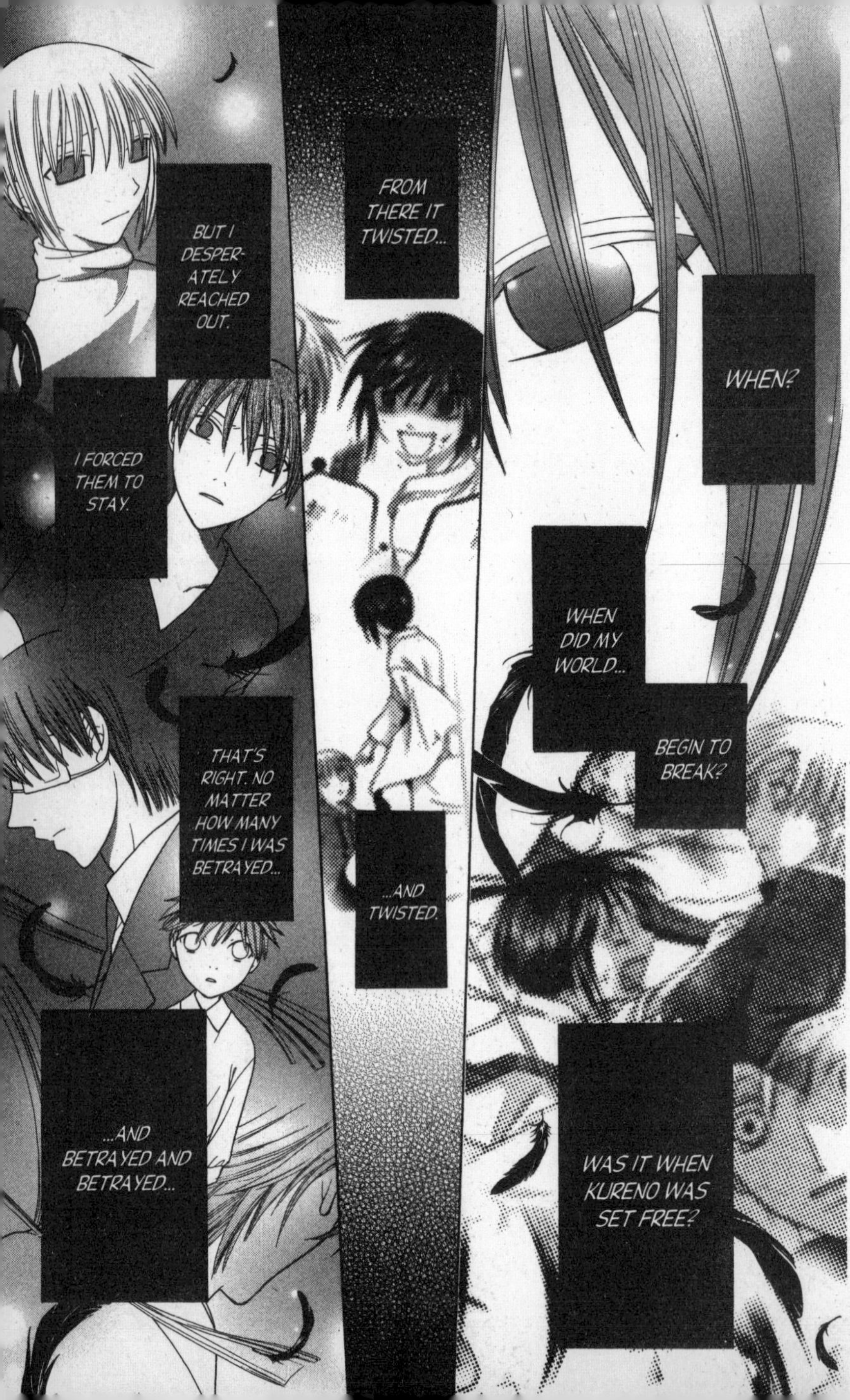
WHEN?
WHEN DID MY WORLD...
BEGIN TO BREAK?
WAS IT WHEN KURENO WAS SET FREE?
FROM THERE IT TWISTED...
...AND TWISTED.
BUT I DESPERATELY REACHED OUT.
I FORCED THEM TO STAY.
THAT'S RIGHT. NO MATTER HOW MANY TIMES I WAS BETRAYED...
...AND BETRAYED AND BETRAYED...

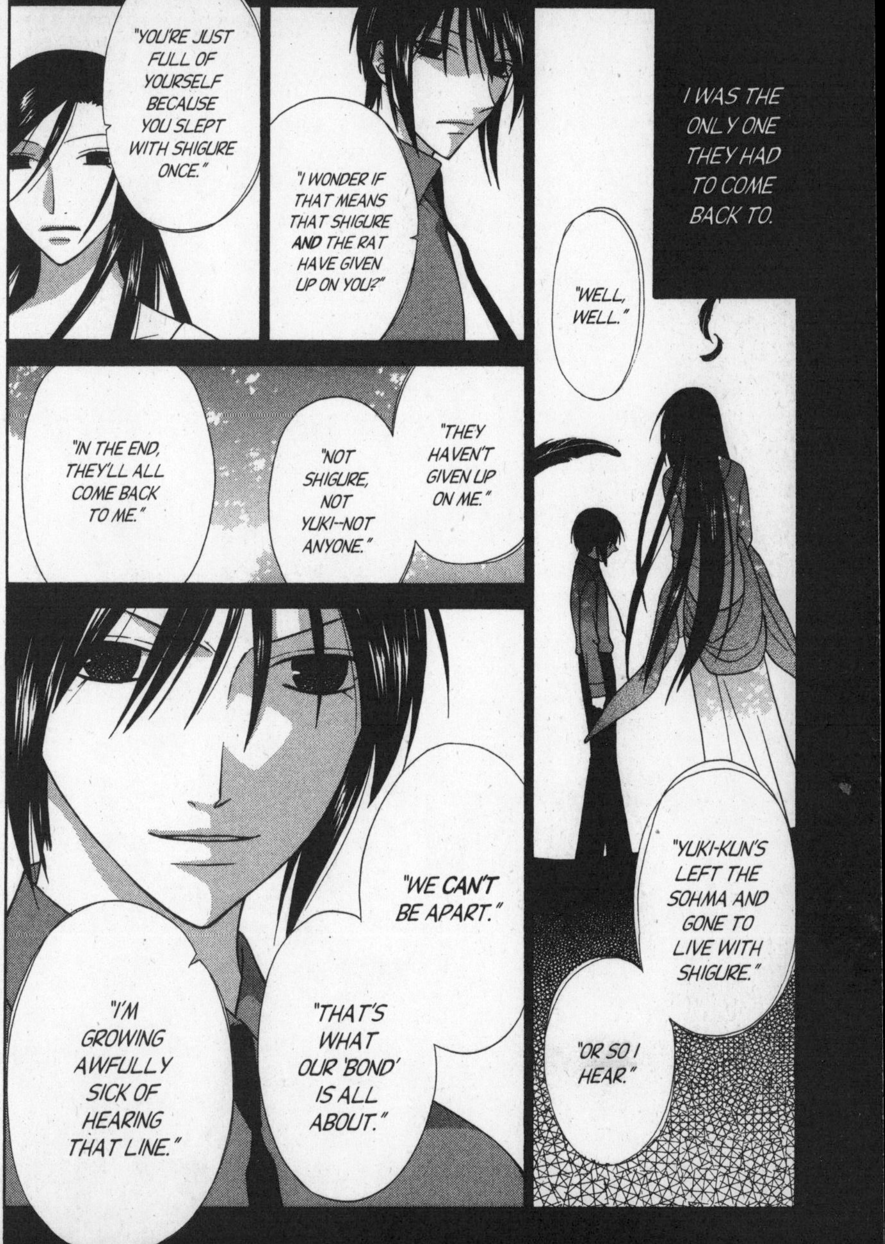
I WAS THE ONLY ONE THEY HAD TO COME BACK TO.
"WELL, WELL."
"YUKI-KUN'S LEFT THE SOHMA AND GONE TO LIVE WITH SHIGURE."
"OR SO I HEAR."
"I WONDER IF THAT MEANS THAT SHIGURE AND THE RAT HAVE GIVEN UP ON YOU?"
"YOU'RE JUST FULL OF YOURSELF BECAUSE YOU SLEPT WITH SHIGURE ONCE."
"THEY HAVEN'T GIVEN UP ON ME."
"NOT SHIGURE, NOT YUKI--NOT ANYONE."
"IN THE END, THEY'LL ALL COME BACK TO ME."
"WE CAN'T BE APART."
"THAT'S WHAT OUR 'BOND' IS ALL ABOUT."
"I'M GROWING AWFULLY SICK OF HEARING THAT LINE."

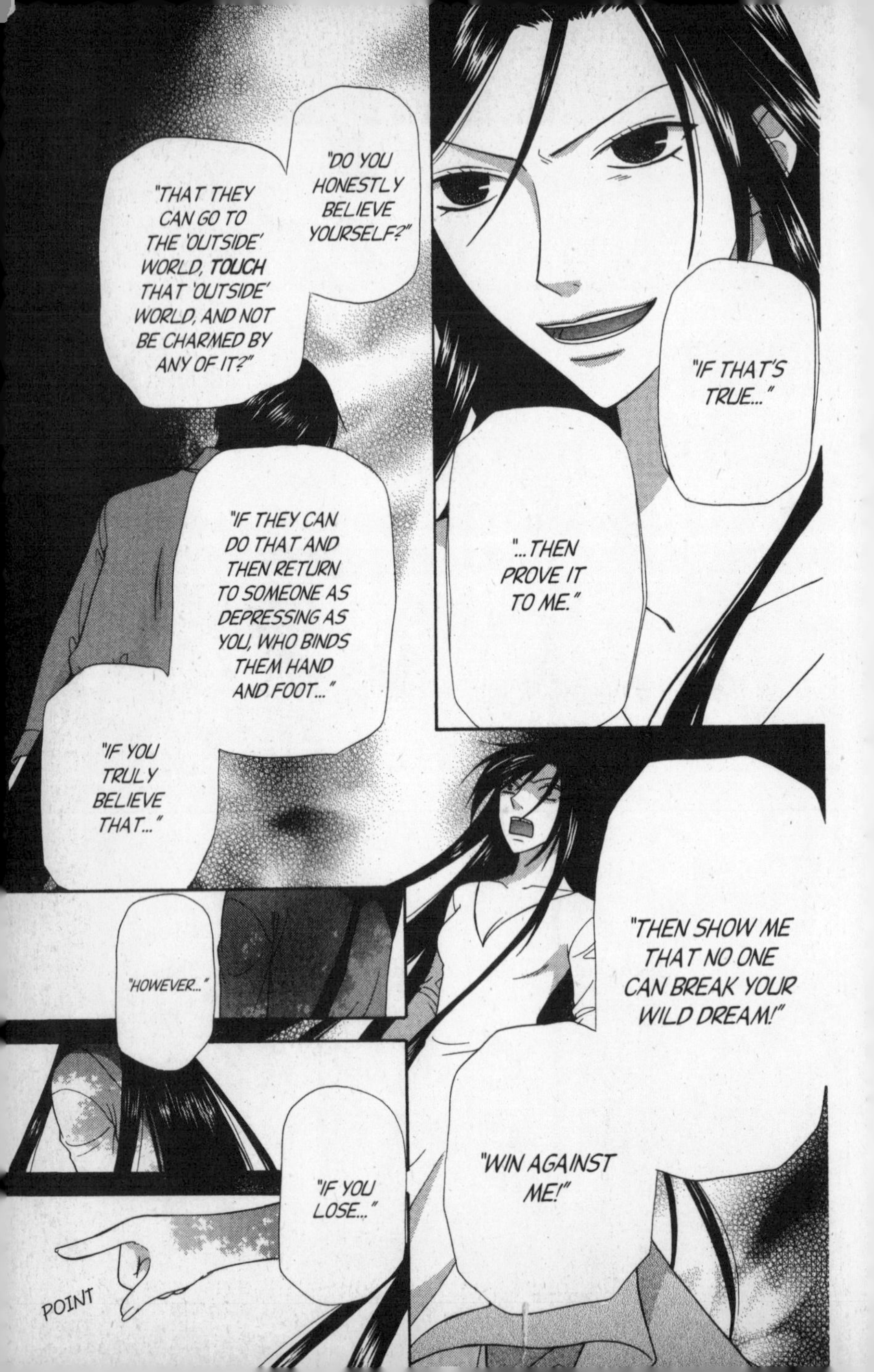
"IF THAT'S TRUE..."
"...THEN PROVE IT TO ME."
"THEN SHOW ME THAT NO ONE CAN BREAK YOUR WILD DREAM!"
"DO YOU HONESTLY BELIEVE YOURSELF?"
"THAT THEY CAN GO TO THE 'OUTSIDE' WORLD, **TOUCH** THAT 'OUTSIDE' WORLD, AND NOT BE CHARMED BY ANY OF IT?"
"IF THEY CAN DO THAT AND THEN RETURN TO SOMEONE AS DEPRESSING AS YOU, WHO BINDS THEM HAND AND FOOT..."
"IF YOU TRULY BELIEVE THAT..."
"HOWEVER..."
"WIN AGAINST ME!"
"IF YOU LOSE..."
POINT

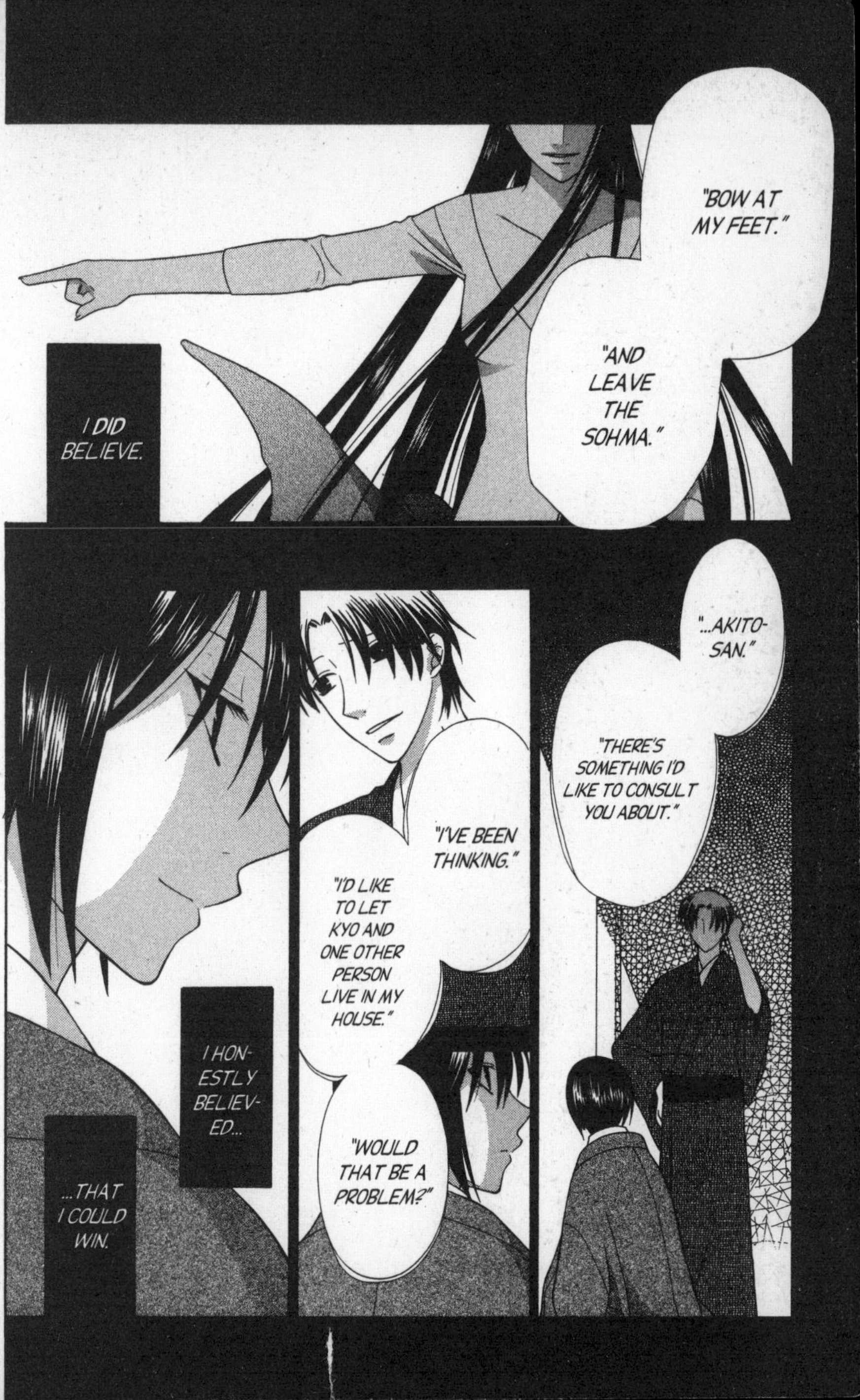
"BOW AT MY FEET."
"AND LEAVE THE SOHMA."
I DID BELIEVE.
"...AKITO-SAN."
"THERE'S SOMETHING I'D LIKE TO CONSULT YOU ABOUT."
"I'VE BEEN THINKING."
"I'D LIKE TO LET KYO AND ONE OTHER PERSON LIVE IN MY HOUSE."
"WOULD THAT BE A PROBLEM?"
I HON-ESTLY BELIEV-ED...
...THAT I COULD WIN.

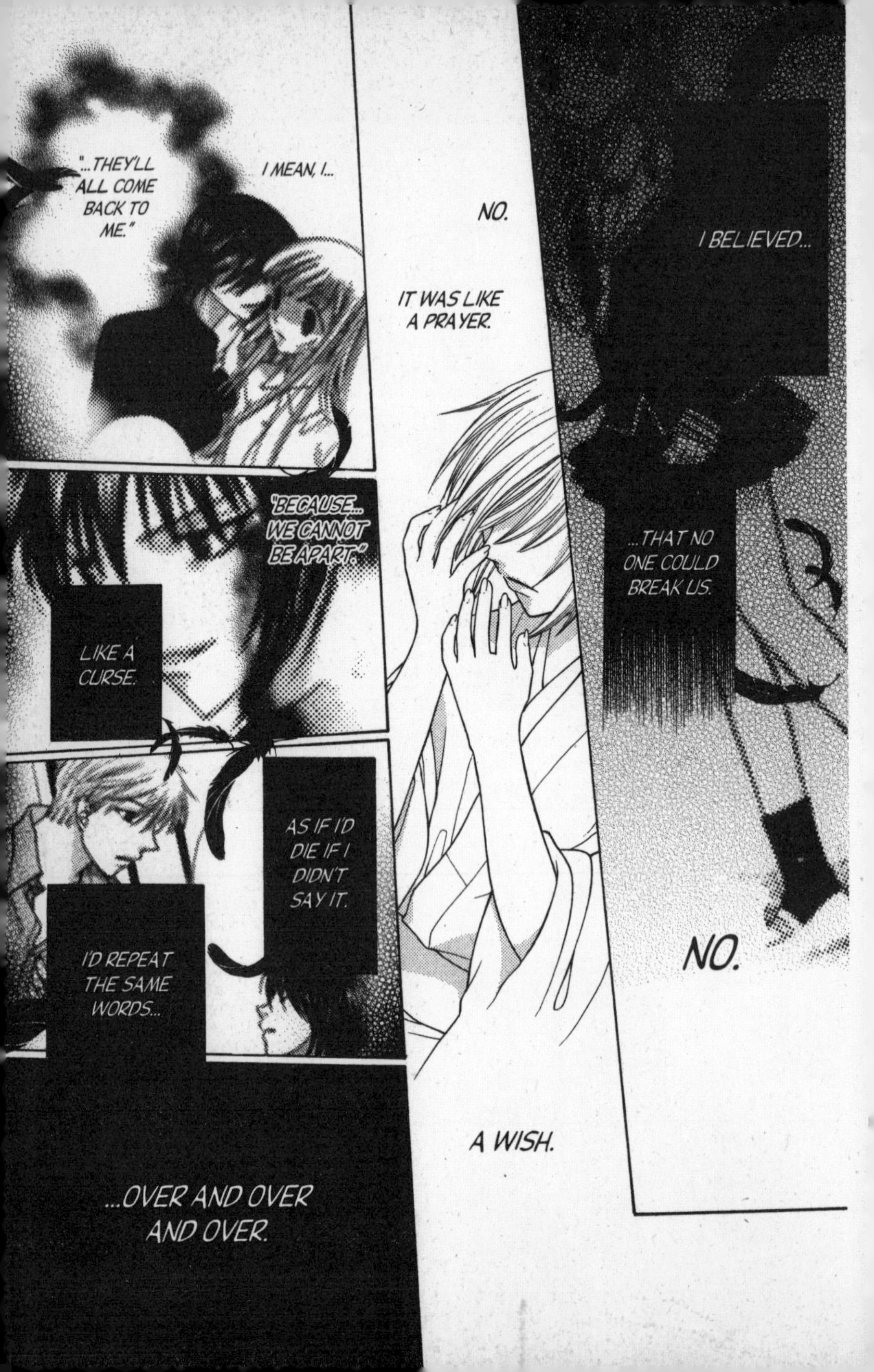
I BELIEVED...
...THAT NO ONE COULD BREAK US.
NO.
NO.
IT WAS LIKE A PRAYER.
A WISH.
I MEAN, I...
"...THEY'LL ALL COME BACK TO ME."
"BECAUSE... WE CANNOT BE APART."
LIKE A CURSE.
AS IF I'D DIE IF I DIDN'T SAY IT.
I'D REPEAT THE SAME WORDS...
...OVER AND OVER AND OVER.

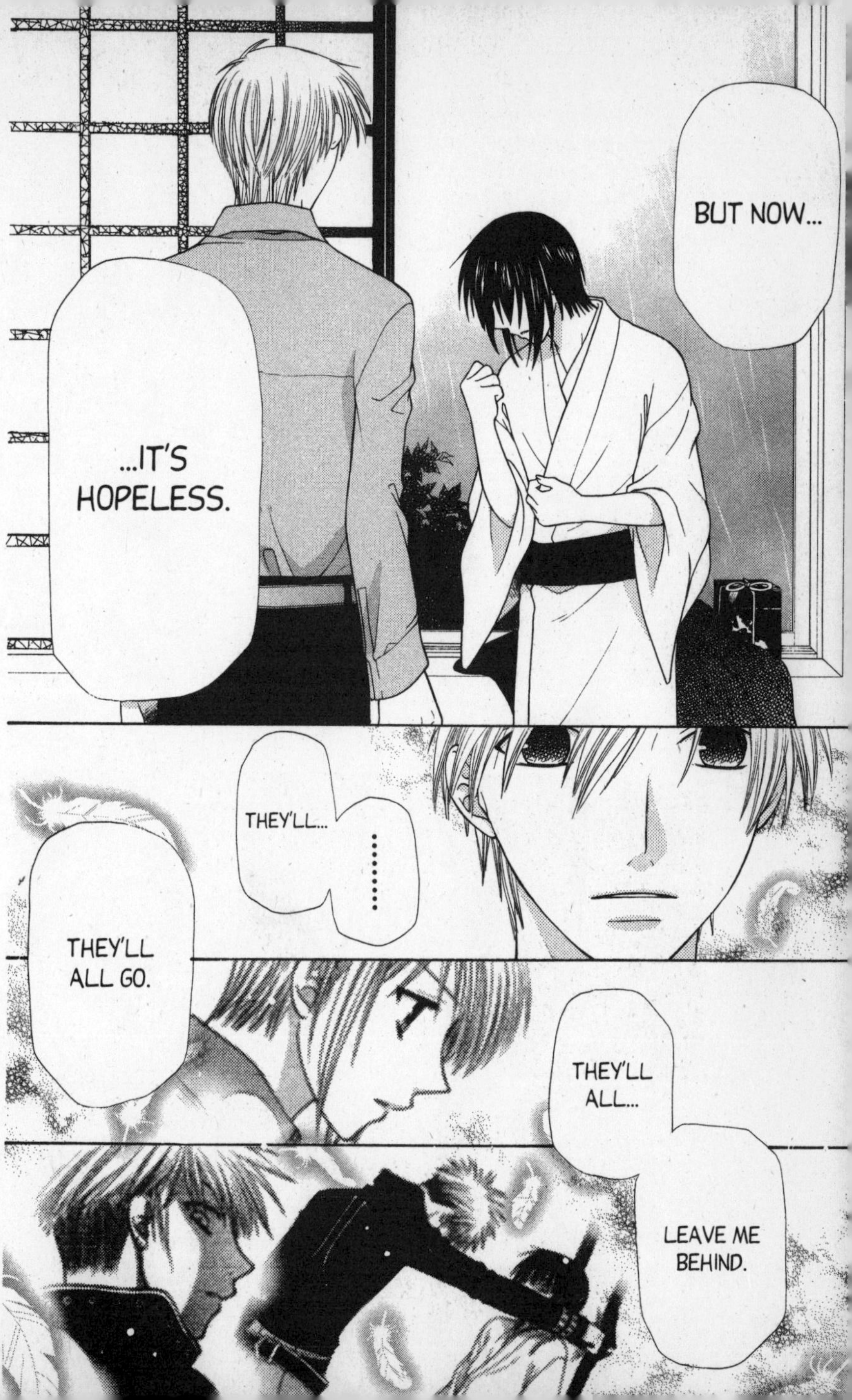
BUT NOW...
...IT'S HOPELESS.
THEY'LL...
....
THEY'LL ALL GO.
THEY'LL ALL...
LEAVE ME BEHIND.

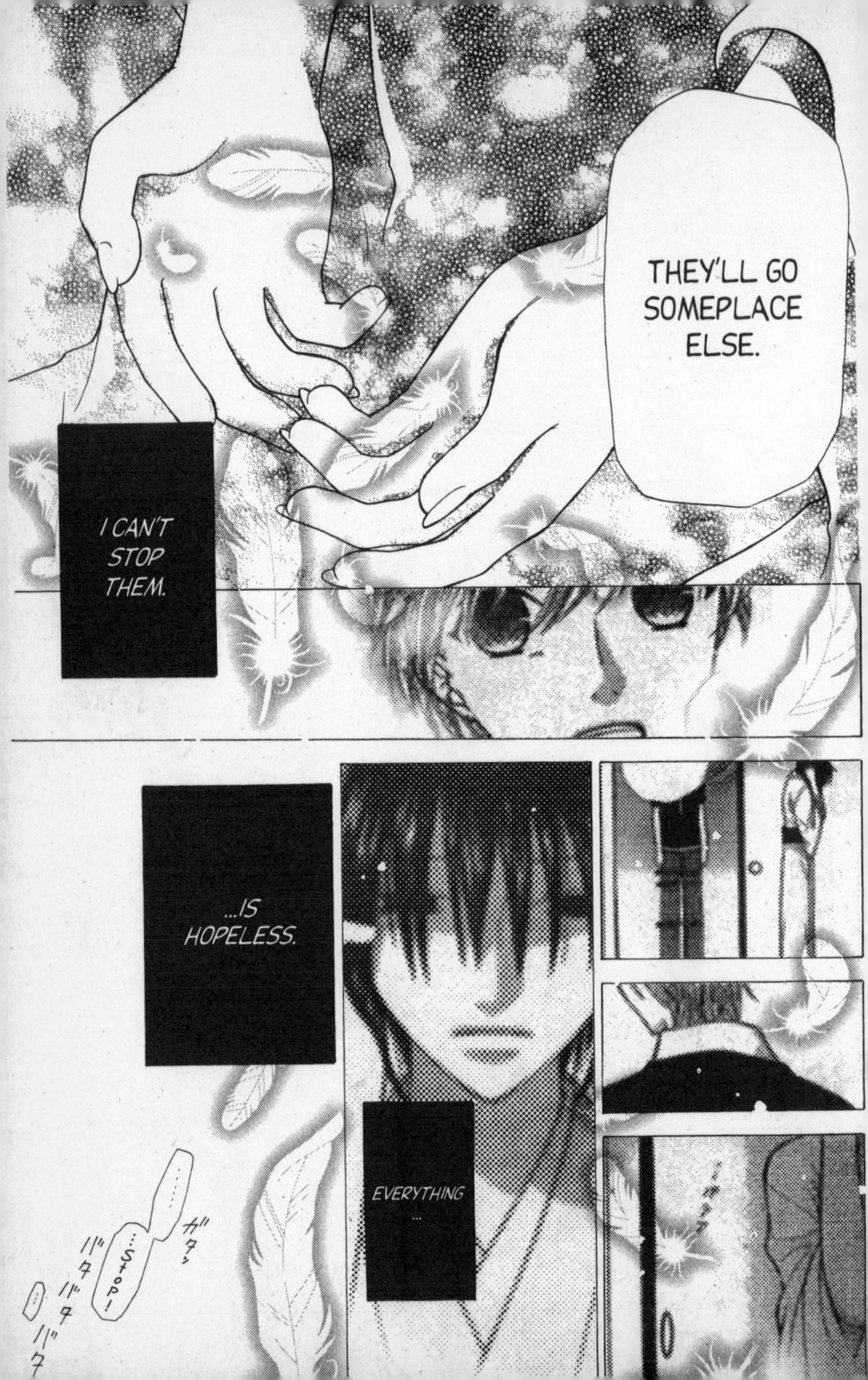
THEY'LL GO SOMEPLACE ELSE.
I CAN'T STOP THEM.
EVERYTHING ...
...IS HOPELESS.
......
...STOP!
ガタッ
バタバタバタ
...

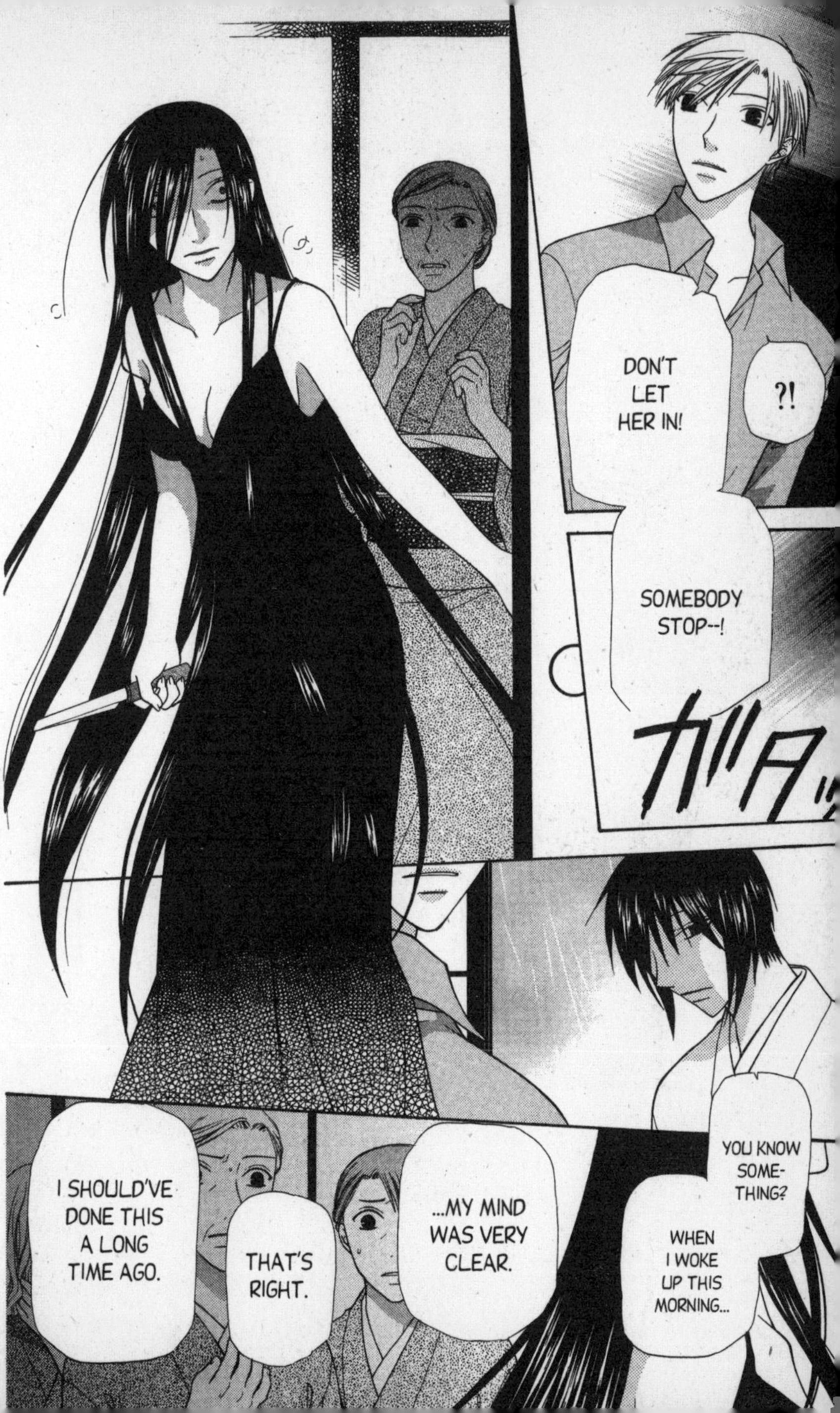
?!
DON'T LET HER IN!
SOMEBODY STOP--!
YOU KNOW SOME-THING?
WHEN I WOKE UP THIS MORNING...
...MY MIND WAS VERY CLEAR.
THAT'S RIGHT.
I SHOULD'VE DONE THIS A LONG TIME AGO.

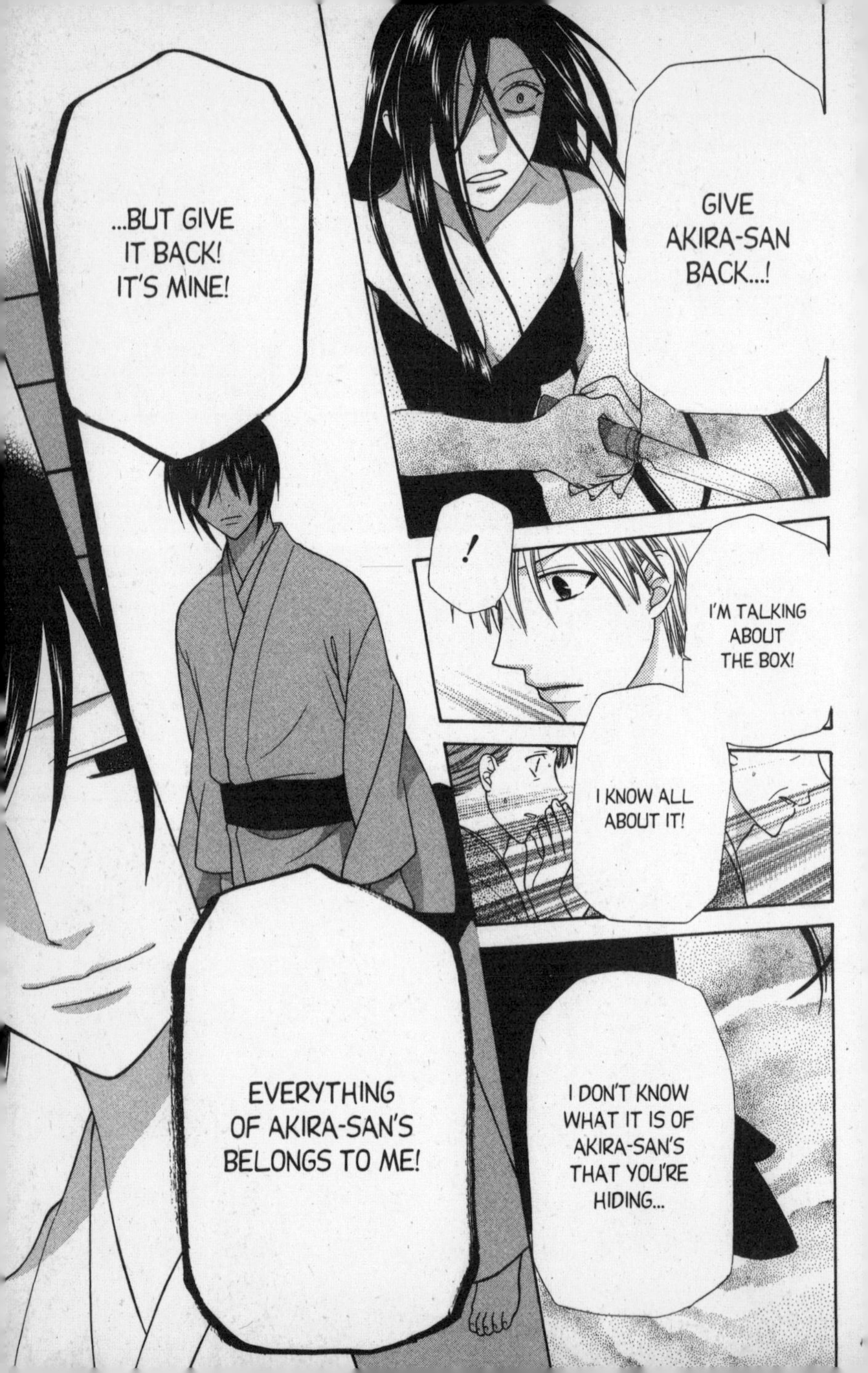
GIVE AKIRA-SAN BACK...!
!
I'M TALKING ABOUT THE BOX!
I KNOW ALL ABOUT IT!
I DON'T KNOW WHAT IT IS OF AKIRA-SAN'S THAT YOU'RE HIDING...
...BUT GIVE IT BACK! IT'S MINE!
EVERYTHING OF AKIRA-SAN'S BELONGS TO ME!

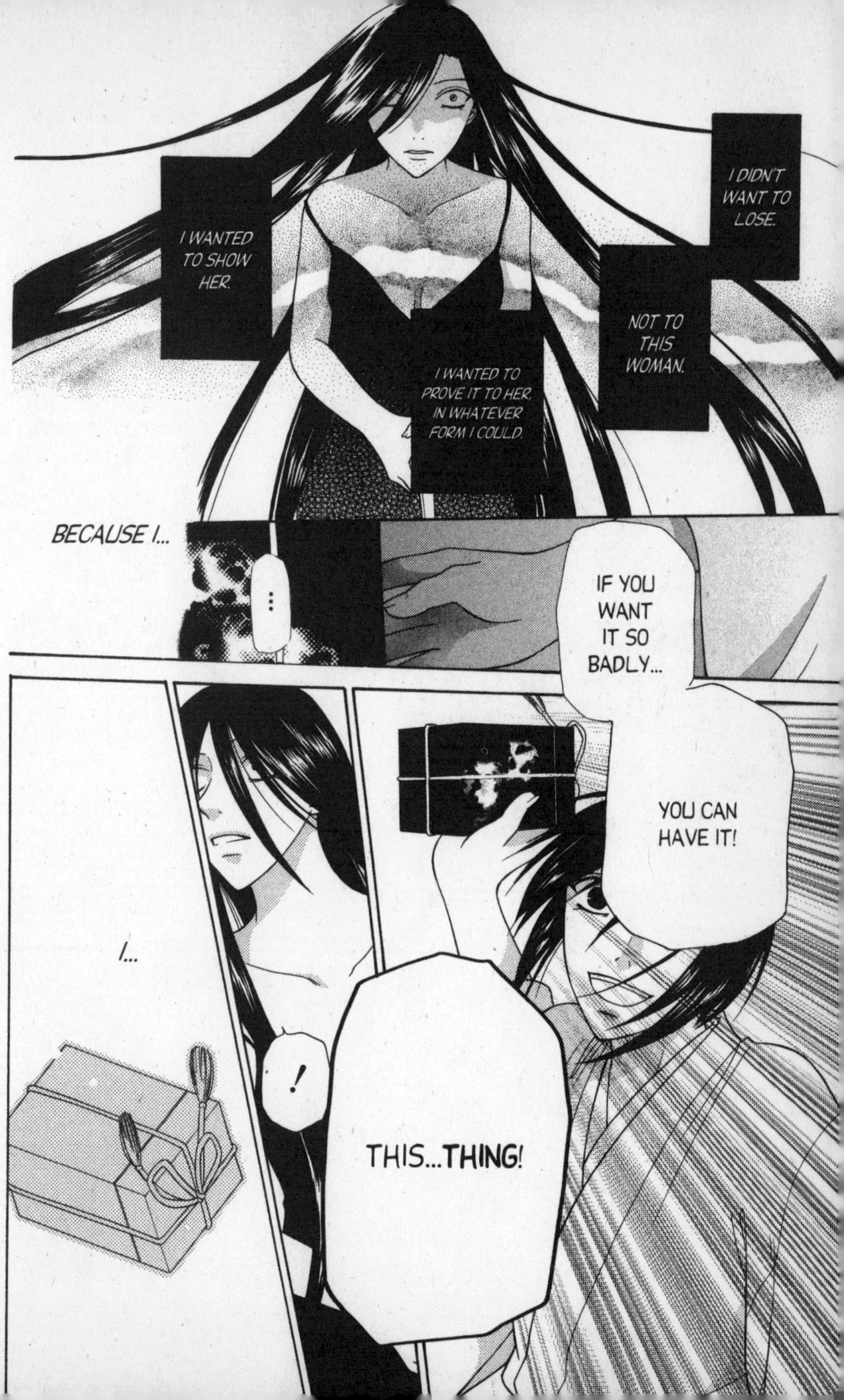

I DIDN'T WANT TO LOSE.
NOT TO THIS WOMAN.
I WANTED TO SHOW HER.
I WANTED TO PROVE IT TO HER, IN WHATEVER FORM I COULD.
IF YOU WANT IT SO BADLY...
...
BECAUSE I...
YOU CAN HAVE IT!
THIS...THING!
!
I...

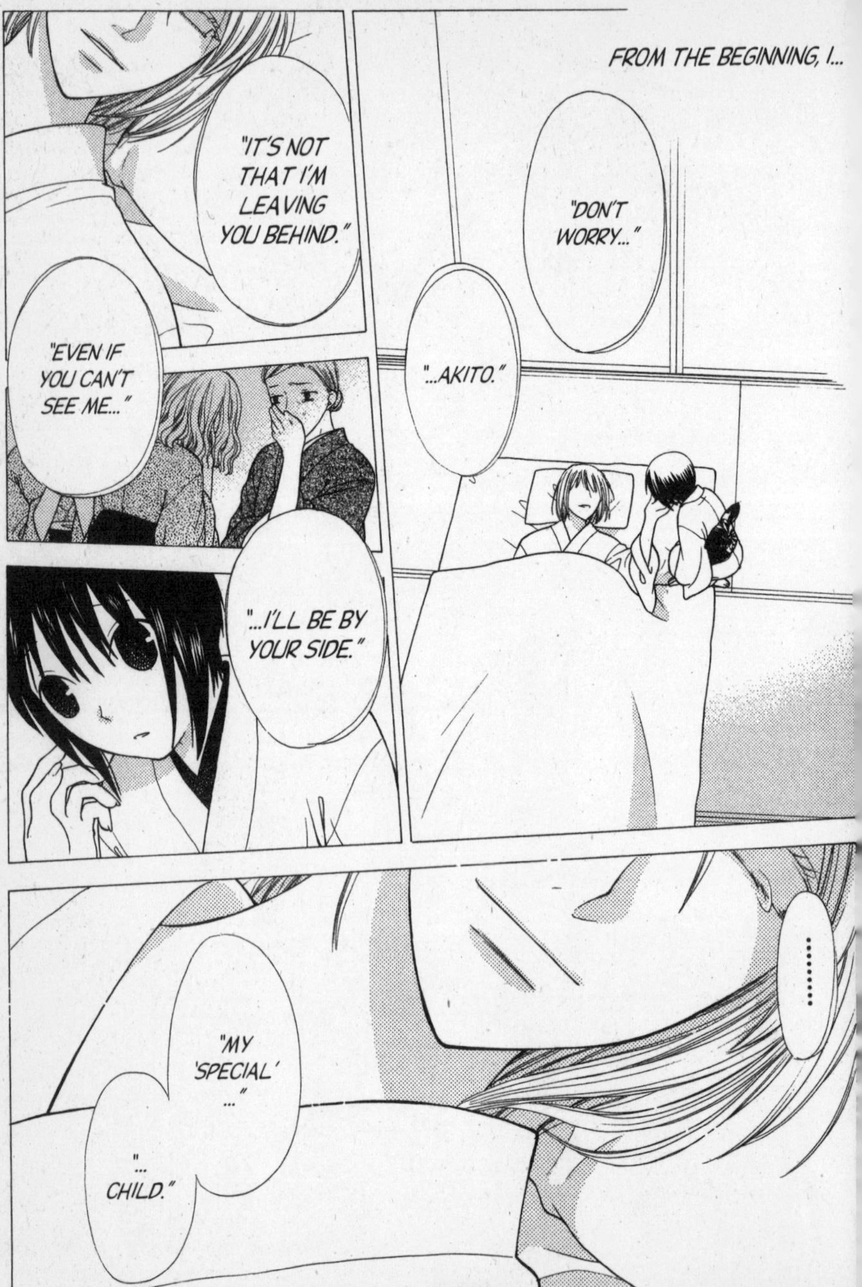
FROM THE BEGINNING, I...
"DON'T WORRY..."
"...AKITO."
"IT'S NOT THAT I'M LEAVING YOU BEHIND."
"EVEN IF YOU CAN'T SEE ME..."
"...I'LL BE BY YOUR SIDE."
....
"MY 'SPECIAL' ..."
"... CHILD."

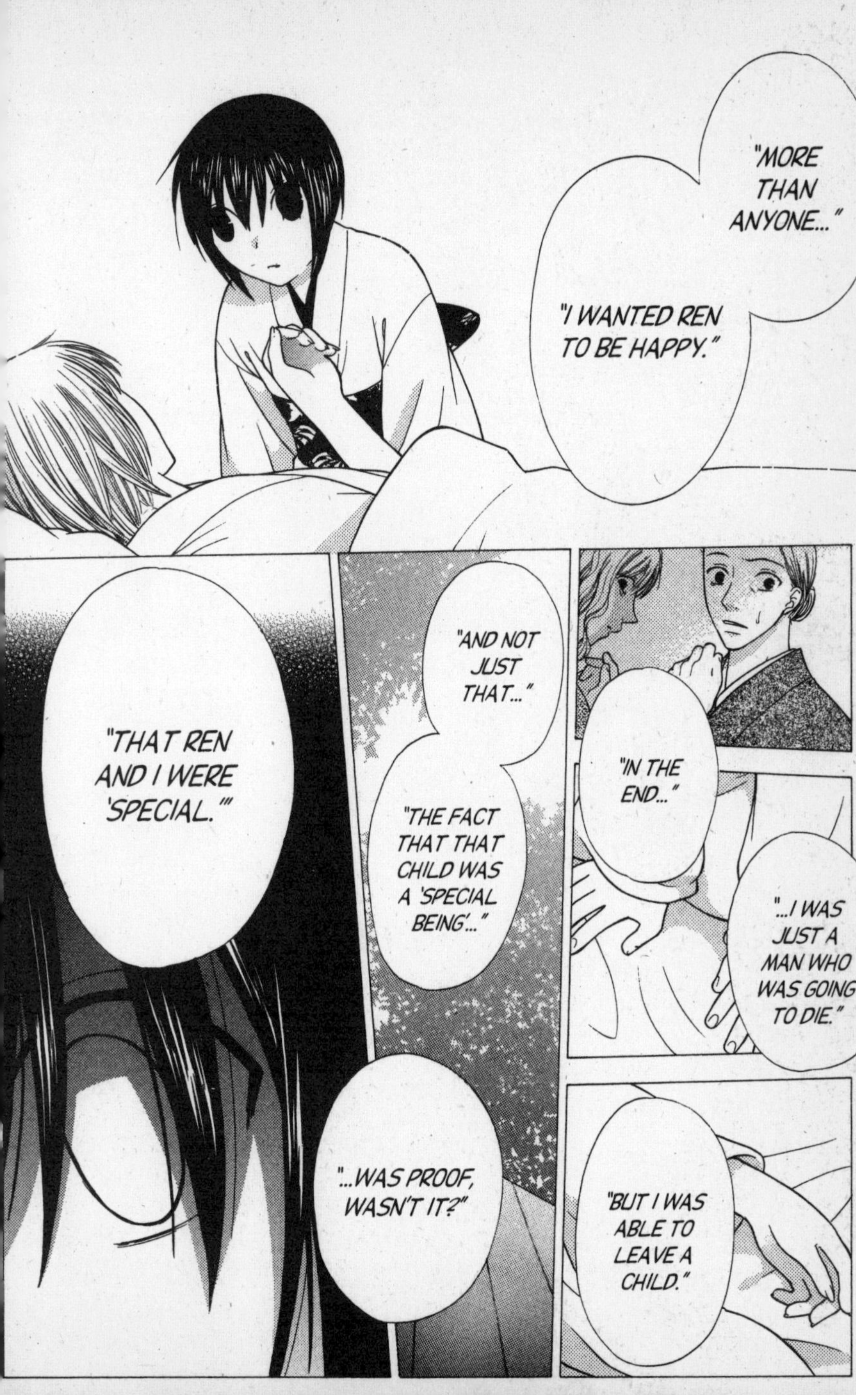
"MORE THAN ANYONE..."
"I WANTED REN TO BE HAPPY."
"IN THE END..."
"...I WAS JUST A MAN WHO WAS GOING TO DIE."
"BUT I WAS ABLE TO LEAVE A CHILD."
"AND NOT JUST THAT..."
"THE FACT THAT THAT CHILD WAS A 'SPECIAL BEING'..."
"...WAS PROOF, WASN'T IT?"
"THAT REN AND I WERE 'SPECIAL.'"

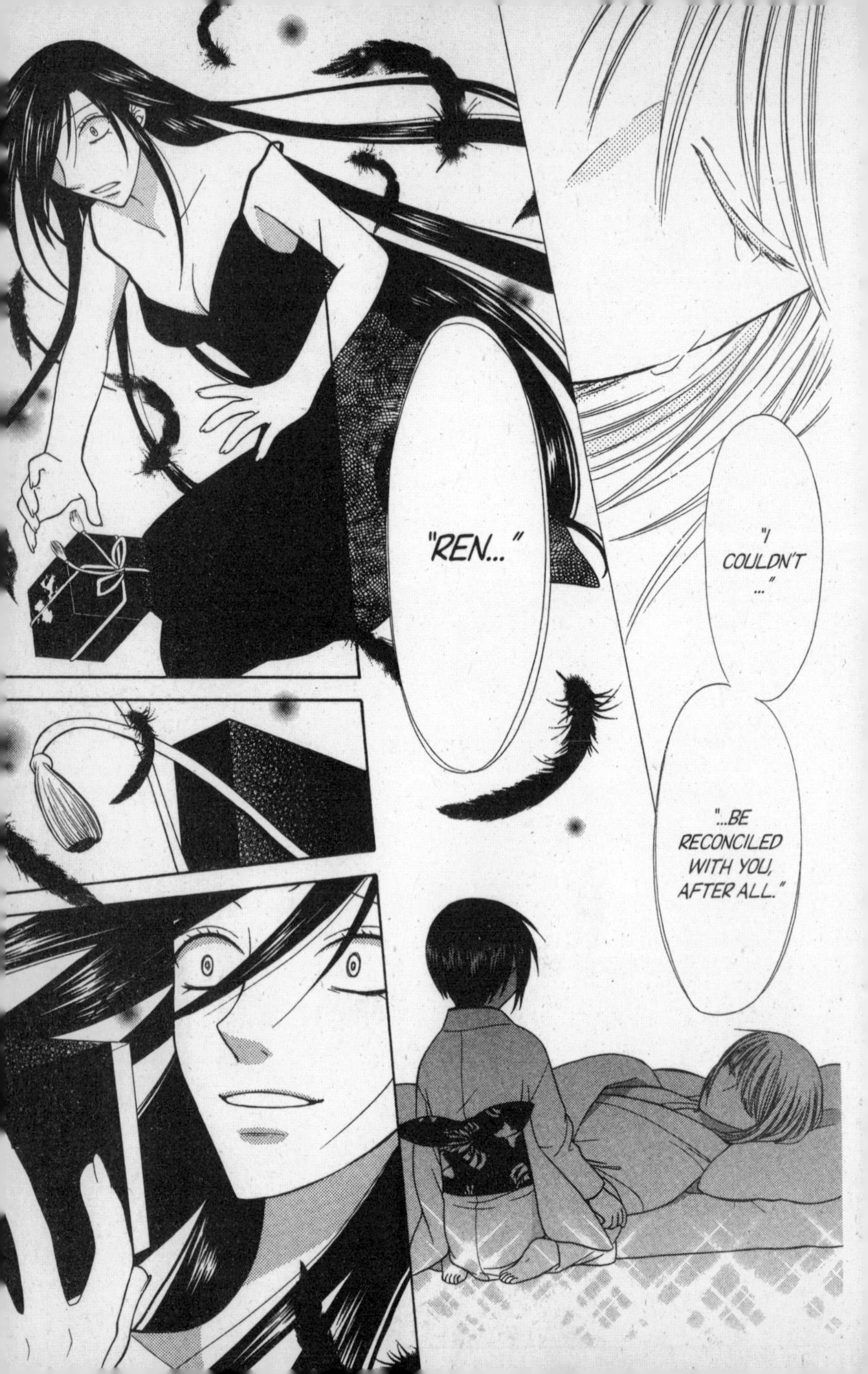
"I COULDN'T ..."
"...BE RECONCILED WITH YOU, AFTER ALL."
"REN..."

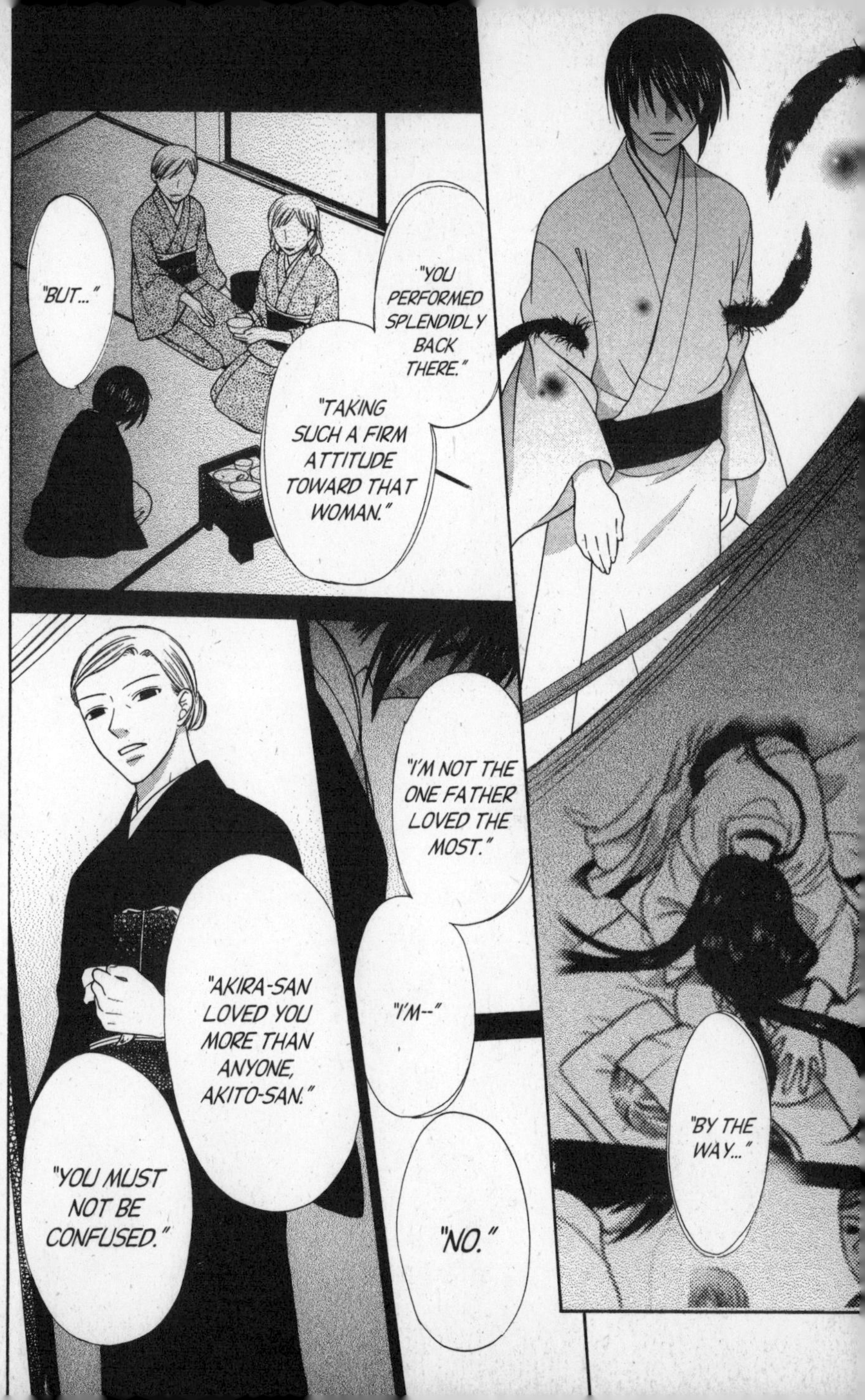
"YOU PERFORMED SPLENDIDLY BACK THERE."
"TAKING SUCH A FIRM ATTITUDE TOWARD THAT WOMAN."
"BUT..."
"BY THE WAY..."
"I'M NOT THE ONE FATHER LOVED THE MOST."
"I'M--"
"NO."
"AKIRA-SAN LOVED YOU MORE THAN ANYONE, AKITO-SAN."
"YOU MUST NOT BE CONFUSED."

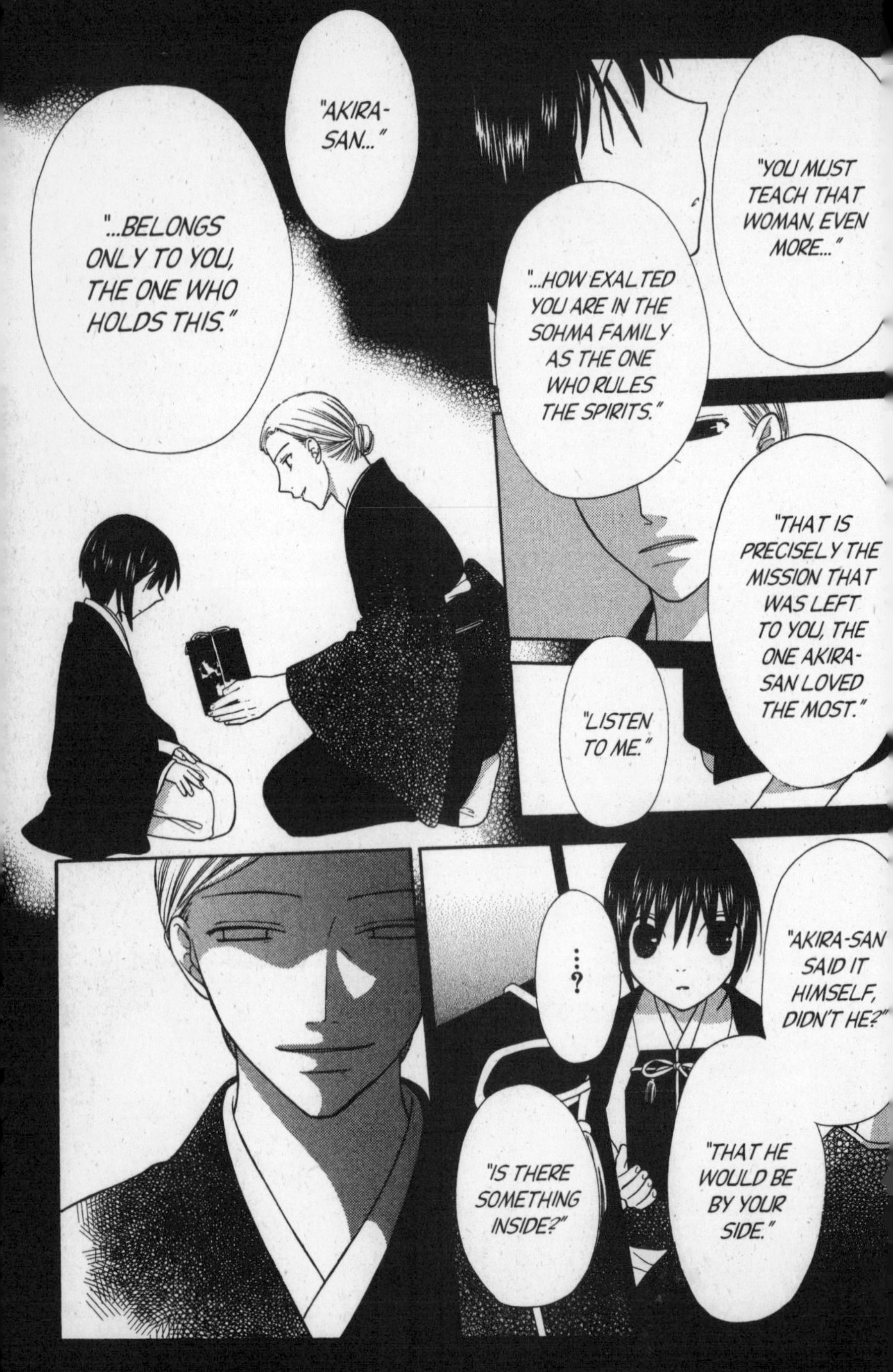
"YOU MUST TEACH THAT WOMAN, EVEN MORE..."
"...HOW EXALTED YOU ARE IN THE SOHMA FAMILY AS THE ONE WHO RULES THE SPIRITS."
"THAT IS PRECISELY THE MISSION THAT WAS LEFT TO YOU, THE ONE AKIRA-SAN LOVED THE MOST."
"LISTEN TO ME."
"AKIRA-SAN..."
"...BELONGS ONLY TO YOU, THE ONE WHO HOLDS THIS."
"AKIRA-SAN SAID IT HIMSELF, DIDN'T HE?"
"THAT HE WOULD BE BY YOUR SIDE."
...?
"IS THERE SOMETHING INSIDE?"

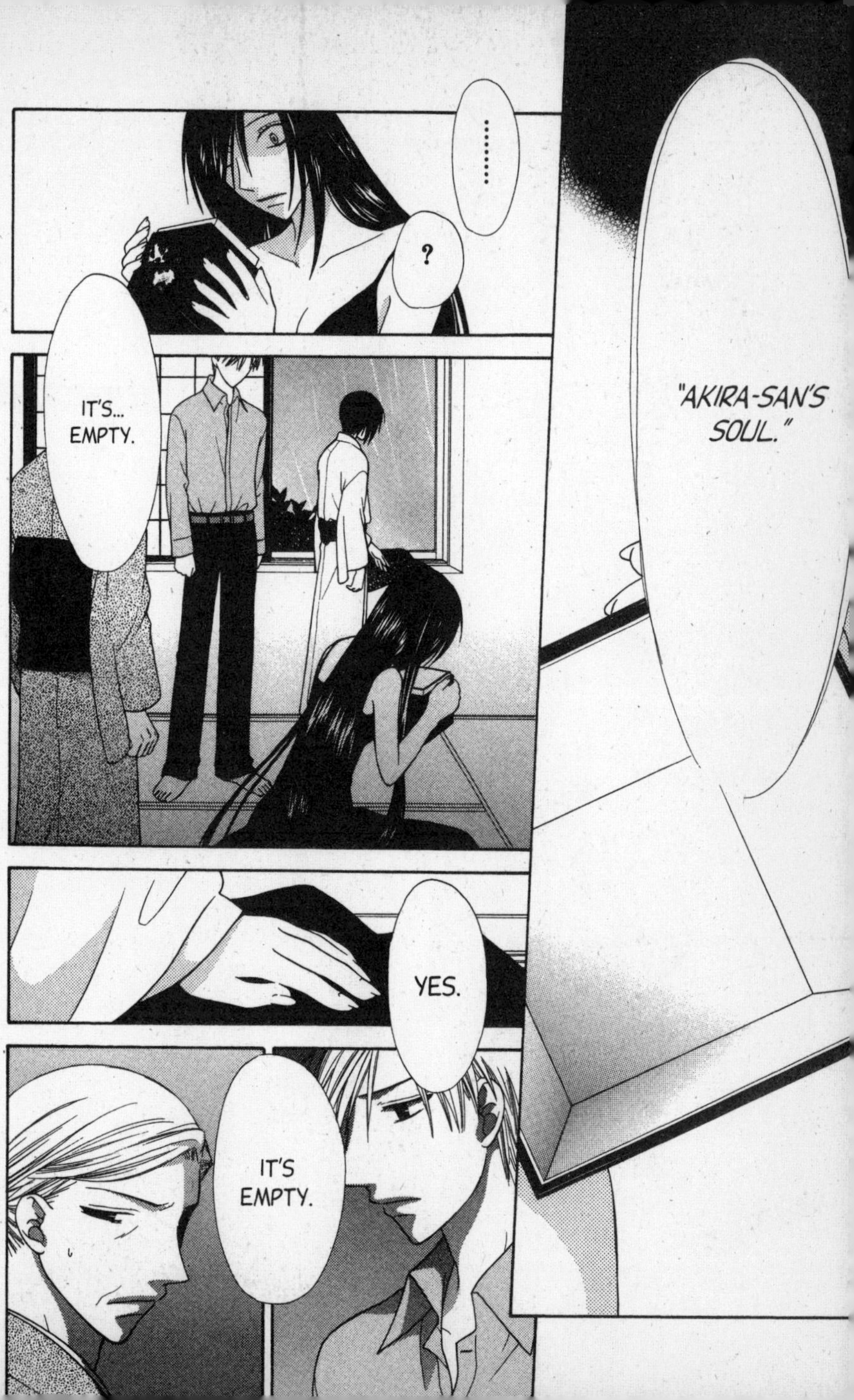
"AKIRA-SAN'S SOUL."
......
?
IT'S... EMPTY.
YES.
IT'S EMPTY.

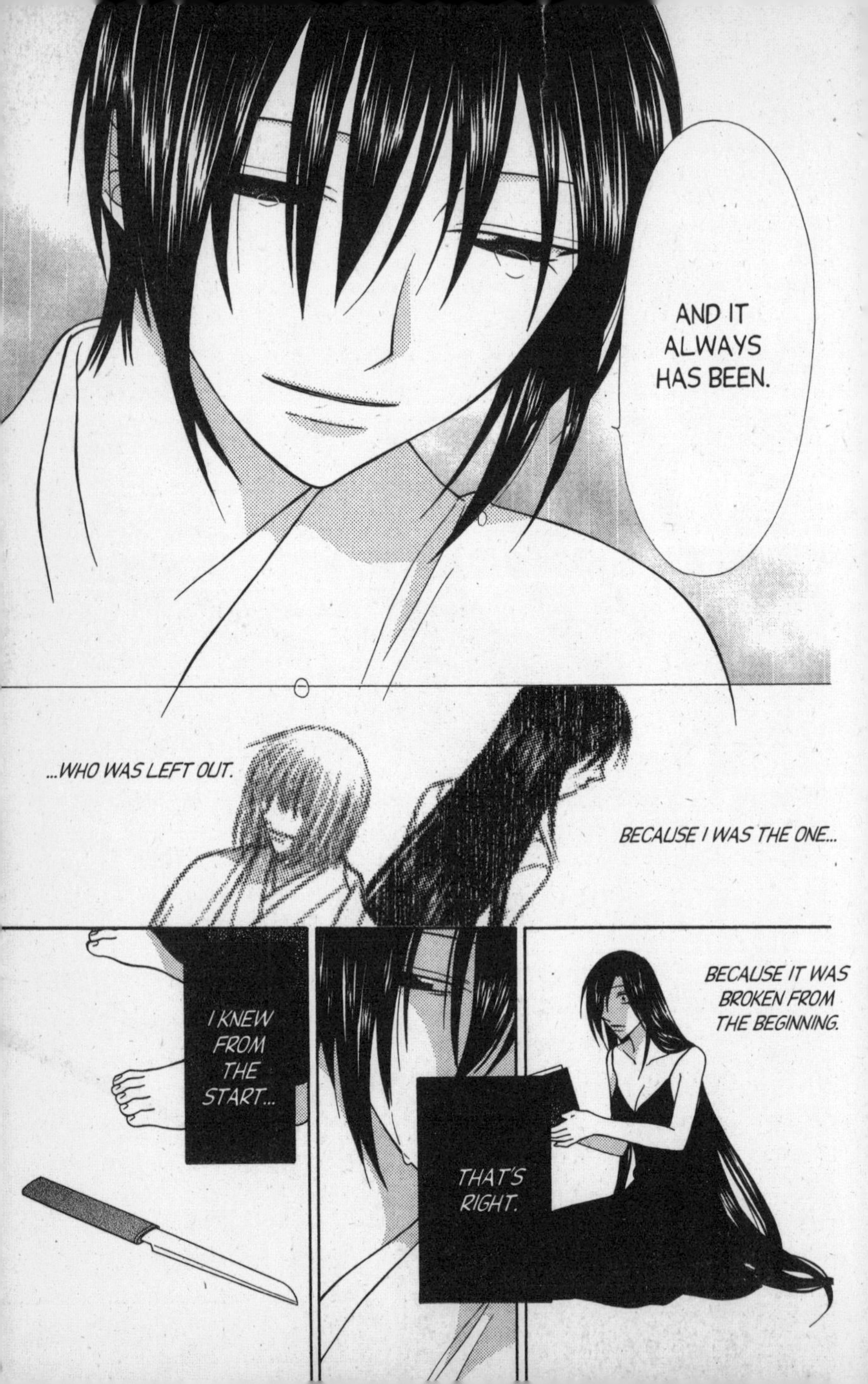
AND IT ALWAYS HAS BEEN.
BECAUSE I WAS THE ONE...
...WHO WAS LEFT OUT.
BECAUSE IT WAS BROKEN FROM THE BEGINNING.
THAT'S RIGHT.
I KNEW FROM THE START...

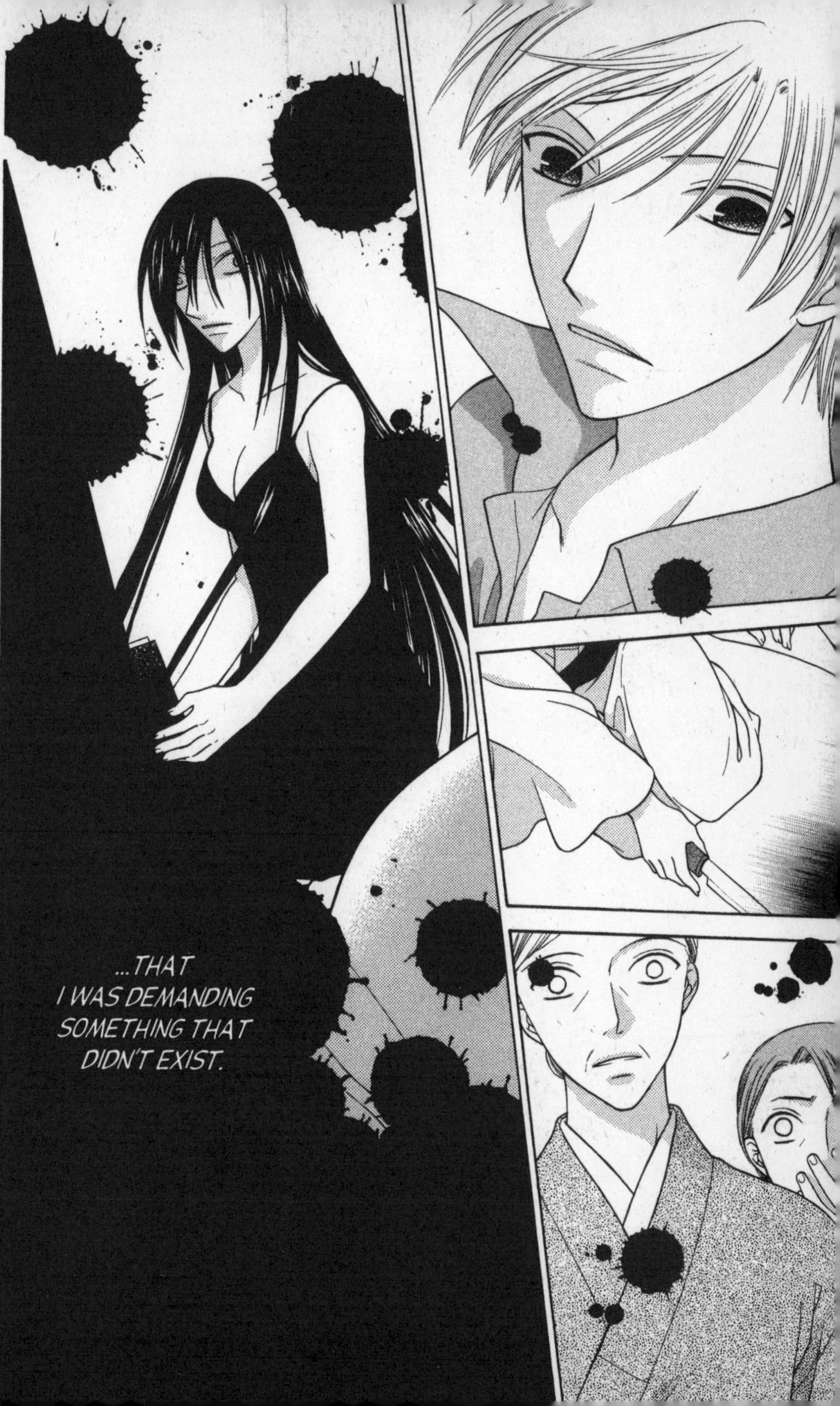
...THAT I WAS DEMANDING SOMETHING THAT DIDN'T EXIST.

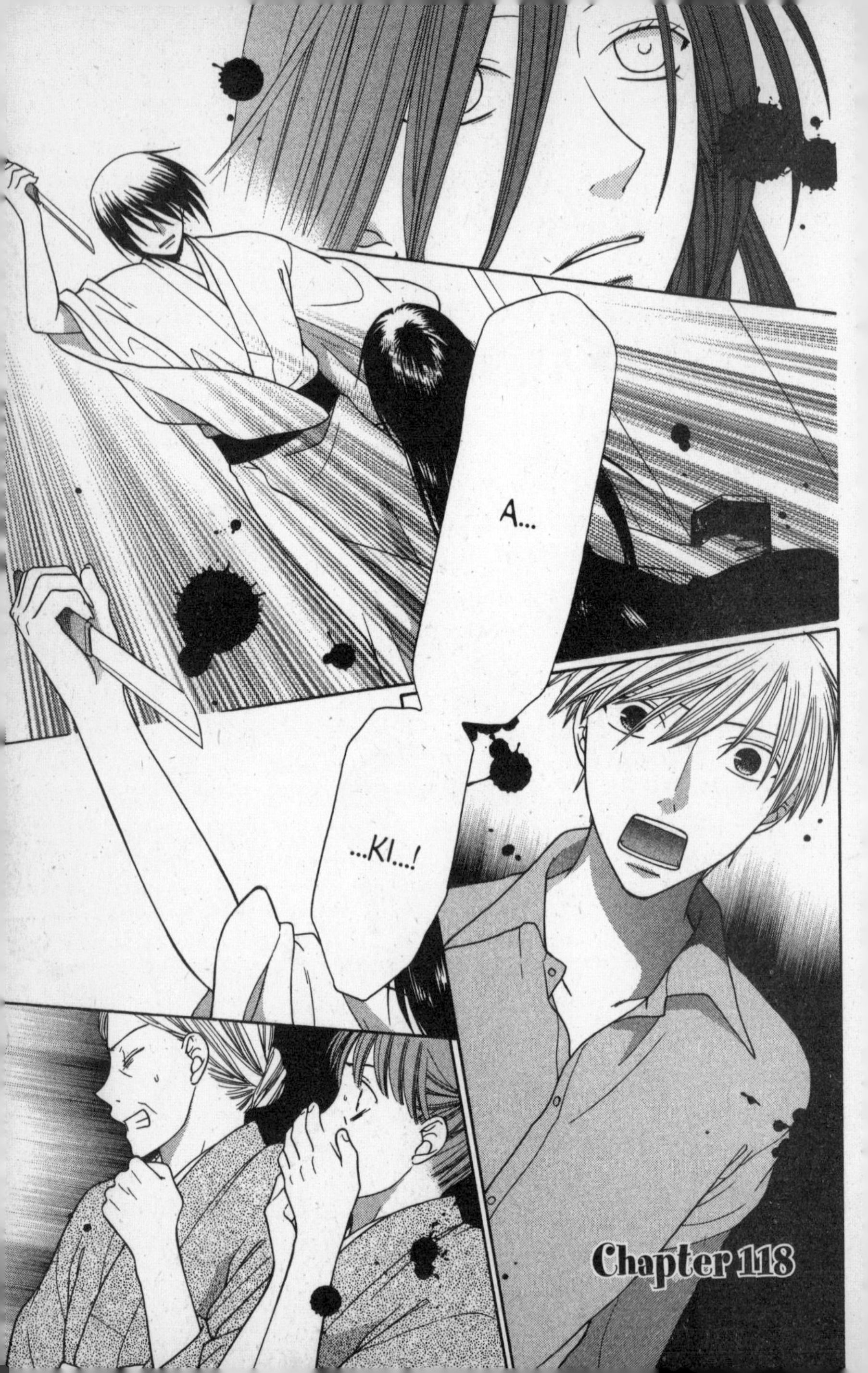
A...
...KI...!
Chapter 118

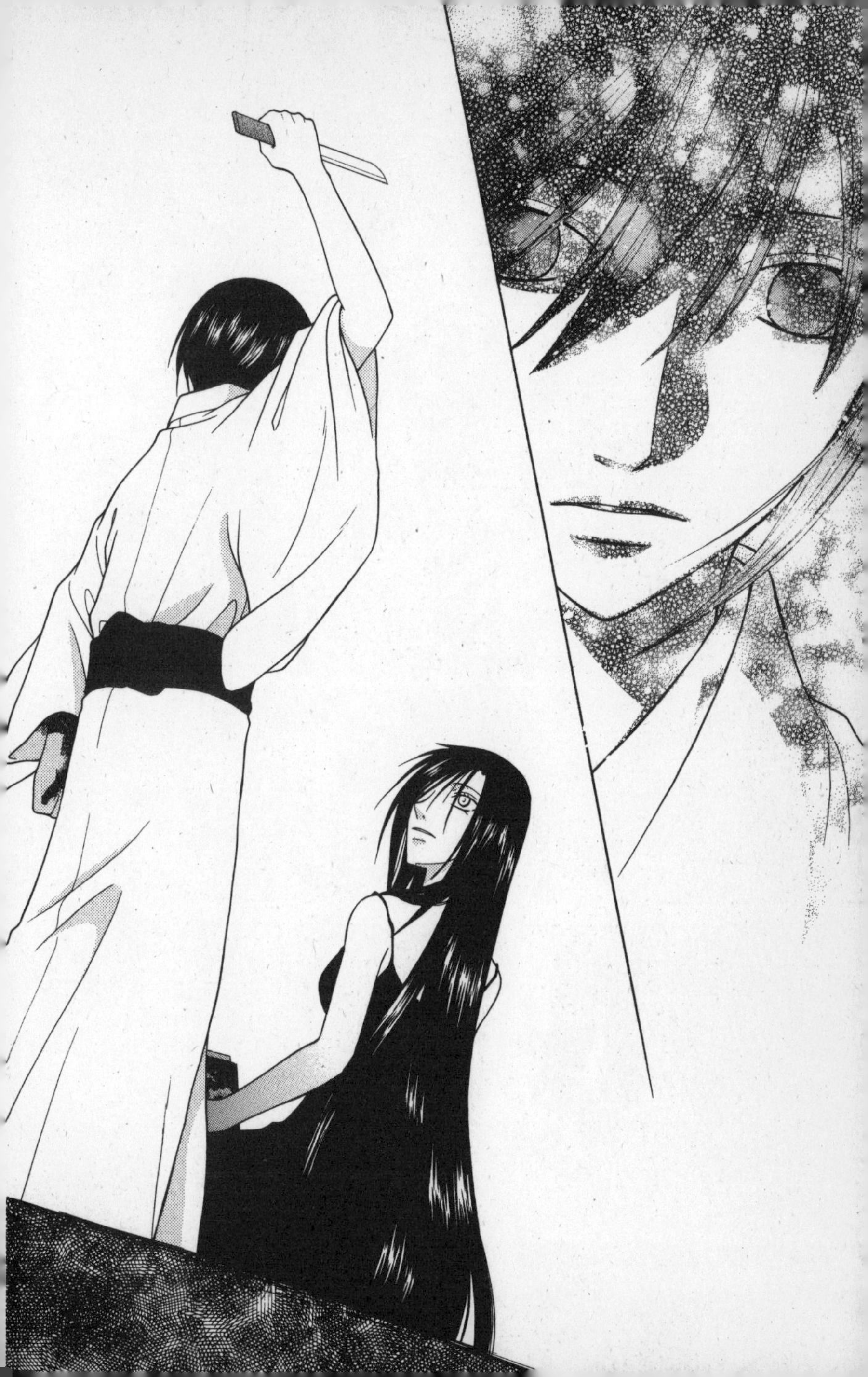

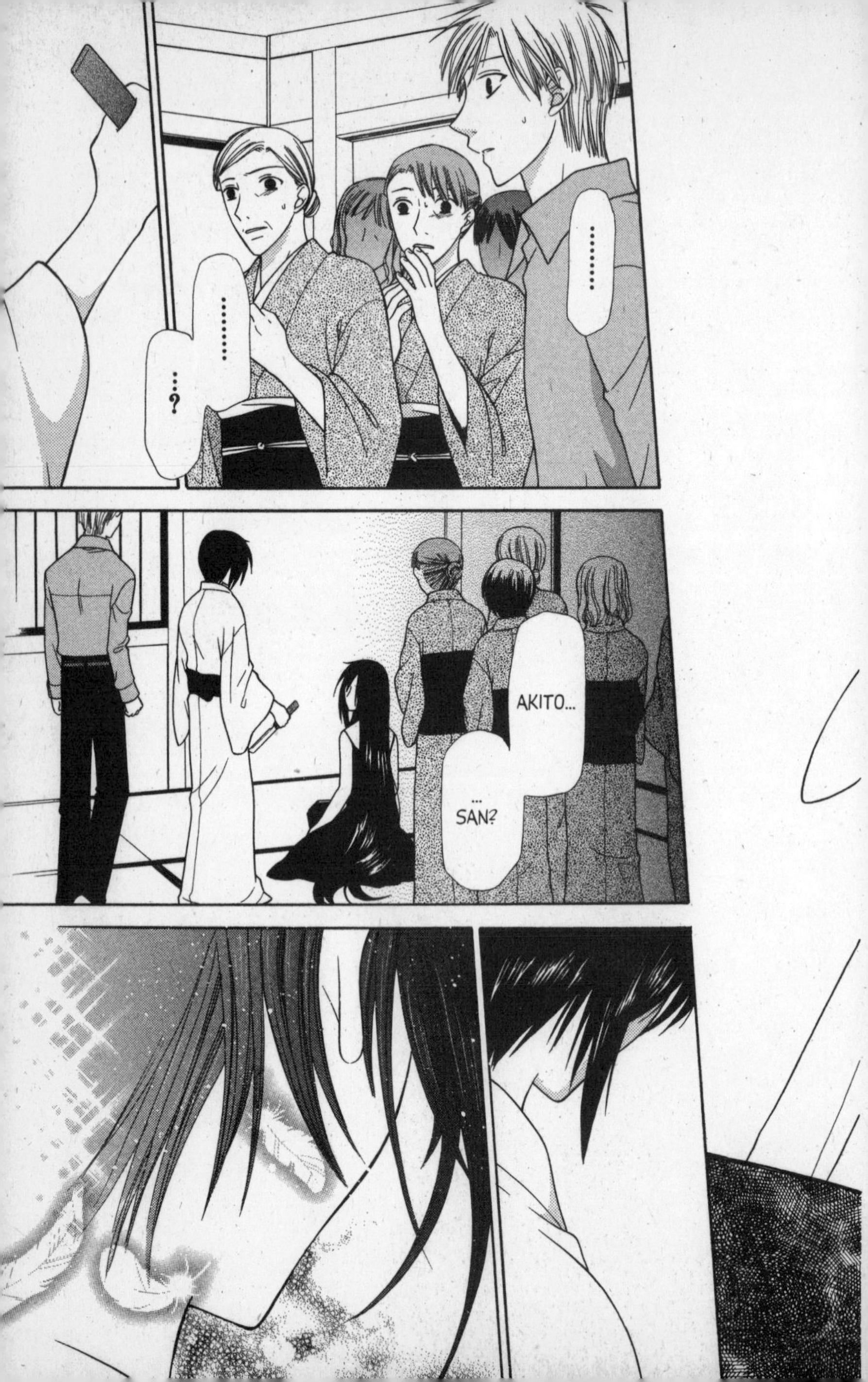
......
....
...?
AKITO...
...SAN?

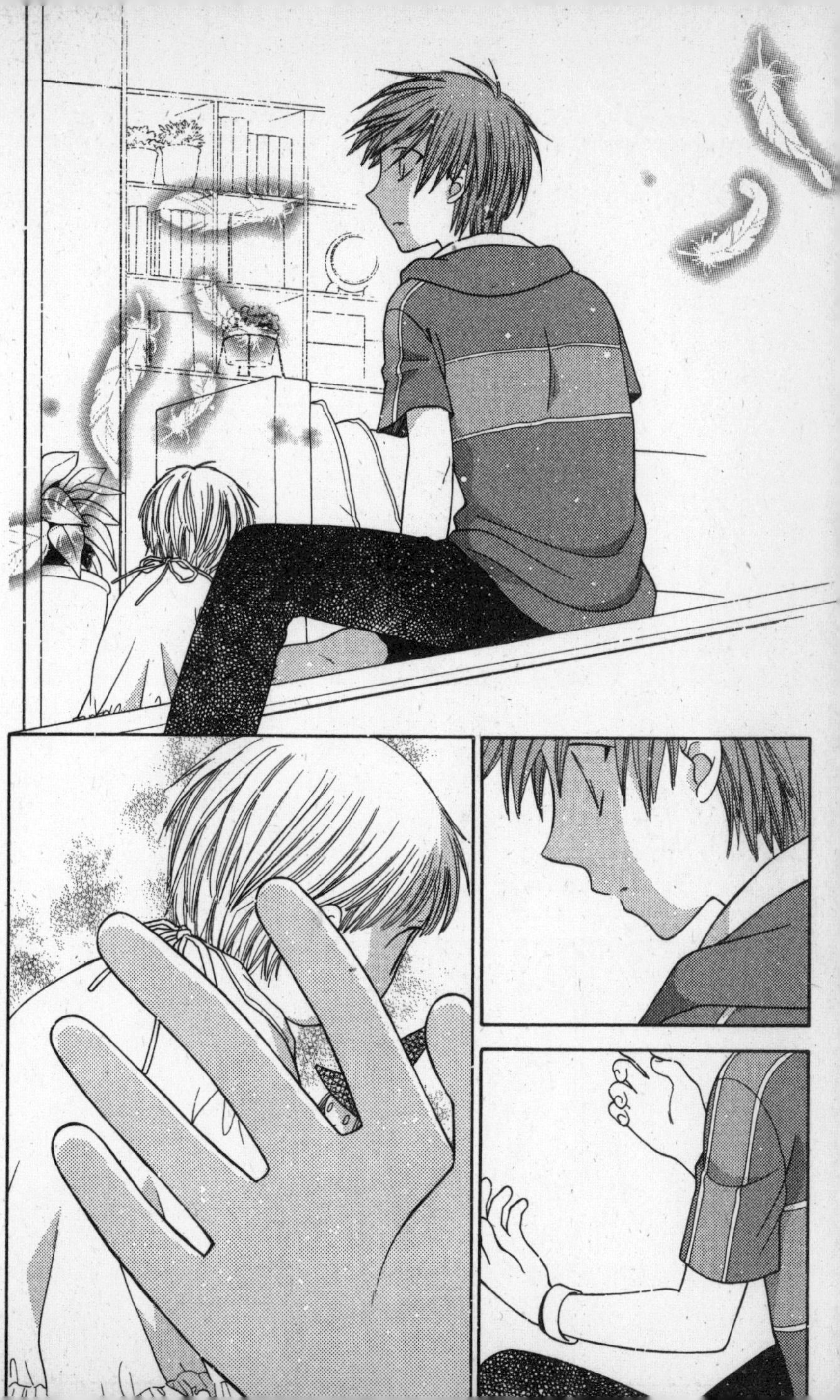

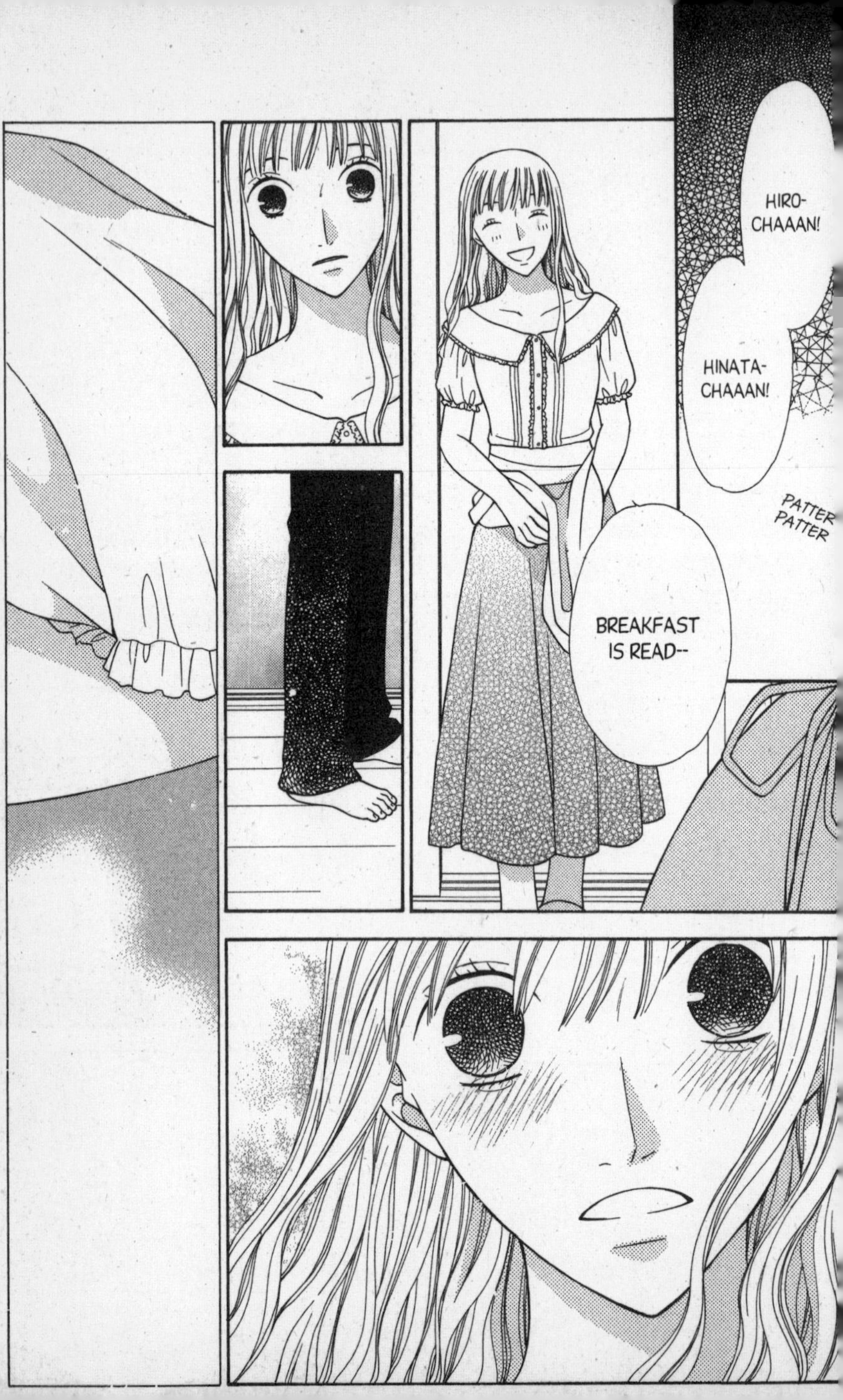
HIRO-CHAAAN!
HINATA-CHAAAN!
PATTER PATTER
BREAKFAST IS READ--

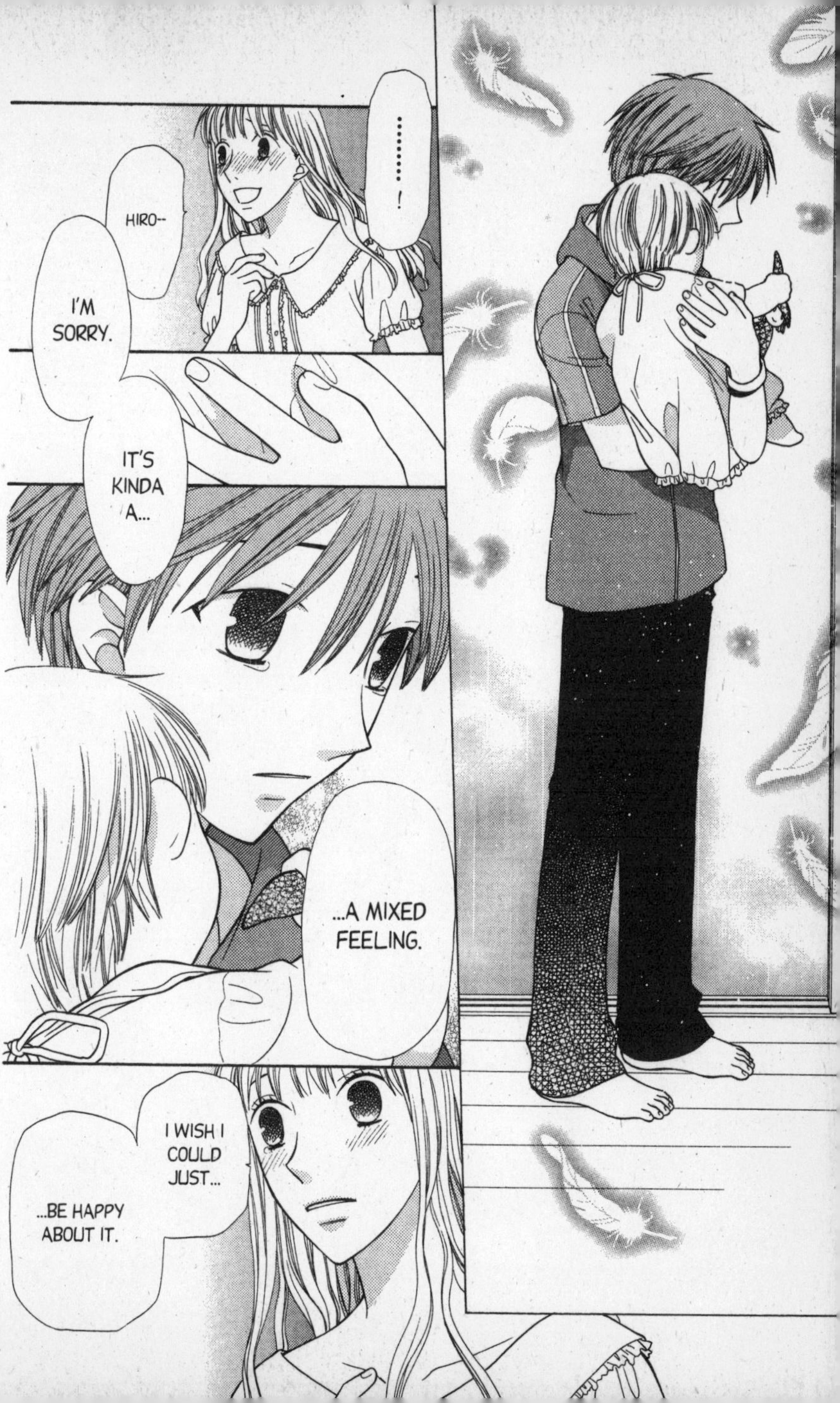
......!
HIRO--
I'M SORRY.
IT'S KINDA A...
...A MIXED FEELING.
I WISH I COULD JUST...
...BE HAPPY ABOUT IT.

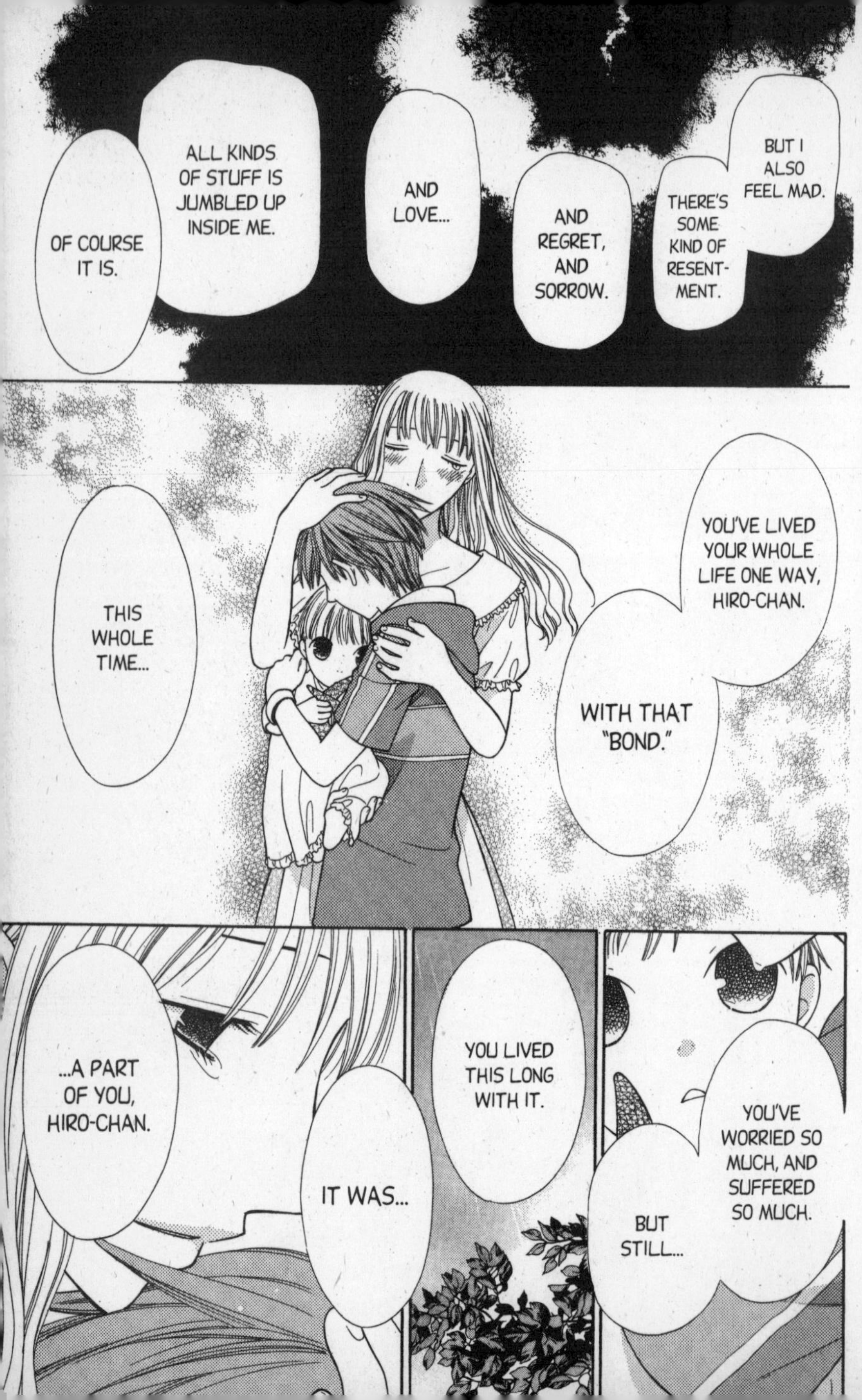
BUT I ALSO FEEL MAD.
THERE'S SOME KIND OF RESENT-MENT.
AND REGRET, AND SORROW.
AND LOVE...
ALL KINDS OF STUFF IS JUMBLED UP INSIDE ME.
OF COURSE IT IS.
YOU'VE LIVED YOUR WHOLE LIFE ONE WAY, HIRO-CHAN.
WITH THAT "BOND."
THIS WHOLE TIME...
YOU'VE WORRIED SO MUCH, AND SUFFERED SO MUCH.
BUT STILL...
YOU LIVED THIS LONG WITH IT.
IT WAS...
...A PART OF YOU, HIRO-CHAN.

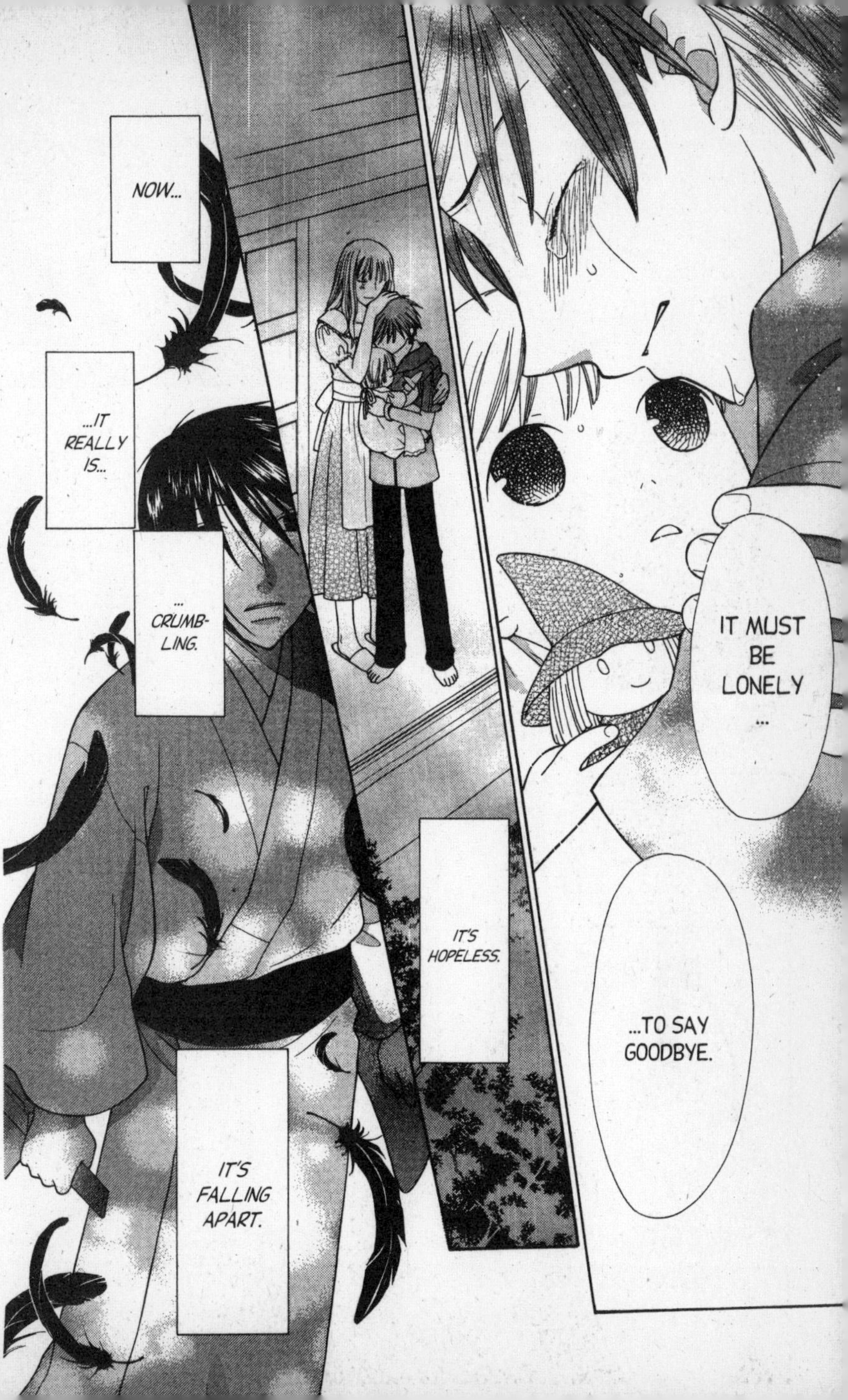
IT MUST BE LONELY ...
...TO SAY GOODBYE.
IT'S HOPELESS.
NOW...
...IT REALLY IS...
... CRUMBLING.
IT'S FALLING APART.

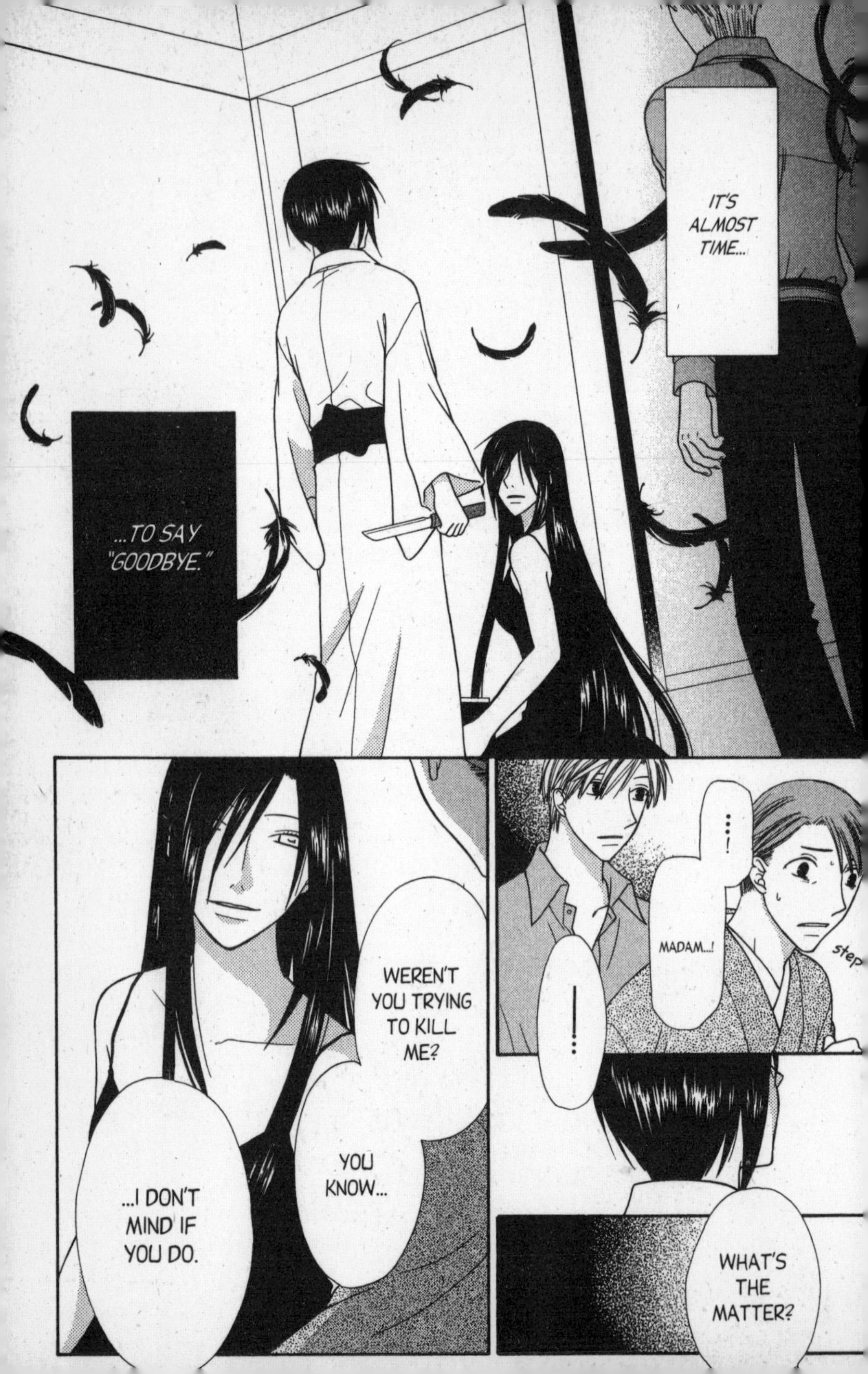
IT'S ALMOST TIME...
...TO SAY "GOODBYE."
...!
step
MADAM...!
...!
WHAT'S THE MATTER?
WEREN'T YOU TRYING TO KILL ME?
YOU KNOW...
...I DON'T MIND IF YOU DO.

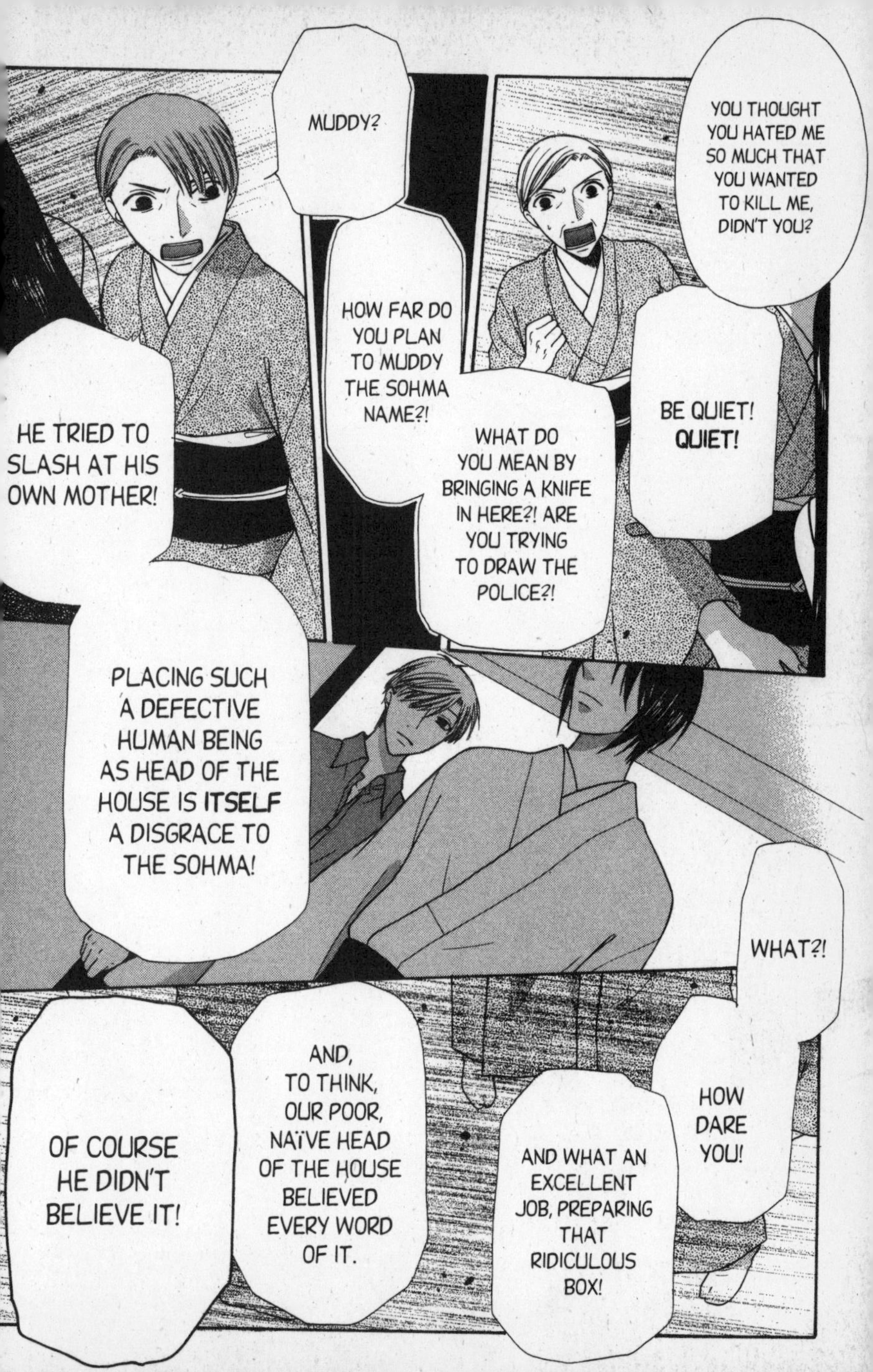
YOU THOUGHT YOU HATED ME SO MUCH THAT YOU WANTED TO KILL ME, DIDN'T YOU?
BE QUIET! **QUIET!**
WHAT DO YOU MEAN BY BRINGING A KNIFE IN HERE?! ARE YOU TRYING TO DRAW THE POLICE?!
MUDDY?
HOW FAR DO YOU PLAN TO MUDDY THE SOHMA NAME?!
HE TRIED TO SLASH AT HIS OWN MOTHER!
WHAT?!
PLACING SUCH A DEFECTIVE HUMAN BEING AS HEAD OF THE HOUSE IS **ITSELF** A DISGRACE TO THE SOHMA!
HOW DARE YOU!
AND WHAT AN EXCELLENT JOB, PREPARING THAT RIDICULOUS BOX!
AND, TO THINK, OUR POOR, NAÏVE HEAD OF THE HOUSE BELIEVED EVERY WORD OF IT.
OF COURSE HE DIDN'T BELIEVE IT!

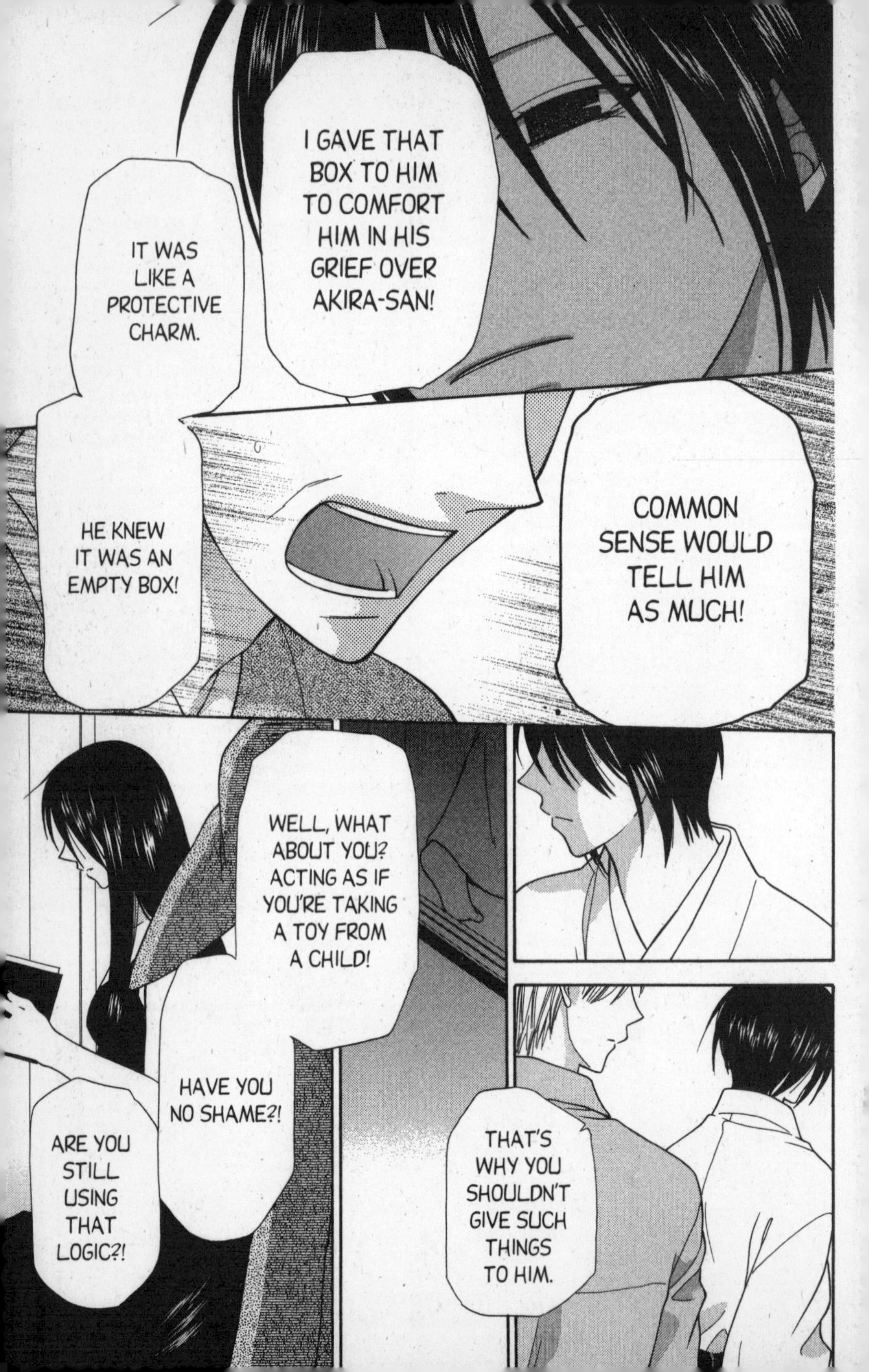
I GAVE THAT BOX TO HIM TO COMFORT HIM IN HIS GRIEF OVER AKIRA-SAN!
IT WAS LIKE A PROTECTIVE CHARM.
COMMON SENSE WOULD TELL HIM AS MUCH!
HE KNEW IT WAS AN EMPTY BOX!
THAT'S WHY YOU SHOULDN'T GIVE SUCH THINGS TO HIM.
WELL, WHAT ABOUT YOU? ACTING AS IF YOU'RE TAKING A TOY FROM A CHILD!
HAVE YOU NO SHAME?!
ARE YOU STILL USING THAT LOGIC?!

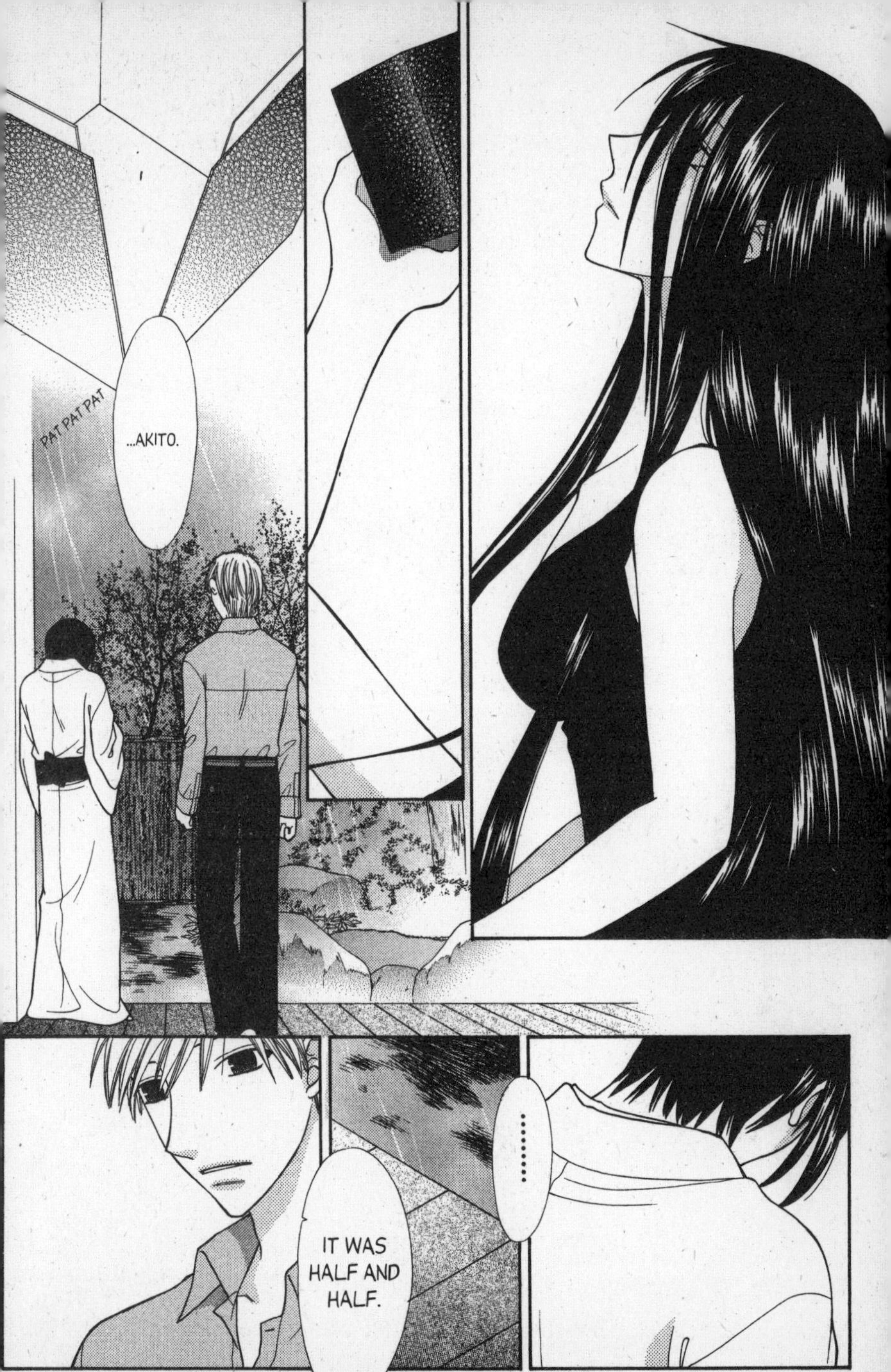
...AKITO.
PAT PAT PAT
......
IT WAS HALF AND HALF.

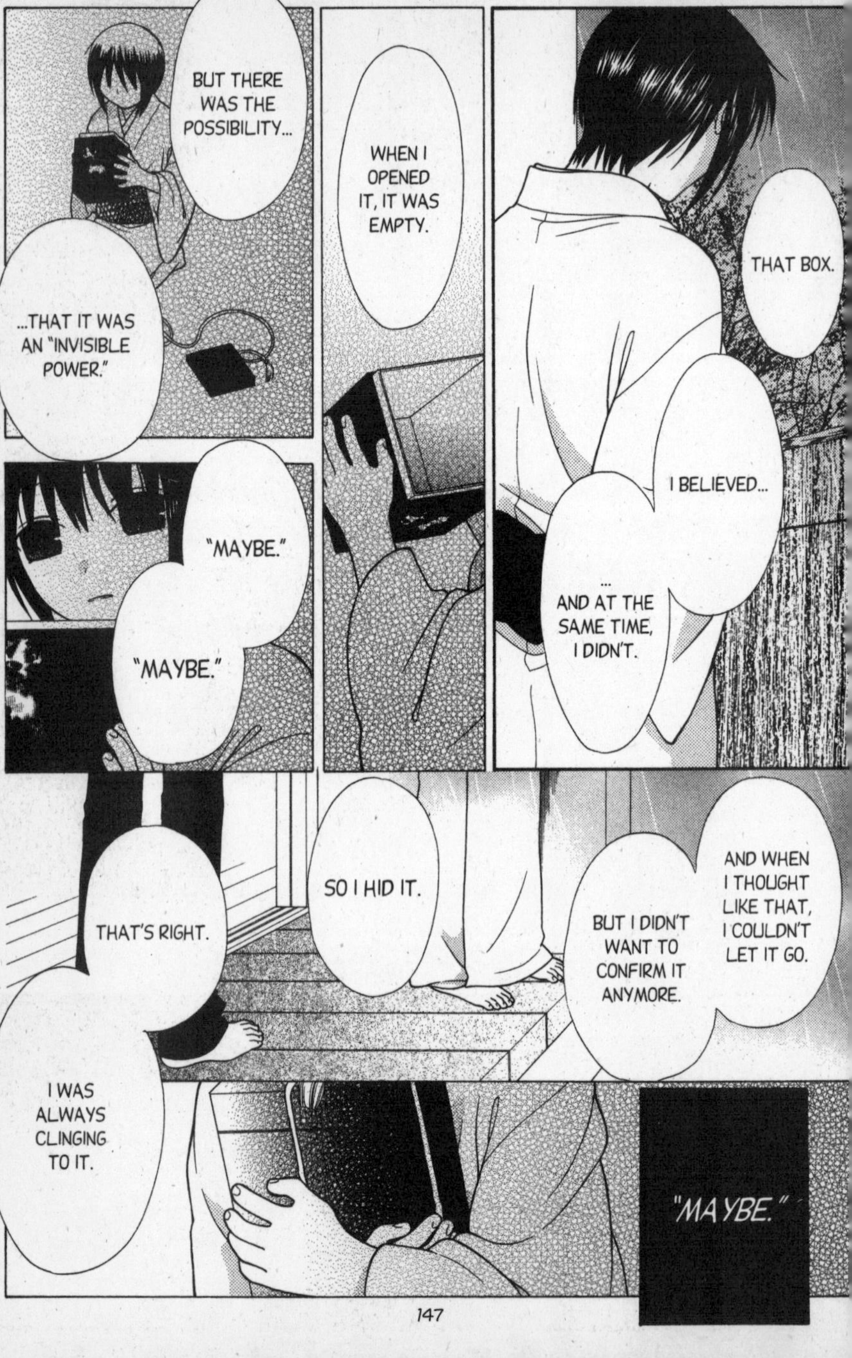
THAT BOX.
I BELIEVED...
...AND AT THE SAME TIME, I DIDN'T.
WHEN I OPENED IT, IT WAS EMPTY.
BUT THERE WAS THE POSSIBILITY...
...THAT IT WAS AN "INVISIBLE POWER."
"MAYBE."
"MAYBE."
AND WHEN I THOUGHT LIKE THAT, I COULDN'T LET IT GO.
BUT I DIDN'T WANT TO CONFIRM IT ANYMORE.
SO I HID IT.
THAT'S RIGHT.
"MAYBE."
I WAS ALWAYS CLINGING TO IT.

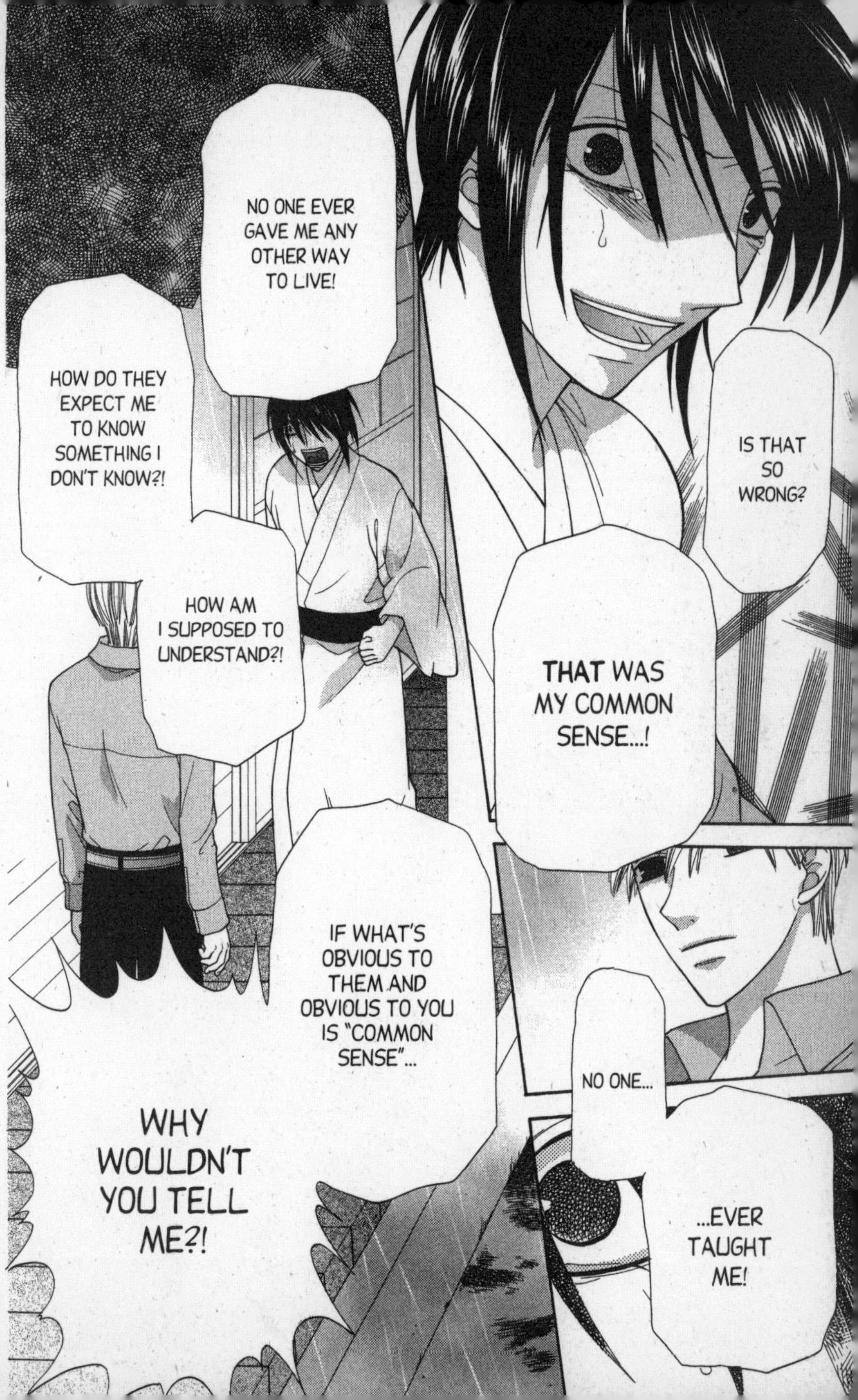
IS THAT SO WRONG?
THAT WAS MY COMMON SENSE...!
NO ONE...
...EVER TAUGHT ME!
NO ONE EVER GAVE ME ANY OTHER WAY TO LIVE!
HOW DO THEY EXPECT ME TO KNOW SOMETHING I DON'T KNOW?!
HOW AM I SUPPOSED TO UNDERSTAND?!
IF WHAT'S OBVIOUS TO THEM AND OBVIOUS TO YOU IS "COMMON SENSE"...
WHY WOULDN'T YOU TELL ME?!

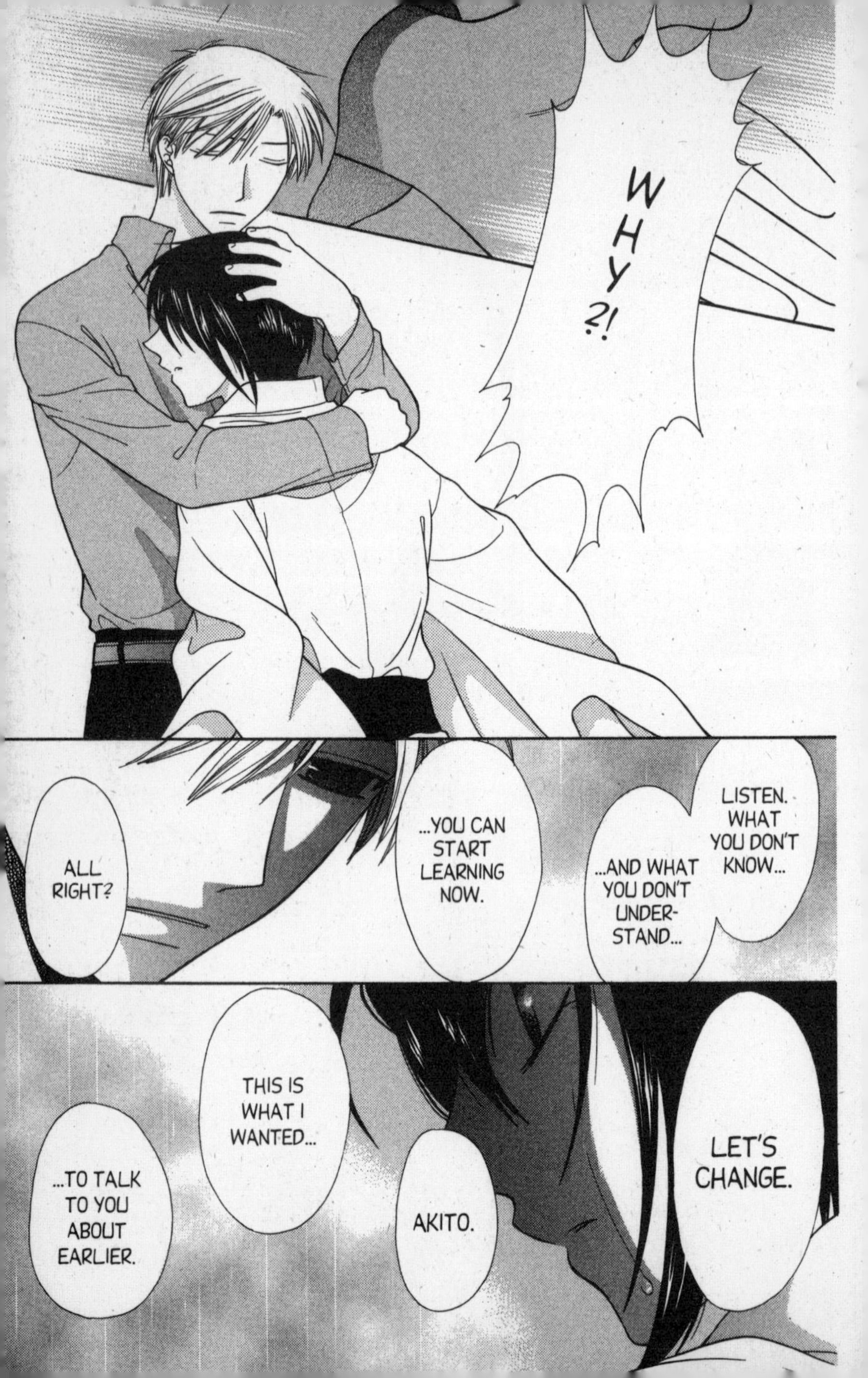
WHY?!
LISTEN. WHAT YOU DON'T KNOW...
...AND WHAT YOU DON'T UNDER-STAND...
...YOU CAN START LEARNING NOW.
ALL RIGHT?
LET'S CHANGE.
AKITO.
THIS IS WHAT I WANTED...
...TO TALK TO YOU ABOUT EARLIER.

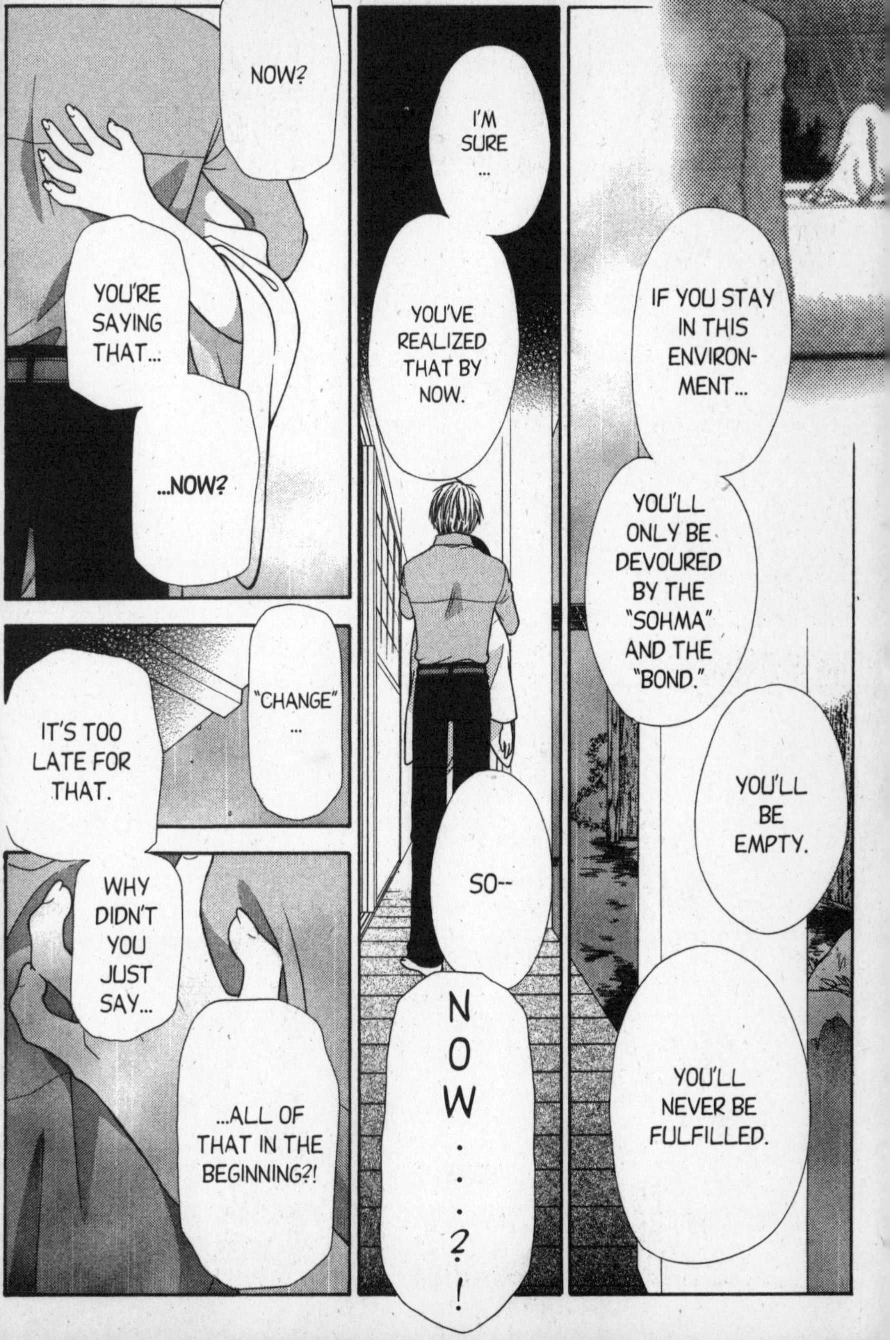
IF YOU STAY IN THIS ENVIRONMENT...
YOU'LL ONLY BE DEVOURED BY THE "SOHMA" AND THE "BOND."
YOU'LL BE EMPTY.
YOU'LL NEVER BE FULFILLED.
I'M SURE ...
YOU'VE REALIZED THAT BY NOW.
SO--
NOW...?!
NOW?
YOU'RE SAYING THAT...
...NOW?
"CHANGE" ...
IT'S TOO LATE FOR THAT.
WHY DIDN'T YOU JUST SAY...
...ALL OF THAT IN THE BEGINNING?!

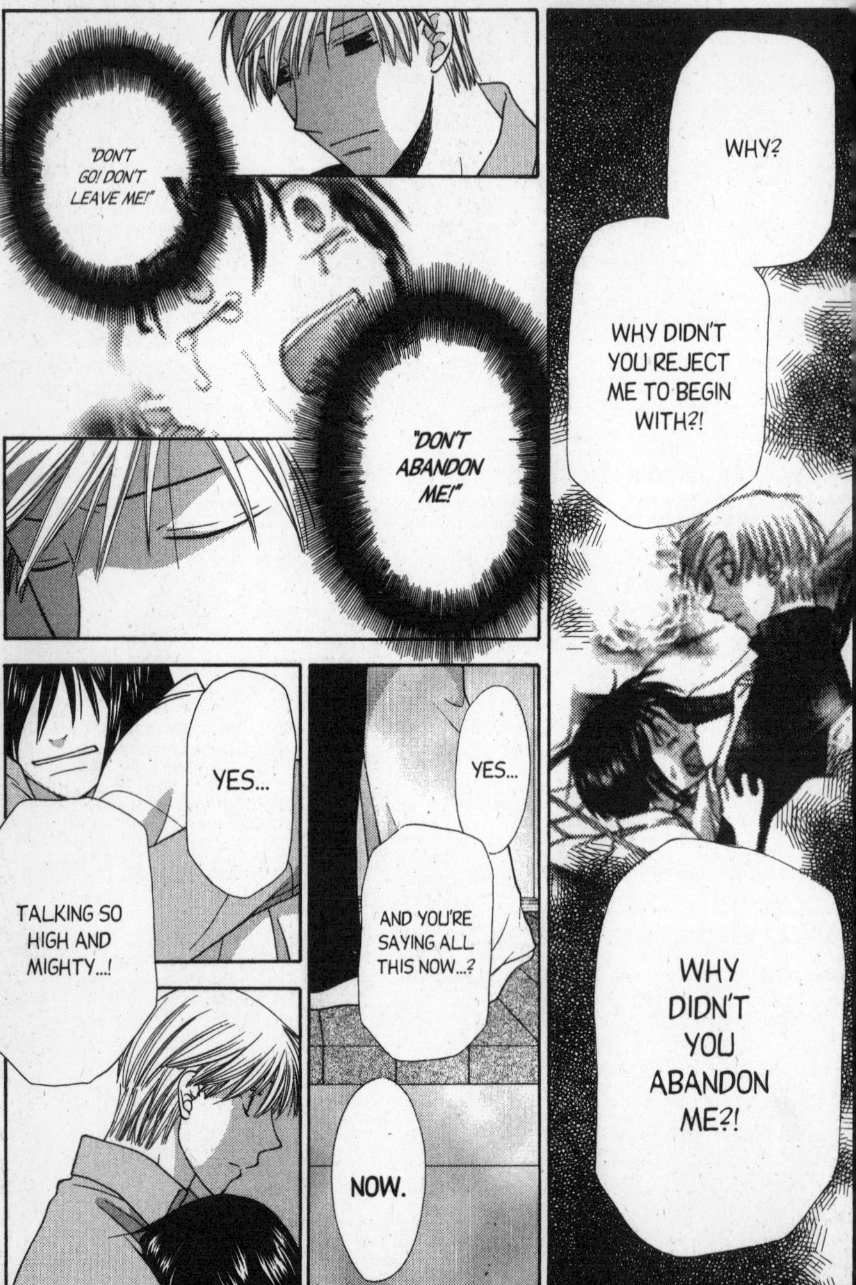
WHY?
WHY DIDN'T YOU REJECT ME TO BEGIN WITH?!
WHY DIDN'T YOU ABANDON ME?!
"DON'T GO! DON'T LEAVE ME!"
"DON'T ABANDON ME!"
YES...
AND YOU'RE SAYING ALL THIS NOW...?
NOW.
YES...
TALKING SO HIGH AND MIGHTY...!

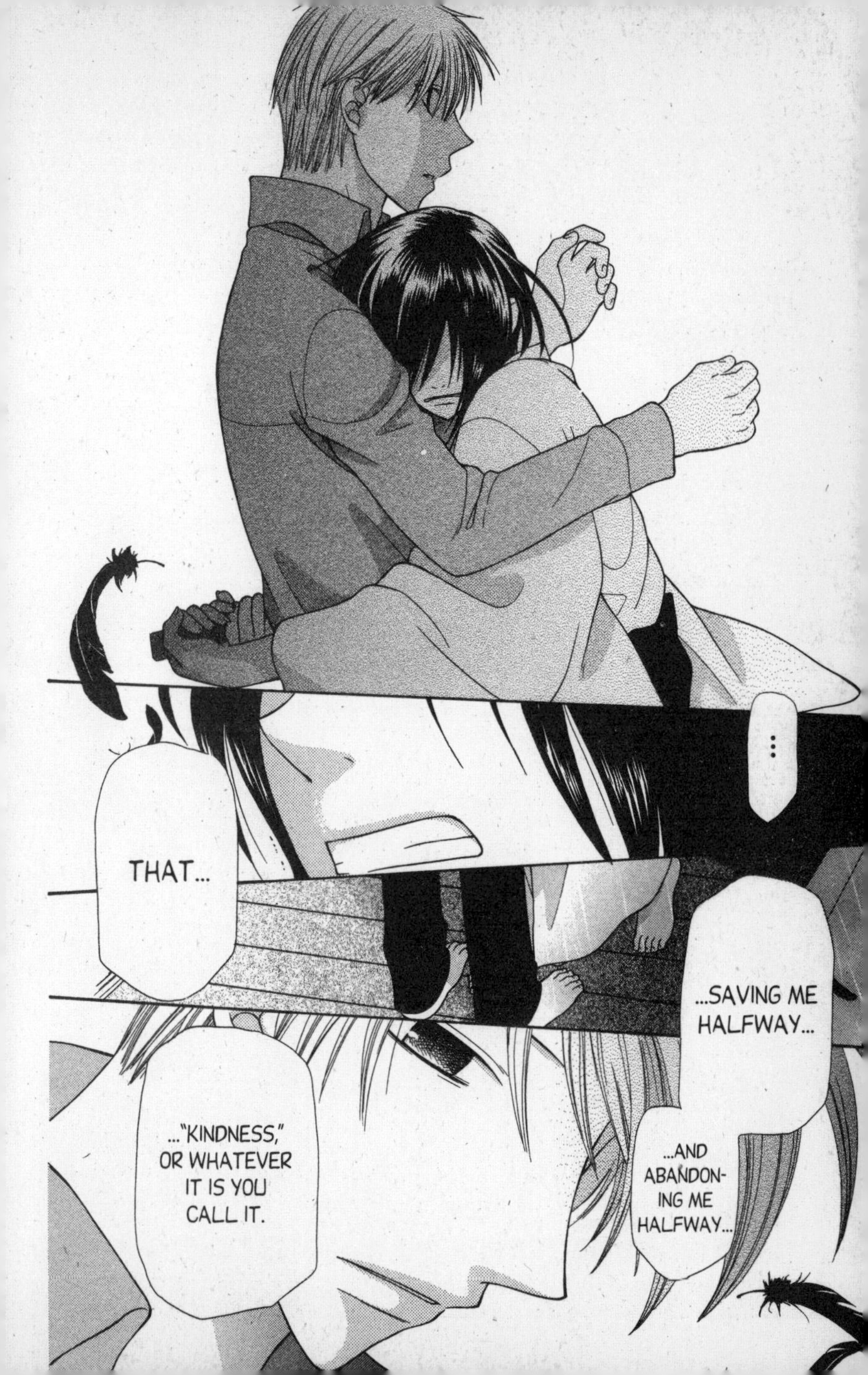
...
THAT...
...SAVING ME HALFWAY...
...AND ABANDONING ME HALFWAY...
..."KINDNESS," OR WHATEVER IT IS YOU CALL IT.

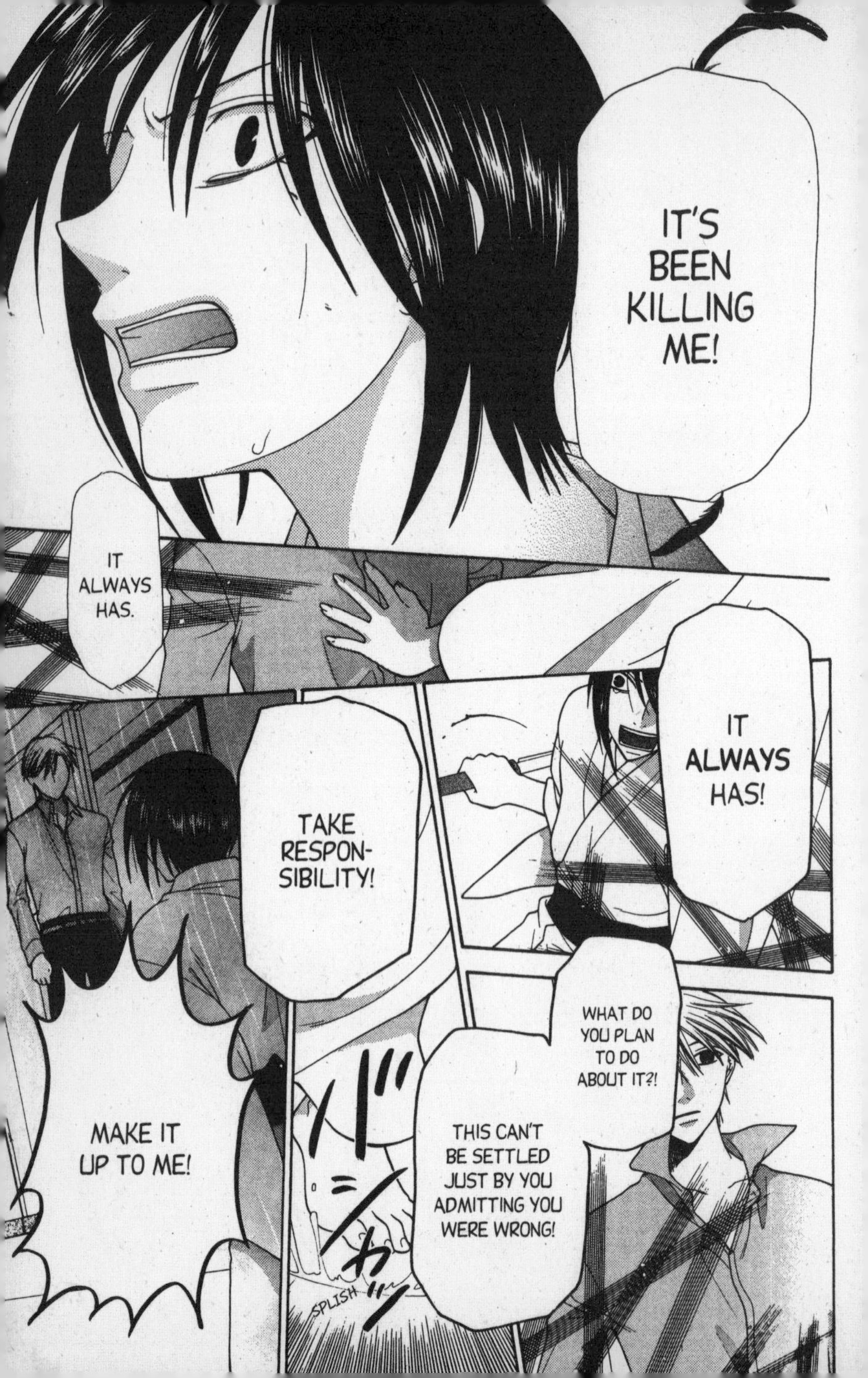
IT'S BEEN KILLING ME!
IT ALWAYS HAS.
IT ALWAYS HAS!
WHAT DO YOU PLAN TO DO ABOUT IT?!
THIS CAN'T BE SETTLED JUST BY YOU ADMITTING YOU WERE WRONG!
SPLISH
TAKE RESPON-SIBILITY!
MAKE IT UP TO ME!

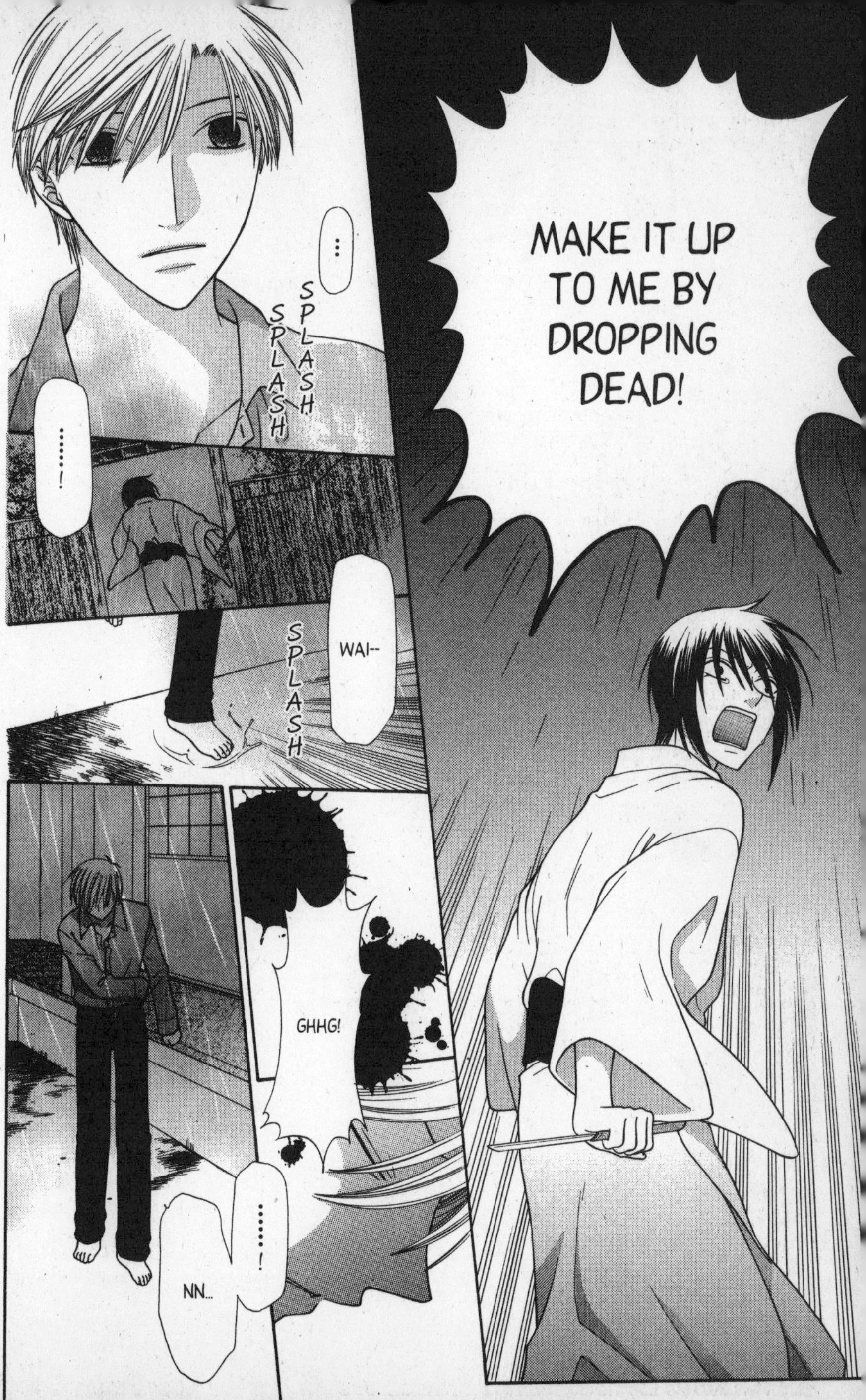
MAKE IT UP TO ME BY DROPPING DEAD!
...
SPLASH SPLASH
......!
SPLASH
WAI--
GHHG!
......!
NN...

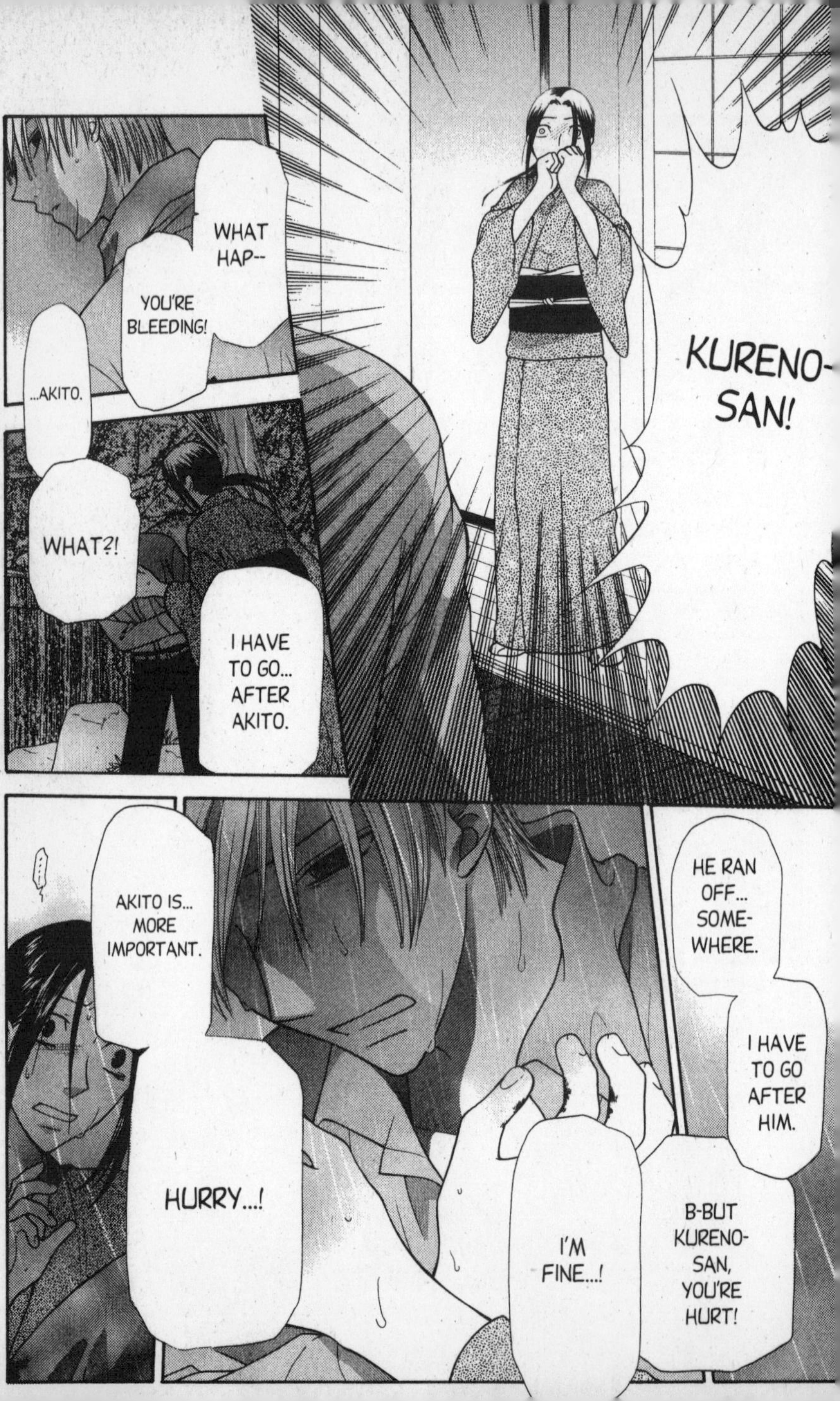
KURENO-SAN!
WHAT HAP--
YOU'RE BLEEDING!
...AKITO.
WHAT?!
I HAVE TO GO... AFTER AKITO.
HE RAN OFF... SOME-WHERE.
I HAVE TO GO AFTER HIM.
B-BUT KURENO-SAN, YOU'RE HURT!
I'M FINE...!
AKITO IS... MORE IMPORTANT.
HURRY...!

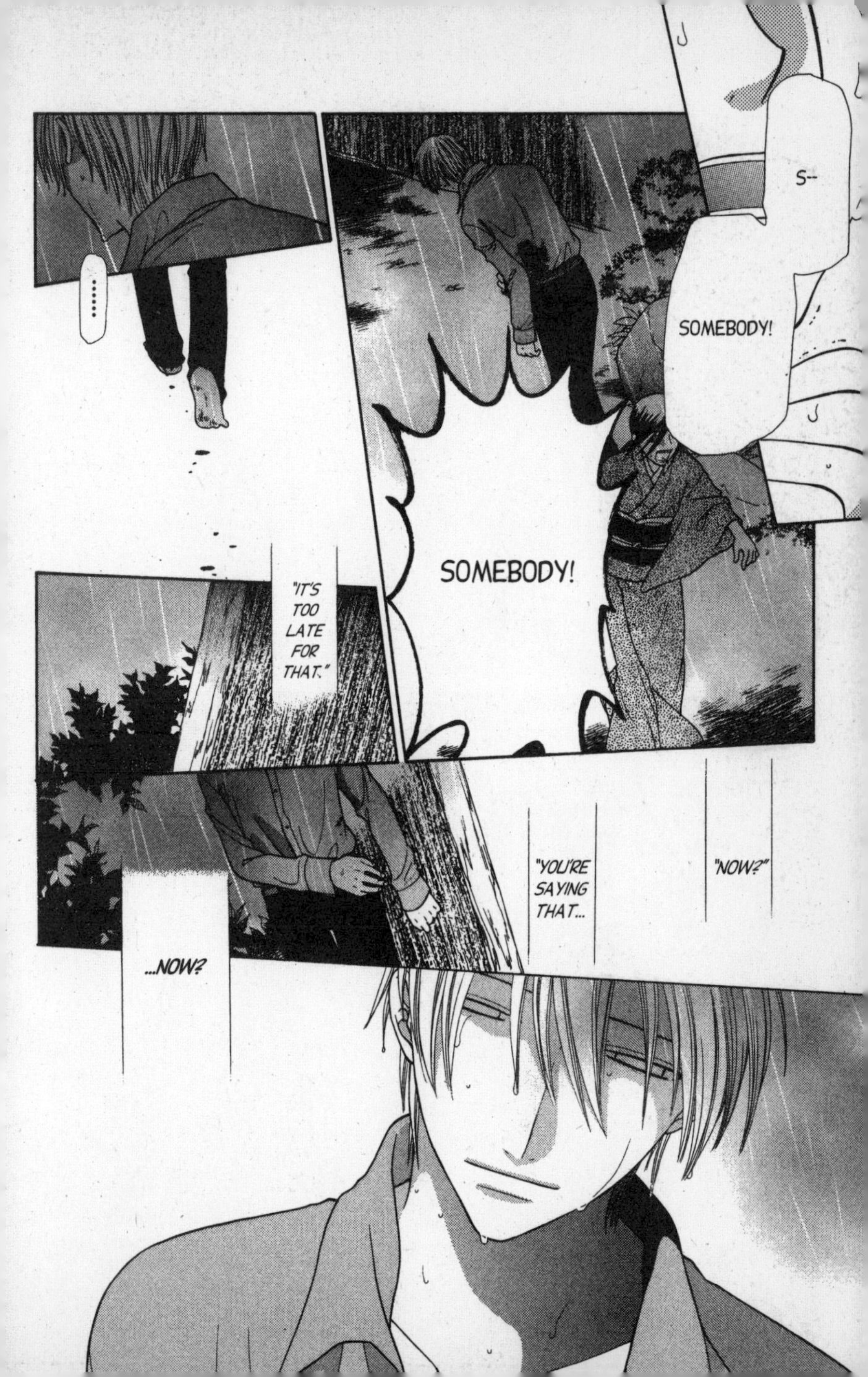
S--
SOMEBODY!
SOMEBODY!
......
"IT'S TOO LATE FOR THAT."
"YOU'RE SAYING THAT...
"NOW?"
...NOW?

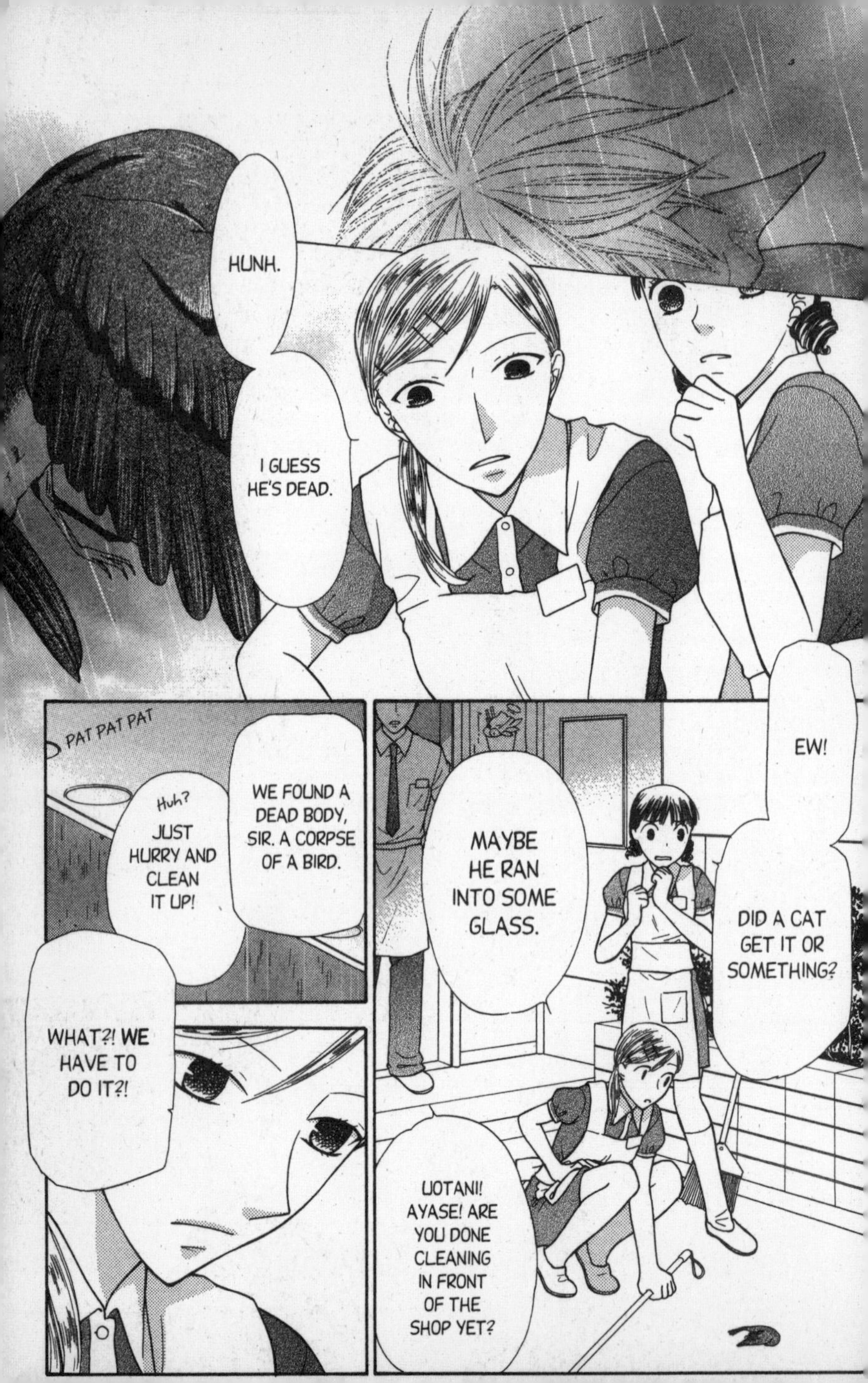
HUNH.
I GUESS HE'S DEAD.
EW!
DID A CAT GET IT OR SOMETHING?
MAYBE HE RAN INTO SOME GLASS.
UOTANI! AYASE! ARE YOU DONE CLEANING IN FRONT OF THE SHOP YET?
PAT PAT PAT
WE FOUND A DEAD BODY, SIR. A CORPSE OF A BIRD.
Huh?
JUST HURRY AND CLEAN IT UP!
WHAT?! WE HAVE TO DO IT?!

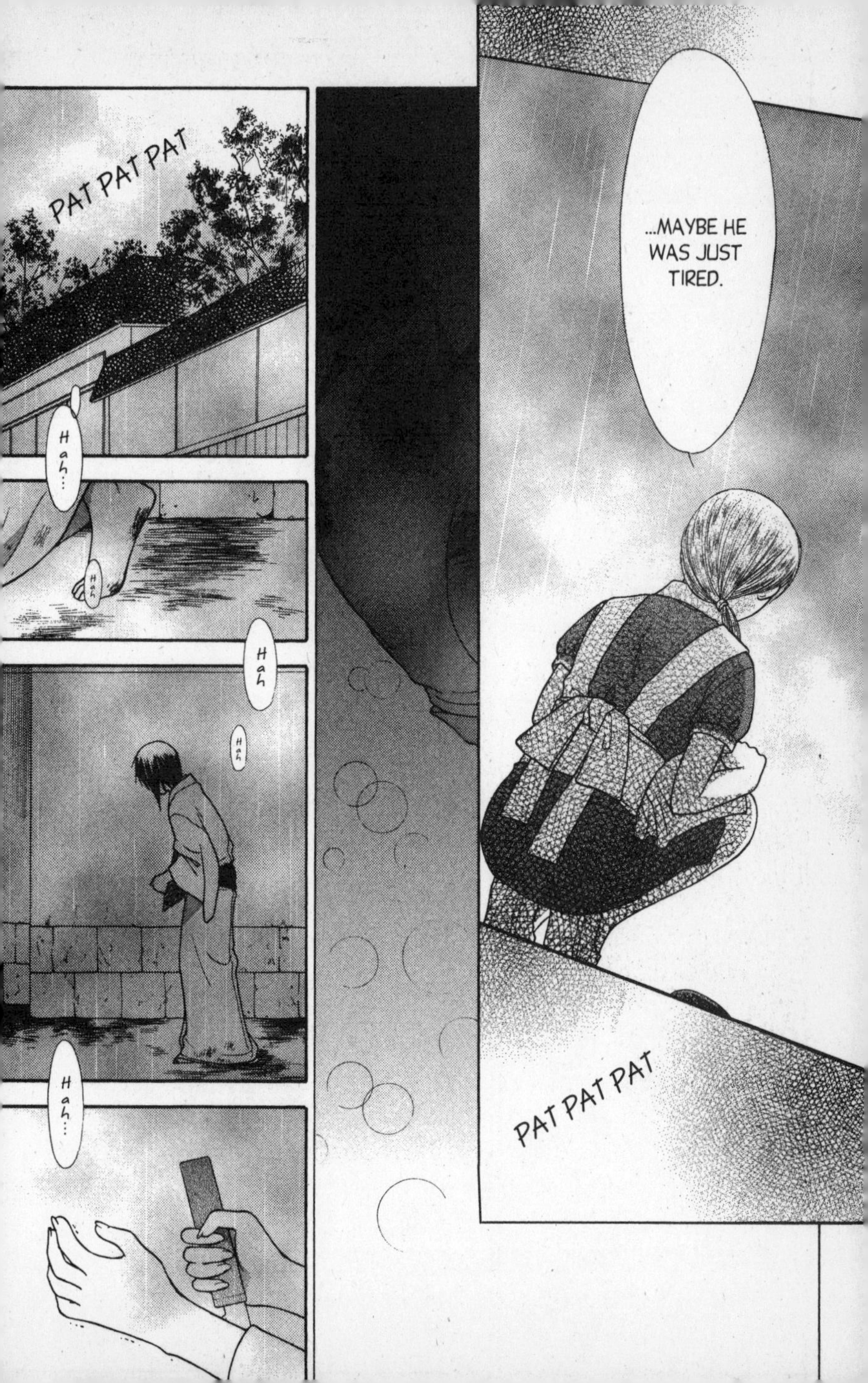
...MAYBE HE WAS JUST TIRED.
PAT PAT PAT
PAT PAT PAT
Hah...
Hah
Hah
Hah
Hah...

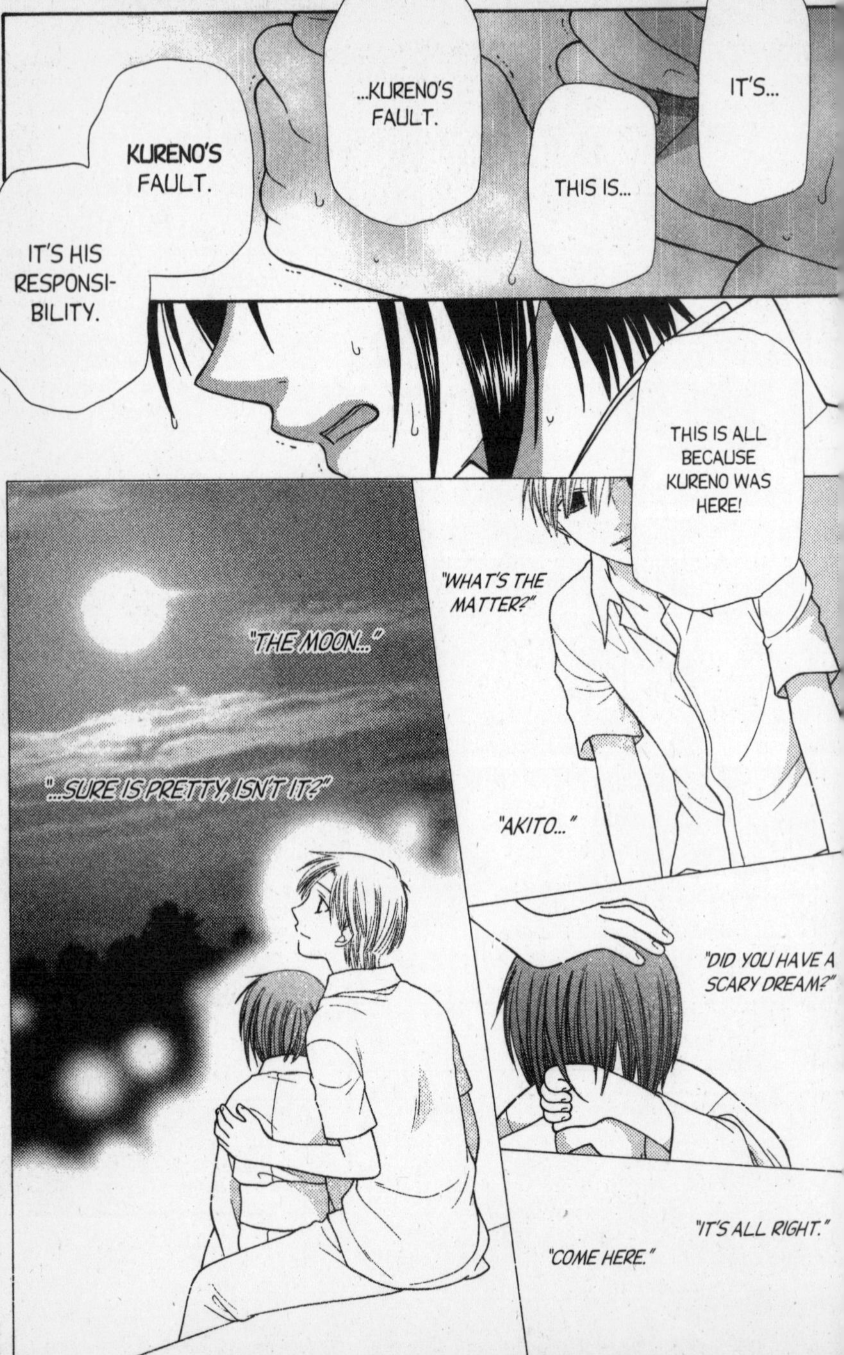
IT'S...
THIS IS...
...KURENO'S FAULT.
KURENO'S FAULT.
IT'S HIS RESPONSIBILITY.
THIS IS ALL BECAUSE KURENO WAS HERE!
"WHAT'S THE MATTER?"
"AKITO..."
"DID YOU HAVE A SCARY DREAM?"
"IT'S ALL RIGHT."
"COME HERE."
"THE MOON..."
"...SURE IS PRETTY, ISN'T IT?"

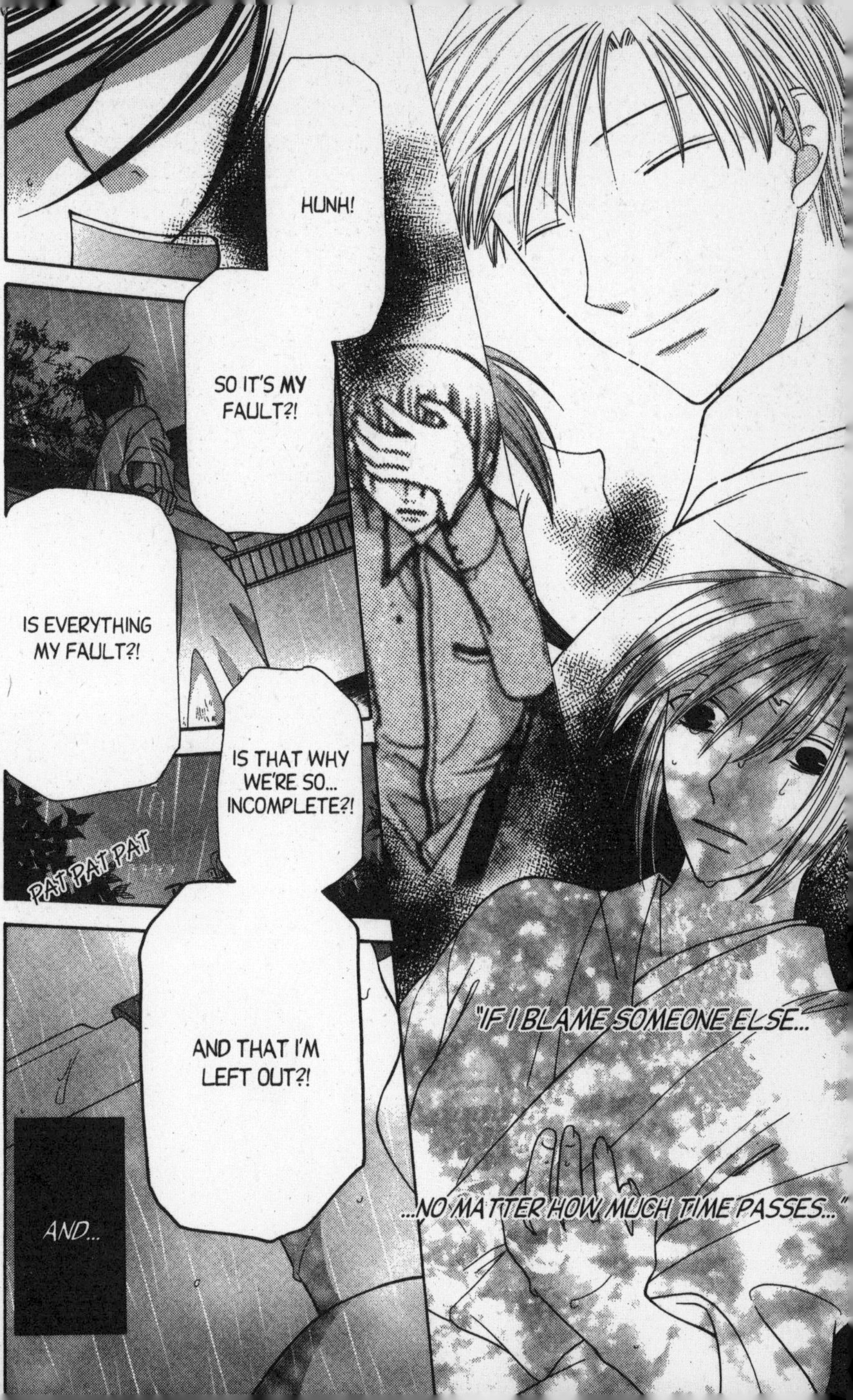
HUNH!
SO IT'S MY FAULT?!
IS EVERYTHING MY FAULT?!
IS THAT WHY WE'RE SO... INCOMPLETE?!
PAT PAT PAT
AND THAT I'M LEFT OUT?!
AND...
"IF I BLAME SOMEONE ELSE...
...NO MATTER HOW MUCH TIME PASSES..."

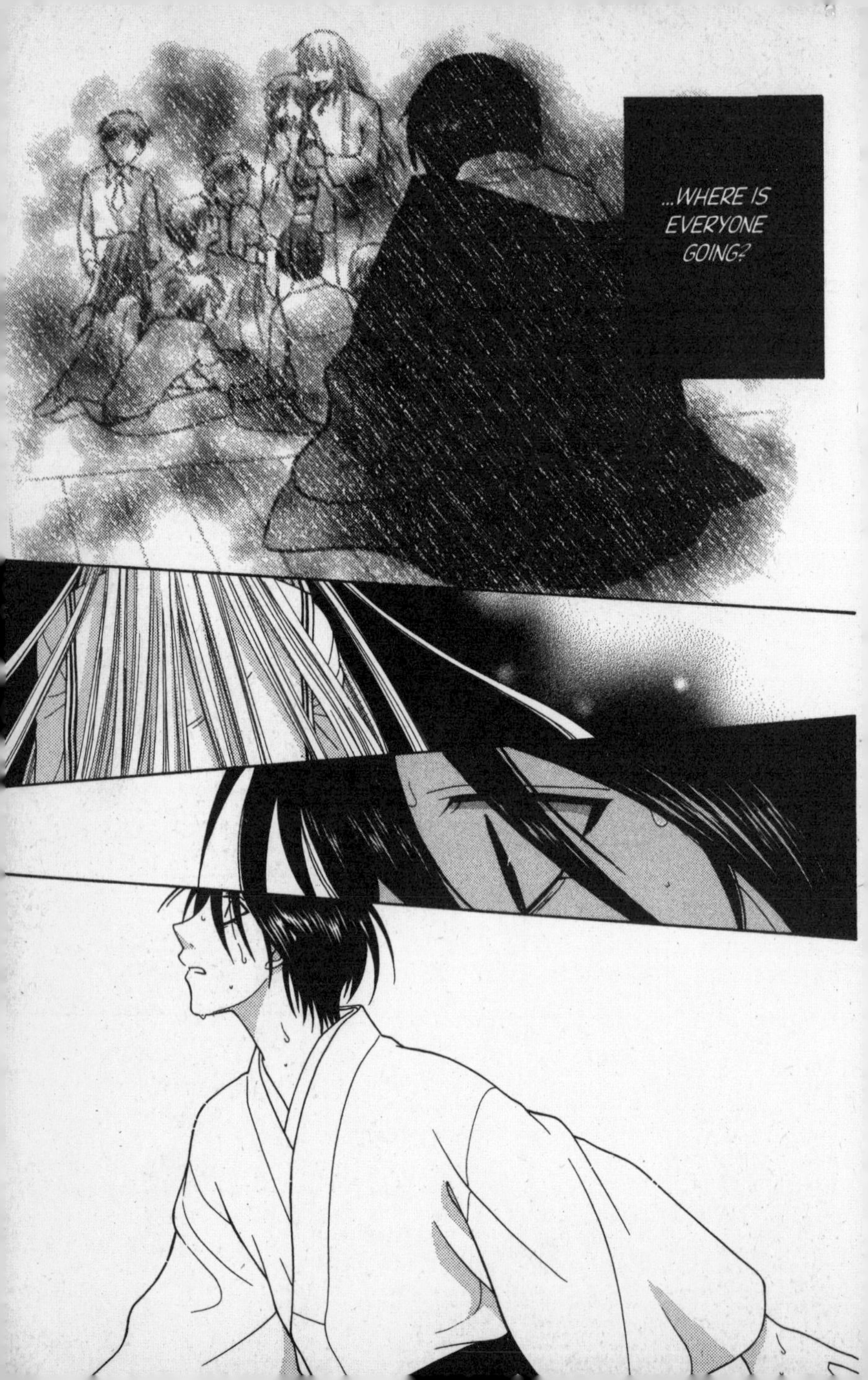
...WHERE IS EVERYONE GOING?

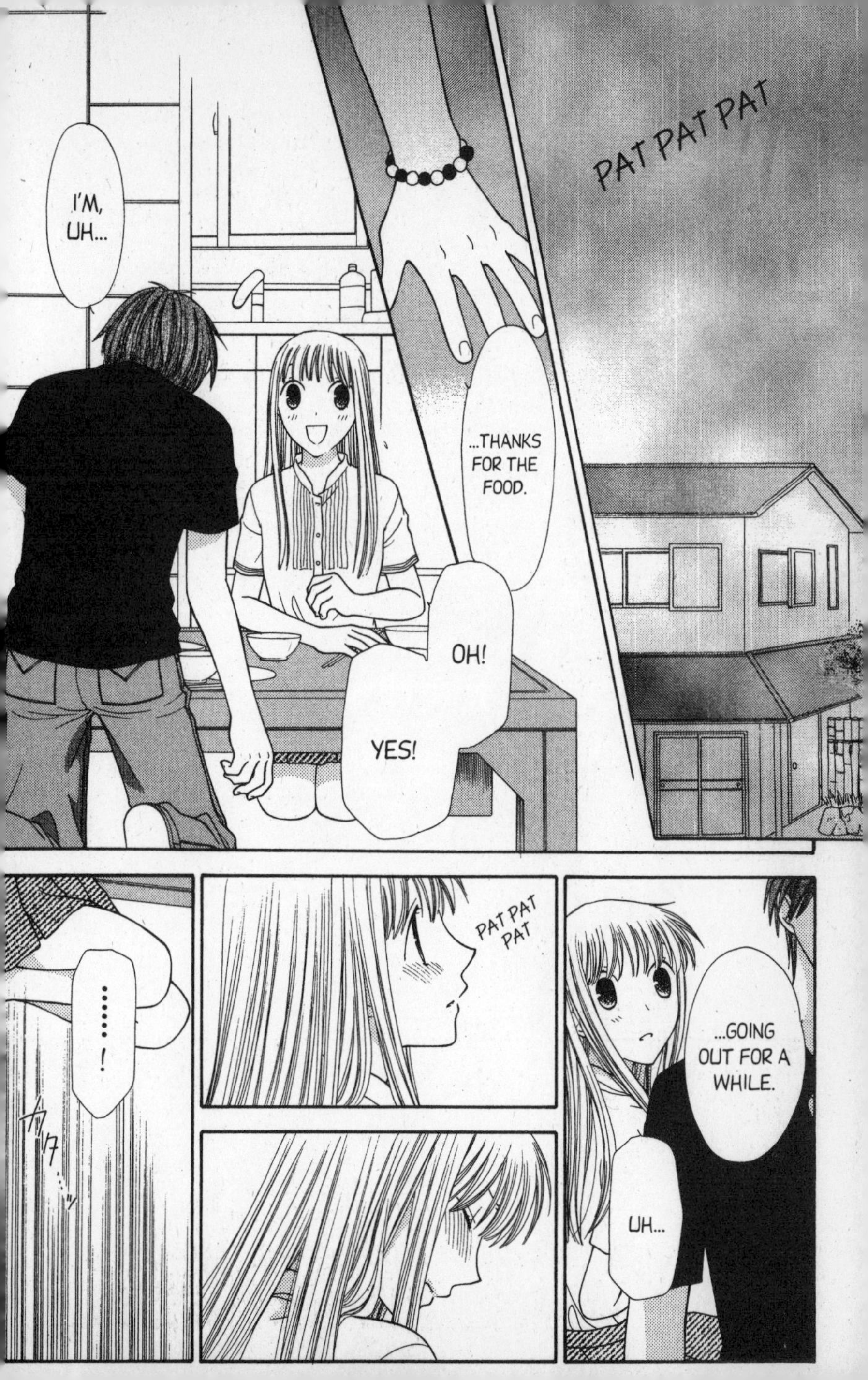
PAT PAT PAT
...THANKS FOR THE FOOD.
OH!
YES!
I'M, UH...
...GOING OUT FOR A WHILE.
UH...
PAT PAT PAT
......!

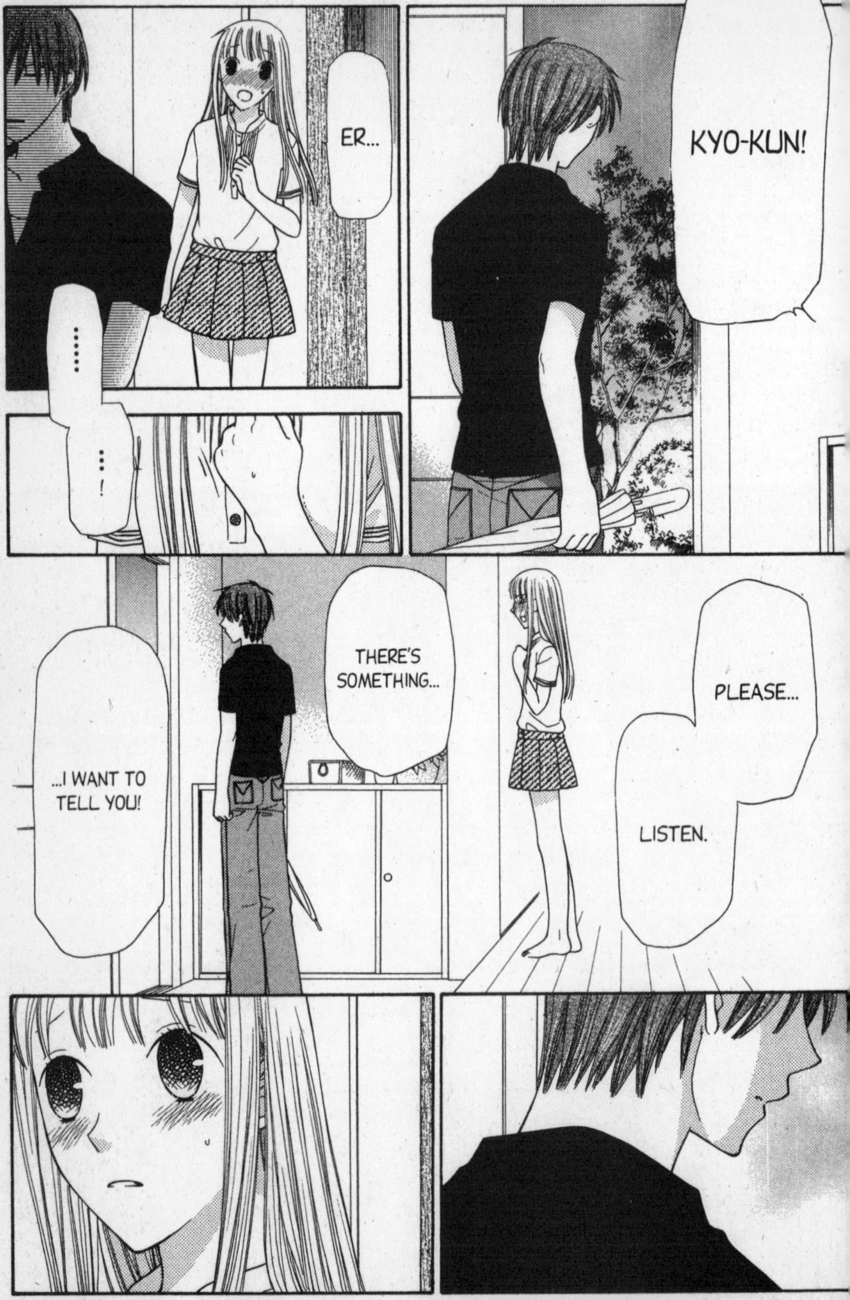
KYO-KUN!
ER...
......
...!
PLEASE...
LISTEN.
THERE'S SOMETHING...
...I WANT TO TELL YOU!

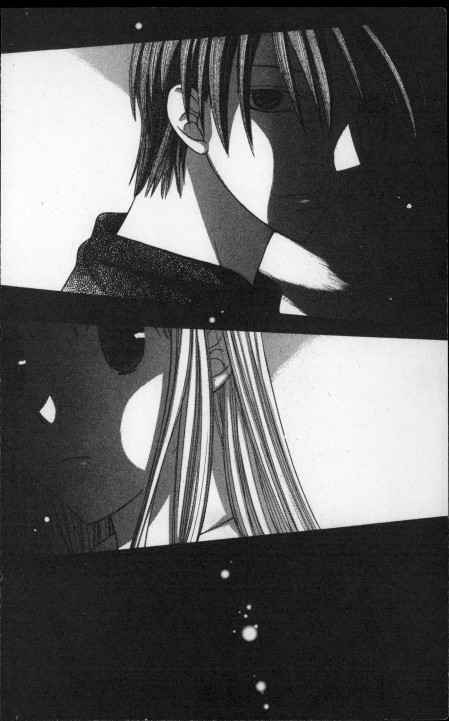

Chapter 119

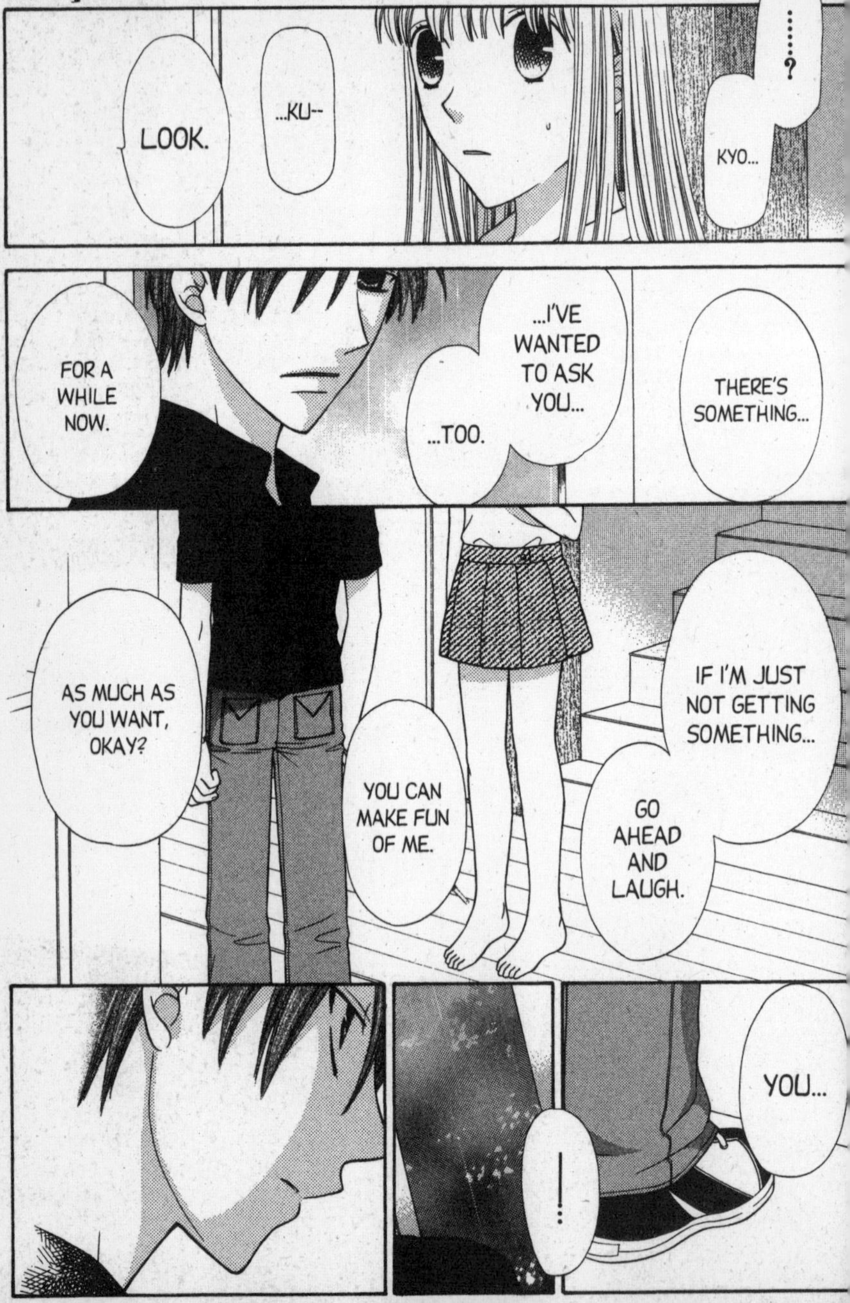
......?
KYO...
...KU--
LOOK.
THERE'S SOMETHING...
...I'VE WANTED TO ASK YOU...
...TOO.
FOR A WHILE NOW.
IF I'M JUST NOT GETTING SOMETHING...
GO AHEAD AND LAUGH.
YOU CAN MAKE FUN OF ME.
AS MUCH AS YOU WANT, OKAY?
YOU...
......!

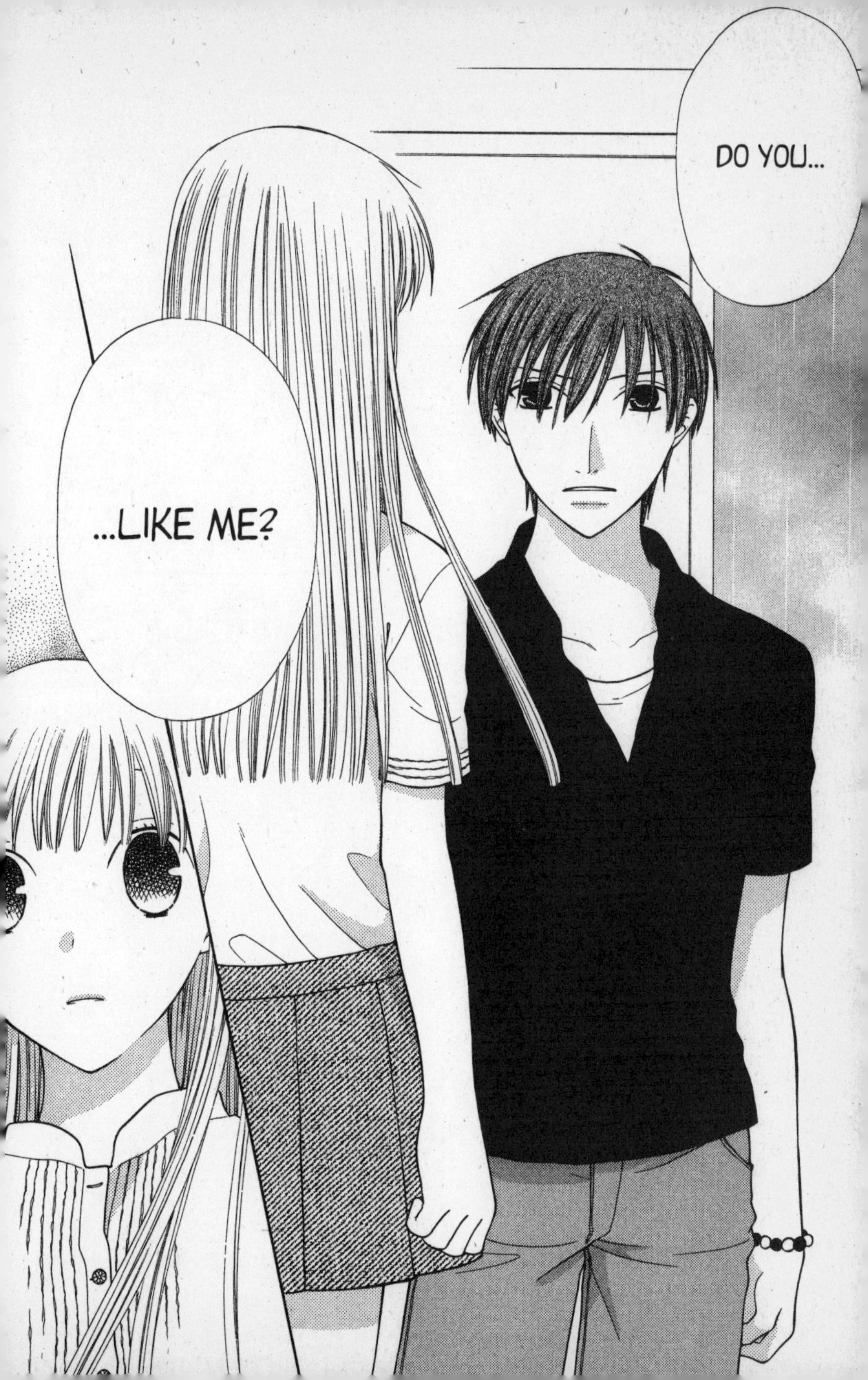
DO YOU...
...LIKE ME?

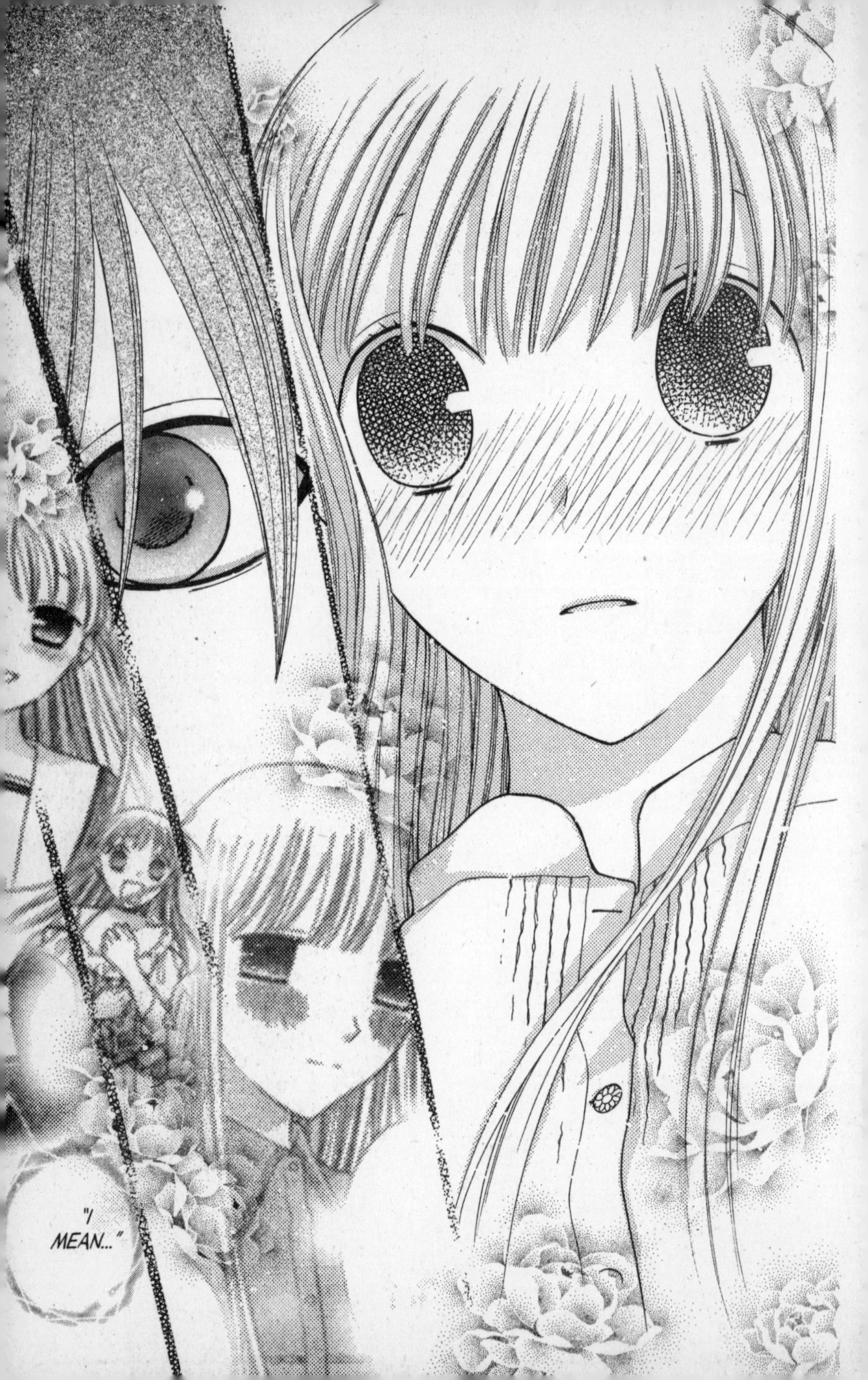
"I MEAN..."

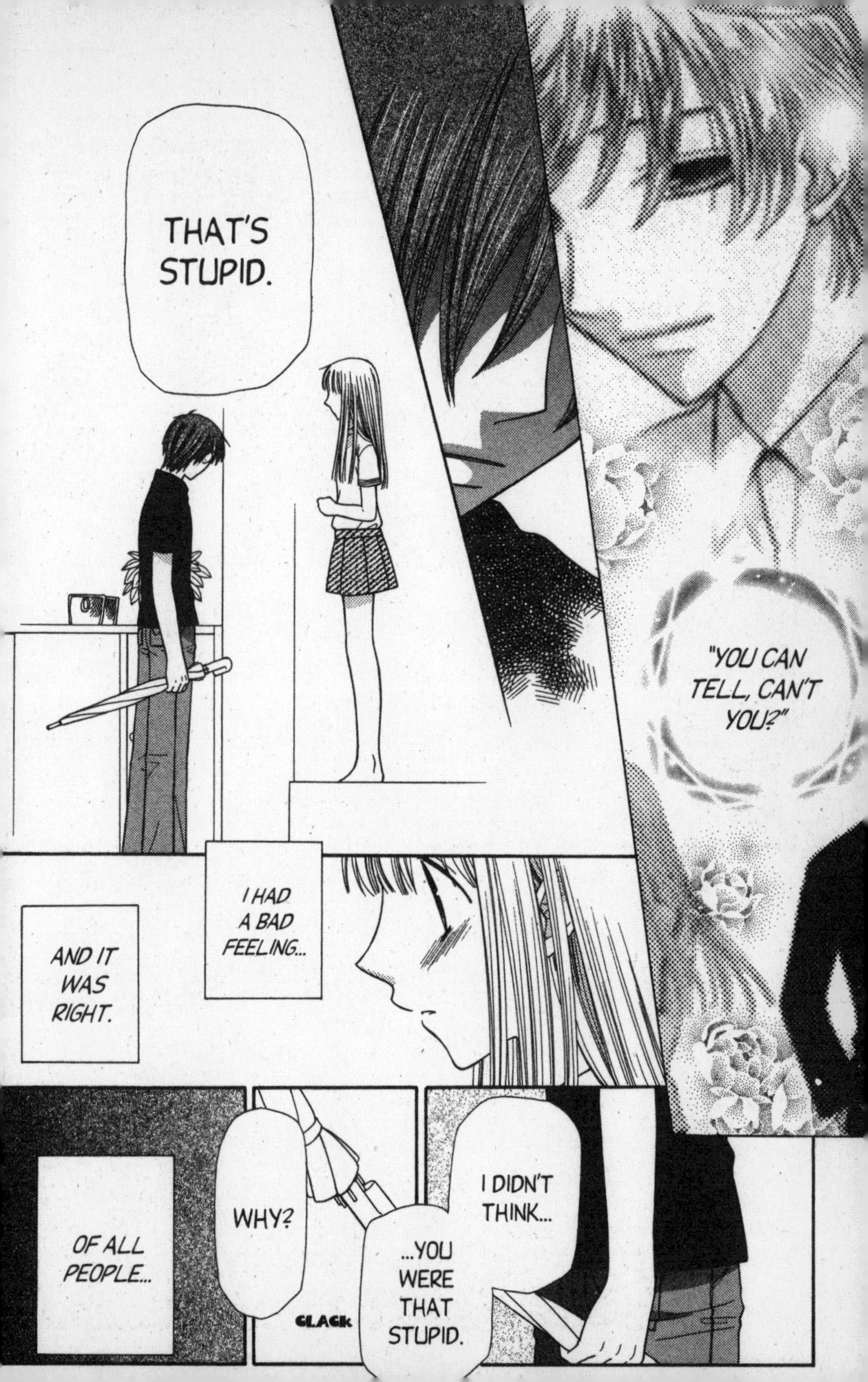
"YOU CAN TELL, CAN'T YOU?"
THAT'S STUPID.
I HAD A BAD FEELING...
AND IT WAS RIGHT.
I DIDN'T THINK...
...YOU WERE THAT STUPID.
WHY?
CLACK
OF ALL PEOPLE...

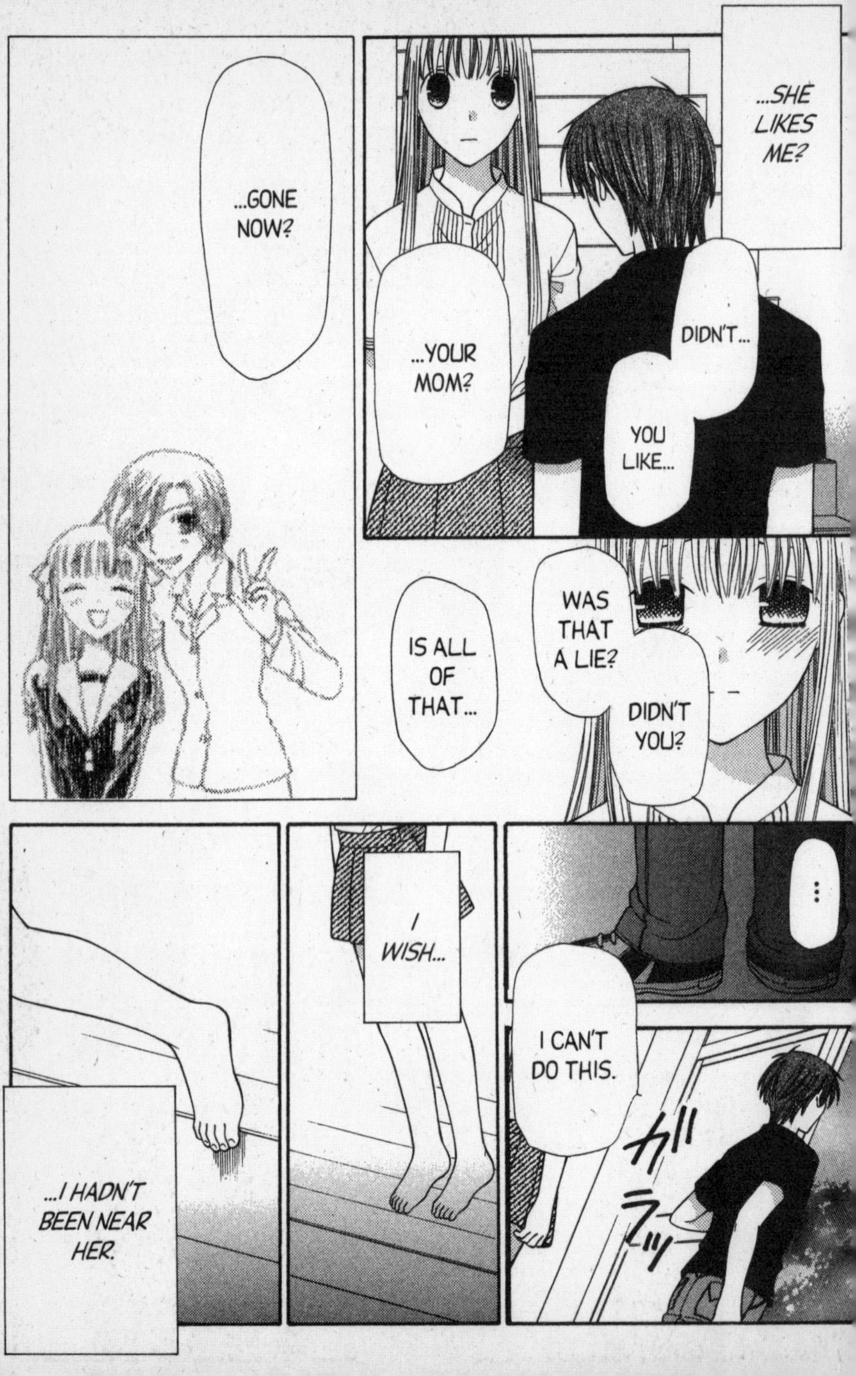
...SHE LIKES ME?
DIDN'T...
YOU LIKE...
...YOUR MOM?
WAS THAT A LIE?
DIDN'T YOU?
IS ALL OF THAT...
...GONE NOW?
...
I CAN'T DO THIS.
ガラッ
I WISH...
...I HADN'T BEEN NEAR HER.

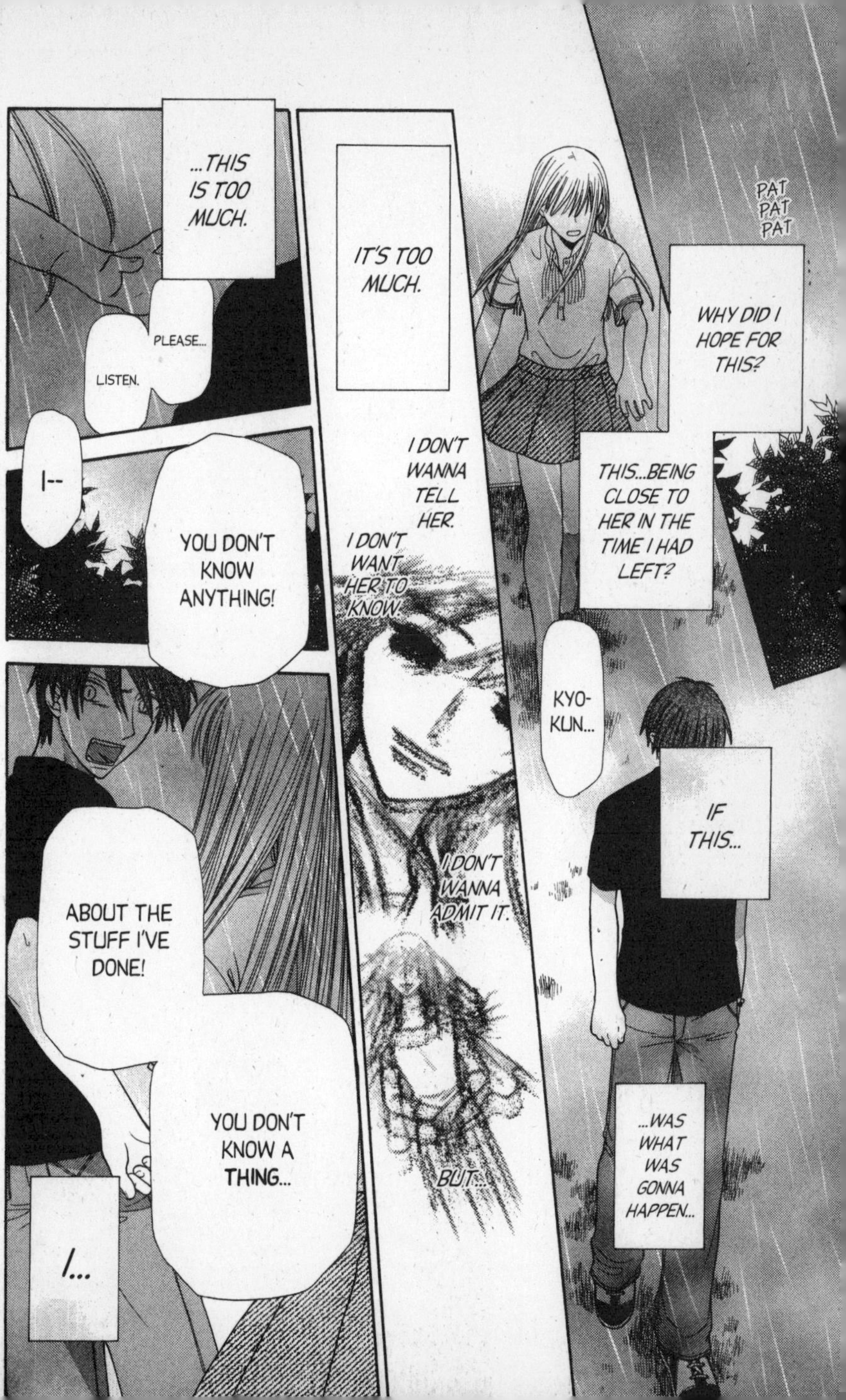
PAT PAT PAT
WHY DID I HOPE FOR THIS?
THIS...BEING CLOSE TO HER IN THE TIME I HAD LEFT?
KYO-KUN...
IF THIS...
...WAS WHAT WAS GONNA HAPPEN...
IT'S TOO MUCH.
I DON'T WANNA TELL HER.
I DON'T WANT HER TO KNOW.
I DON'T WANNA ADMIT IT.
BUT...
...THIS IS TOO MUCH.
PLEASE...
LISTEN.
I--
YOU DON'T KNOW ANYTHING!
ABOUT THE STUFF I'VE DONE!
YOU DON'T KNOW A THING...
I...

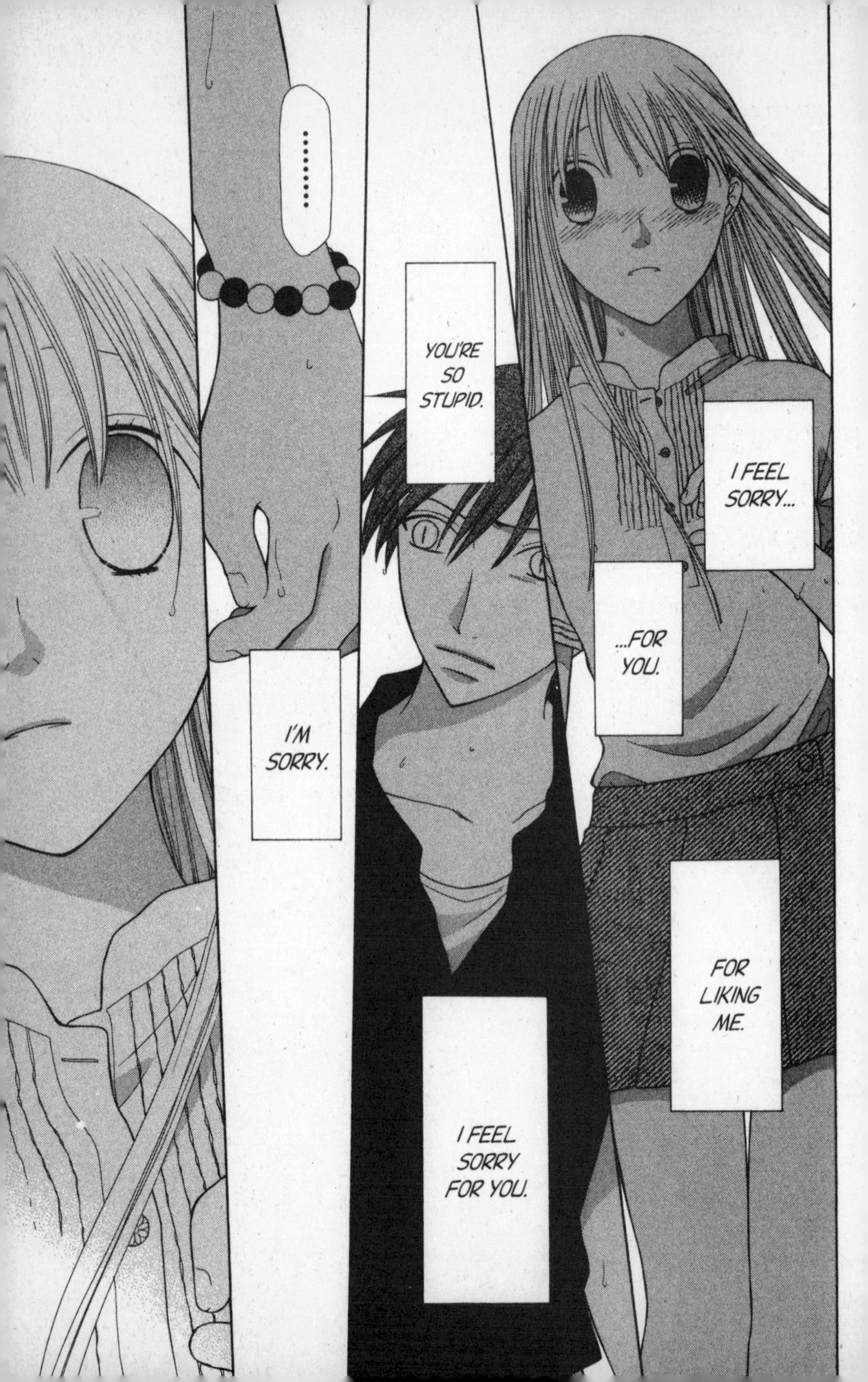
I FEEL SORRY...
...FOR YOU.
FOR LIKING ME.
YOU'RE SO STUPID.
I FEEL SORRY FOR YOU.
......
I'M SORRY.

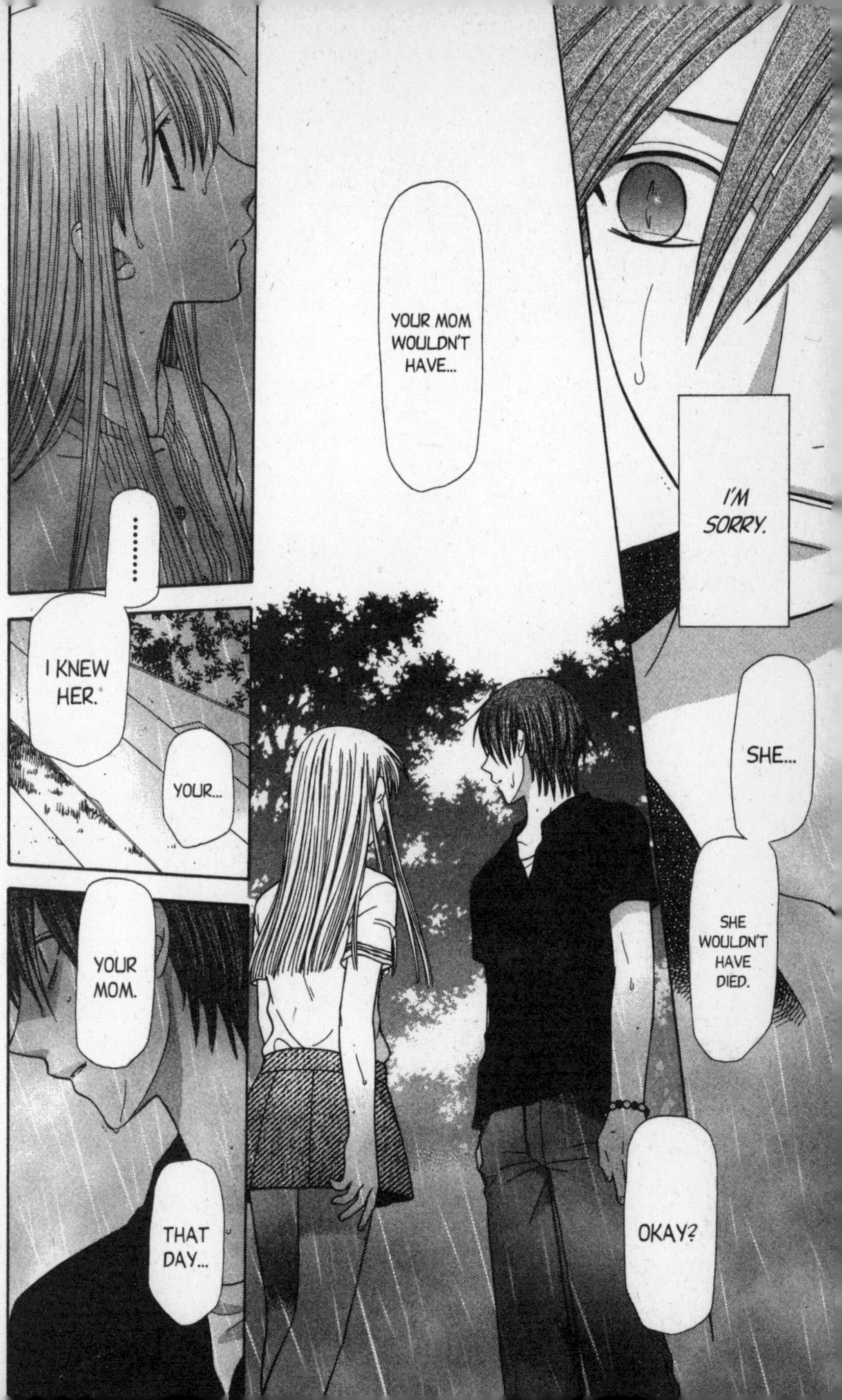
......
I KNEW HER.
YOUR...
YOUR MOM.
THAT DAY...
YOUR MOM WOULDN'T HAVE...
SHE...
SHE WOULDN'T HAVE DIED.
OKAY?
I'M SORRY.

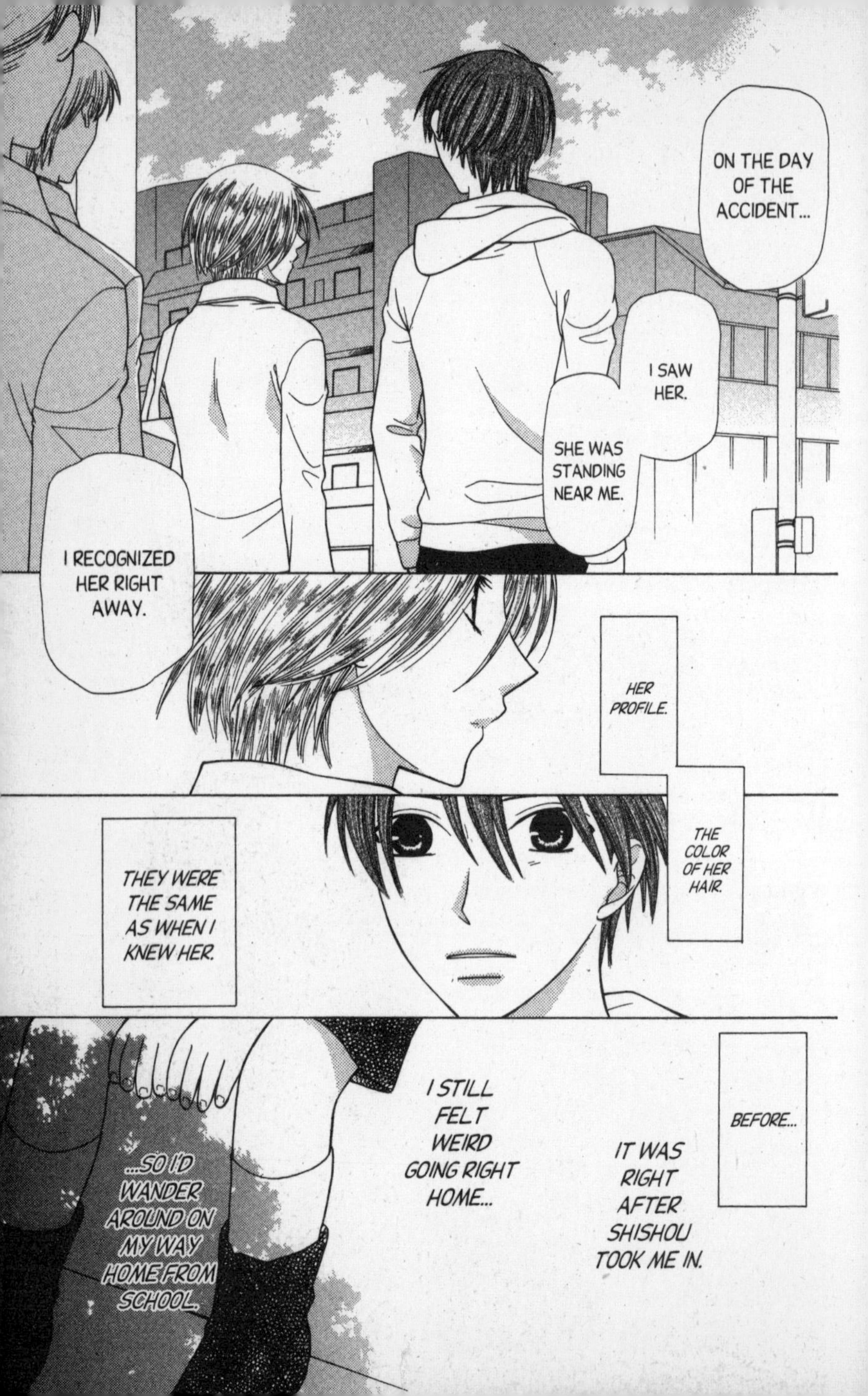
ON THE DAY OF THE ACCIDENT...
I SAW HER.
SHE WAS STANDING NEAR ME.
I RECOGNIZED HER RIGHT AWAY.
HER PROFILE.
THE COLOR OF HER HAIR.
THEY WERE THE SAME AS WHEN I KNEW HER.
BEFORE...
IT WAS RIGHT AFTER SHISHOU TOOK ME IN.
I STILL FELT WEIRD GOING RIGHT HOME...
...SO I'D WANDER AROUND ON MY WAY HOME FROM SCHOOL.

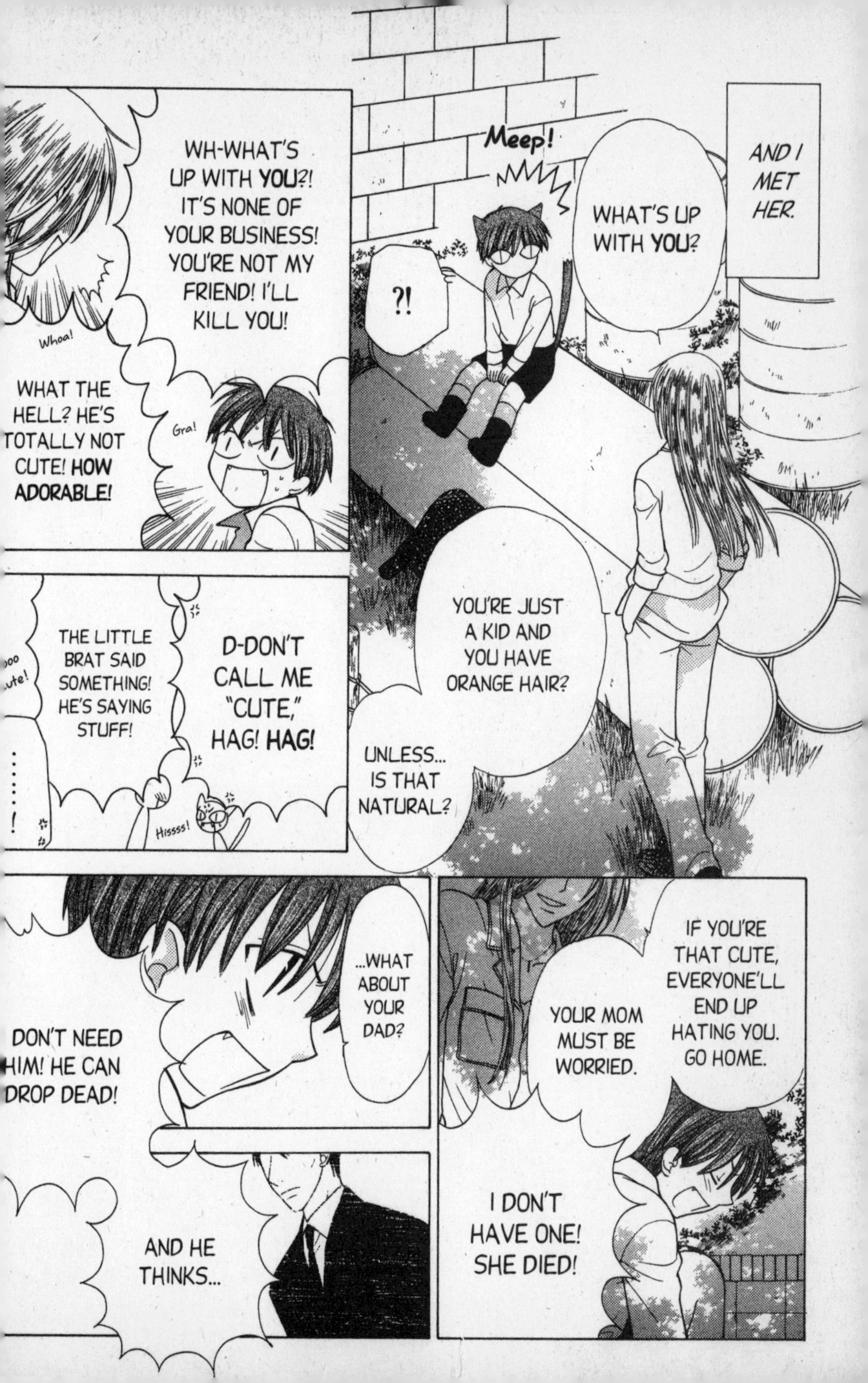
AND I MET HER.
Meep!
WHAT'S UP WITH YOU?
?!
YOU'RE JUST A KID AND YOU HAVE ORANGE HAIR?
UNLESS... IS THAT NATURAL?
WH-WHAT'S UP WITH YOU?! IT'S NONE OF YOUR BUSINESS! YOU'RE NOT MY FRIEND! I'LL KILL YOU!
Whoa!
WHAT THE HELL? HE'S TOTALLY NOT CUTE! HOW ADORABLE!
Gra!
D-DON'T CALL ME "CUTE," HAG! HAG!
THE LITTLE BRAT SAID SOMETHING! HE'S SAYING STUFF!
Hissss!
......!
IF YOU'RE THAT CUTE, EVERYONE'LL END UP HATING YOU. GO HOME.
YOUR MOM MUST BE WORRIED.
I DON'T HAVE ONE! SHE DIED!
...WHAT ABOUT YOUR DAD?
DON'T NEED HIM! HE CAN DROP DEAD!
AND HE THINKS...

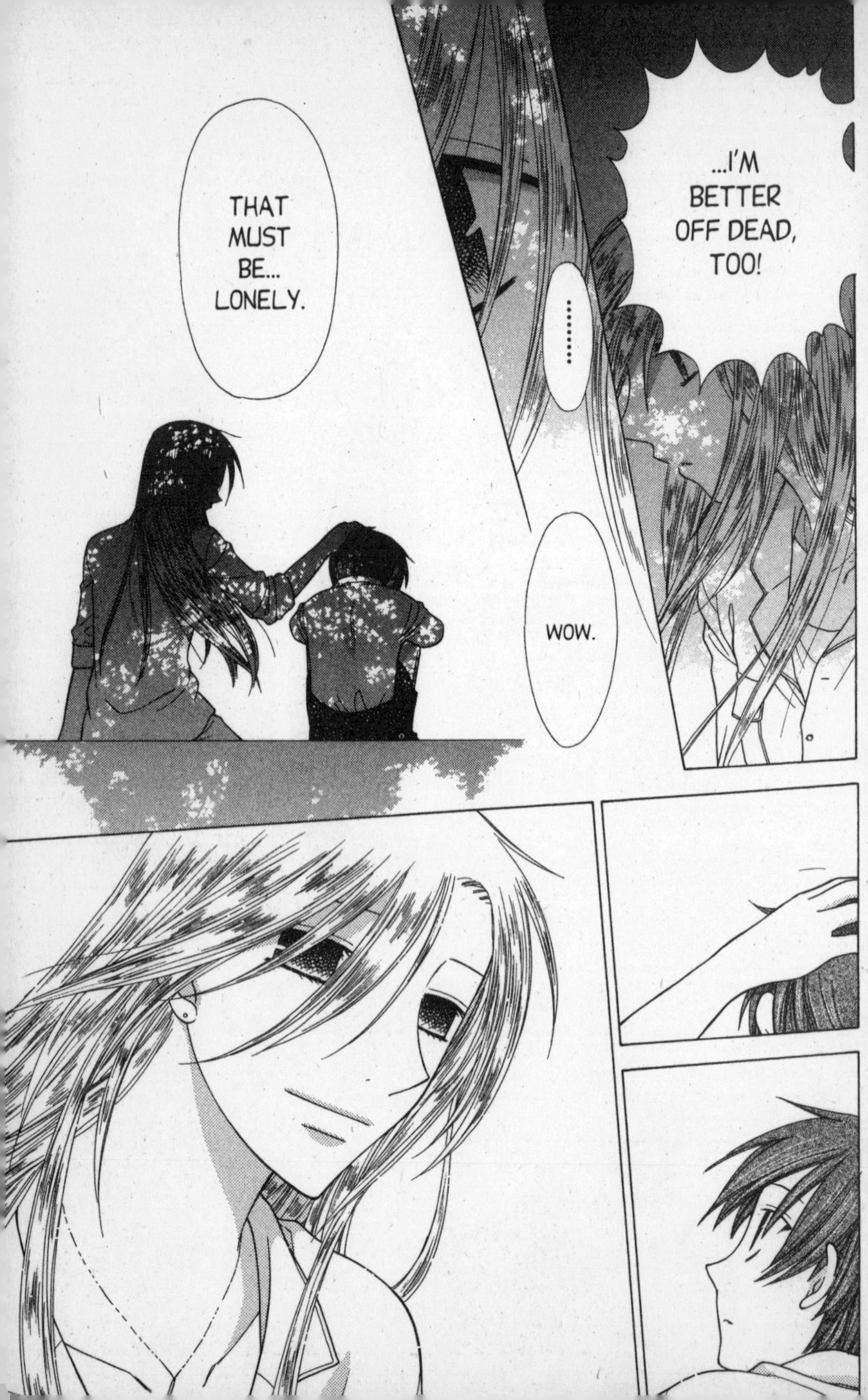
...I'M BETTER OFF DEAD, TOO!
......
WOW.
THAT MUST BE... LONELY.

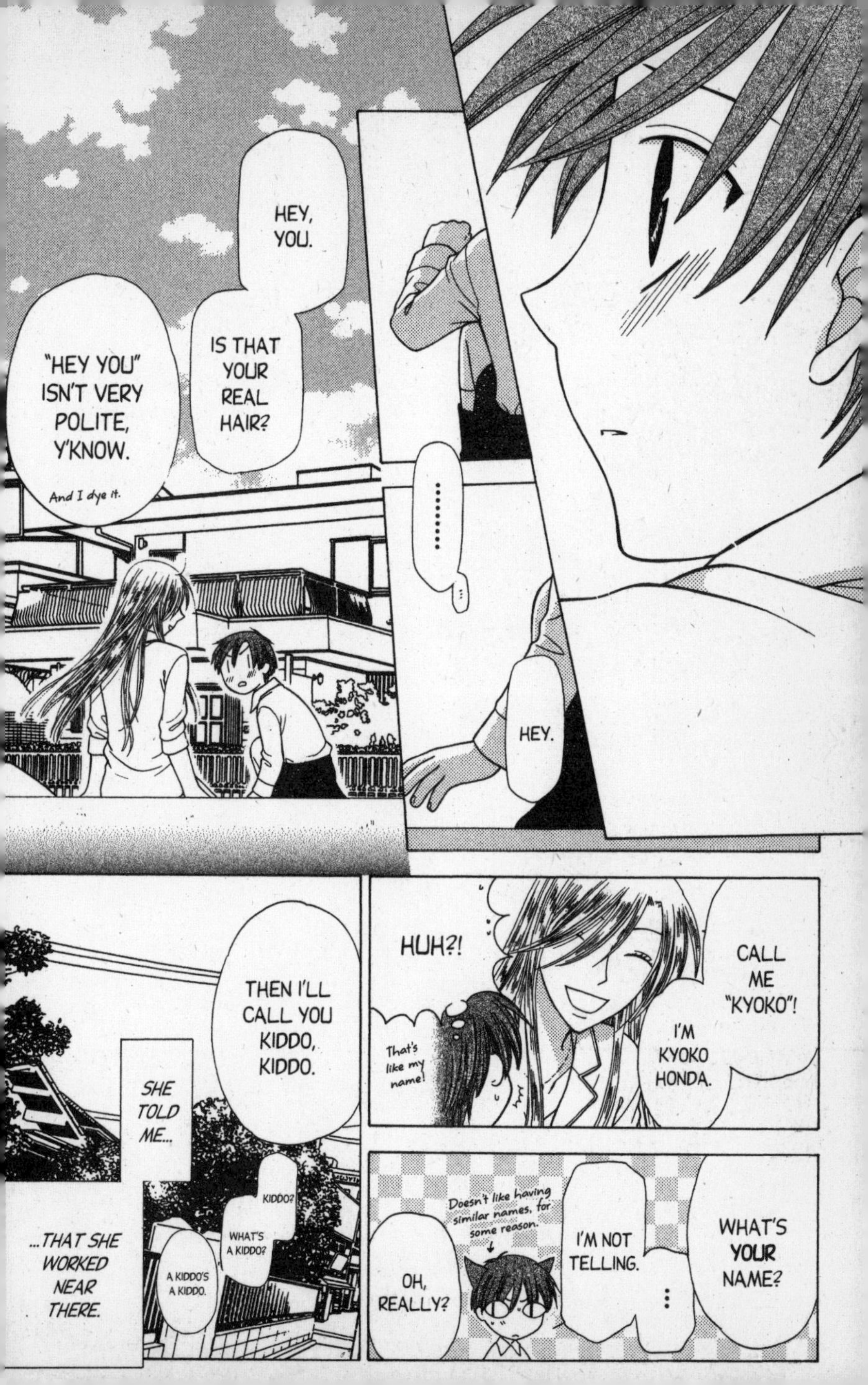

......
...
HEY.
HEY, YOU.
IS THAT YOUR REAL HAIR?
"HEY YOU" ISN'T VERY POLITE, Y'KNOW.
And I dye it.
CALL ME "KYOKO"!
I'M KYOKO HONDA.
HUH?!
That's like my name!
WHAT'S YOUR NAME?
...
I'M NOT TELLING.
Doesn't like having similar names, for some reason.
OH, REALLY?
THEN I'LL CALL YOU KIDDO, KIDDO.
SHE TOLD ME...
KIDDO?
WHAT'S A KIDDO?
A KIDDO'S A KIDDO.
...THAT SHE WORKED NEAR THERE.

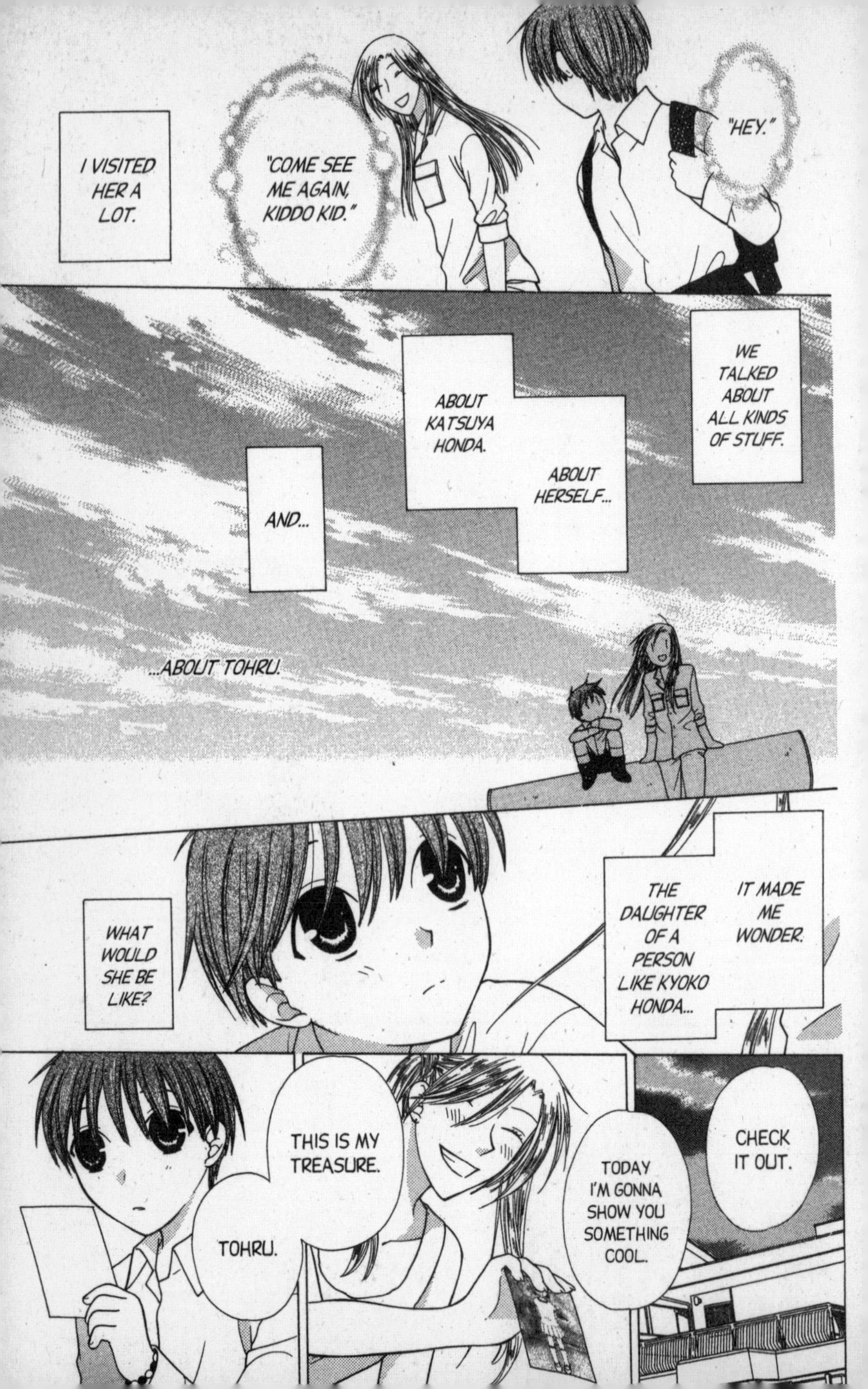
"HEY."
"COME SEE ME AGAIN, KIDDO KID."
I VISITED HER A LOT.
WE TALKED ABOUT ALL KINDS OF STUFF.
ABOUT KATSUYA HONDA.
ABOUT HERSELF...
AND...
...ABOUT TOHRU.
IT MADE ME WONDER.
THE DAUGHTER OF A PERSON LIKE KYOKO HONDA...
WHAT WOULD SHE BE LIKE?
CHECK IT OUT.
TODAY I'M GONNA SHOW YOU SOMETHING COOL.
THIS IS MY TREASURE.
TOHRU.

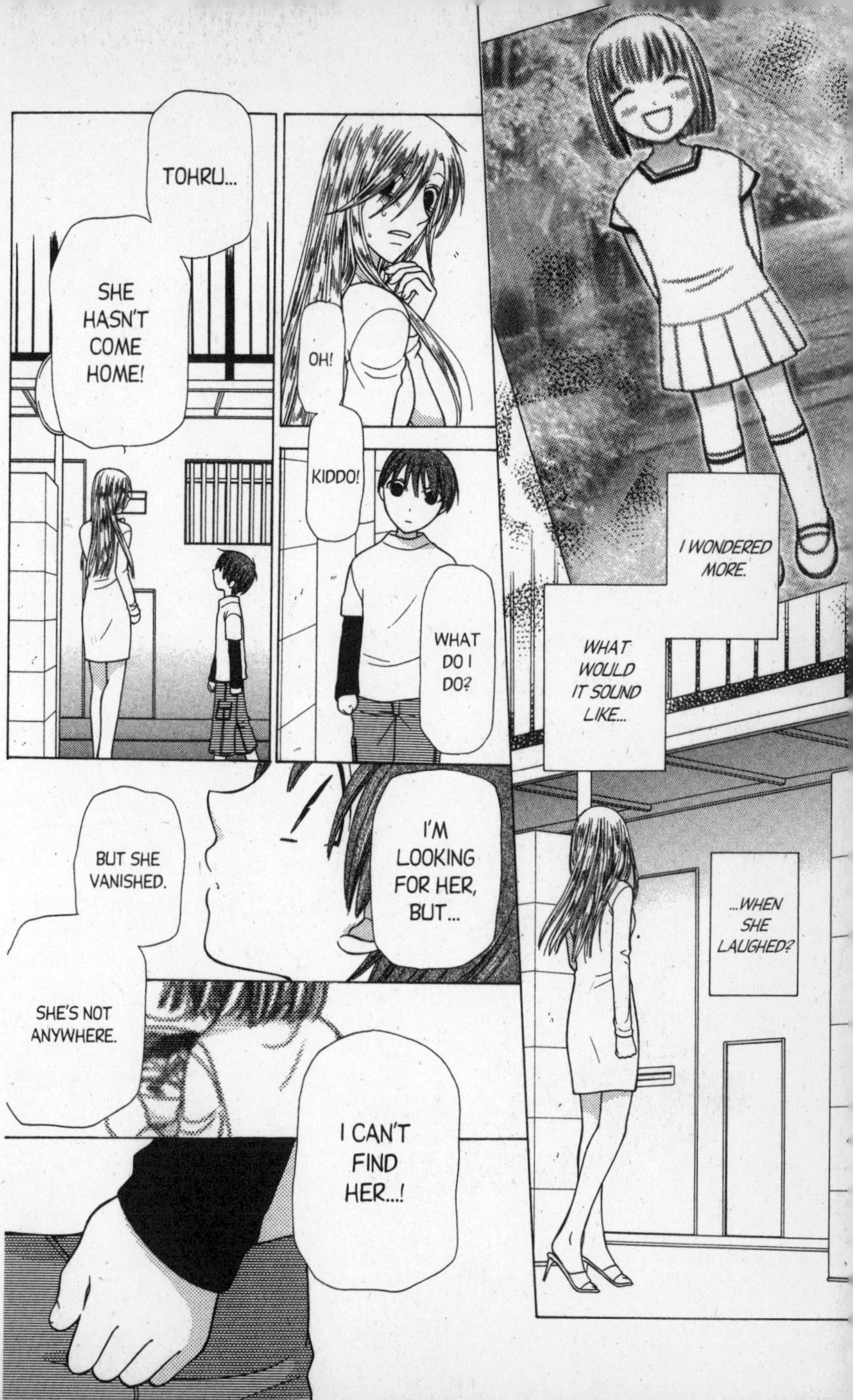
I WONDERED MORE.
WHAT WOULD IT SOUND LIKE...
...WHEN SHE LAUGHED?
OH!
KIDDO!
WHAT DO I DO?
TOHRU...
SHE HASN'T COME HOME!
I'M LOOKING FOR HER, BUT...
BUT SHE VANISHED.
SHE'S NOT ANYWHERE.
I CAN'T FIND HER...!

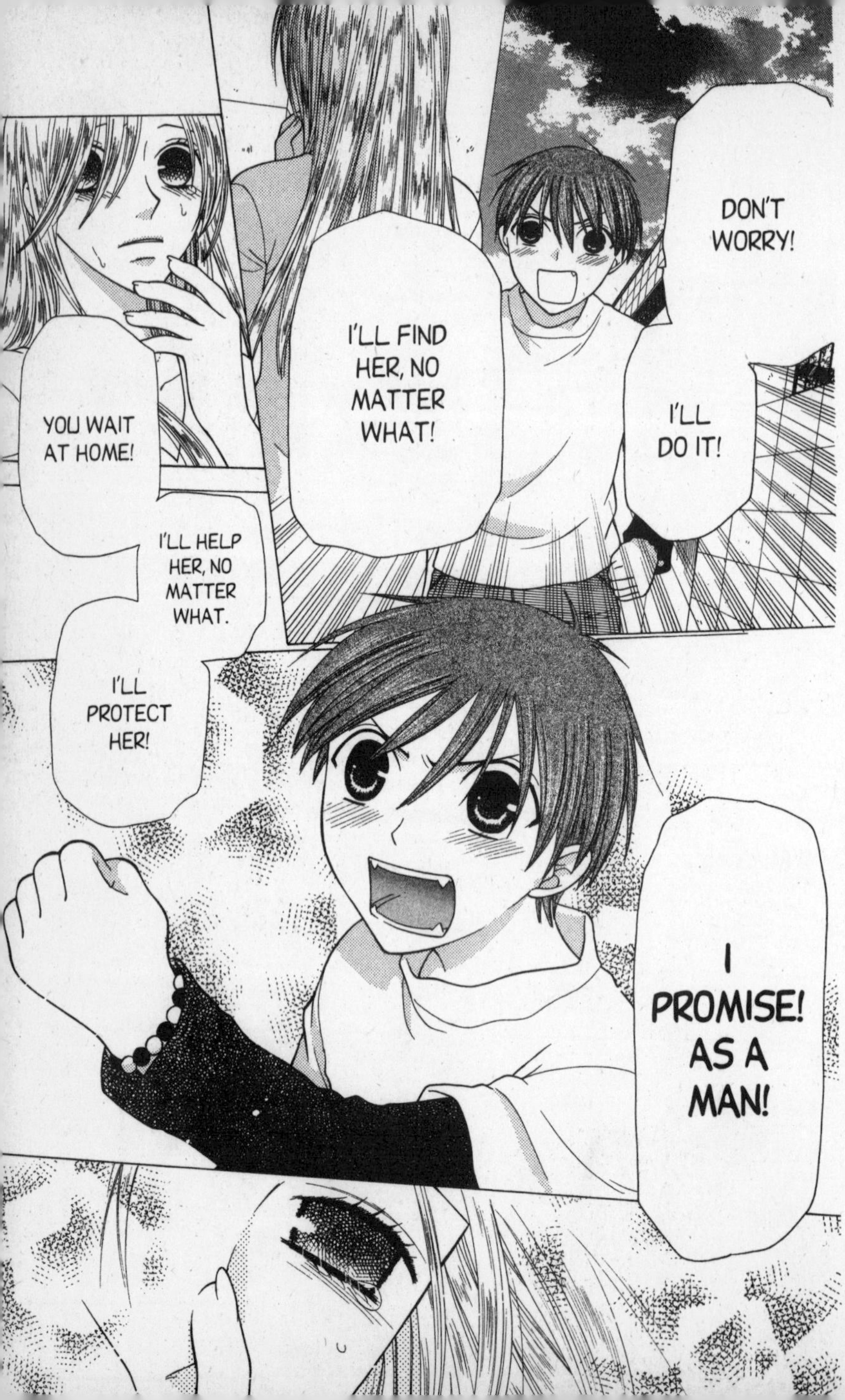
DON'T WORRY!
I'LL DO IT!
I'LL FIND HER, NO MATTER WHAT!
YOU WAIT AT HOME!
I'LL HELP HER, NO MATTER WHAT.
I'LL PROTECT HER!
I PROMISE! AS A MAN!

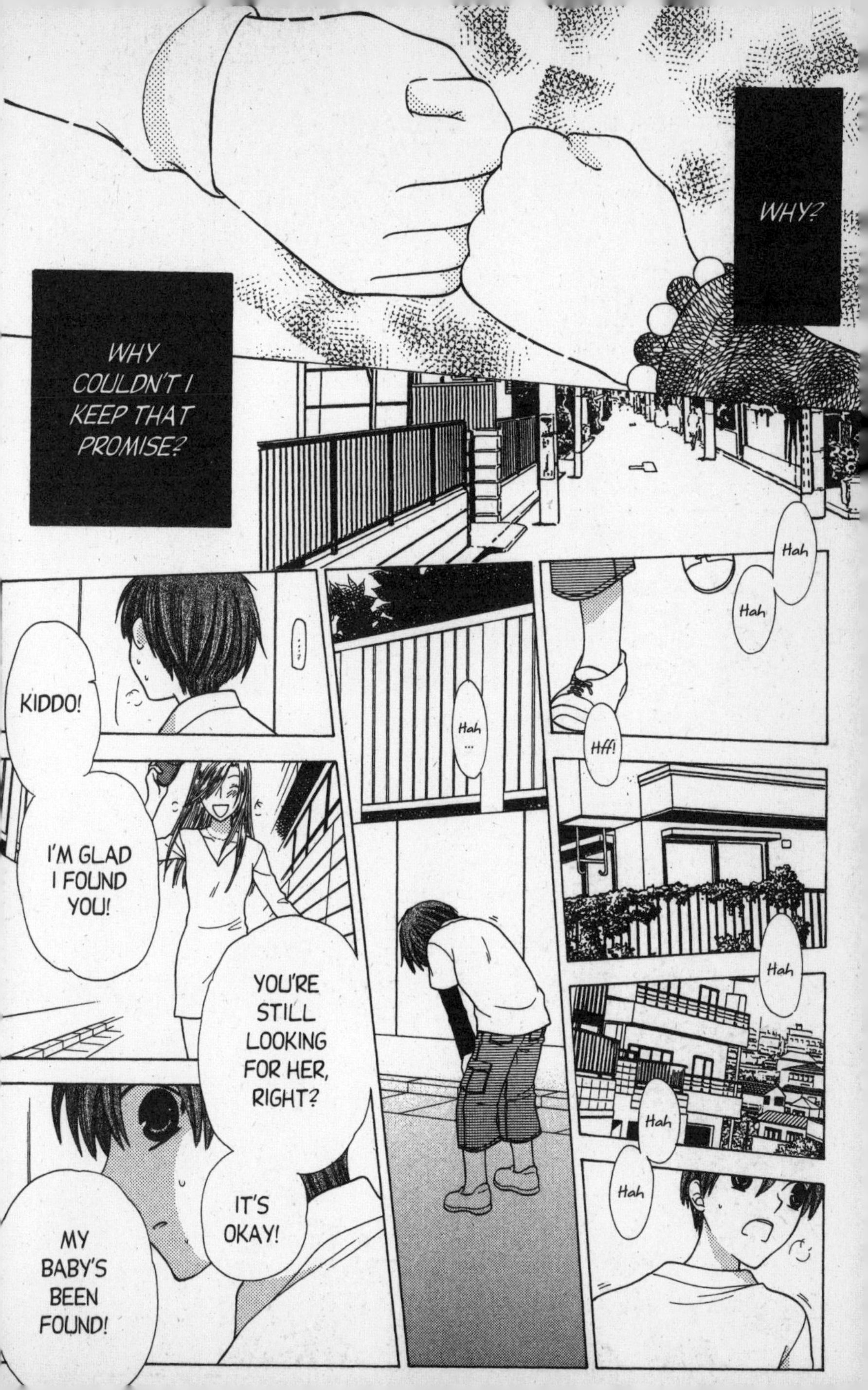
WHY?
WHY COULDN'T I KEEP THAT PROMISE?
Hah
Hah
Hff!
Hah
Hah
Hah
Hah ...
...?
KIDDO!
I'M GLAD I FOUND YOU!
YOU'RE STILL LOOKING FOR HER, RIGHT?
IT'S OKAY!
MY BABY'S BEEN FOUND!

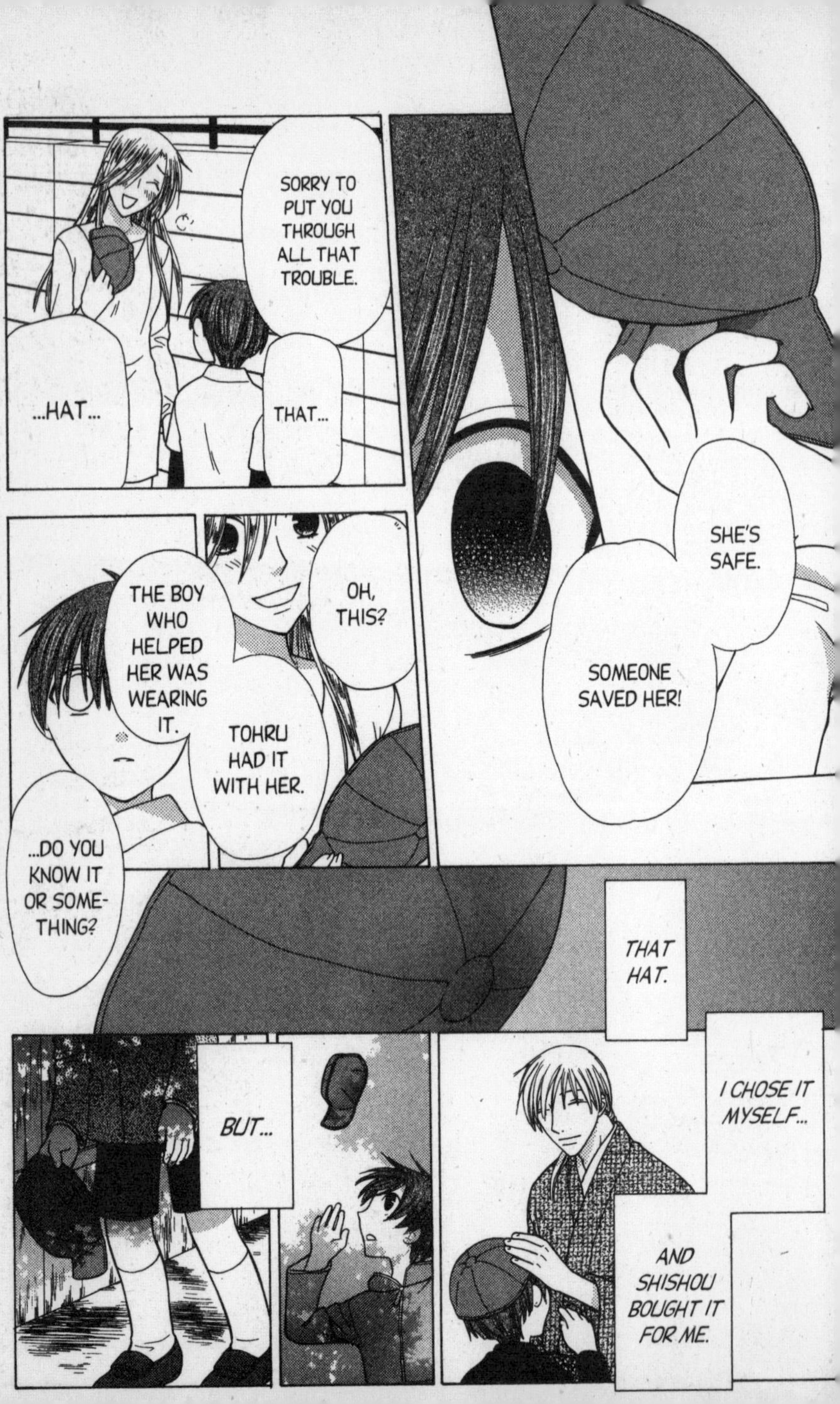
SHE'S SAFE.
SOMEONE SAVED HER!
SORRY TO PUT YOU THROUGH ALL THAT TROUBLE.
THAT...
...HAT...
OH, THIS?
THE BOY WHO HELPED HER WAS WEARING IT.
TOHRU HAD IT WITH HER.
...DO YOU KNOW IT OR SOME-THING?
THAT HAT.
I CHOSE IT MYSELF...
AND SHISHOU BOUGHT IT FOR ME.
BUT...

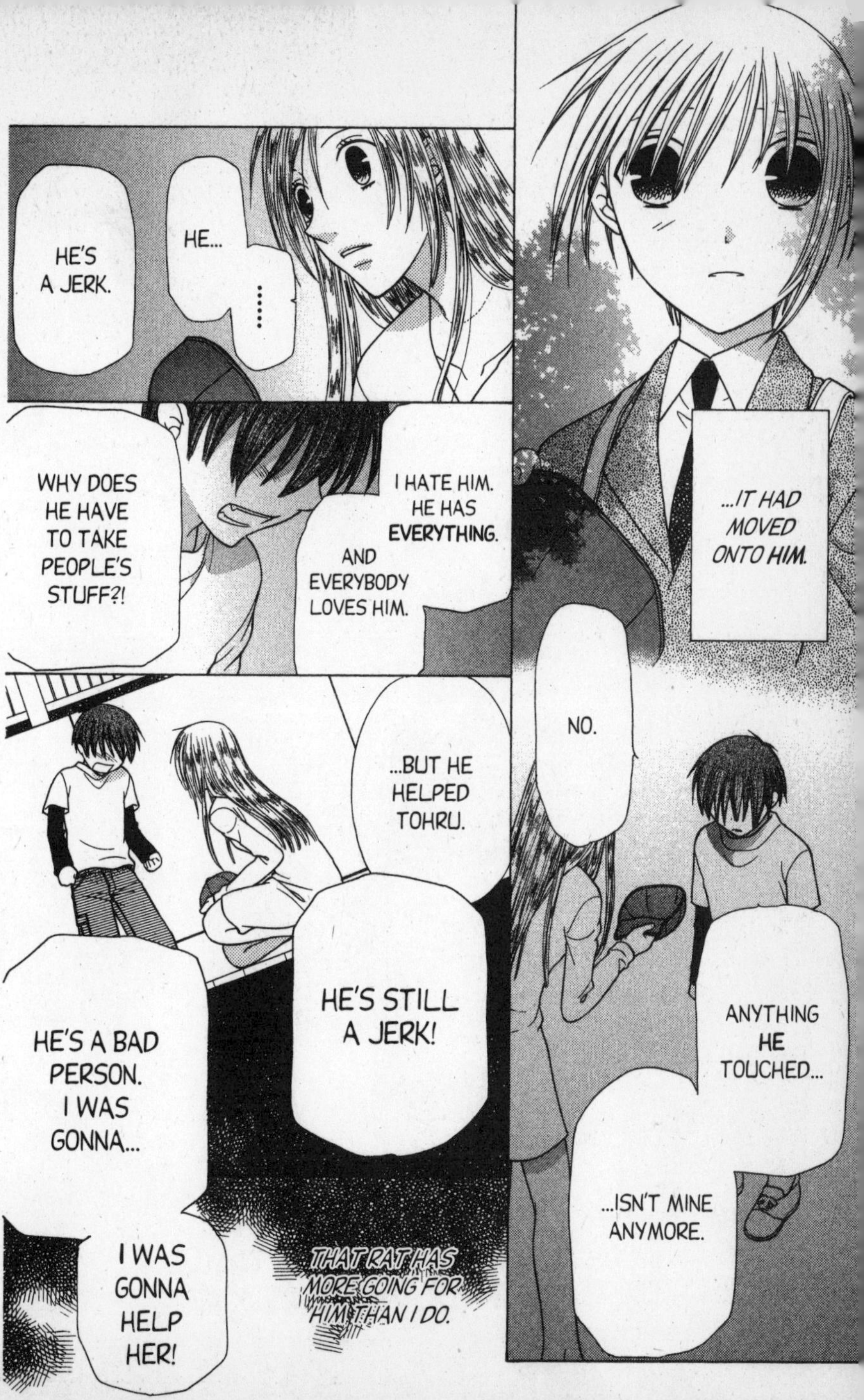
...IT HAD MOVED ONTO HIM.
NO.
ANYTHING HE TOUCHED...
...ISN'T MINE ANYMORE.
HE...
......
HE'S A JERK.
I HATE HIM. HE HAS EVERYTHING.
AND EVERYBODY LOVES HIM.
WHY DOES HE HAVE TO TAKE PEOPLE'S STUFF?!
...BUT HE HELPED TOHRU.
HE'S STILL A JERK!
HE'S A BAD PERSON. I WAS GONNA...
THAT RAT HAS MORE GOING FOR HIM THAN I DO.
I WAS GONNA HELP HER!

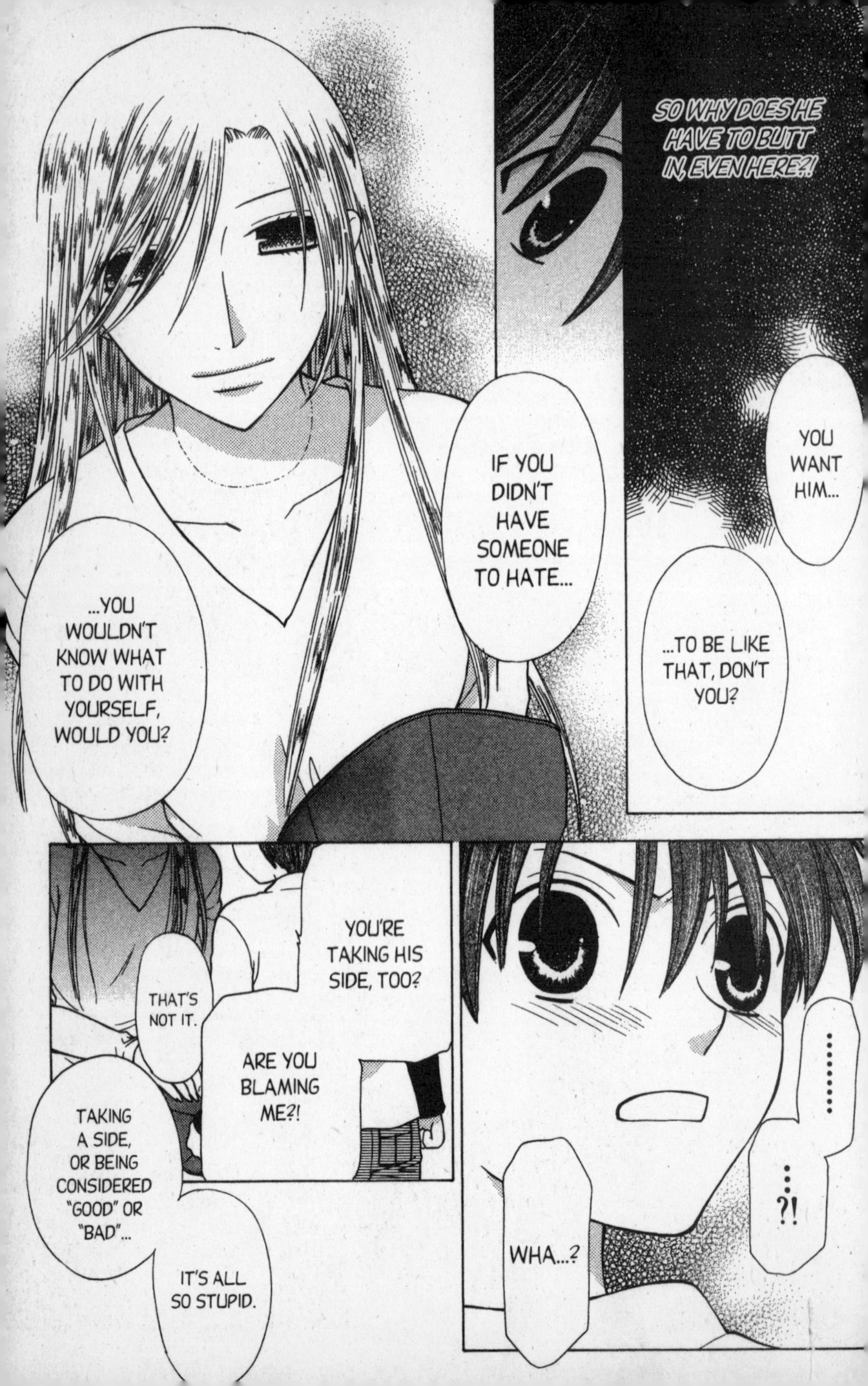
SO WHY DOES HE HAVE TO BUTT IN, EVEN HERE?!
YOU WANT HIM...
...TO BE LIKE THAT, DON'T YOU?
IF YOU DIDN'T HAVE SOMEONE TO HATE...
...YOU WOULDN'T KNOW WHAT TO DO WITH YOURSELF, WOULD YOU?
....
...?!
WHA...?
YOU'RE TAKING HIS SIDE, TOO?
ARE YOU BLAMING ME?!
THAT'S NOT IT.
TAKING A SIDE, OR BEING CONSIDERED "GOOD" OR "BAD"...
IT'S ALL SO STUPID.

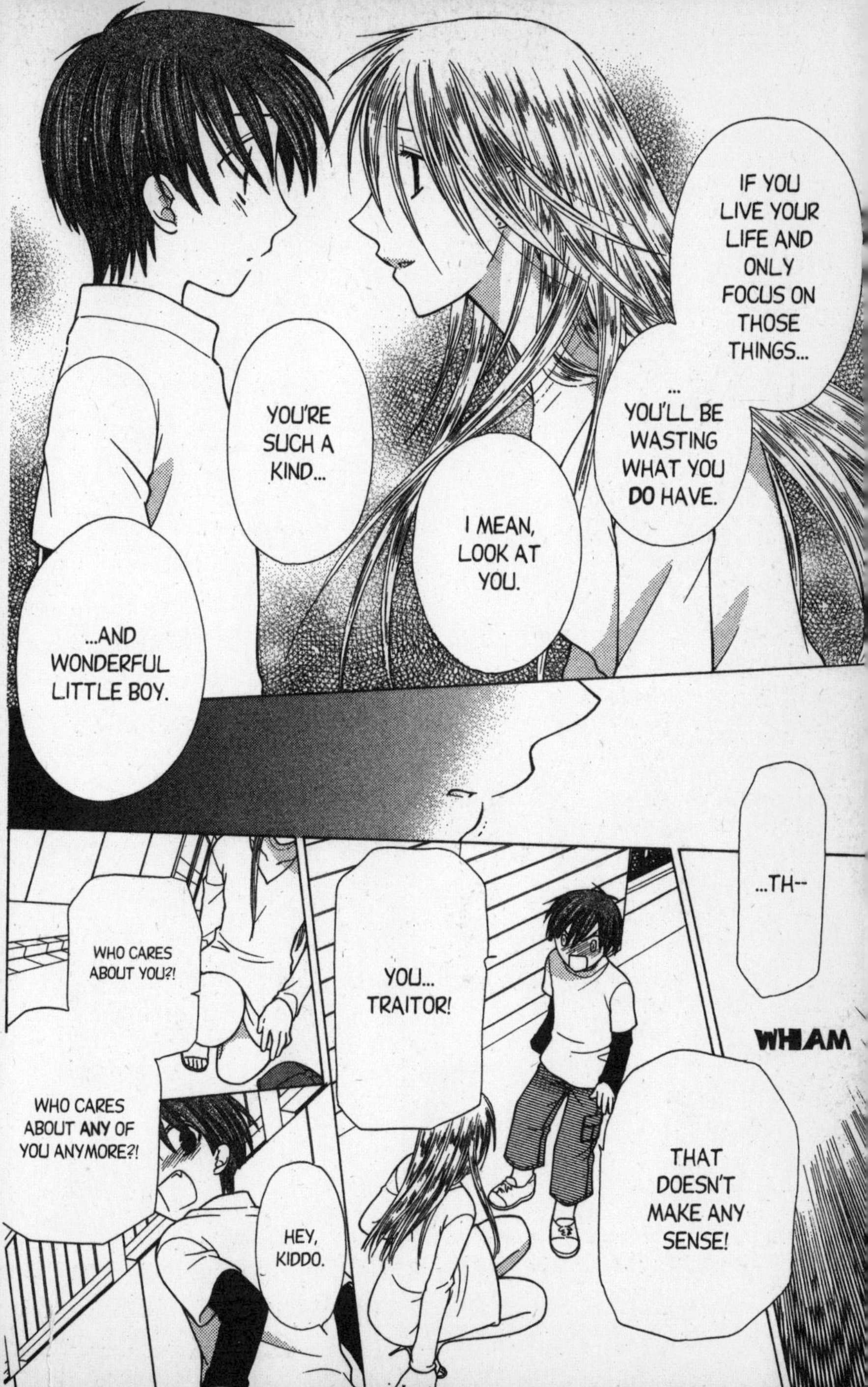
IF YOU LIVE YOUR LIFE AND ONLY FOCUS ON THOSE THINGS...
...YOU'LL BE WASTING WHAT YOU DO HAVE.
I MEAN, LOOK AT YOU.
YOU'RE SUCH A KIND...
...AND WONDERFUL LITTLE BOY.
...TH--
WHAM
THAT DOESN'T MAKE ANY SENSE!
YOU... TRAITOR!
HEY, KIDDO.
WHO CARES ABOUT YOU?!
WHO CARES ABOUT ANY OF YOU ANYMORE?!

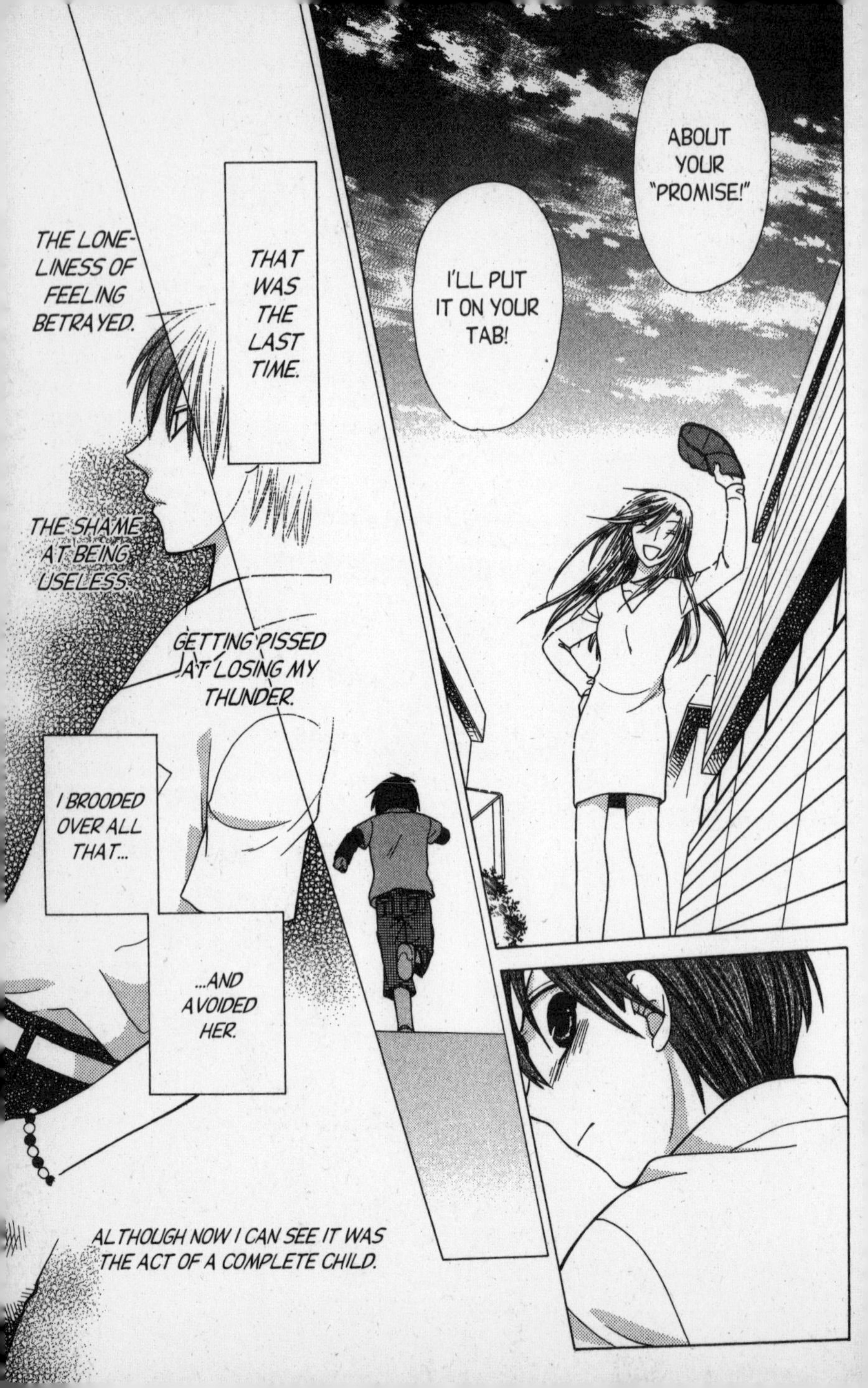

ABOUT YOUR "PROMISE!"
I'LL PUT IT ON YOUR TAB!
THAT WAS THE LAST TIME.
THE LONE-LINESS OF FEELING BETRAYED.
THE SHAME AT BEING USELESS.
GETTING PISSED AT LOSING MY THUNDER.
I BROODED OVER ALL THAT...
...AND AVOIDED HER.
ALTHOUGH NOW I CAN SEE IT WAS THE ACT OF A COMPLETE CHILD.

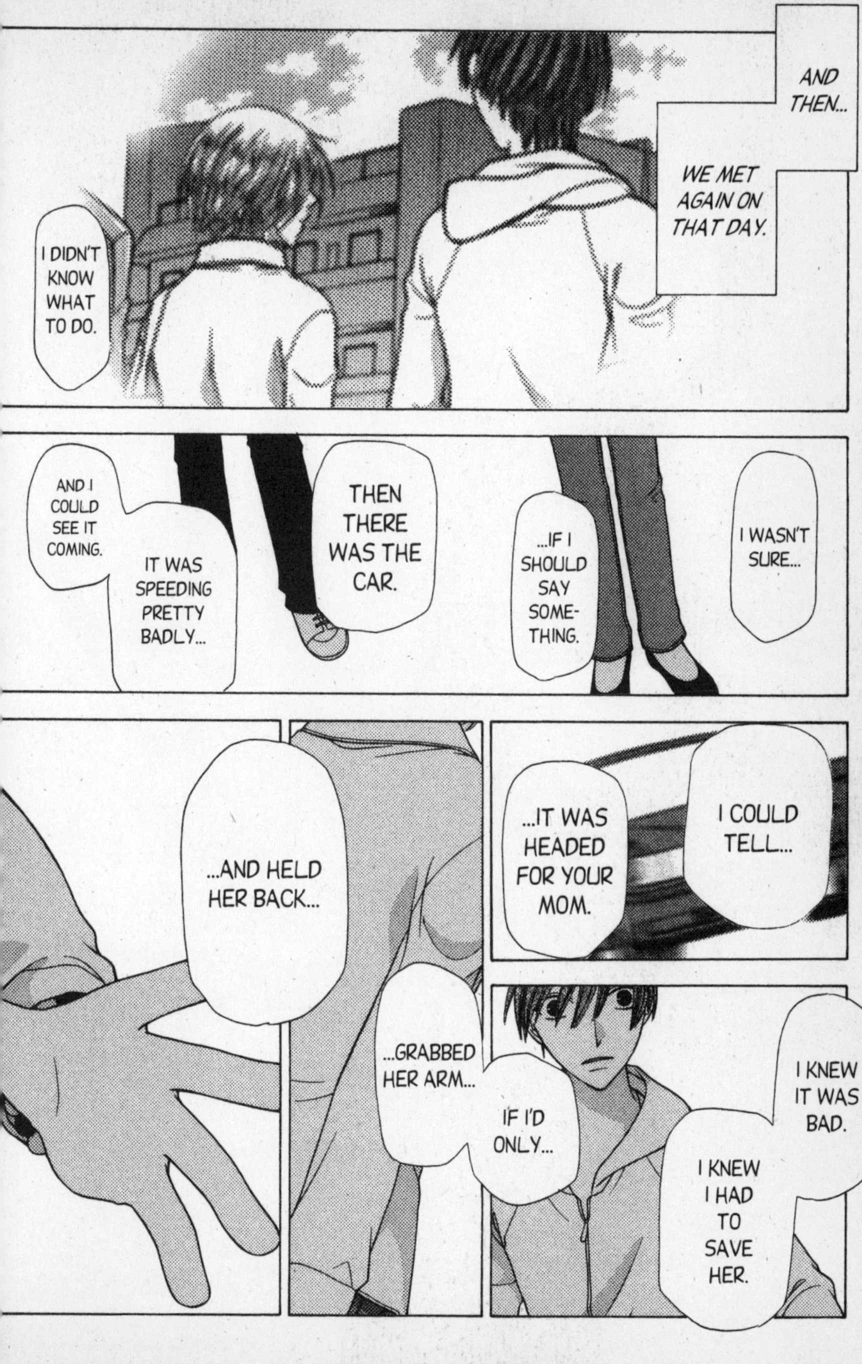
AND THEN...
WE MET AGAIN ON THAT DAY.
I DIDN'T KNOW WHAT TO DO.
I WASN'T SURE...
...IF I SHOULD SAY SOME-THING.
THEN THERE WAS THE CAR.
IT WAS SPEEDING PRETTY BADLY...
AND I COULD SEE IT COMING.
I COULD TELL...
...IT WAS HEADED FOR YOUR MOM.
I KNEW IT WAS BAD.
I KNEW I HAD TO SAVE HER.
IF I'D ONLY...
...GRABBED HER ARM...
...AND HELD HER BACK...

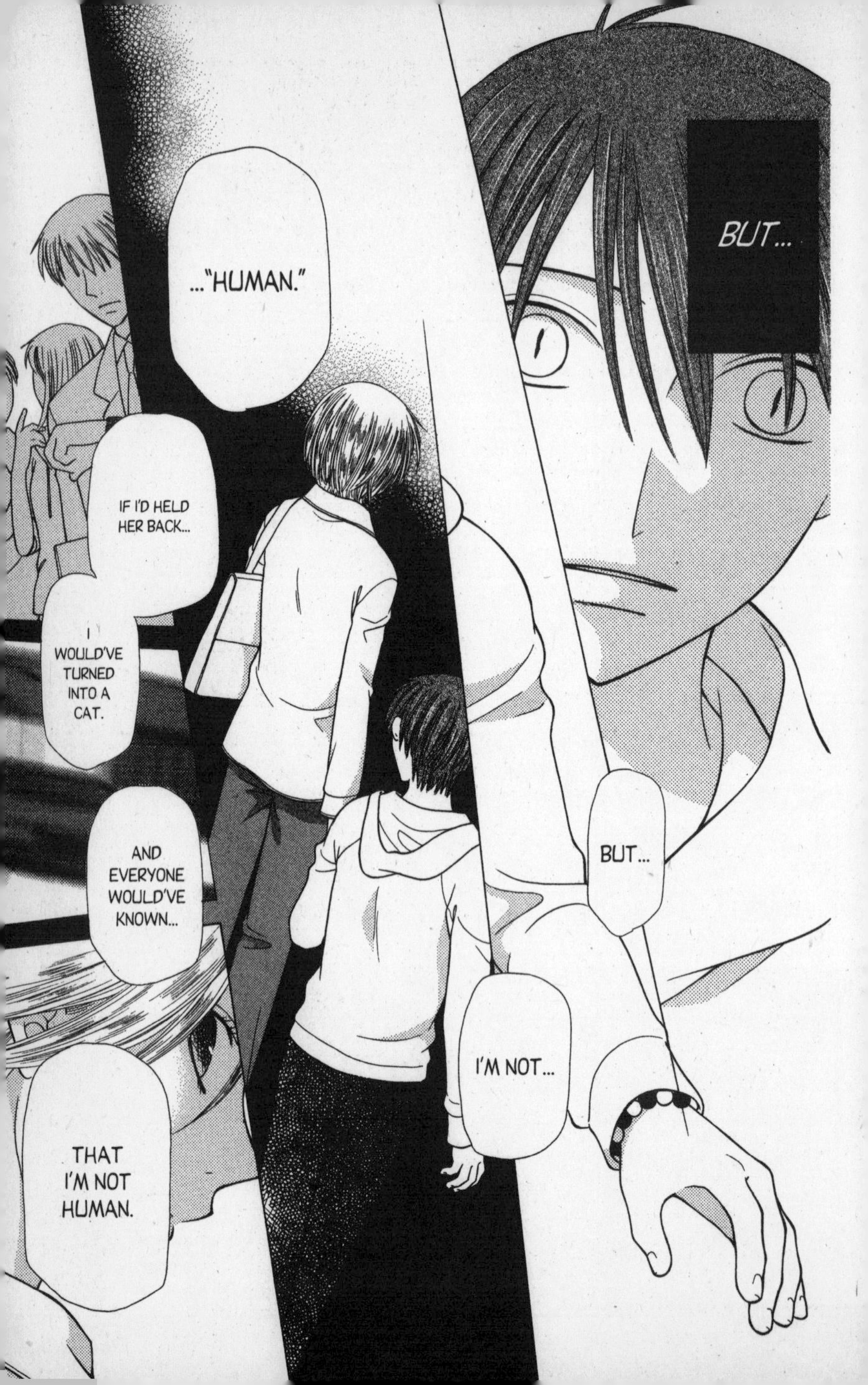
BUT...
BUT...
I'M NOT...
..."HUMAN."
IF I'D HELD HER BACK...
I WOULD'VE TURNED INTO A CAT.
AND EVERYONE WOULD'VE KNOWN...
THAT I'M NOT HUMAN.

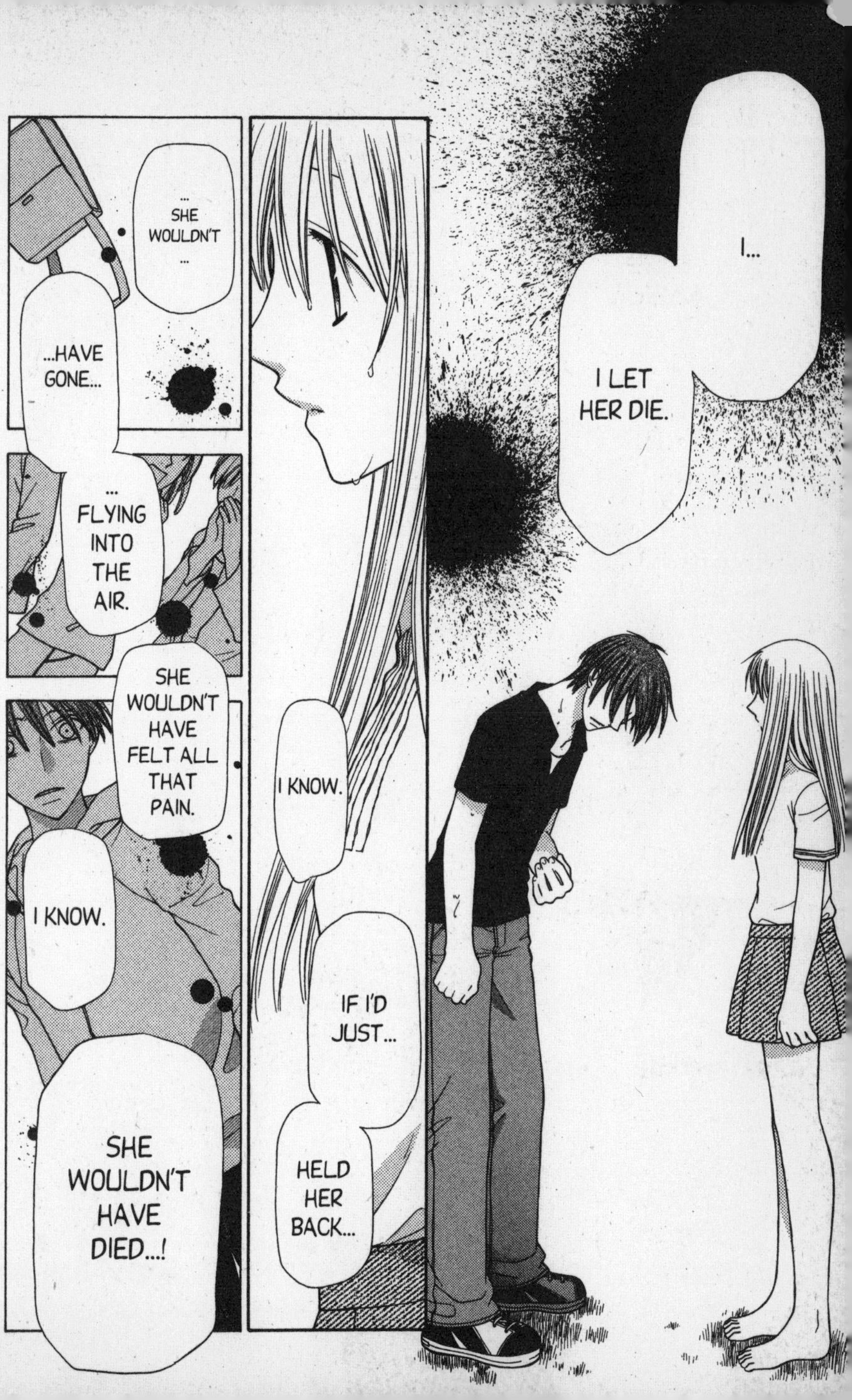
I...
I LET HER DIE.
I KNOW.
IF I'D JUST...
HELD HER BACK...
... SHE WOULDN'T ...
...HAVE GONE...
... FLYING INTO THE AIR.
SHE WOULDN'T HAVE FELT ALL THAT PAIN.
I KNOW.
SHE WOULDN'T HAVE DIED...!

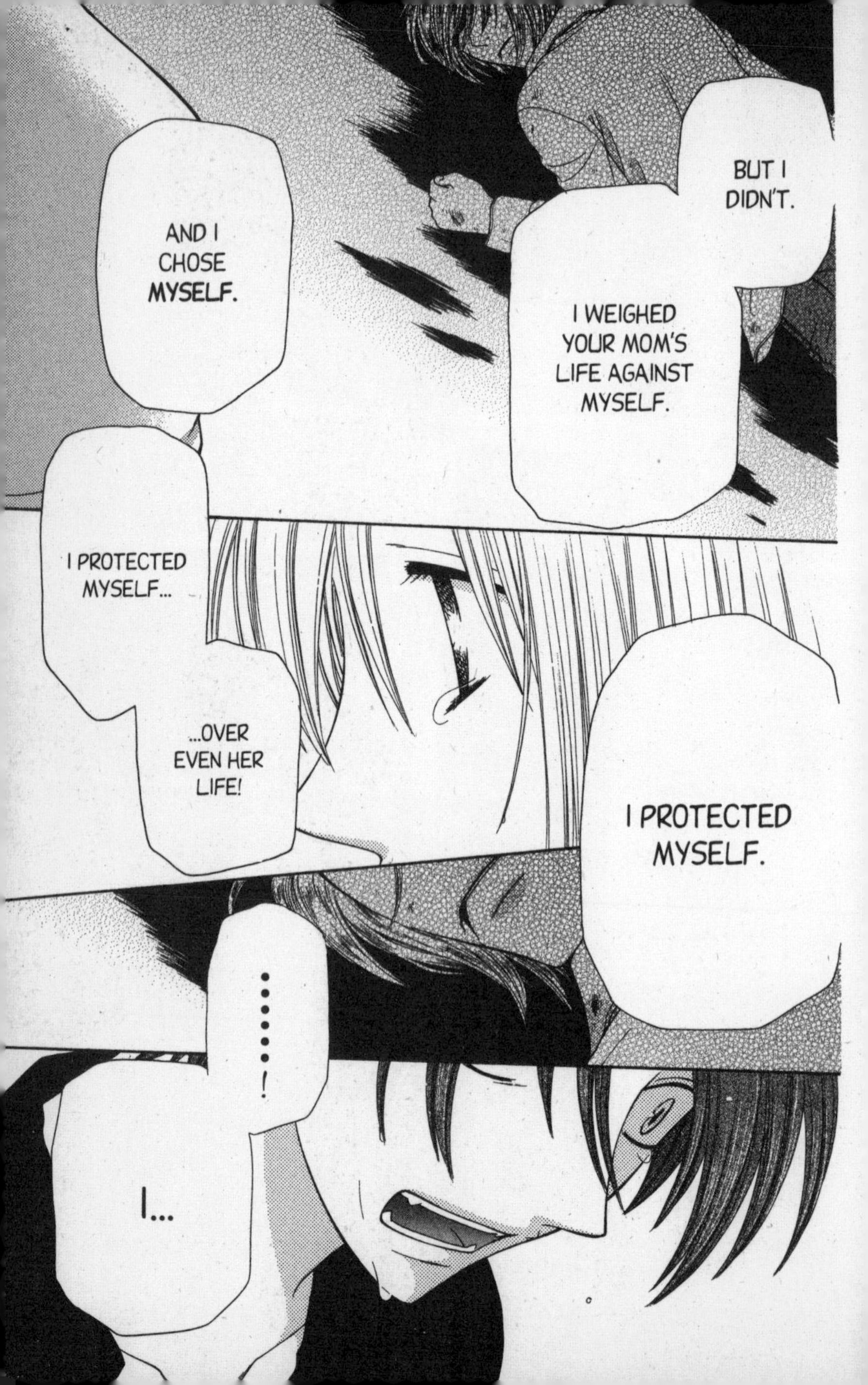
BUT I DIDN'T.
I WEIGHED YOUR MOM'S LIFE AGAINST MYSELF.
AND I CHOSE MYSELF.
I PROTECTED MYSELF...
...OVER EVEN HER LIFE!
I PROTECTED MYSELF.
......!
I...

I HATE MYSELF FOR BEING LIKE THIS.
I DESPISE MYSELF.
I'D RATHER...
THINGS WOULD BE BETTER IF I WAS GONE.
IF I'D JUST DISAPPEAR.
BUT IN THE END, I ALWAYS PROTECT MYSELF.
I INDULGE MYSELF...
....AND RUN AWAY.
ALWAYS.
ALWAYS.
ALWAYS.
EVEN NOW.

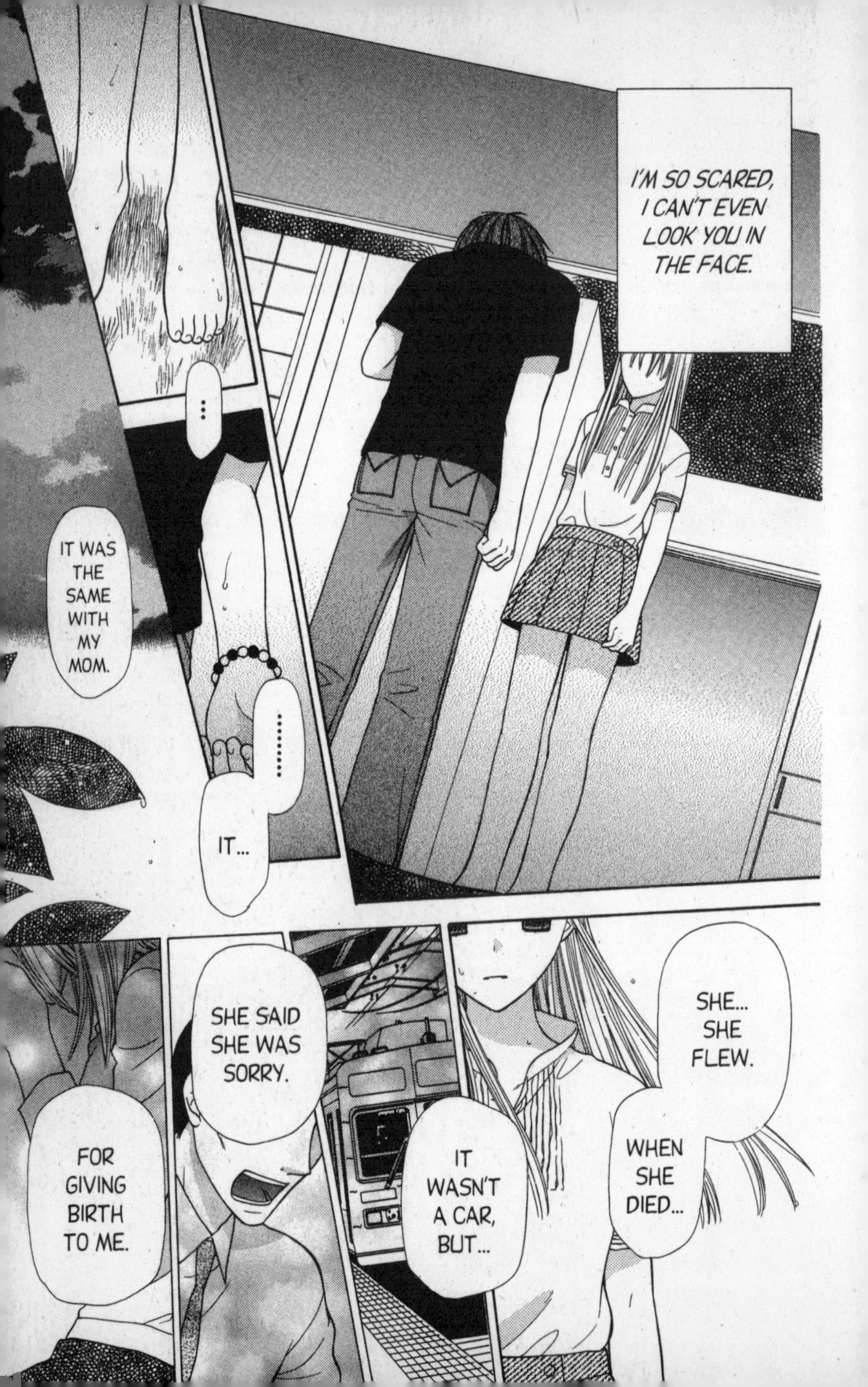
I'M SO SCARED, I CAN'T EVEN LOOK YOU IN THE FACE.
...
......
IT...
IT WAS THE SAME WITH MY MOM.
SHE... SHE FLEW.
WHEN SHE DIED...
IT WASN'T A CAR, BUT...
SHE SAID SHE WAS SORRY.
FOR GIVING BIRTH TO ME.

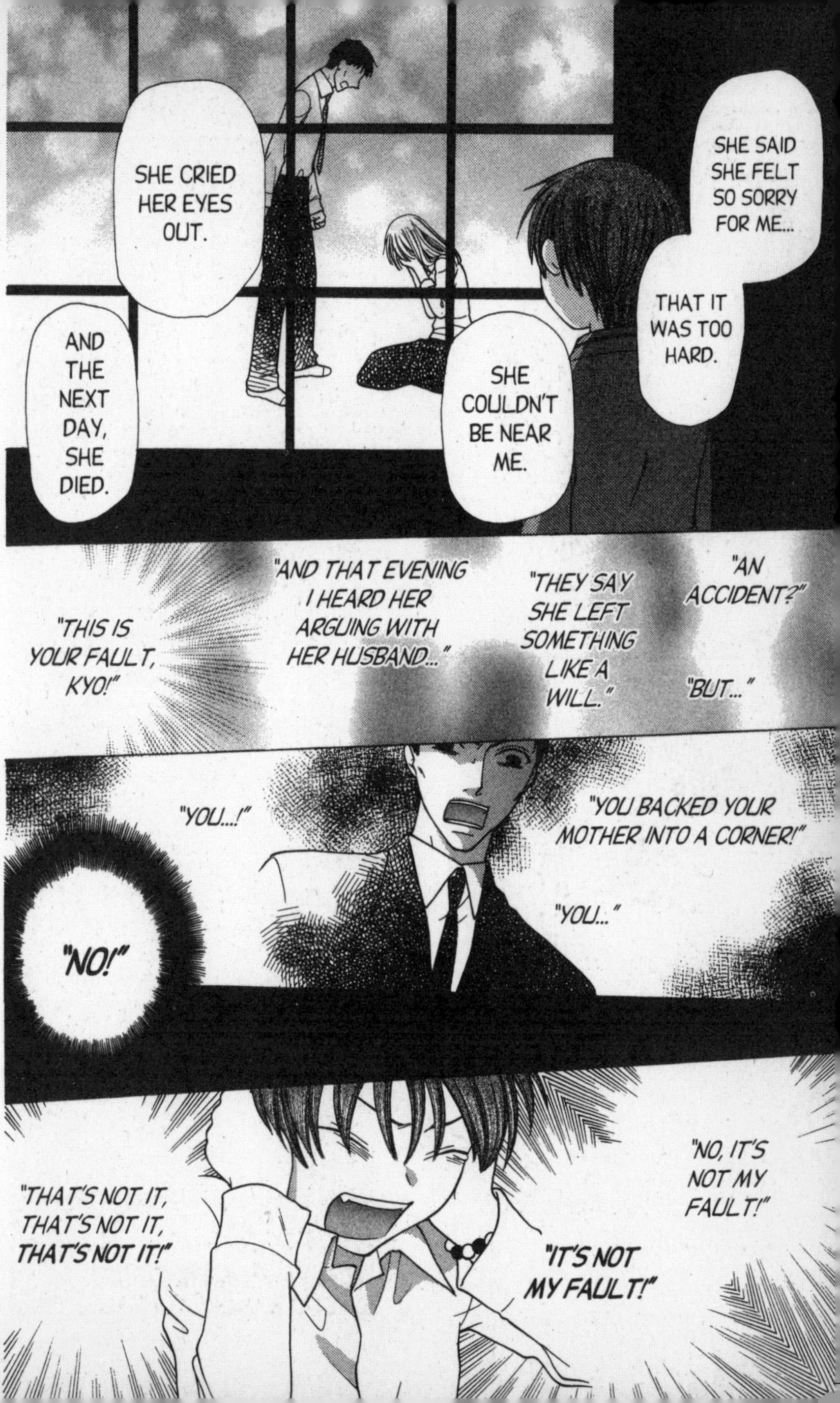
SHE SAID SHE FELT SO SORRY FOR ME...
THAT IT WAS TOO HARD.
SHE COULDN'T BE NEAR ME.
SHE CRIED HER EYES OUT.
AND THE NEXT DAY, SHE DIED.
"AN ACCIDENT?"
"BUT..."
"THEY SAY SHE LEFT SOMETHING LIKE A WILL."
"AND THAT EVENING I HEARD HER ARGUING WITH HER HUSBAND..."
"THIS IS YOUR FAULT, KYO!"
"YOU BACKED YOUR MOTHER INTO A CORNER!"
"YOU..."
"YOU...!"
"NO!"
"NO, IT'S NOT MY FAULT!"
"IT'S NOT MY FAULT!"
"THAT'S NOT IT, THAT'S NOT IT, THAT'S NOT IT!"

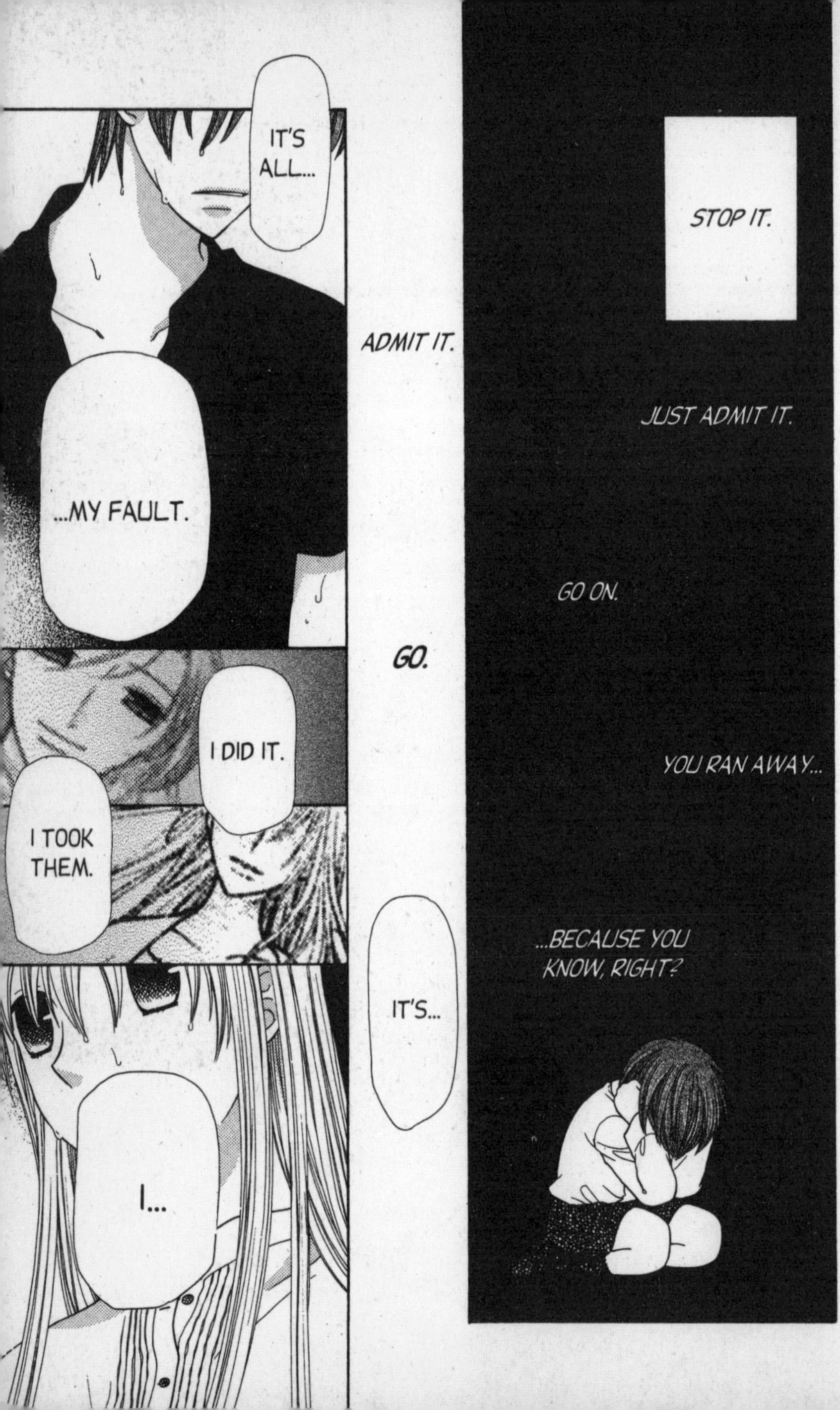
STOP IT.
JUST ADMIT IT.
GO ON.
YOU RAN AWAY...
...BECAUSE YOU KNOW, RIGHT?
ADMIT IT.
GO.
IT'S...
IT'S ALL...
...MY FAULT.
I DID IT.
I TOOK THEM.
I...

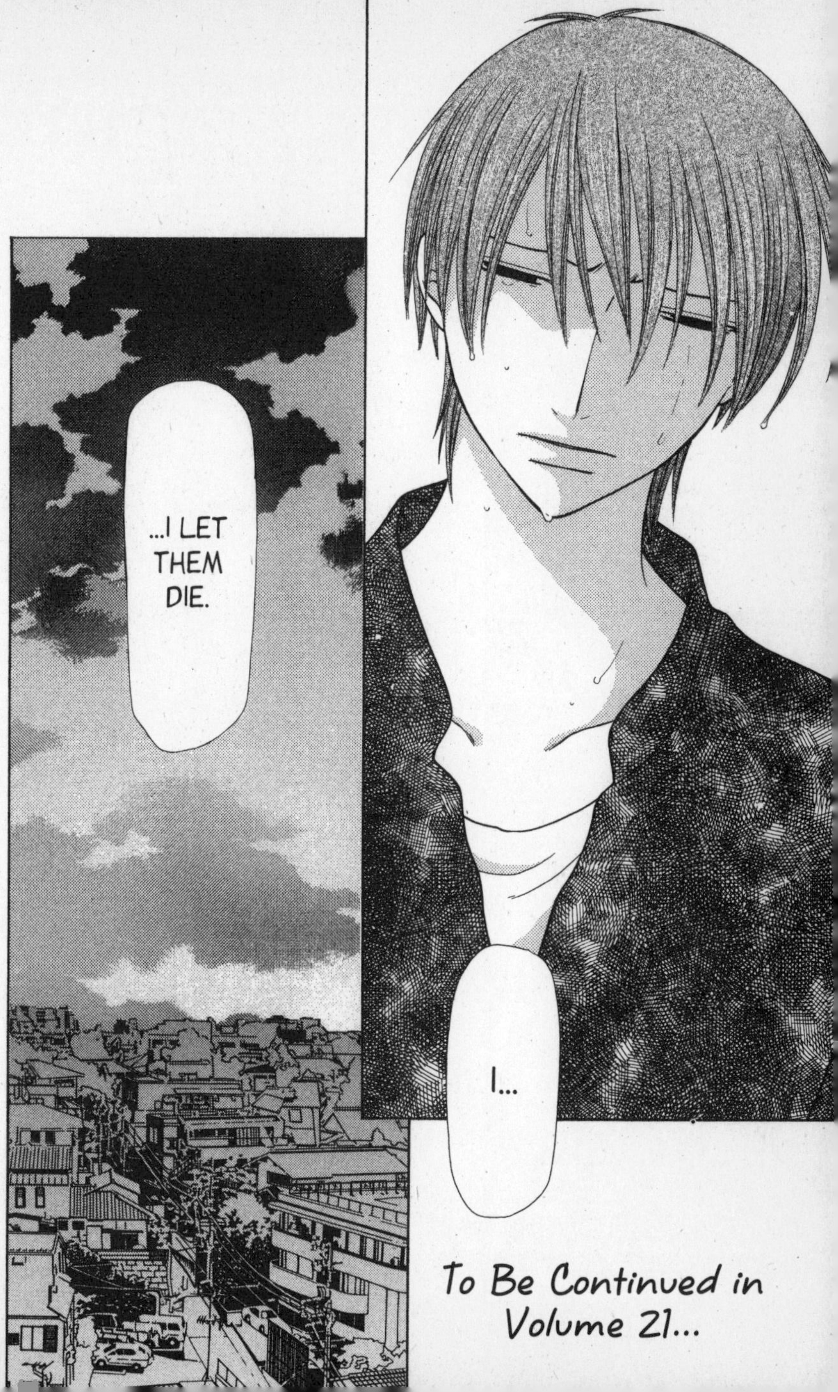
I...
...I LET THEM DIE.

To Be Continued in Volume 21...

I feel so grateful!

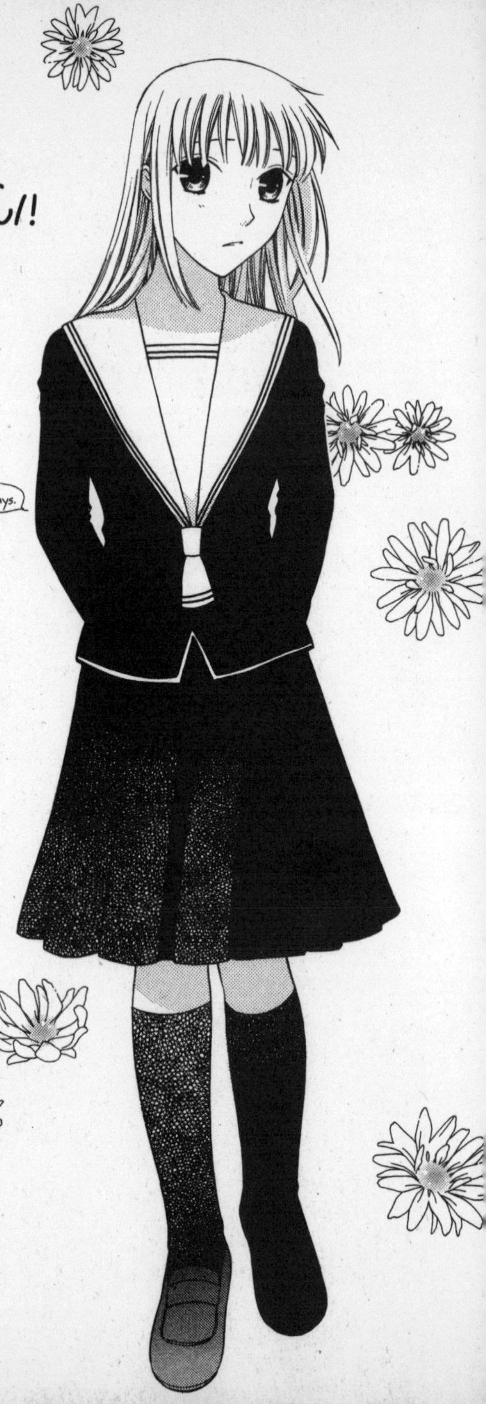
....
...she says.

Harada-sama, Araki-sama,
Mother-sama, Editor-sama...

And everyone who reads
and supports this manga.

Who will I have next...?

This has been
Natsuki Takaya.

Next time in...

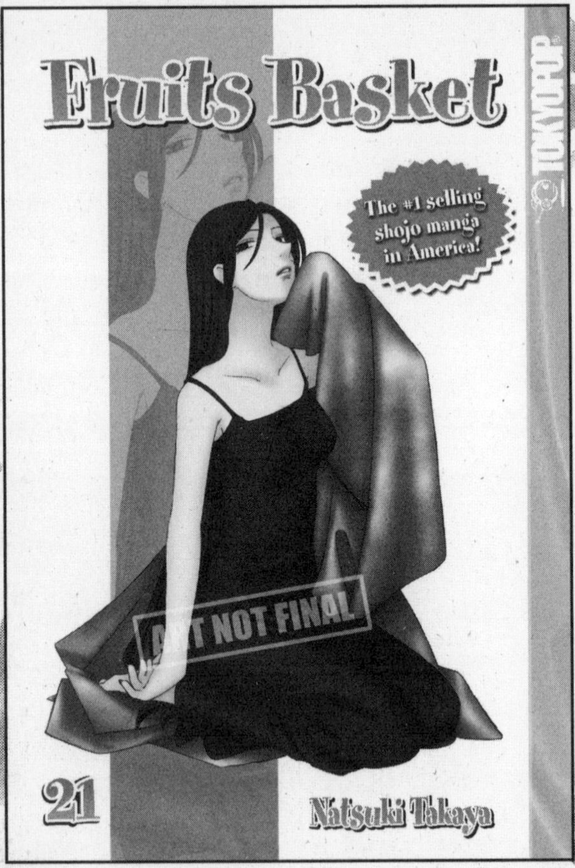

Fruits Basket
TOKYOPOP
The #1 selling shojo manga in America!
ART NOT FINAL
21
Natsuki Takaya

Coming Clean

Kyo reveals all, telling Tohru about his role in her mother's death. Kyo explains that he overcame his guilt by blaming everything on Yuki, but he now realizes that he was only running away from his own feelings. How will he react when Tohru says that she still loves him?

Fruits Basket Volume 21
Available November 2008

Fans Basket

I can't believe there are only a few volumes of Fruits Basket left! And even though the series is coming to an end, I continue to receive more and more fan art! One thing is certain, your dedication is not ending anytime soon! Take our first piece of fan art in this edition of Fans Basket, for example... Amazing!

- Paul Morrissey, Editor

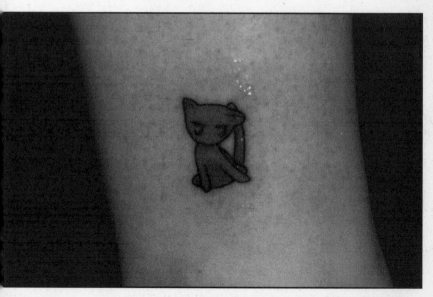

Maria Hoffman
Age 20
Bay Shore, NY

Whoa! Maria, you are the ultimate fan! You know, TOKYOPOP is publishing the *Fruits Basket Sticker Book*, and it contains temporary tattoos...so you didn't need to go out and get a real one! Nonetheless, I admire the dedication!

Hannah Lees
Age 24
Los Angeles, CA

Awwwww... Tohru and Kyo look so cozy
in your sketch, Hannah! Adorable!

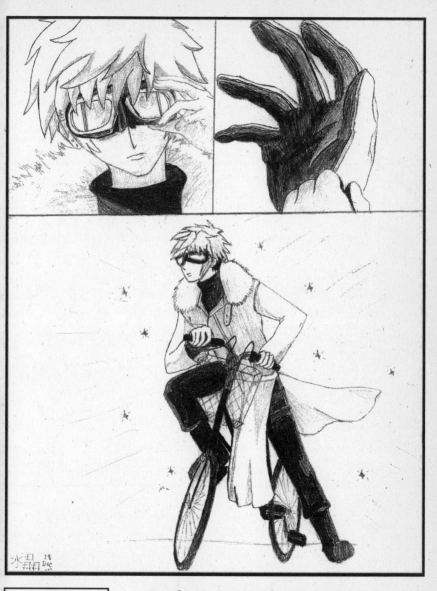

Crystal Styron
Age 17
Murfreesboro, NC

Haru looks soooo cool on his bike! And I love the panels showing him putting on the goggles and the glove. Nice work!

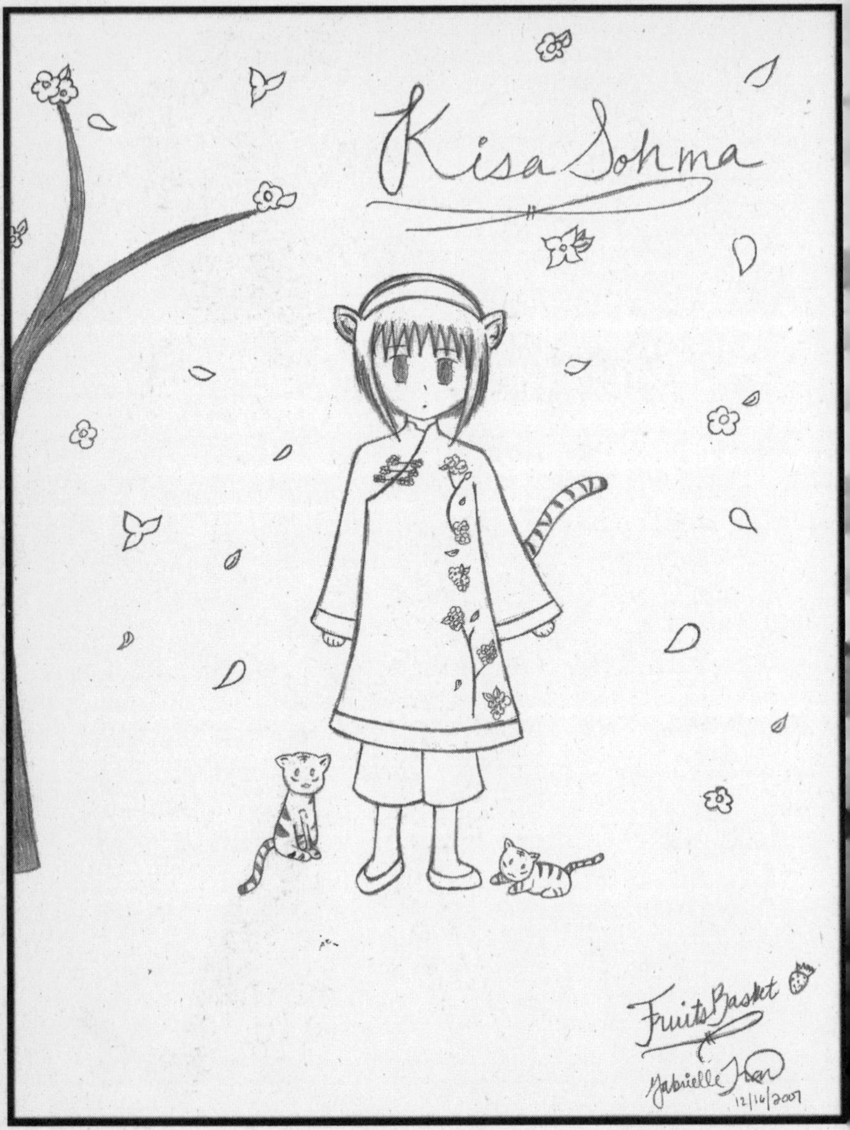
Kisa Sohma
Fruits Basket
12/16/2007

Gabby Tran
Age 13
Pass Christian, MS

Thanks for drawing such an cute sketch of Kisa, Gabby! The flowers on Kisa's outfit are a particularly nice touch.

"The Birdcage"

Jaili Noehlin
Age 30
Mexico City, Mexico

In her letter, Jaili wrote that the Furuba characters reminded her of caged birds, and that notion inspired her to draw this amazing piece of art! Gorgeous work, Jaili!

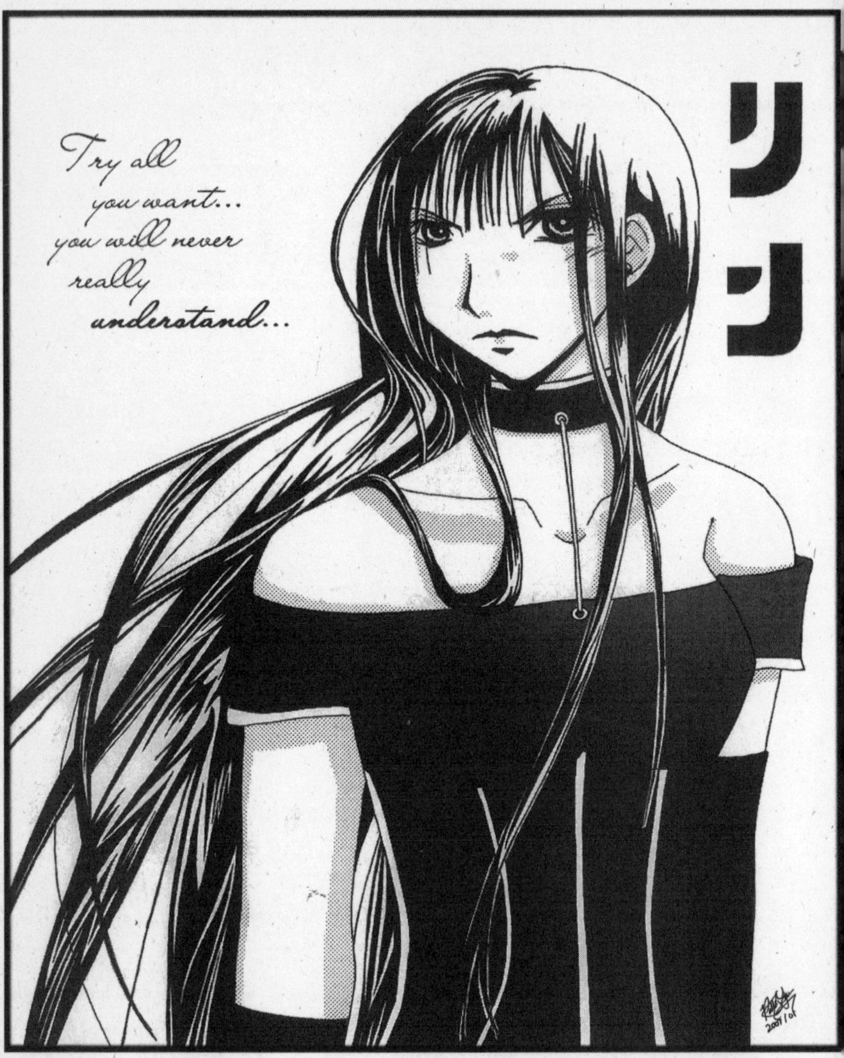
Try all
you want...
you will never
really
understand...
リン

Patty You
Age 16
Cerritos, CA

This is such an intense picture of Rin! You've totally captured Rin's strength and sense of determination, Patty.

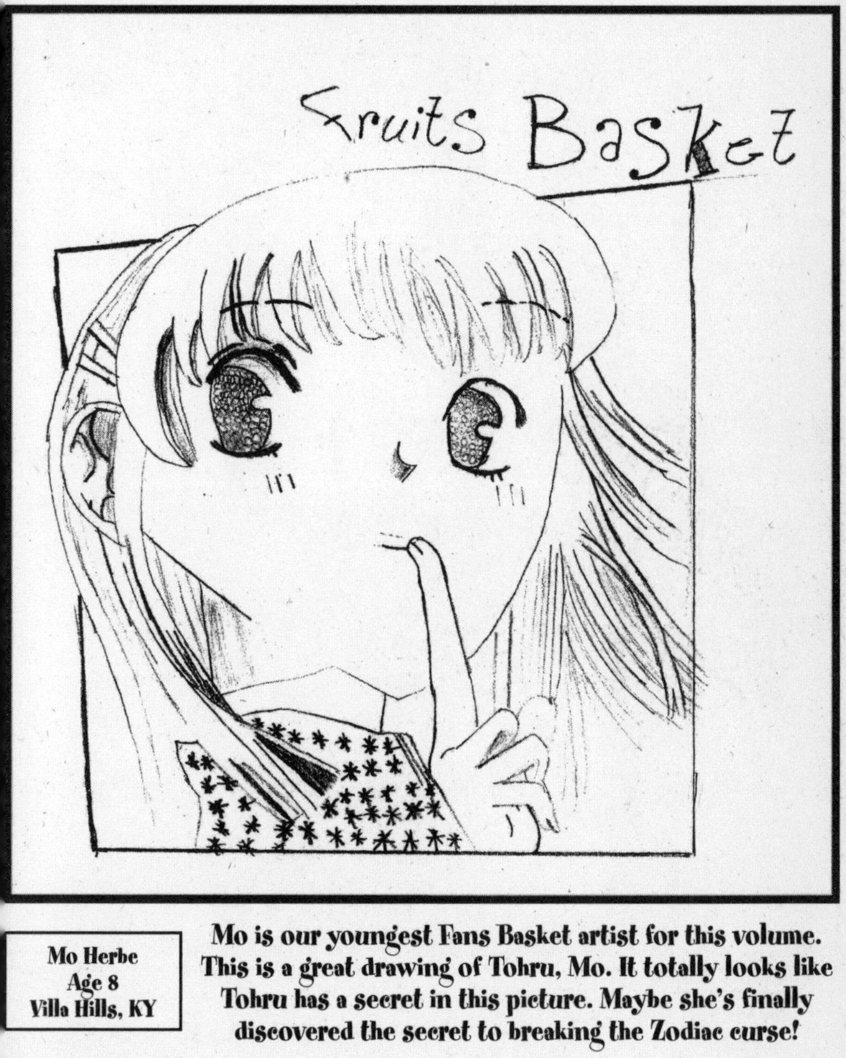
Fruits Basket

Mo Herbe
Age 8
Villa Hills, KY

Mo is our youngest Fans Basket artist for this volume. This is a great drawing of Tohru, Mo. It totally looks like Tohru has a secret in this picture. Maybe she's finally discovered the secret to breaking the Zodiac curse!

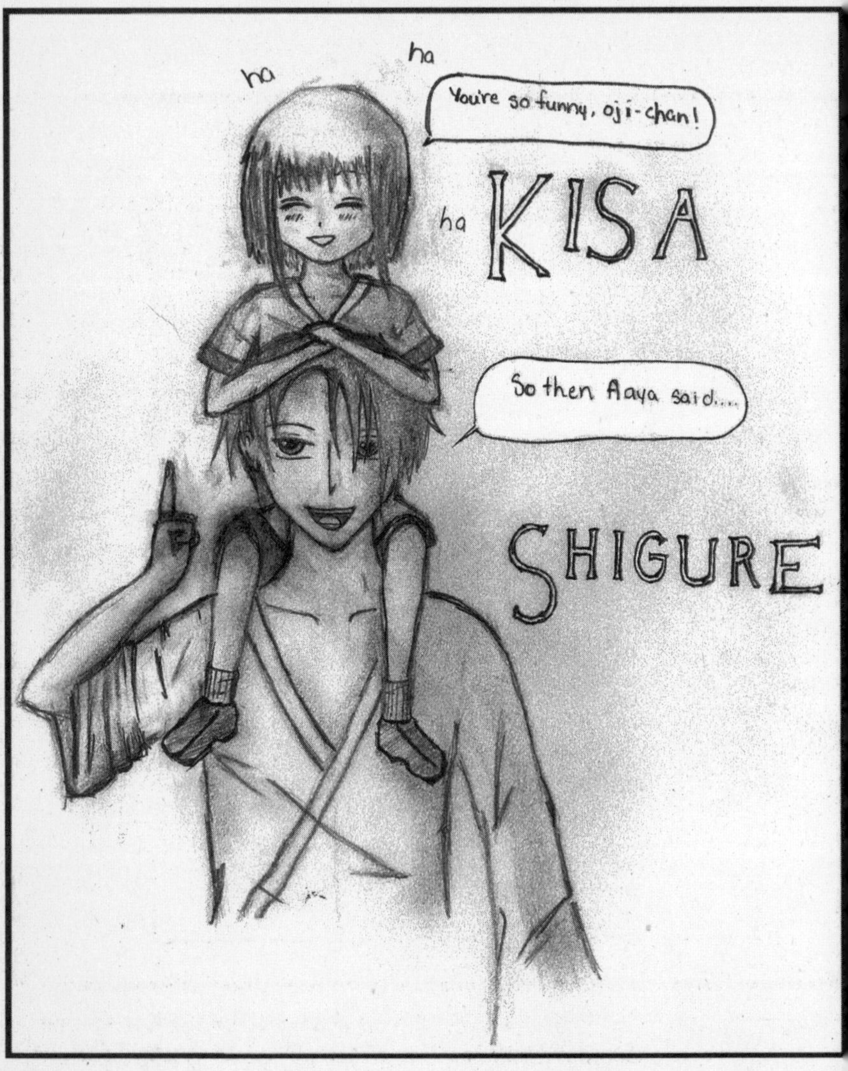
ha
ha
You're so funny, oji-chan!
ha KISA
So then Aaya said....
SHIGURE

Tyler Withrow
Age 14
Richmond, VA

This is such an endearing drawing, Tyler. It's very playful and sweet. Thanks for sending it in!

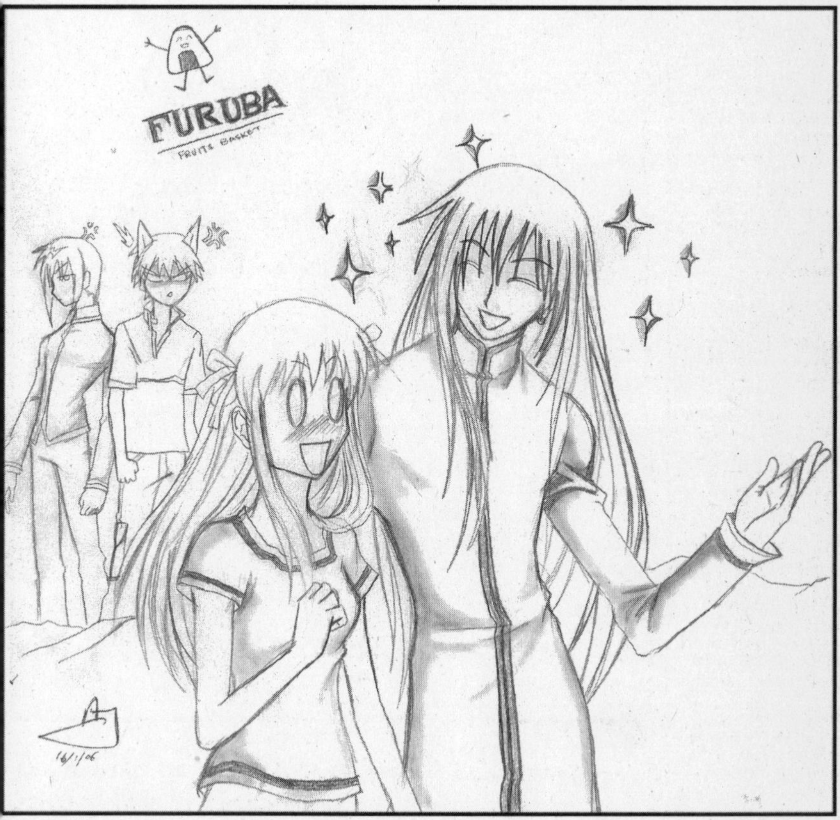
FURUBA
FRUITS BASKET

Ashley Jamieson
Age 18
New Zealand

Ashley's picture certainly made me chuckle. All the expressions are priceless, but I particularly like Kyo stewing in the background. Hmmm...I wonder if Tohru and Ayame would be a good couple...?

Do you want to share your love for *Fruits Basket* with fans around the world? "Fans Basket" is taking submissions of fan art, poetry, cosplay photos, or any other Furuba fun you'd like to share!

How to submit:

1) Send your work via regular mail (NOT e-mail) to:

"Fans Basket"
c/o TOKYOPOP
5900 Wilshire Blvd.
Suite 2000
Los Angeles, CA 90036

2) All work should be in black-and-white and no larger than 8.5" x 11". (And try not to fold it too many times!)

3) Anything you send will not be returned. If you want to keep your original, it's fine to send us a copy.

4) Please include your full name, age, city and state for us to print with your work. If you'd rather us use a pen name, please include that, too.

5) IMPORTANT: If you're under the age of 18, you must have your parent's permission in order for us to print your work. Any submissions without a signed note of parental consent cannot be used.

6) For full details, please check out our website: http://www.tokyopop.com/aboutus/fanart.php

Disclaimer: Anything you send to us becomes the exclusive property of TOKYOPOP Inc. and, as we said before, will not be returned to you. We will have the right to print, reproduce, distribute, or modify the artwork for use in future volumes of *Fruits Basket* or on the web royalty-free.

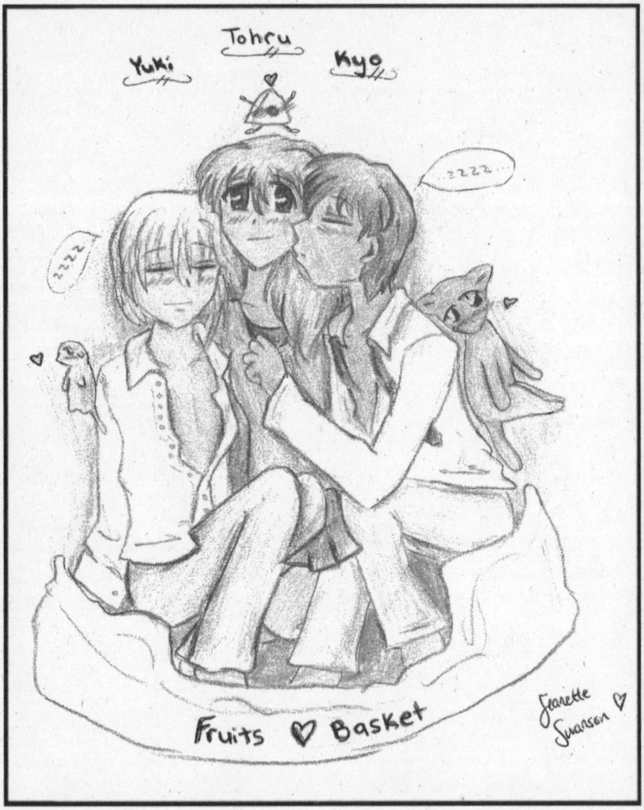

Tohru
Yuki
Kyo
zzzz...
zzzz
Fruits ♡ Basket
Jeanette Swanson ♡

Jeanette Swanson
Age 14
Seattle, WA

Tohru looks rather embarrassed in this drawing—as if having two boys fawning all over her makes her uncomfortable!

TOKYOPOP.com

WHERE MANGA LIVES!

▶ JOIN the
TOKYOPOP community:
www.TOKYOPOP.com

COME AND PREVIEW THE HOTTEST MANGA AROUND!

CREATE...
UPLOAD...
DOWNLOAD...
BLOG...
CHAT...
VOTE...
LIVE!!!!

WWW.TOKYOPOP.COM HAS:

• Exclusives
• News
• Contests
• Games
• Rising Stars of Manga
• iManga
• and more...

TOKYOPOP.COM 2.0
NOW LIVE!

© Branded Entertainment LLC, TOKYOPOP Inc., and Russell Productions, Inc.

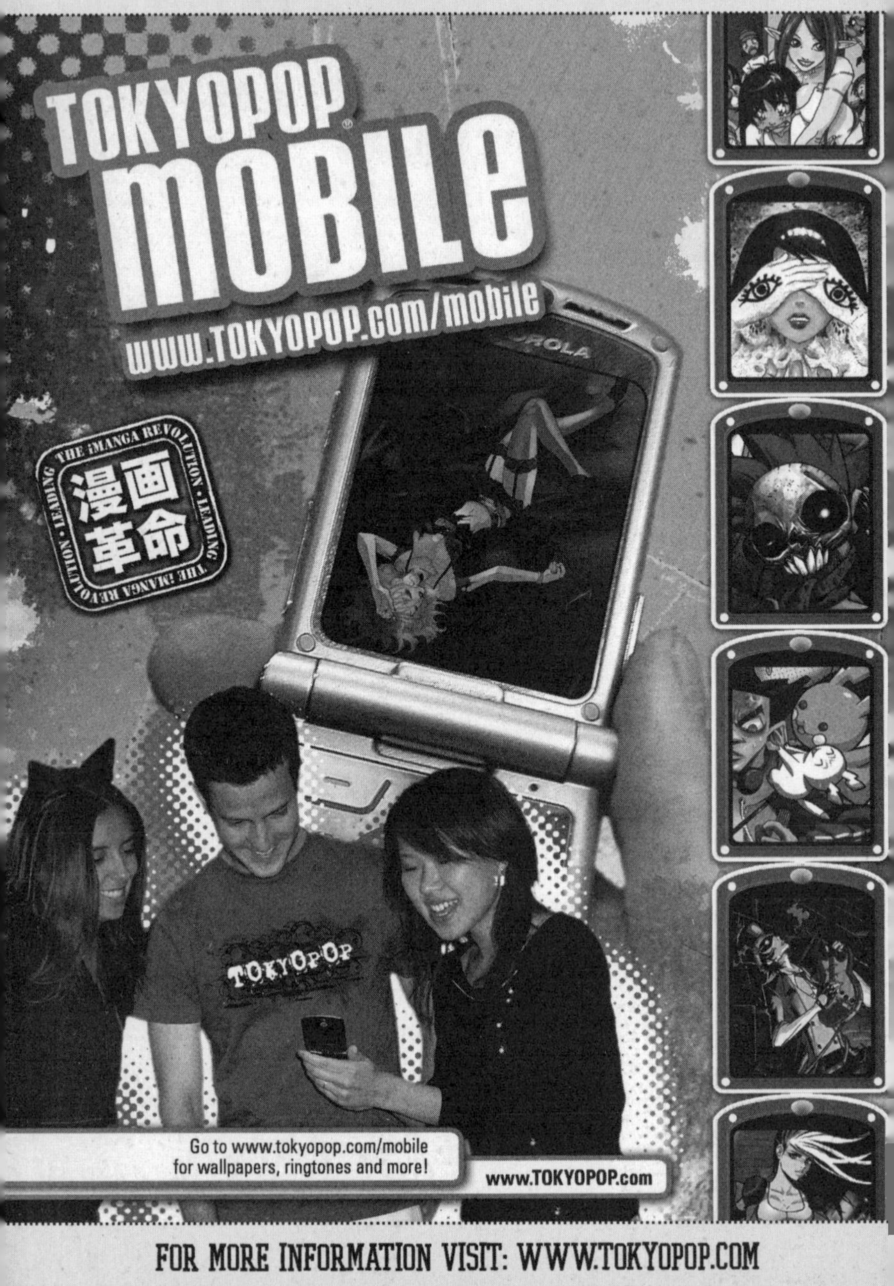
TOKYOPOP MOBILE
www.TOKYOPOP.com/mobile
THE iMANGA REVOLUTION · LEADING · THE iMANGA REVOLUTION · LEADING
漫画革命
TOKYOPOP
Go to www.tokyopop.com/mobile
for wallpapers, ringtones and more!
www.TOKYOPOP.com

FOR MORE INFORMATION VISIT: WWW.TOKYOPOP.COM

TOKYOPOP MANGA SUPPLEMENT

SUPER HYPER
AUDIOTISTIC
SONIC REVOLUTION!!!

www.myspace.com/tokyopop

www.TOKYOPOP.com

Available at the iTunes Music Store
and everywhere music downloads
are available. Keyword: TOKYOPOP

New releases every month!
Check out these great albums
AVAILABLE NOW!!!

©2007 TOKYOPOP Inc.

FOR MORE INFORMATION VISIT: WWW.TOKYOPOP.COM

From the creator of *Peace Maker*

ヴァッサロード

+

Nanae Chrono

The Vatican has employed a new assassin who's a vampire, *and* a cyborg. If you think he sounds nasty, wait 'till you see his master! When these two hot guys collide, the good times and carnage will roll like a head off a guillotine!

© NANAE CHRONO/MAG Garden

FOR MORE INFORMATION VISIT: WWW.TOKYOPOP.COM

TOKYOPOP MANGA SUPPLEMENT

AS SEEN ON CARTOON NETWORK

TRINITY BLOOD™

Trinity Blood Volume 7
While lost in the city, Ion and Esther meet a
strange young tea-seller who reveals that
Radu may be alive…but not before a fight for
their survival against Dietrich's vampire
zombie soldiers!

ACTION

OT OLDER TEEN AGE 15+

LET THE BLOODLETTING CONTINUE

THE SOURCE MATERIAL FOR THE ANIME AND MANGA

THE ADVENTURES CONTINUE IN THESE EXCITING TRINITY BLOOD NOVELS

POP FICTION

Trinity Blood
Rage Against the Moons
Volumes 1, 2 and 3

Trinity Blood
Reborn on the Mars
Volumes 1 and 2

Trinity Blood Volume 7 © Kiyo KYUJJYO 2006 © Sunao YOSHIDA 2006 / KADOKAWA SHOTEN
Trinity Blood: Rage Against The Moons, Volume 3 © Sunao YOSHIDA 2001 / KADOKAWA SHOTEN
Trinity Blood: Reborn on the Mars, Volume 2 © Sunao YOSHIDA 2000, 2001 / KADOKAWA SHOTEN

FOR MORE INFORMATION VISIT: WWW.TOKYOPOP.COM

TOKYOPOP MANGA SUPPLEMENT

Hotel AFRICA™

Hotel AFRICA
VOLUME TWO
By Hee Jung Park

Anything can happen at the Hotel Africa

Tales of heartbreak, irony, and redemption are in store when you check in a second time to the Hotel Africa. Continue along with Elvis as he reveals more tales of the desolate hotel and its strange guests.

INCLUDES ORIGINAL COLOR ART!

hee jung park's
fever
one

Also available from Hee Jung Park
Fever

Once you go to Fever, you will never be the same...

Too Long

A girl who attracts suicide victims, a shy record store customer, and the star of a rock band... what could these three have in common? Find out in this moving collection of short stories.

Too Long

© Hee-Jung Park

FOR MORE INFORMATION VISIT: WWW.TOKYOPOP.COM

TOKYOPOP MANGA SUPPLEMENT

ARE YOU TRULY ALIVE?

In the collapsing world of the afterlife, two guardians face the ultimate question: Thaddeus yearns for answers, while Mercutio seeks his true love. Will they be able to find it all before it's too late?

ART BY
ROB STEEN
AND STORY BY
STORMCROW HAYES

A MEDITATIVE AND BROODING EXPLORATION INTO THE ENDLESS POSSIBILITIES OF THE AFTERLIFE.

FANTASY

OT
OLDER TEEN
AGE 16+

© Sam Hayes, Rob Steen and TOKYOPOP Inc.

READ AN ENTIRE CHAPTER FOR FREE: WWW.TOKYOPOP.COM/MANGAONLINE

SPOTLIGHT TOKYOPOP MANGA SUPPLEMENT

DEVIL MAY CRY

DANTE'S HAVING A **HELL** OF A TIME!

THE NEW MANGA NOVEL FROM TOKYOPOP

CHECK OUT TOKYOPOP'S MANGA NOVELS TODAY:
www.TOKYOPOP.com/books/novels
Manga also available from TOKYOPOP!

© SHIN-YA GOIKEDA 2002. © CAPCOM CO., LTD 2001. ALL RIGHTS RESERVED.   DEVIL MAY CRY ™ & © 2006 CAPCOM CO., LTD. ALL RIGHTS RESERVED.

STOP!

This is the back of the book.
You wouldn't want to spoil a great ending!

This book is printed "manga-style," in the authentic Japanese right-to-left format. Since none of the artwork has been flipped or altered, readers get to experience the story just as the creator intended. You've been asking for it, so TOKYOPOP® delivered: authentic, hot-off-the-press, and far more fun!

DIRECTIONS

If this is your first time reading manga-style, here's a quick guide to help you understand how it works.

It's easy... just start in the top right panel and follow the numbers. Have fun, and look for more 100% authentic manga from TOKYOPOP®!